THE WORLD'S GREATEST COMIC MAGAZINE

WRITER: **JONATHAN HICKMAN**

ARTIST: **RON GARNEY** [ISSUES #605-606], **MIKE CHOI** [ISSUE #605.1], **GIUSEPPE CAMUNCOLI** [BREAKDOWNS #607-608], **KARL KESEL** [FINISHES #607-608] & **RYAN STEGMAN** [ISSUES #609-611]

COLOR ARTISTS: **JASON KEITH** [#605-606], **CRIS PETER** [# 605.1] & **PAUL MOUNTS** [# 607-611]

COVER ARTISTS: **RON GARNEY & JASON KEITH** [# 605], **MIKE CHOI & GURU-eFX** [# 605.1, 606-607], **FRANK CHO & JASON KEITH** [# 608] AND **RYAN STEGMAN & PAUL MOUNTS** [# 609-611]

LETTERER: **VIRTUAL CALLIGRAPHY'S CLAYTON COWLES**

ASSISTANT EDITORS: **JOHN DENNING & JAKE THOMAS**

ASSOCIATE EDITOR: **LAUREN SANKOVITCH**

EDITOR: **TOM BREVOORT**

COLLECTION EDITOR: **JENNIFER GRÜNWALD**
ASSISTANT EDITORS: **ALEX STARBUCK & NELSON RIBEIRO**
EDITOR, SPECIAL PROJECTS: **MARK D. BEAZLEY**
SENIOR EDITOR, SPECIAL PROJECTS: **JEFF YOUNGQUIST**
SENIOR VICE PRESIDENT OF SALES: **DAVID GABRIEL**
SVP OF BRAND PLANNING & COMMUNICATIONS: **MICHAEL PASCIULLO**

EDITOR IN CHIEF: **AXEL ALONSO**
CHIEF CREATIVE OFFICER: **JOE QUESADA**
PUBLISHER: **DAN BUCKLEY**
EXECUTIVE PRODUCER: **ALAN FINE**

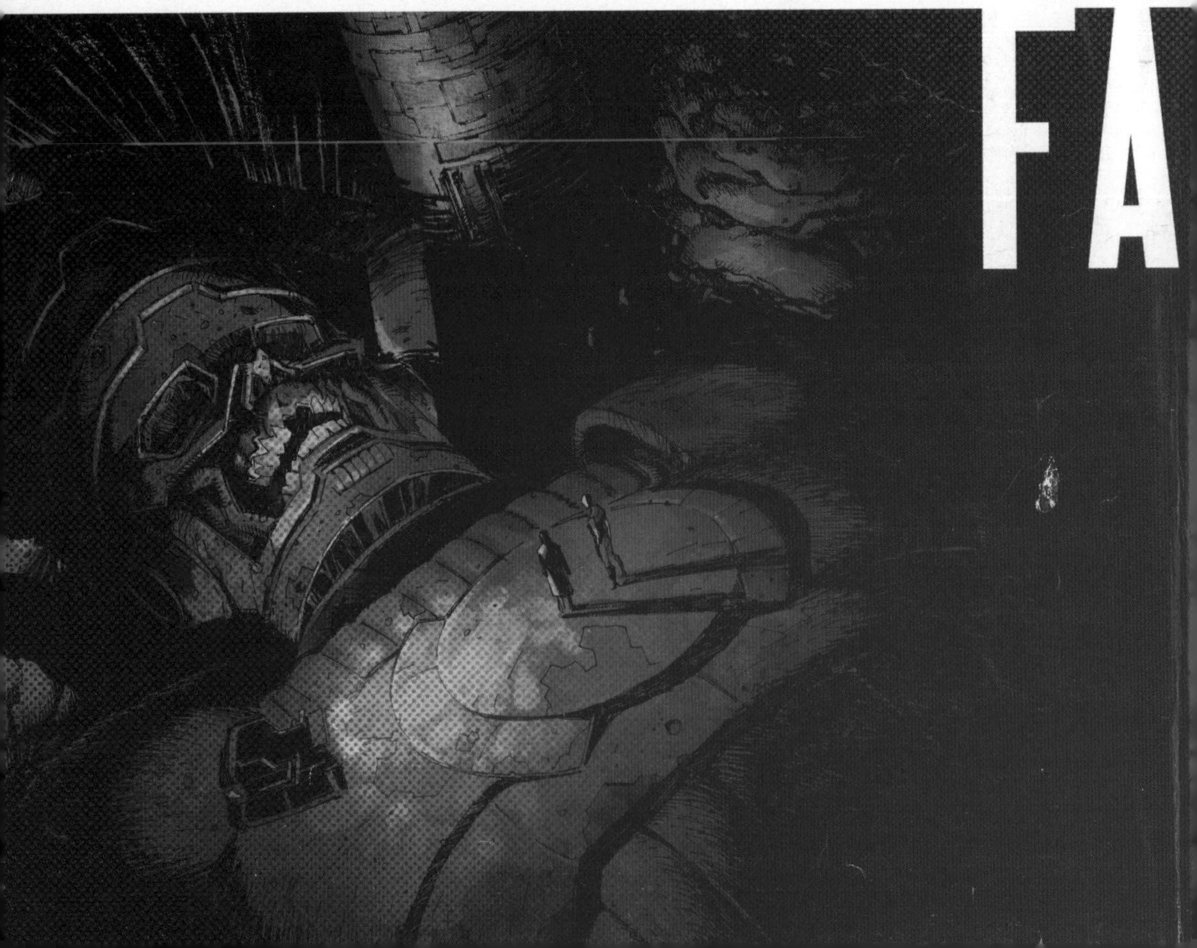
FA

NTASTIC FOUR

UNIFIED FIELD THEORY: STAN LEE & JACK KIRBY

FANTASTIC FOUR BY JONATHAN HICKMAN VOL. 6. Contains material originally published in magazine form as FANTASTIC FOUR #605.1 and #605-611. First printing 2012. Hardcover ISBN# 978-0-7851-6154-7. Softcover ISBN# 978-0-7851-6155-4. Published by MARVEL WORLDWIDE, INC., a subsidiary of MARVEL ENTERTAINMENT, LLC. OFFICE OF PUBLICATION: 135 West 50th Street, New York, NY 10020. Copyright © 2012 and 2013 Marvel Characters, Inc. All rights reserved. Hardcover: $29.99 per copy in the U.S. and $32.99 in Canada (GST #R127032852). Softcover: $24.99 per copy in the U.S. and $27.99 in Canada (GST #R127032852). Canadian Agreement #40668537. All characters featured in this issue and the distinctive names and likenesses thereof, and all related indicia are trademarks of Marvel Characters, Inc. No similarity between any of the names, characters, persons, and/or institutions in this magazine with those of any living or dead person or institution is intended, and any such similarity which may exist is purely coincidental. **Printed in the U.S.A.** ALAN FINE, EVP - Office of the President, Marvel Worldwide, Inc. and EVP & CMO Marvel Characters B.V.; DAN BUCKLEY, Publisher & President - Print, Animation & Digital Divisions; JOE QUESADA, Chief Creative Officer; TOM BREVOORT, SVP of Publishing; DAVID BOGART, SVP of Operations & Procurement, Publishing; RUWAN JAYATILLEKE, SVP & Associate Publisher, Publishing; C.B. CEBULSKI, SVP of Creator & Content Development; DAVID GABRIEL, SVP of Publishing Sales & Circulation; MICHAEL PASCIULLO, SVP of Brand Planning & Communications; JIM O'KEEFE, VP of Operations & Logistics; DAN CARR, Executive Director of Publishing Technology; SUSAN CRESPI, Editorial Operations Manager; ALEX MORALES, Publishing Operations Manager; STAN LEE, Chairman Emeritus. For information regarding advertising in Marvel Comics or on Marvel.com, please contact Niza Disla, Director of Marvel Partnerships, at ndisla@marvel.com. For Marvel subscription inquiries, please call 800-217-9158. **Manufactured between 10/22/2012 and 12/3/2012 (hardcover), and 10/22/2012 and 6/10/2013 (softcover), by R.R. DONNELLEY, INC., SALEM, VA, USA.**

10 9 8 7 6 5 4 3 2 1

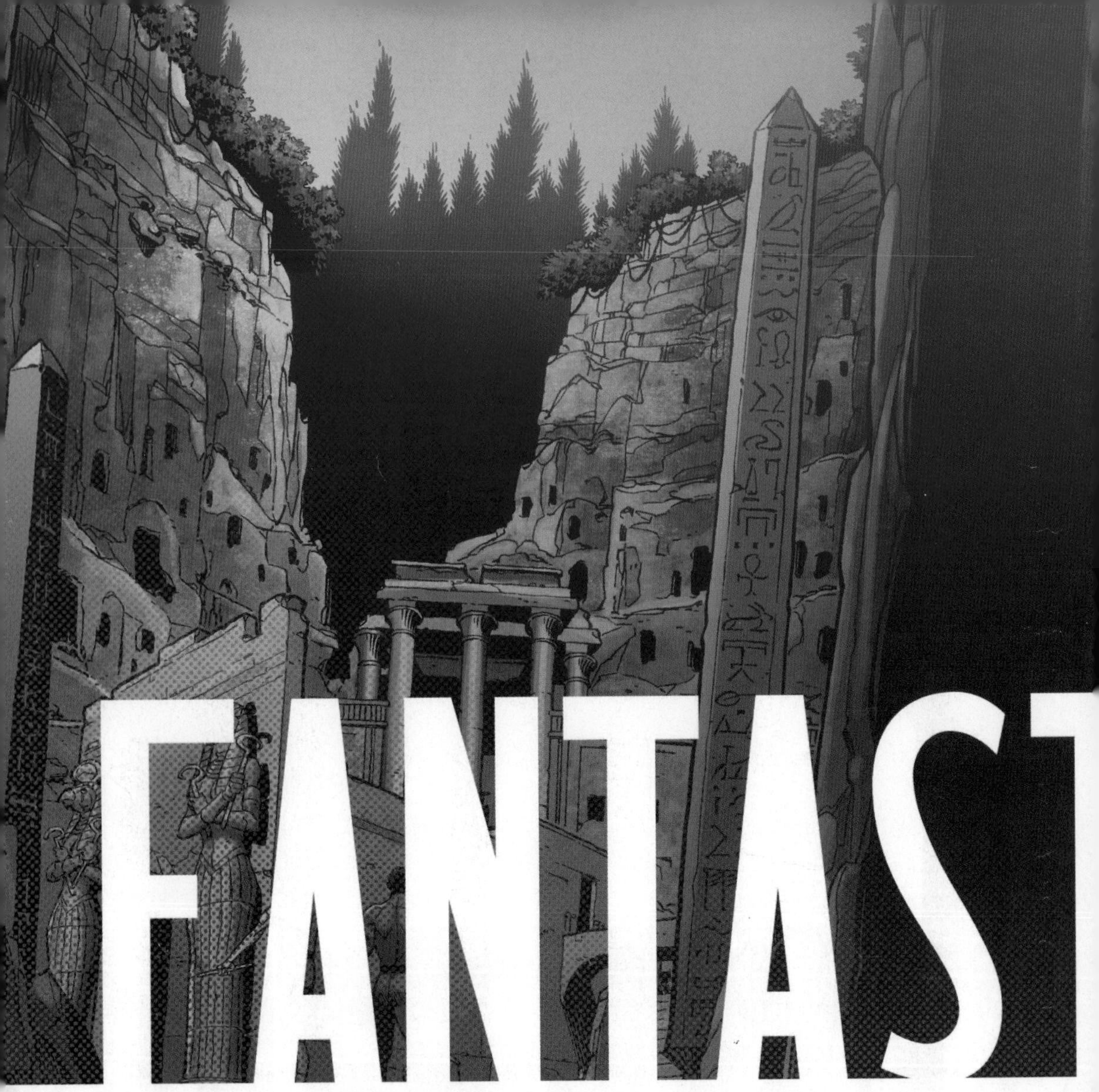
FANTAST

TIC FOUR

VOL **SIX** FOUNDATION

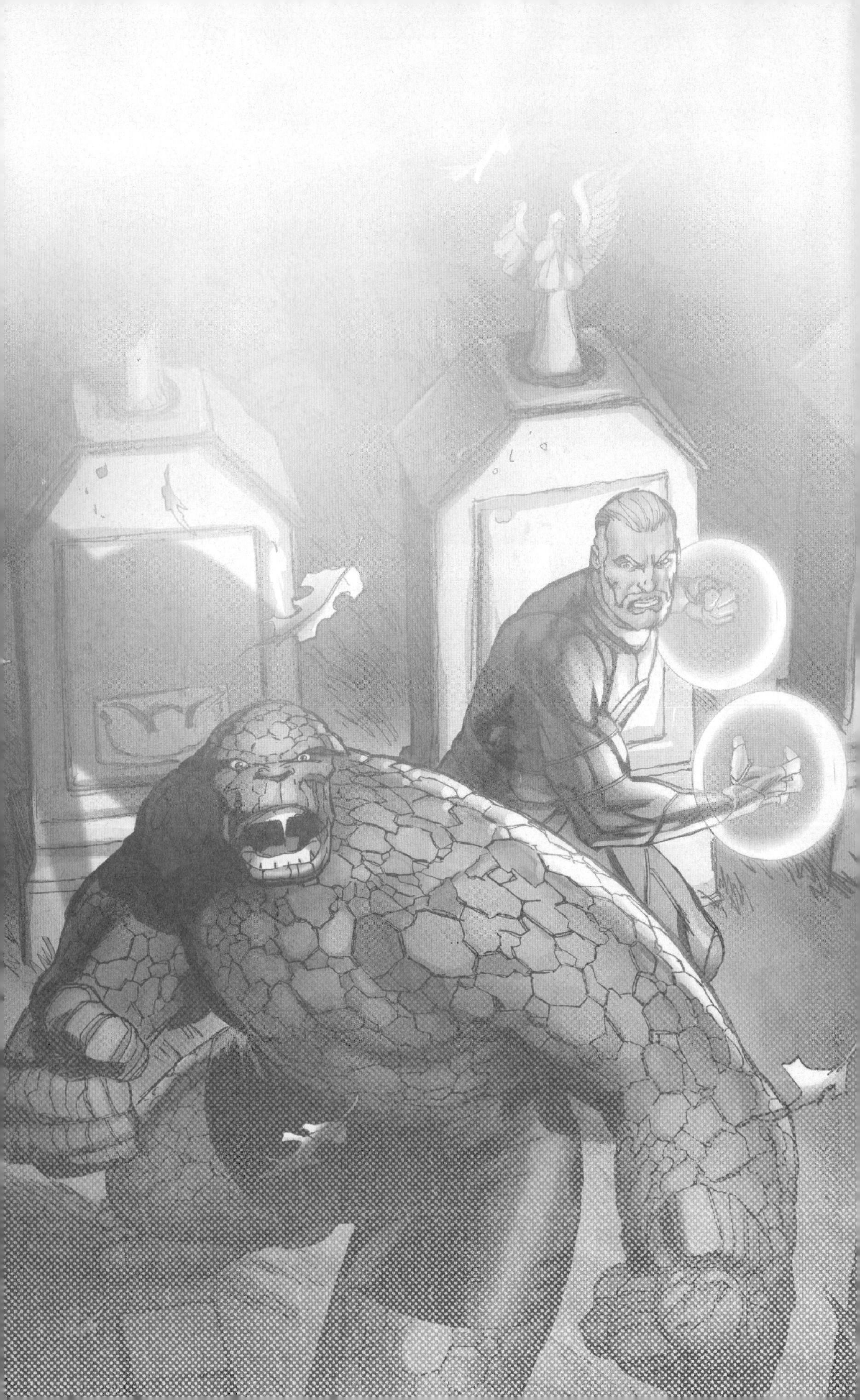

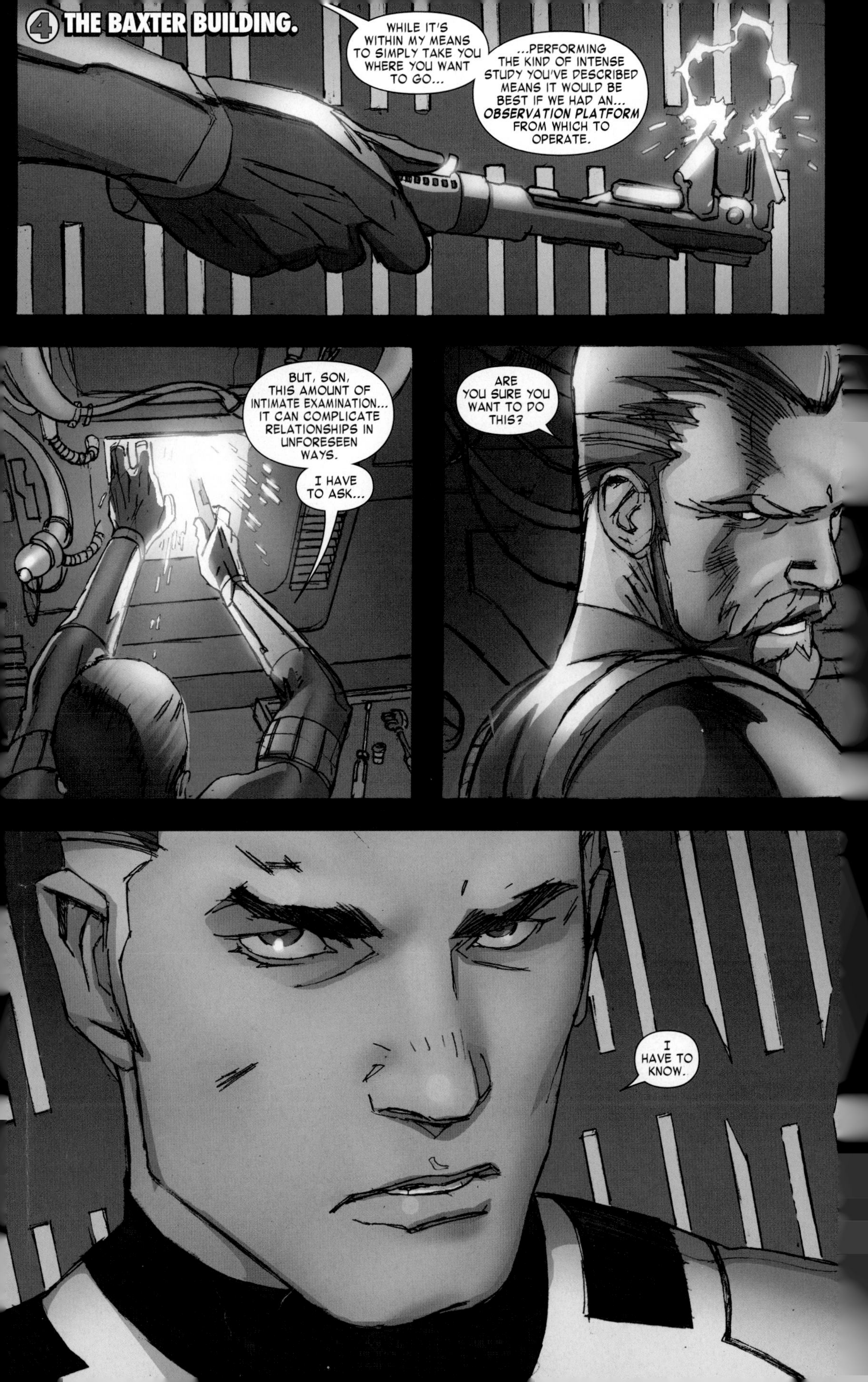
THE BAXTER BUILDING.
WHILE IT'S WITHIN MY MEANS TO SIMPLY TAKE YOU WHERE YOU WANT TO GO...
...PERFORMING THE KIND OF INTENSE STUDY YOU'VE DESCRIBED MEANS IT WOULD BE BEST IF WE HAD AN... OBSERVATION PLATFORM FROM WHICH TO OPERATE.
BUT, SON, THIS AMOUNT OF INTIMATE EXAMINATION... IT CAN COMPLICATE RELATIONSHIPS IN UNFORESEEN WAYS.
I HAVE TO ASK...
ARE YOU SURE YOU WANT TO DO THIS?
I HAVE TO KNOW.

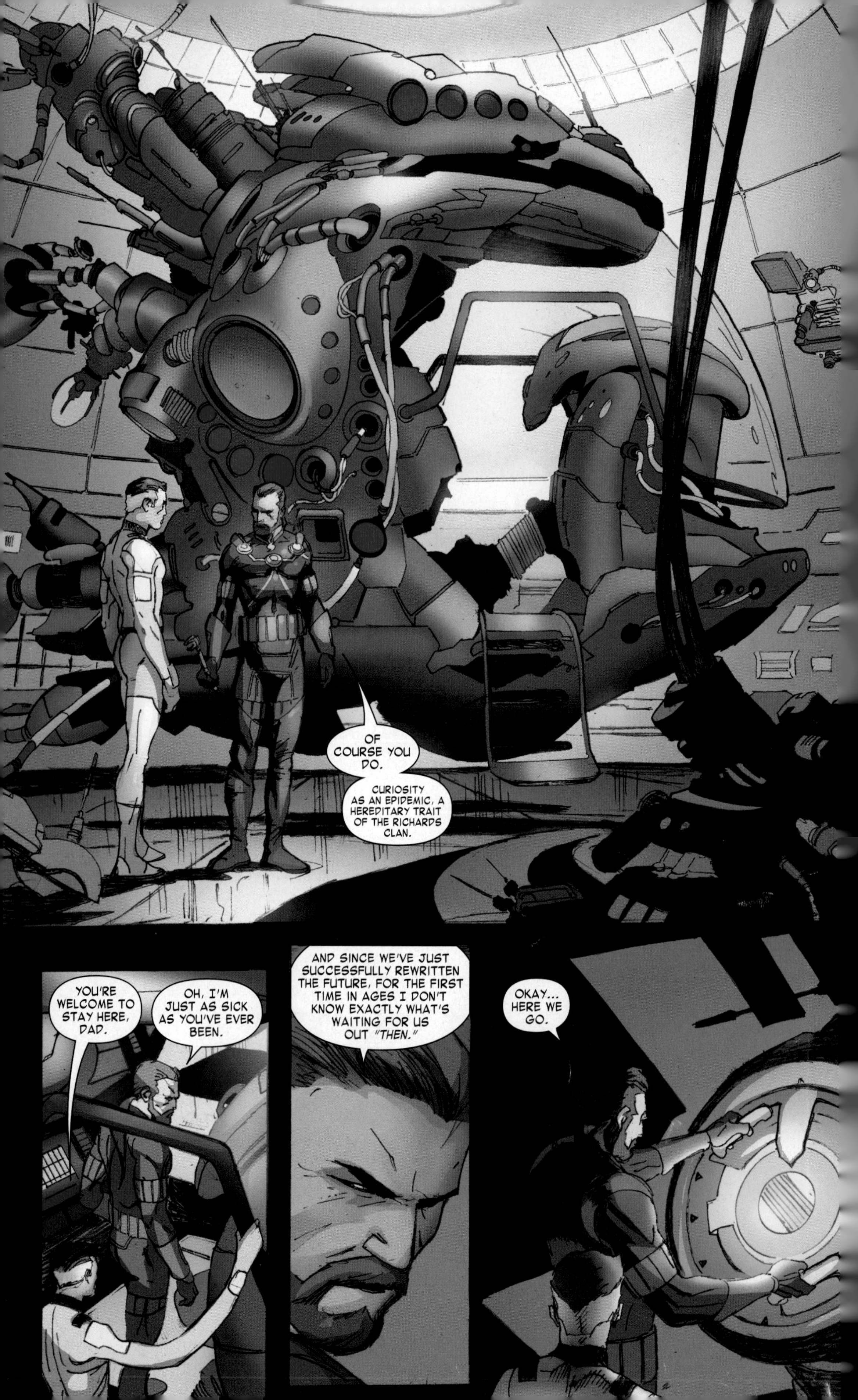
OF COURSE YOU DO.
CURIOSITY AS AN EPIDEMIC, A HEREDITARY TRAIT OF THE RICHARDS CLAN.
YOU'RE WELCOME TO STAY HERE, DAD.
OH, I'M JUST AS SICK AS YOU'VE EVER BEEN.
AND SINCE WE'VE JUST SUCCESSFULLY REWRITTEN THE FUTURE, FOR THE FIRST TIME IN AGES I DON'T KNOW EXACTLY WHAT'S WAITING FOR US OUT "THEN."
OKAY... HERE WE GO.

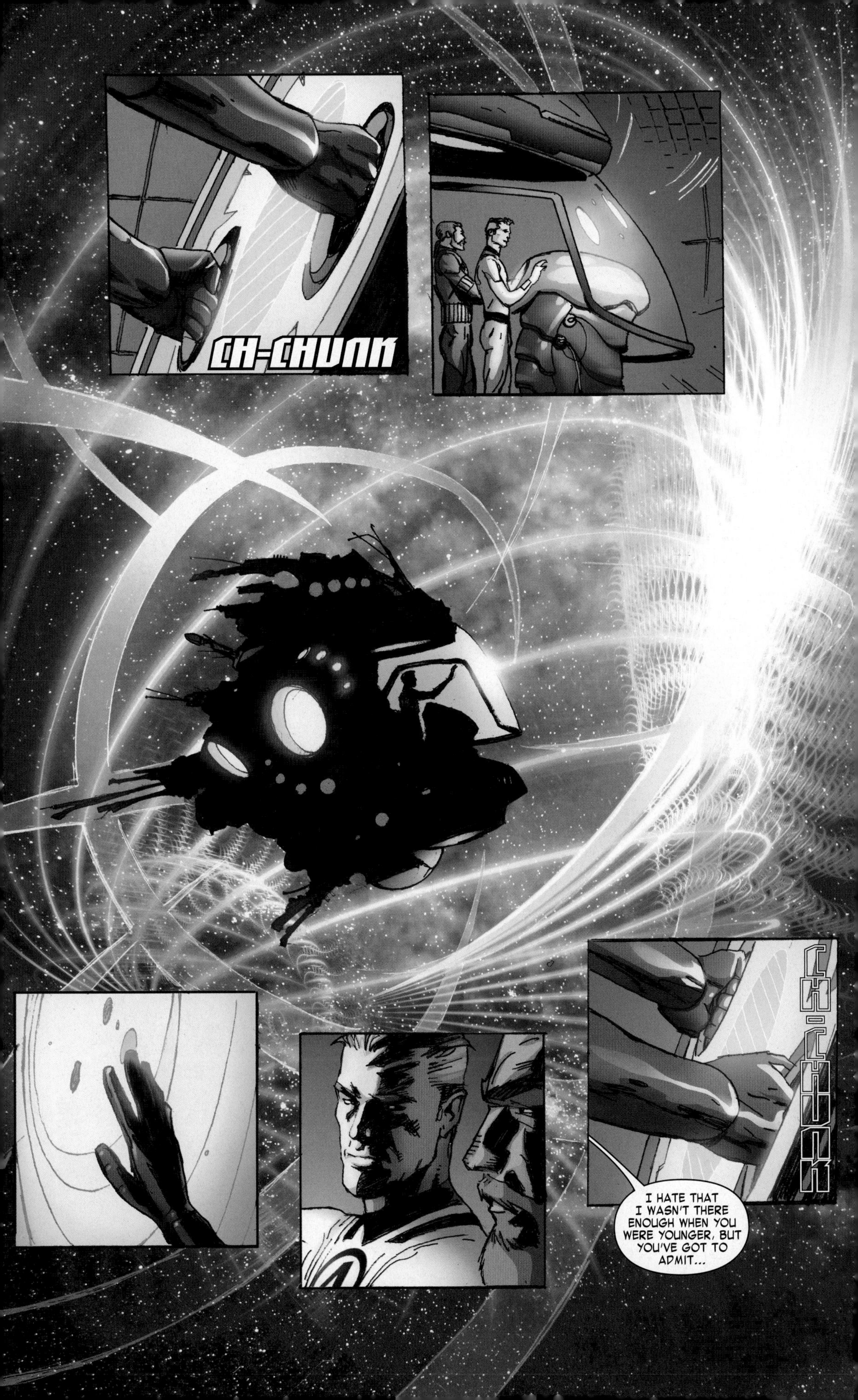
CH-CHUNK
CH-CHUNK
I HATE THAT I WASN'T THERE ENOUGH WHEN YOU WERE YOUNGER, BUT YOU'VE GOT TO ADMIT...

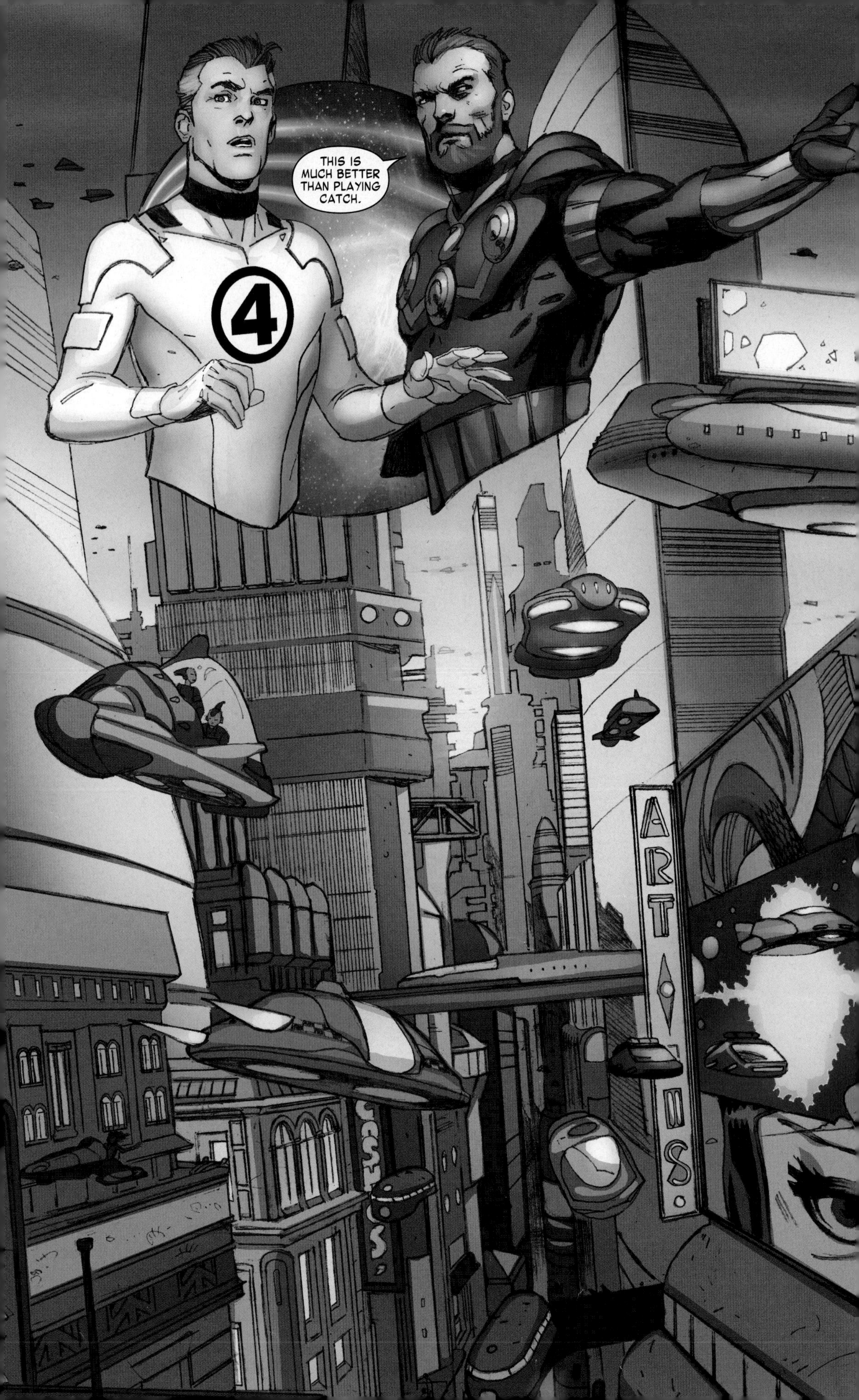
THIS IS MUCH BETTER THAN PLAYING CATCH.
ARTS

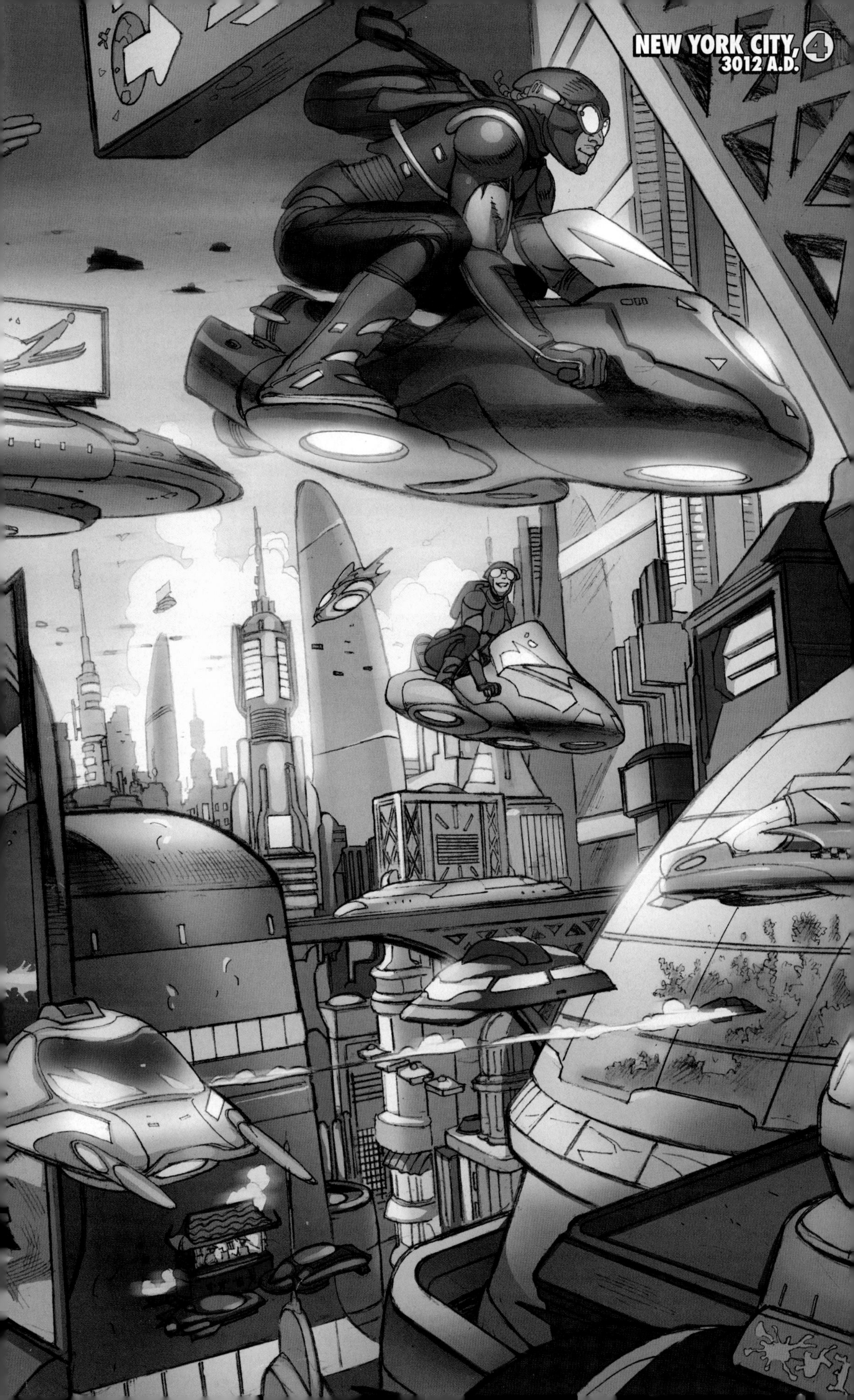
NEW YORK CITY, 3012 A.D.

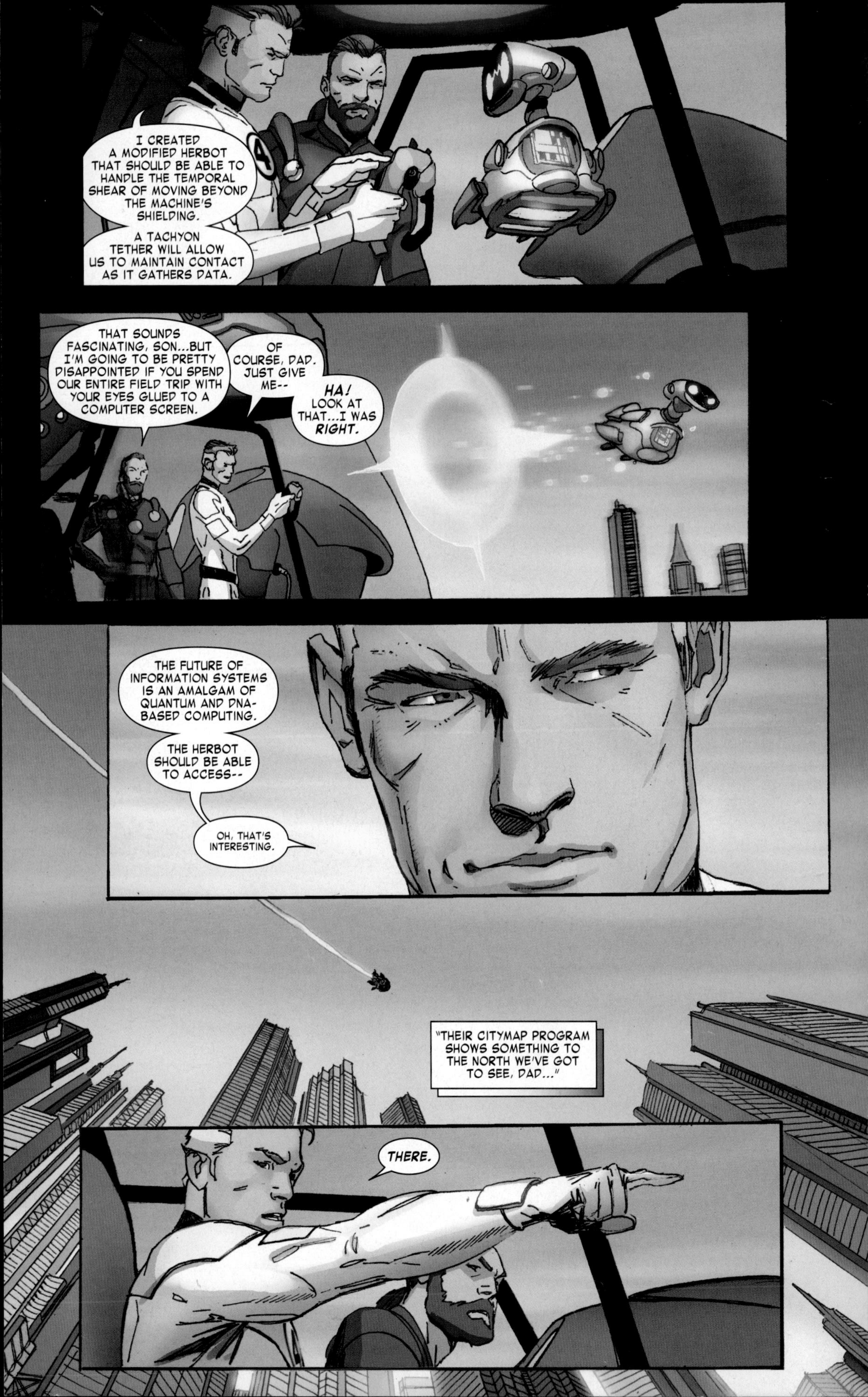
I CREATED A MODIFIED HERBOT THAT SHOULD BE ABLE TO HANDLE THE TEMPORAL SHEAR OF MOVING BEYOND THE MACHINE'S SHIELDING.
A TACHYON TETHER WILL ALLOW US TO MAINTAIN CONTACT AS IT GATHERS DATA.
THAT SOUNDS FASCINATING, SON...BUT I'M GOING TO BE PRETTY DISAPPOINTED IF YOU SPEND OUR ENTIRE FIELD TRIP WITH YOUR EYES GLUED TO A COMPUTER SCREEN.
OF COURSE, DAD. JUST GIVE ME--
HA! LOOK AT THAT...I WAS RIGHT.
THE FUTURE OF INFORMATION SYSTEMS IS AN AMALGAM OF QUANTUM AND DNA-BASED COMPUTING.
THE HERBOT SHOULD BE ABLE TO ACCESS--
OH, THAT'S INTERESTING.
"THEIR CITYMAP PROGRAM SHOWS SOMETHING TO THE NORTH WE'VE GOT TO SEE, DAD..."
THERE.

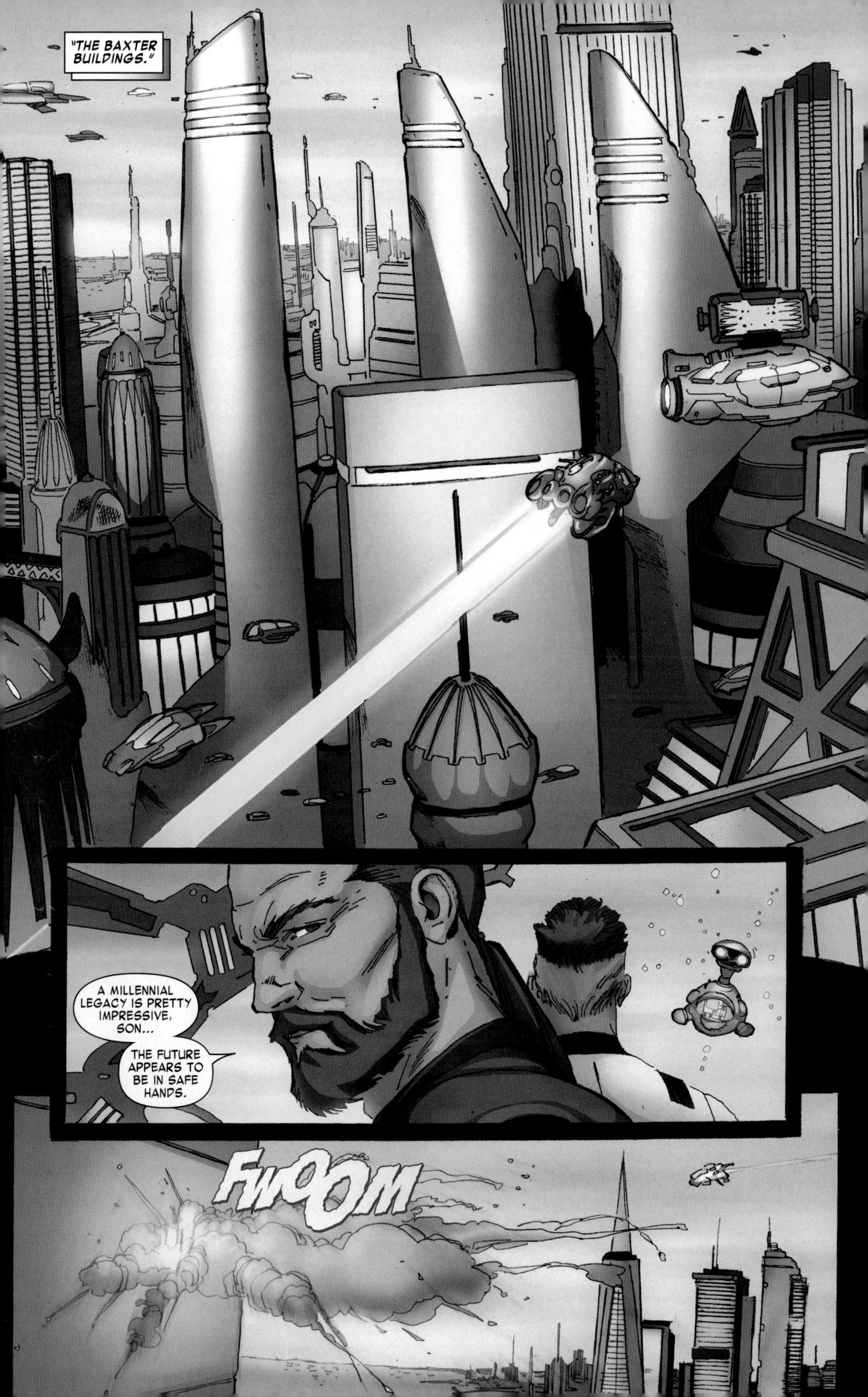
"THE BAXTER BUILDINGS."
A MILLENNIAL LEGACY IS PRETTY IMPRESSIVE, SON...
THE FUTURE APPEARS TO BE IN SAFE HANDS.
FWOOM

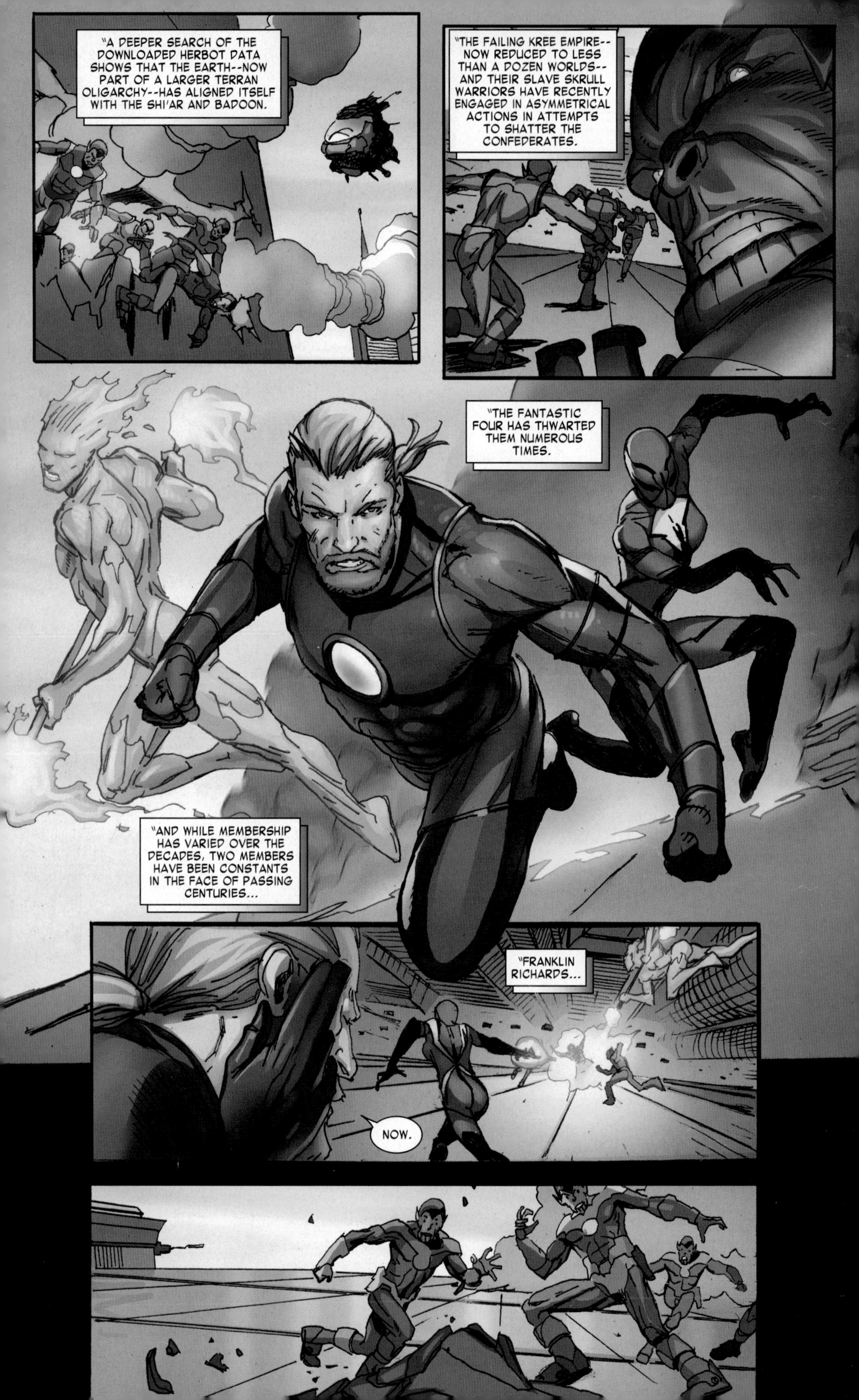
"A DEEPER SEARCH OF THE DOWNLOADED HERBOT DATA SHOWS THAT THE EARTH--NOW PART OF A LARGER TERRAN OLIGARCHY--HAS ALIGNED ITSELF WITH THE SHI'AR AND BADOON.
"THE FAILING KREE EMPIRE--NOW REDUCED TO LESS THAN A DOZEN WORLDS--AND THEIR SLAVE SKRULL WARRIORS HAVE RECENTLY ENGAGED IN ASYMMETRICAL ACTIONS IN ATTEMPTS TO SHATTER THE CONFEDERATES.
"THE FANTASTIC FOUR HAS THWARTED THEM NUMEROUS TIMES.
"AND WHILE MEMBERSHIP HAS VARIED OVER THE DECADES, TWO MEMBERS HAVE BEEN CONSTANTS IN THE FACE OF PASSING CENTURIES...
"FRANKLIN RICHARDS...
NOW.

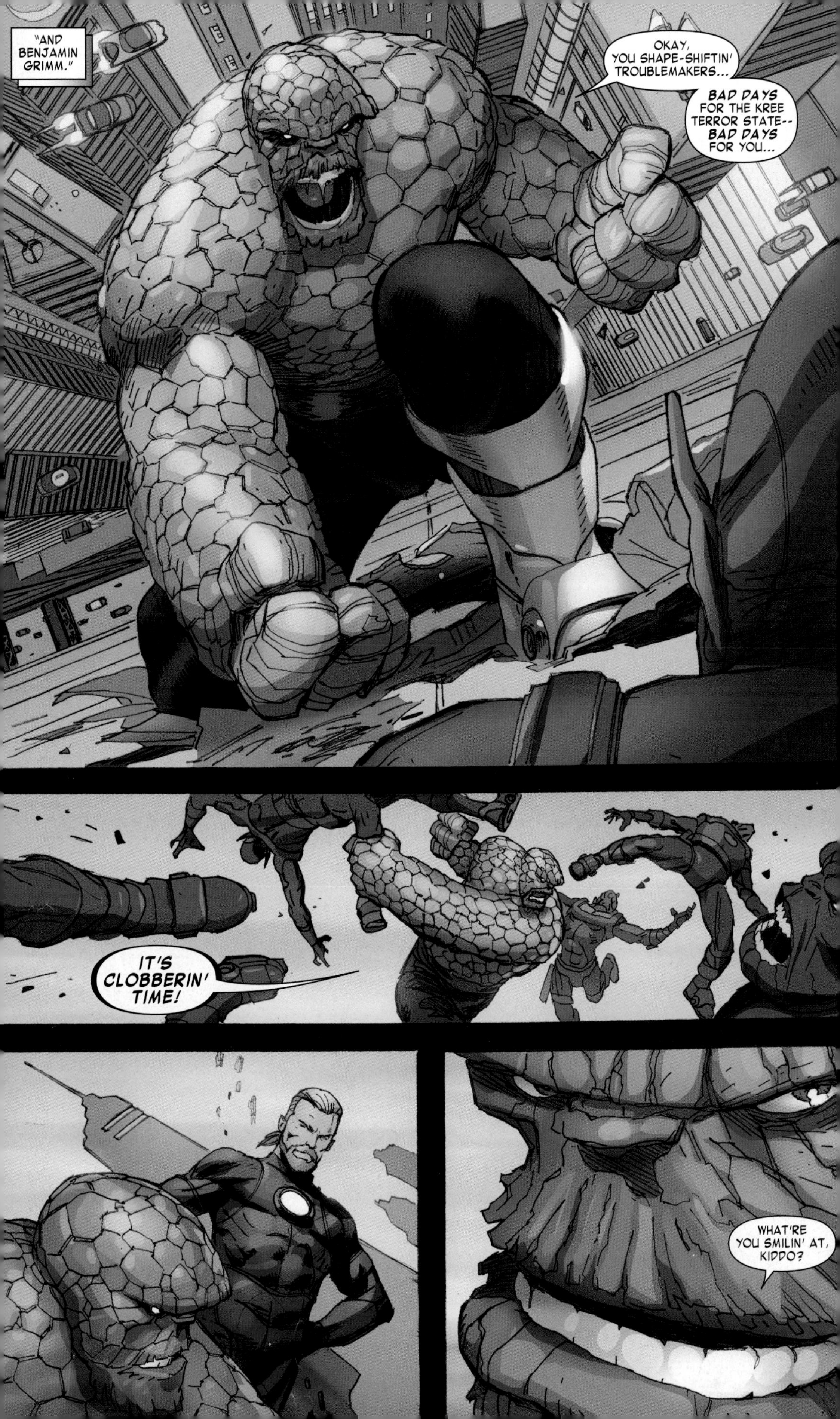
"AND BENJAMIN GRIMM."
OKAY, YOU SHAPE-SHIFTIN' TROUBLEMAKERS...
BAD DAYS FOR THE KREE TERROR STATE-- BAD DAYS FOR YOU...
IT'S CLOBBERIN' TIME!
WHAT'RE YOU SMILIN' AT, KIDDO?

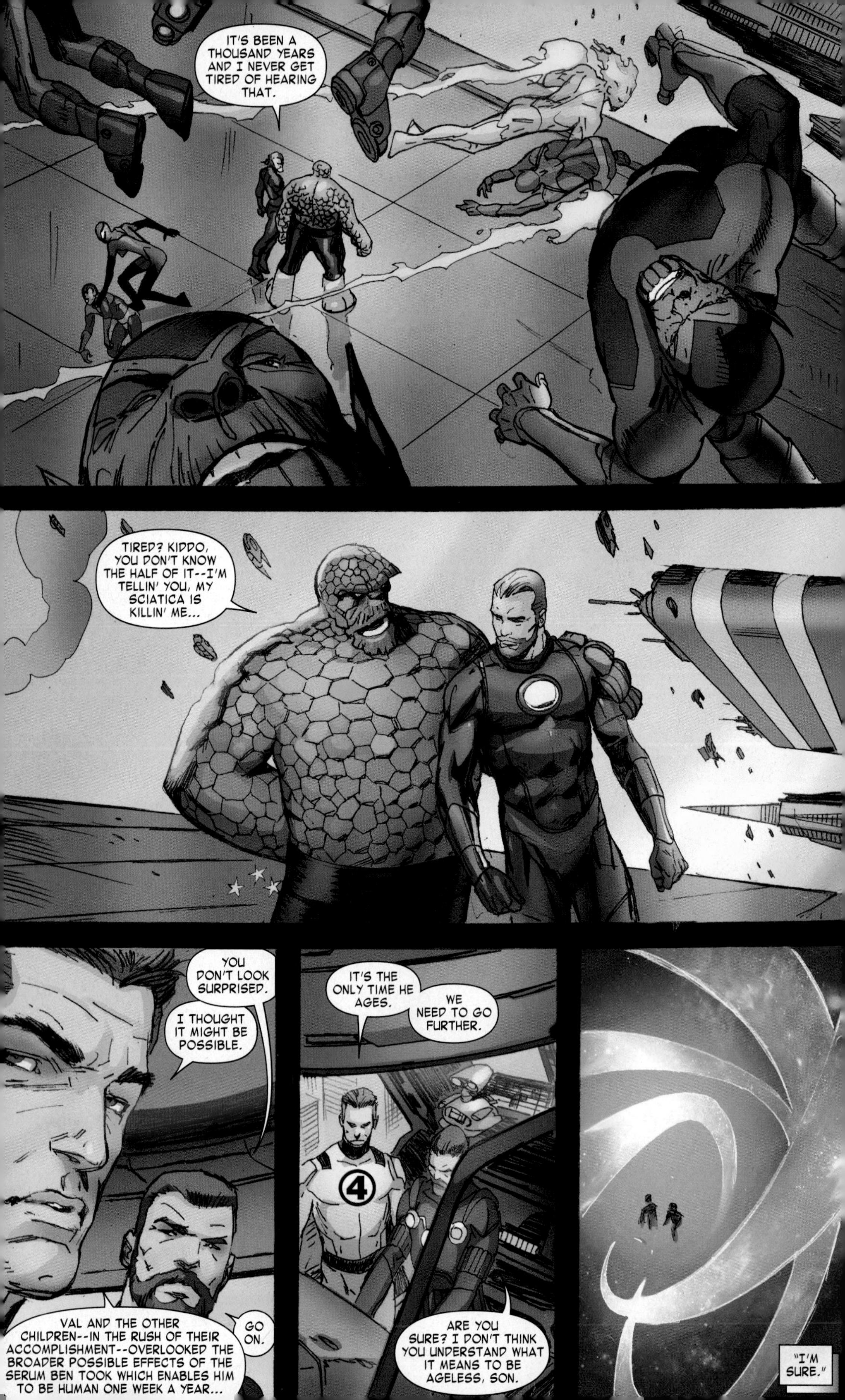
IT'S BEEN A THOUSAND YEARS AND I NEVER GET TIRED OF HEARING THAT.
TIRED? KIDDO, YOU DON'T KNOW THE HALF OF IT--I'M TELLIN' YOU, MY SCIATICA IS KILLIN' ME...
YOU DON'T LOOK SURPRISED.
I THOUGHT IT MIGHT BE POSSIBLE.
VAL AND THE OTHER CHILDREN--IN THE RUSH OF THEIR ACCOMPLISHMENT--OVERLOOKED THE BROADER POSSIBLE EFFECTS OF THE SERUM BEN TOOK WHICH ENABLES HIM TO BE HUMAN ONE WEEK A YEAR...
GO ON.
IT'S THE ONLY TIME HE AGES.
WE NEED TO GO FURTHER.
ARE YOU SURE? I DON'T THINK YOU UNDERSTAND WHAT IT MEANS TO BE AGELESS, SON.
"I'M SURE."

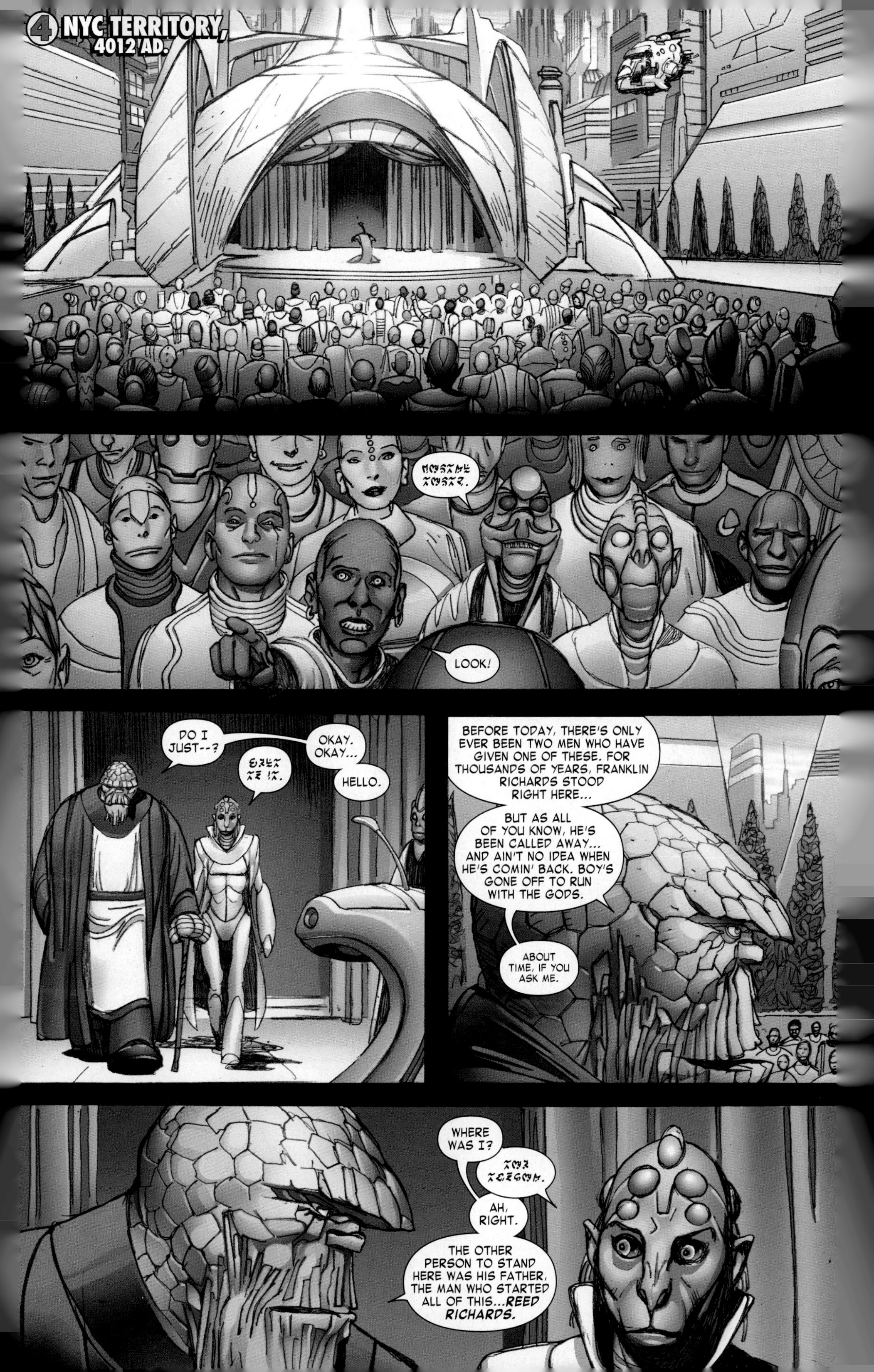

NYC TERRITORY, 4012 AD.
LOOK!
DO I JUST--?
OKAY. OKAY...
HELLO.
BEFORE TODAY, THERE'S ONLY EVER BEEN TWO MEN WHO HAVE GIVEN ONE OF THESE. FOR THOUSANDS OF YEARS, FRANKLIN RICHARDS STOOD RIGHT HERE...
BUT AS ALL OF YOU KNOW, HE'S BEEN CALLED AWAY... AND AIN'T NO IDEA WHEN HE'S COMIN' BACK. BOY'S GONE OFF TO RUN WITH THE GODS.
ABOUT TIME, IF YOU ASK ME.
WHERE WAS I?
AH, RIGHT.
THE OTHER PERSON TO STAND HERE WAS HIS FATHER, THE MAN WHO STARTED ALL OF THIS...REED RICHARDS.

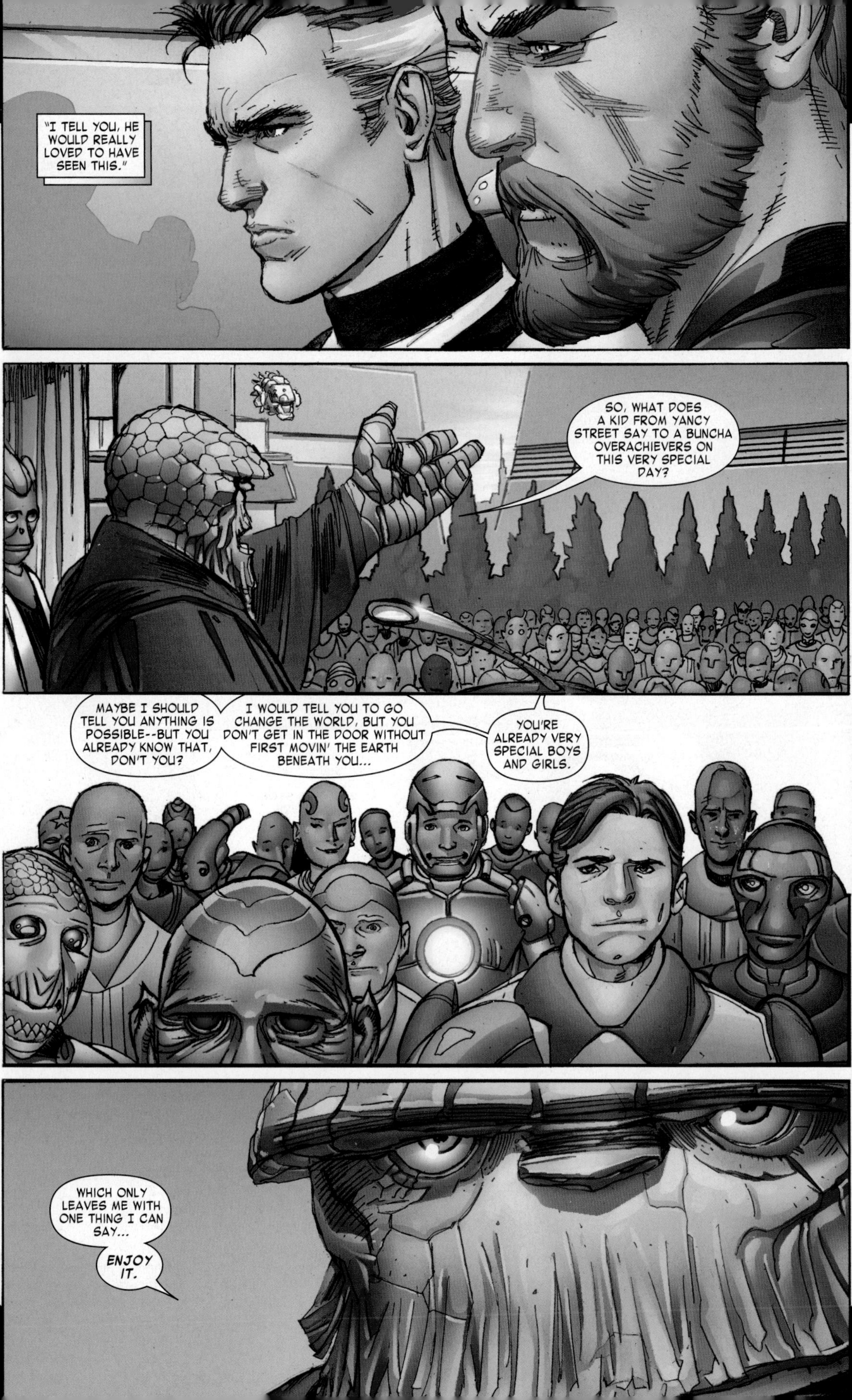
"I TELL YOU, HE WOULD REALLY LOVED TO HAVE SEEN THIS."
SO, WHAT DOES A KID FROM YANCY STREET SAY TO A BUNCHA OVERACHIEVERS ON THIS VERY SPECIAL DAY?
YOU'RE ALREADY VERY SPECIAL BOYS AND GIRLS.
I WOULD TELL YOU TO GO CHANGE THE WORLD, BUT YOU DON'T GET IN THE DOOR WITHOUT FIRST MOVIN' THE EARTH BENEATH YOU...
MAYBE I SHOULD TELL YOU ANYTHING IS POSSIBLE--BUT YOU ALREADY KNOW THAT, DON'T YOU?
WHICH ONLY LEAVES ME WITH ONE THING I CAN SAY...
ENJOY IT.

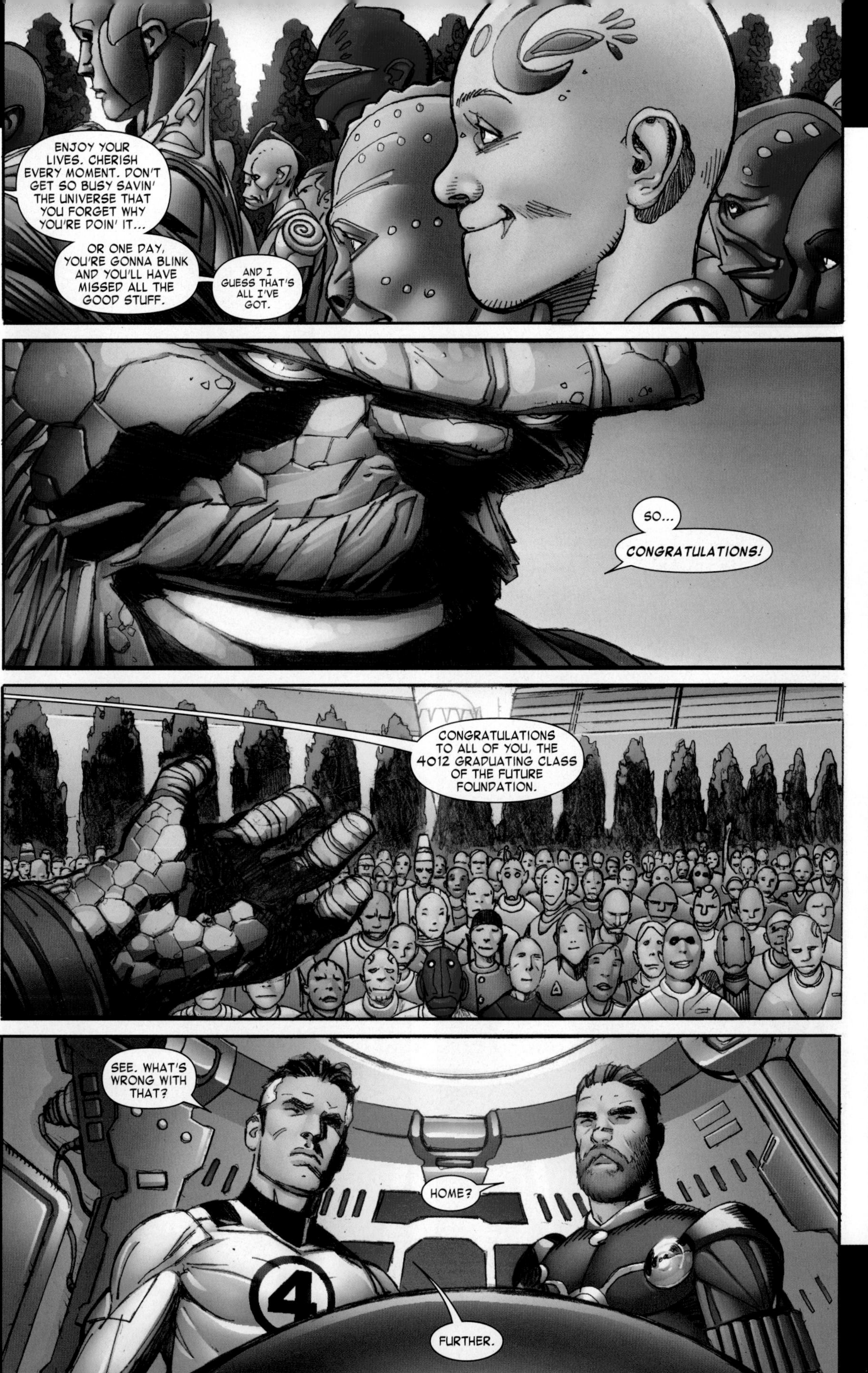
ENJOY YOUR LIVES. CHERISH EVERY MOMENT. DON'T GET SO BUSY SAVIN' THE UNIVERSE THAT YOU FORGET WHY YOU'RE DOIN' IT...
OR ONE DAY, YOU'RE GONNA BLINK AND YOU'LL HAVE MISSED ALL THE GOOD STUFF.
AND I GUESS THAT'S ALL I'VE GOT.
SO...
CONGRATULATIONS!
CONGRATULATIONS TO ALL OF YOU, THE 4012 GRADUATING CLASS OF THE FUTURE FOUNDATION.
SEE. WHAT'S WRONG WITH THAT?
HOME?
FURTHER.

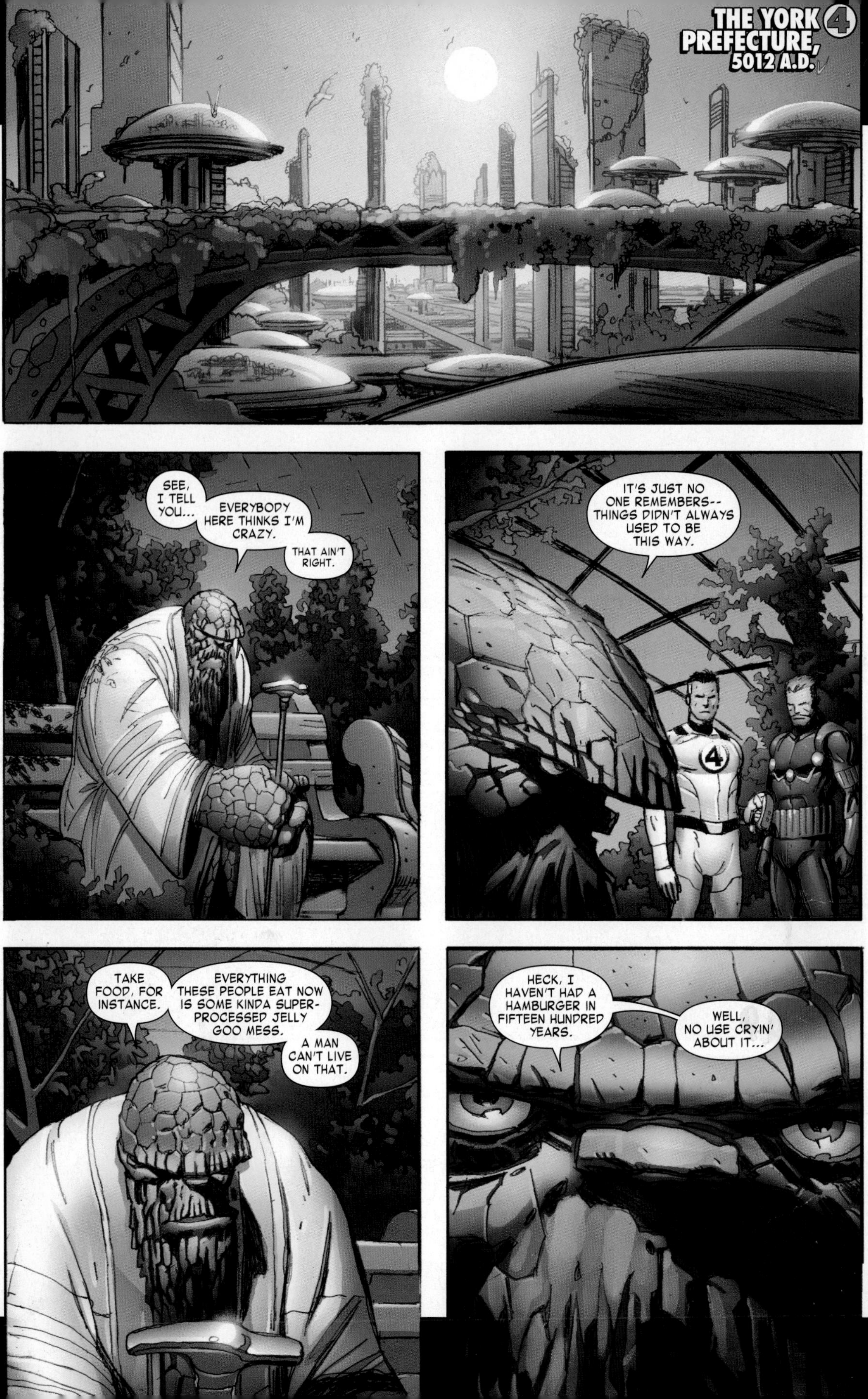
THE YORK PREFECTURE, 5012 A.D.
SEE, I TELL YOU...
EVERYBODY HERE THINKS I'M CRAZY.
THAT AIN'T RIGHT.
IT'S JUST NO ONE REMEMBERS-- THINGS DIDN'T ALWAYS USED TO BE THIS WAY.
TAKE FOOD, FOR INSTANCE.
EVERYTHING THESE PEOPLE EAT NOW IS SOME KINDA SUPER-PROCESSED JELLY GOO MESS.
A MAN CAN'T LIVE ON THAT.
HECK, I HAVEN'T HAD A HAMBURGER IN FIFTEEN HUNDRED YEARS.
WELL, NO USE CRYIN' ABOUT IT...

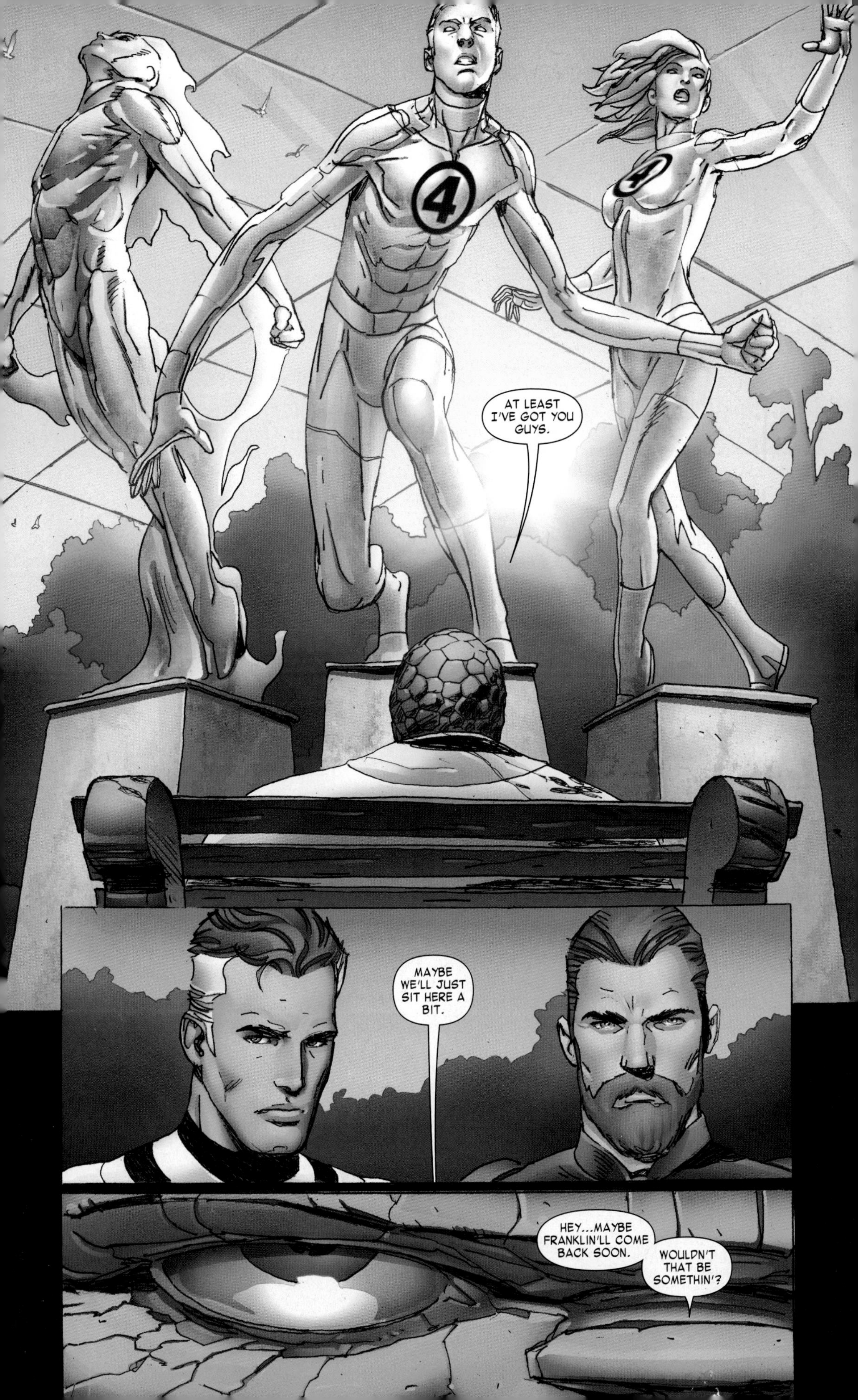
AT LEAST I'VE GOT YOU GUYS.
MAYBE WE'LL JUST SIT HERE A BIT.
HEY...MAYBE FRANKLIN'LL COME BACK SOON.
WOULDN'T THAT BE SOMETHIN'?

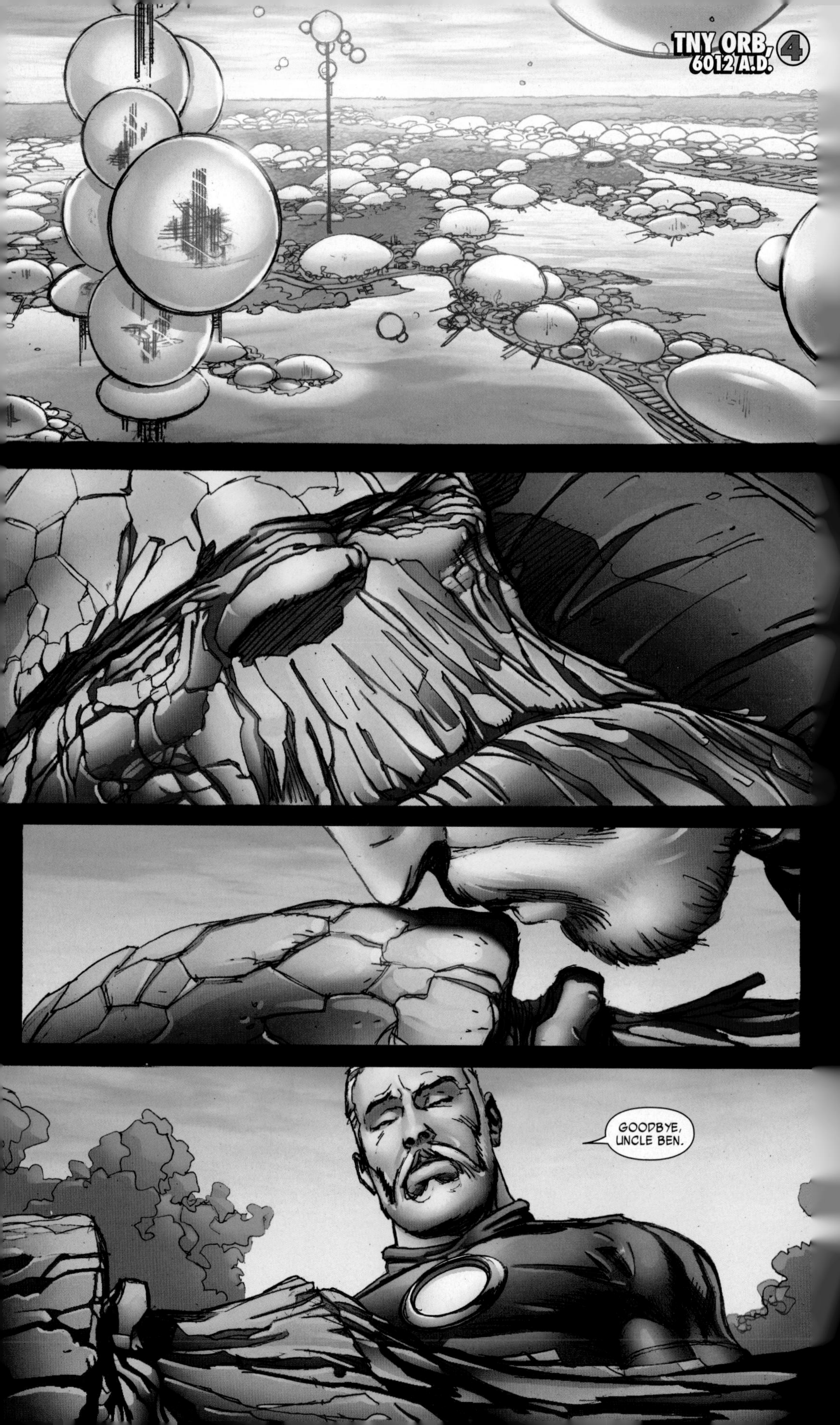
TNY ORB, 6012 A.D.
4
GOODBYE, UNCLE BEN.

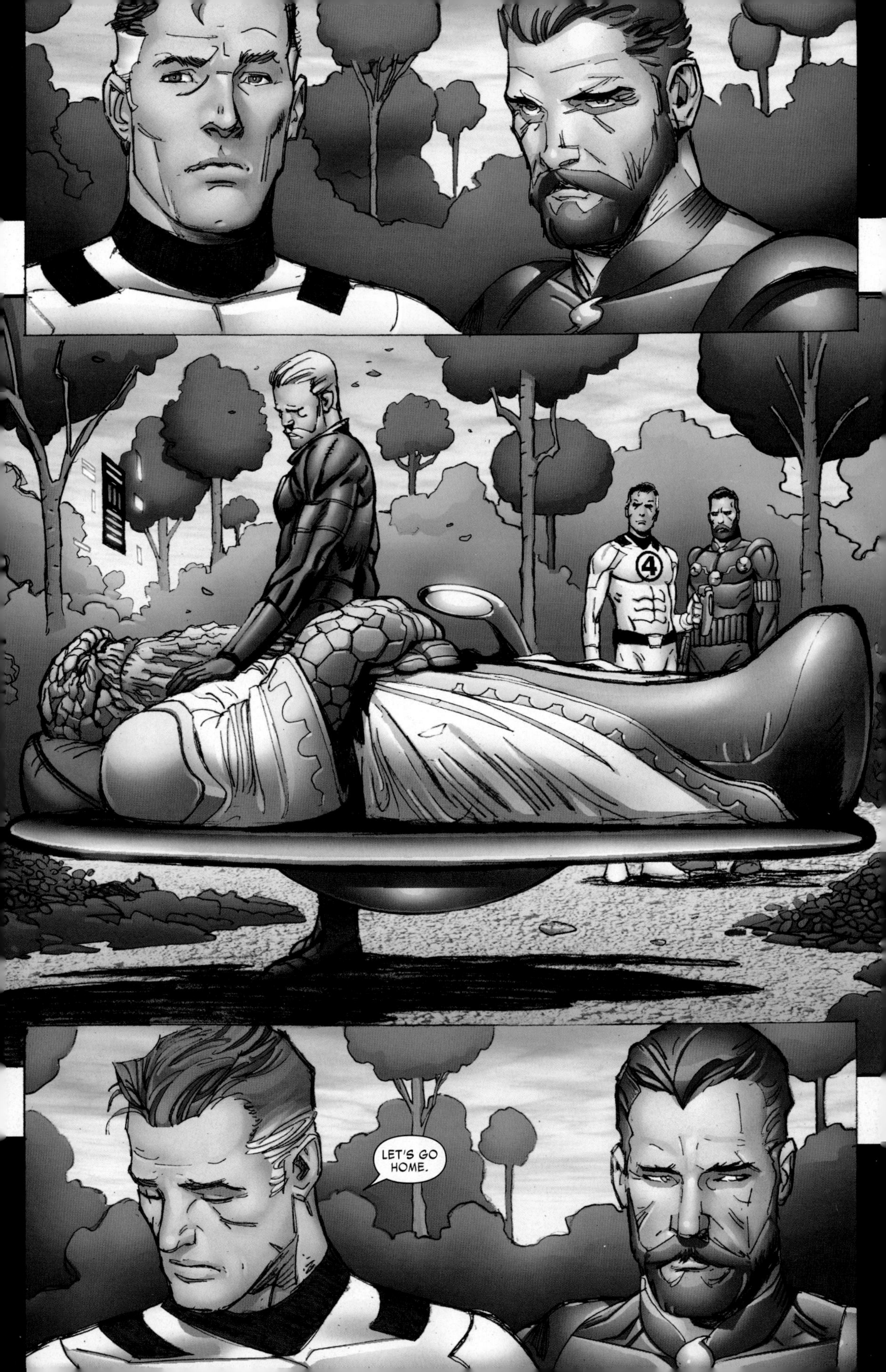
LET'S GO HOME.

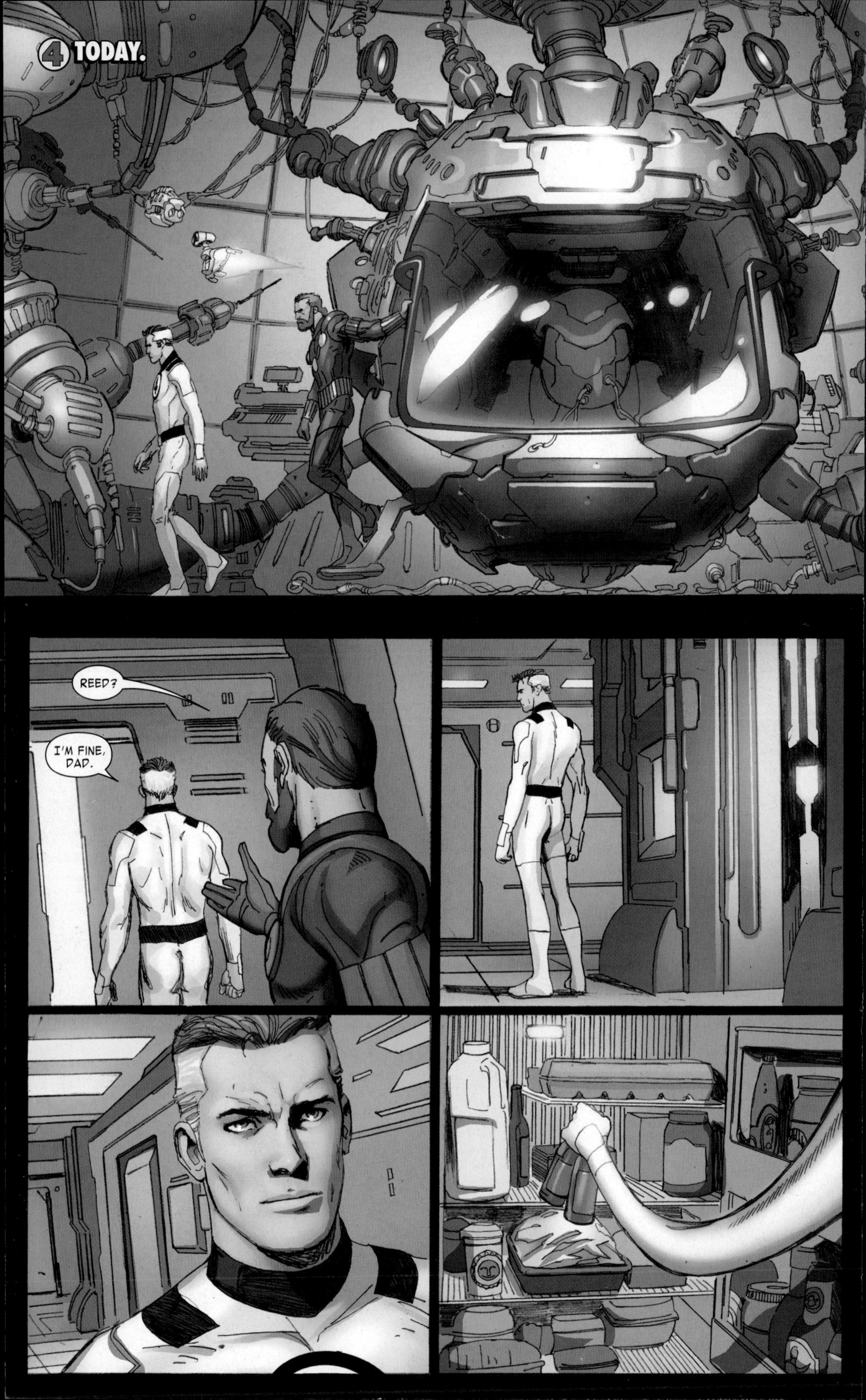
4 TODAY.
REED?
I'M FINE, DAD.

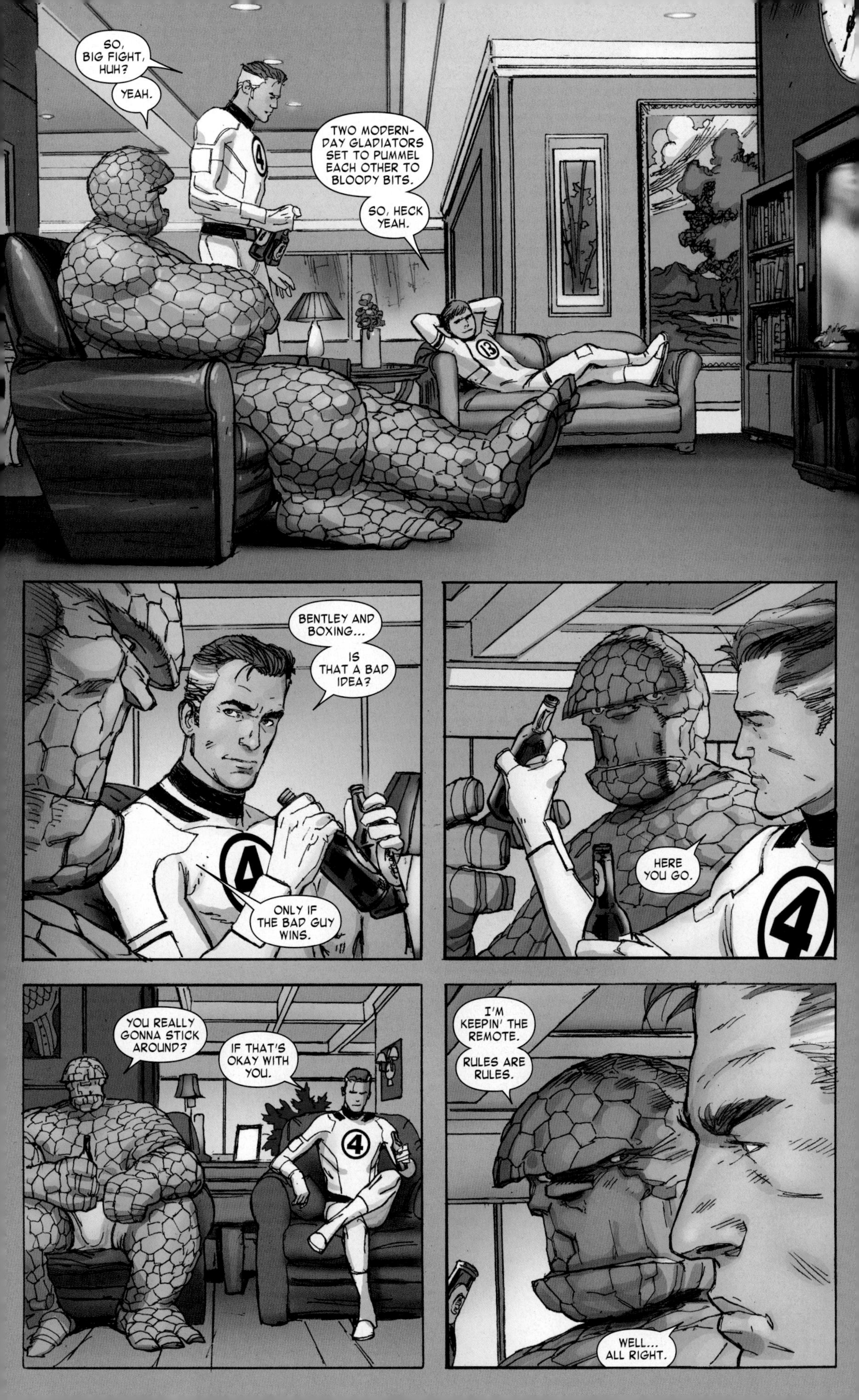
SO, BIG FIGHT, HUH?
YEAH.
TWO MODERN-DAY GLADIATORS SET TO PUMMEL EACH OTHER TO BLOODY BITS.
SO, HECK YEAH.
BENTLEY AND BOXING...
IS THAT A BAD IDEA?
ONLY IF THE BAD GUY WINS.
HERE YOU GO.
YOU REALLY GONNA STICK AROUND?
IF THAT'S OKAY WITH YOU.
I'M KEEPIN' THE REMOTE.
RULES ARE RULES.
WELL... ALL RIGHT.

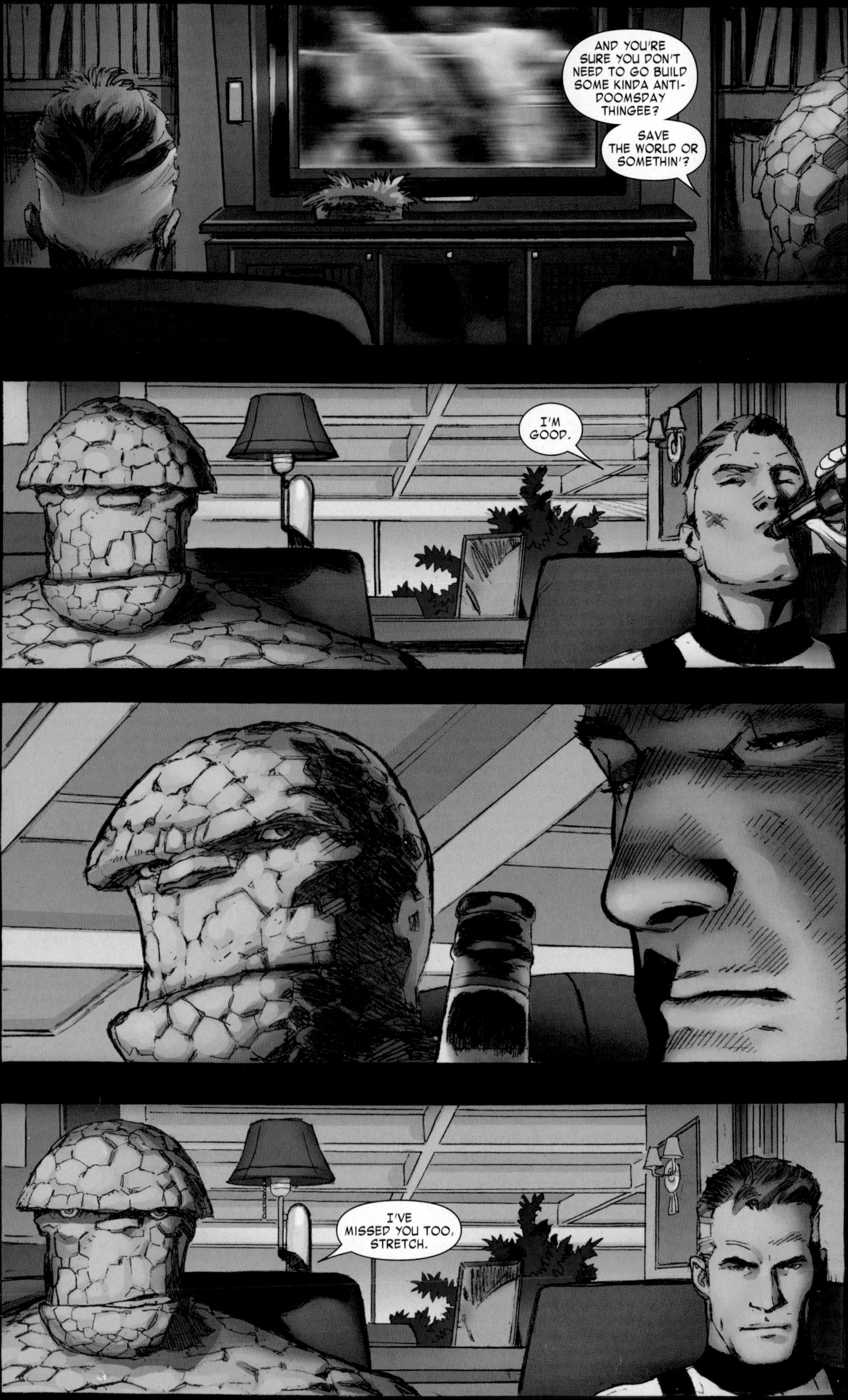
AND YOU'RE SURE YOU DON'T NEED TO GO BUILD SOME KINDA ANTI-DOOMSDAY THINGEE?
SAVE THE WORLD OR SOMETHIN'?
I'M GOOD.
I'VE MISSED YOU TOO, STRETCH.

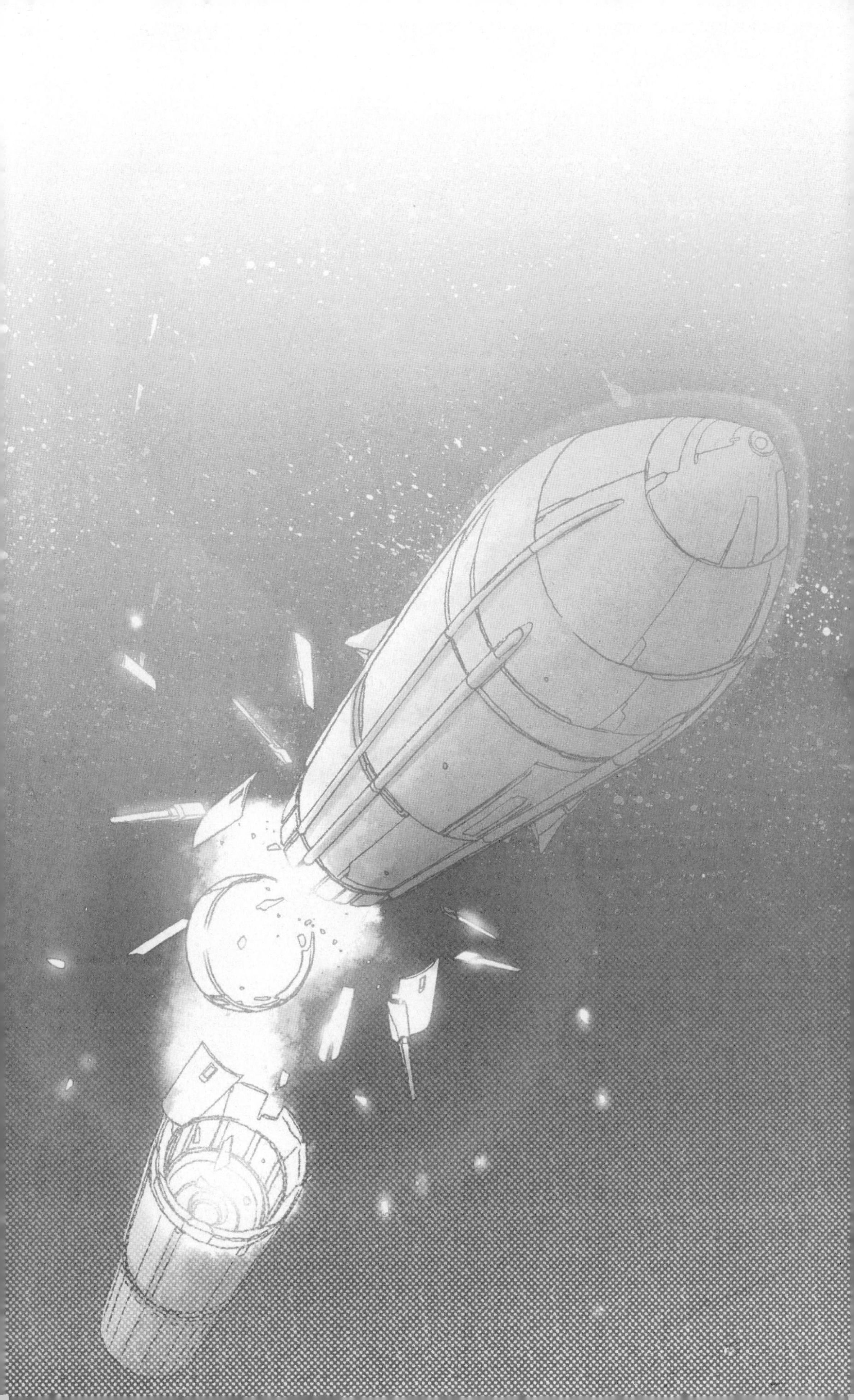

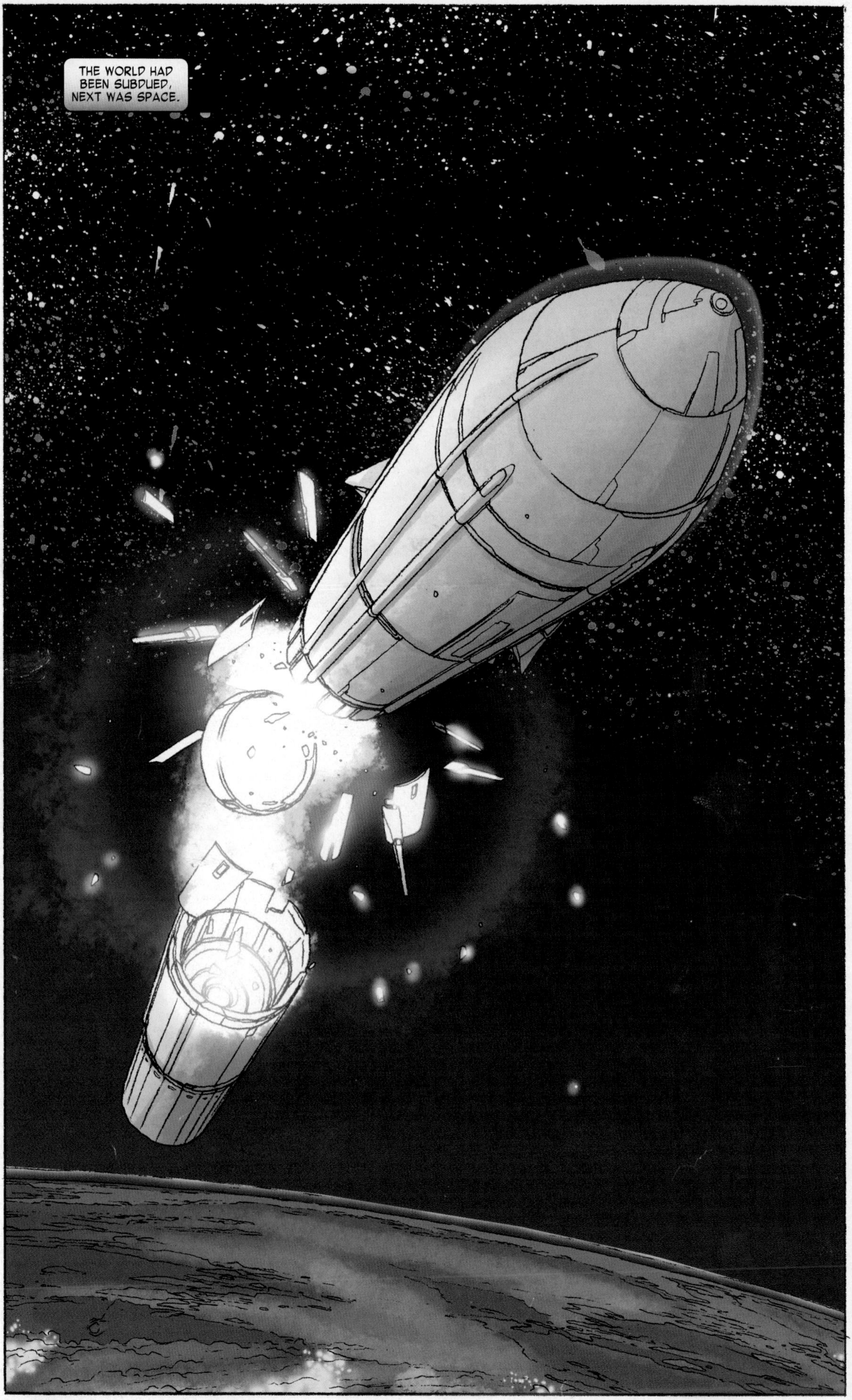
THE WORLD HAD BEEN SUBDUED, NEXT WAS SPACE.

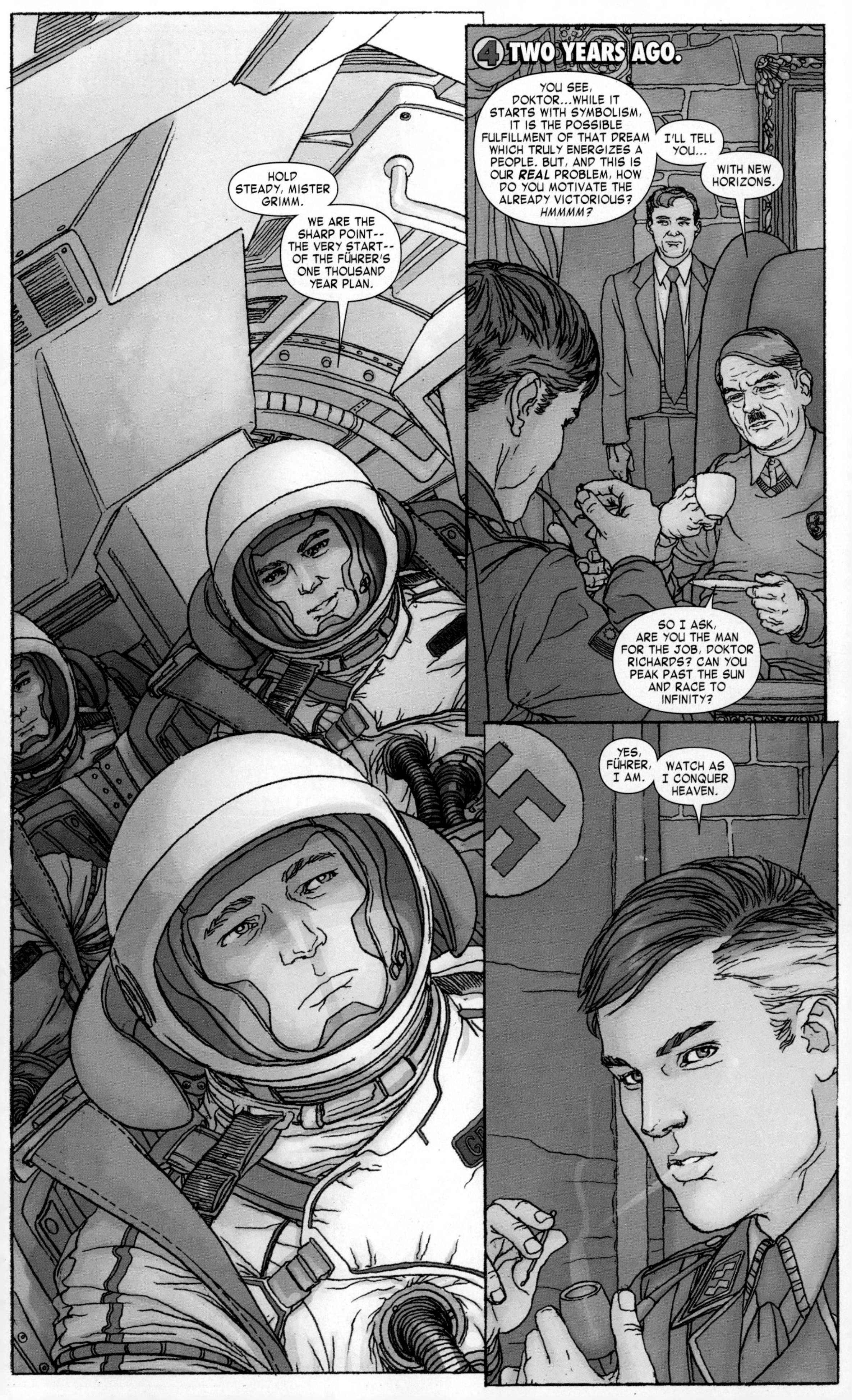
HOLD STEADY, MISTER GRIMM.
WE ARE THE SHARP POINT-- THE VERY START-- OF THE FÜHRER'S ONE THOUSAND YEAR PLAN.
4 TWO YEARS AGO.
YOU SEE, DOKTOR...WHILE IT STARTS WITH SYMBOLISM, IT IS THE POSSIBLE FULFILLMENT OF THAT DREAM WHICH TRULY ENERGIZES A PEOPLE. BUT, AND THIS IS OUR REAL PROBLEM, HOW DO YOU MOTIVATE THE ALREADY VICTORIOUS? HMMMM?
I'LL TELL YOU...
WITH NEW HORIZONS.
SO I ASK, ARE YOU THE MAN FOR THE JOB, DOKTOR RICHARDS? CAN YOU PEAK PAST THE SUN AND RACE TO INFINITY?
YES, FÜHRER, I AM.
WATCH AS I CONQUER HEAVEN.

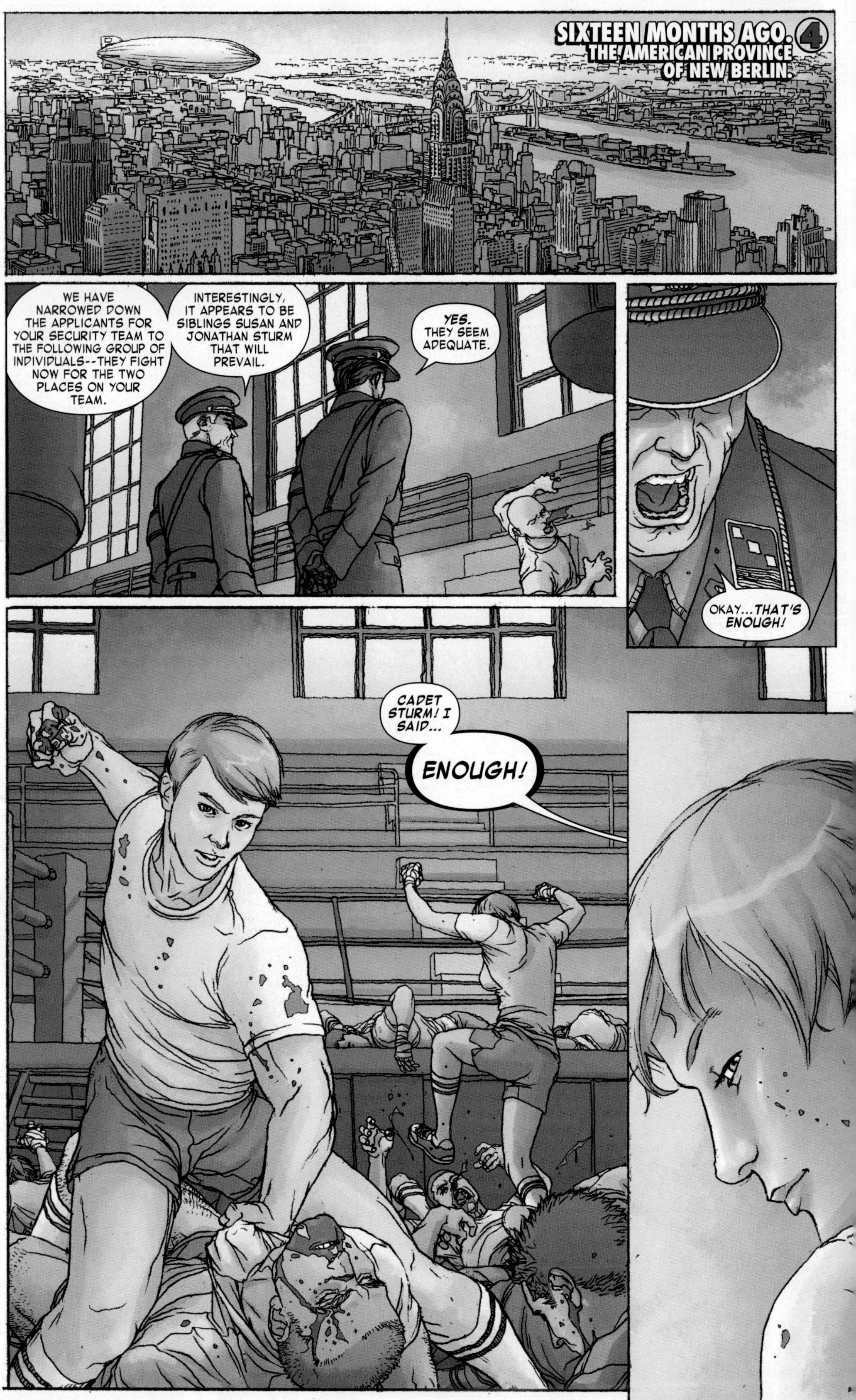

SIXTEEN MONTHS AGO.
4
THE AMERICAN PROVINCE OF NEW BERLIN.
WE HAVE NARROWED DOWN THE APPLICANTS FOR YOUR SECURITY TEAM TO THE FOLLOWING GROUP OF INDIVIDUALS--THEY FIGHT NOW FOR THE TWO PLACES ON YOUR TEAM.
INTERESTINGLY, IT APPEARS TO BE SIBLINGS SUSAN AND JONATHAN STURM THAT WILL PREVAIL.
YES. THEY SEEM ADEQUATE.
OKAY...THAT'S ENOUGH!
CADET STURM! I SAID...
ENOUGH!

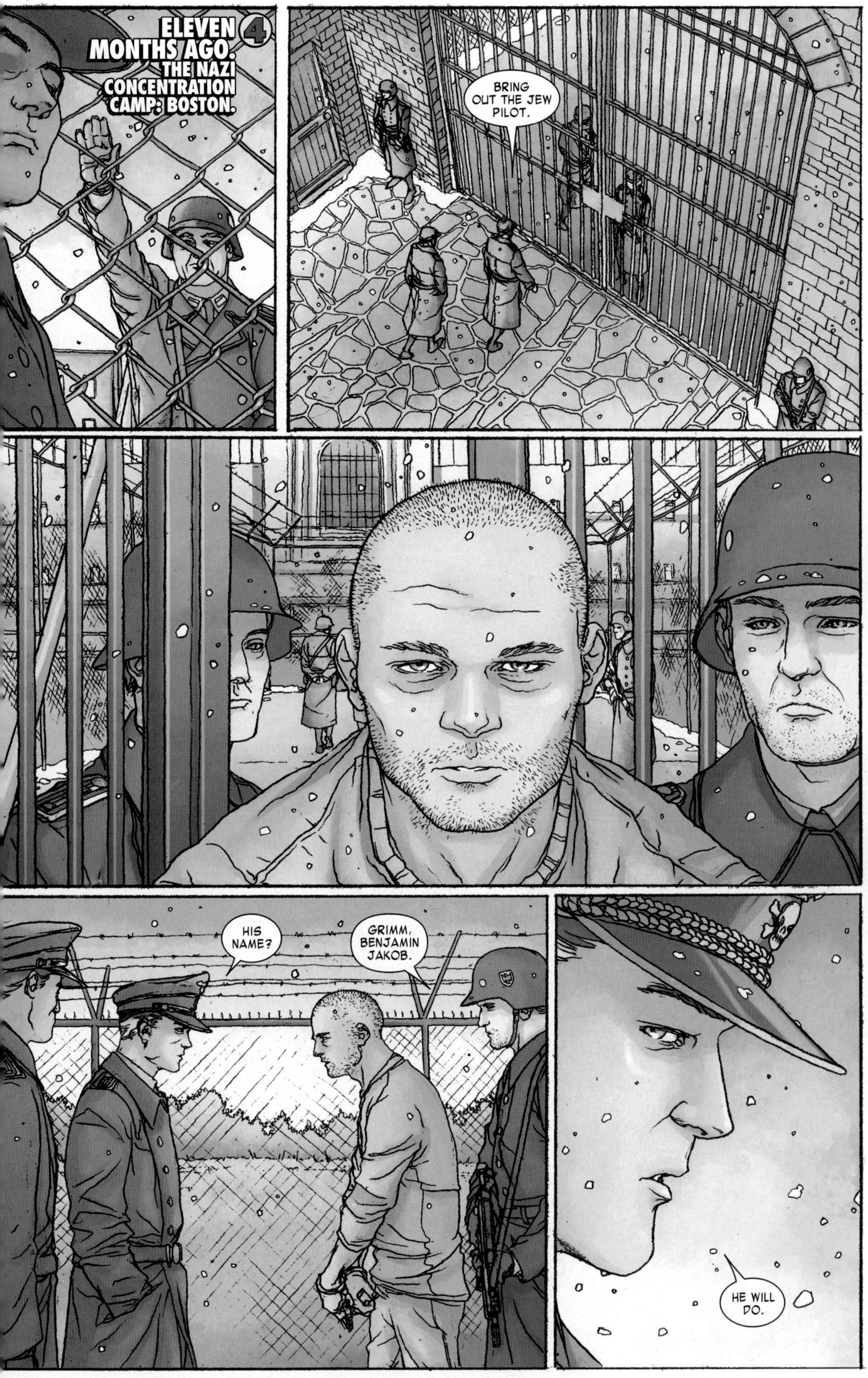
ELEVEN MONTHS AGO. THE NAZI CONCENTRATION CAMP: BOSTON.
BRING OUT THE JEW PILOT.
HIS NAME?
GRIMM, BENJAMIN JAKOB.
HE WILL DO.

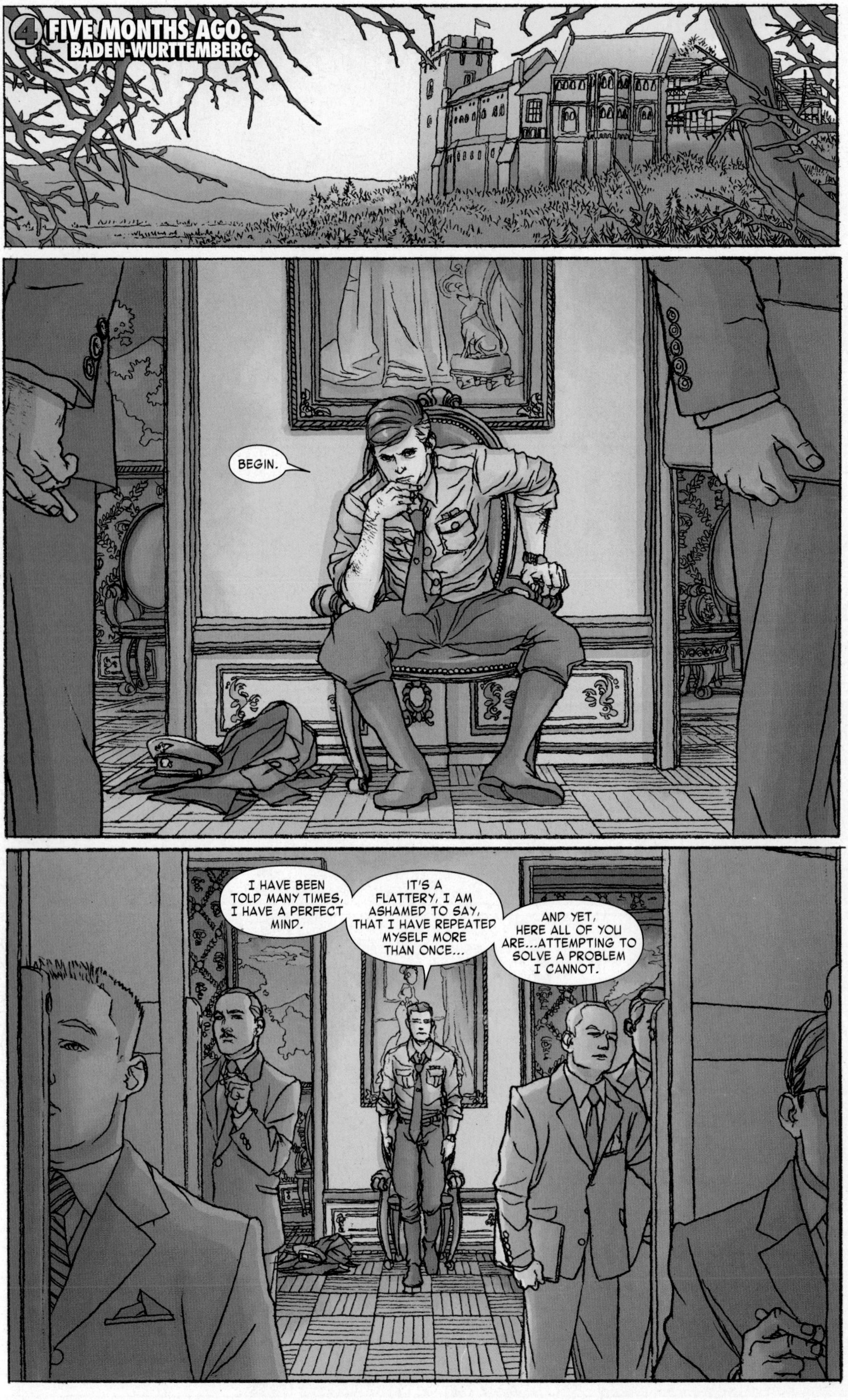
4
FIVE MONTHS AGO.
BADEN-WURTTEMBERG.
BEGIN.
I HAVE BEEN TOLD MANY TIMES, I HAVE A PERFECT MIND.
IT'S A FLATTERY, I AM ASHAMED TO SAY, THAT I HAVE REPEATED MYSELF MORE THAN ONCE...
AND YET, HERE ALL OF YOU ARE...ATTEMPTING TO SOLVE A PROBLEM I CANNOT.

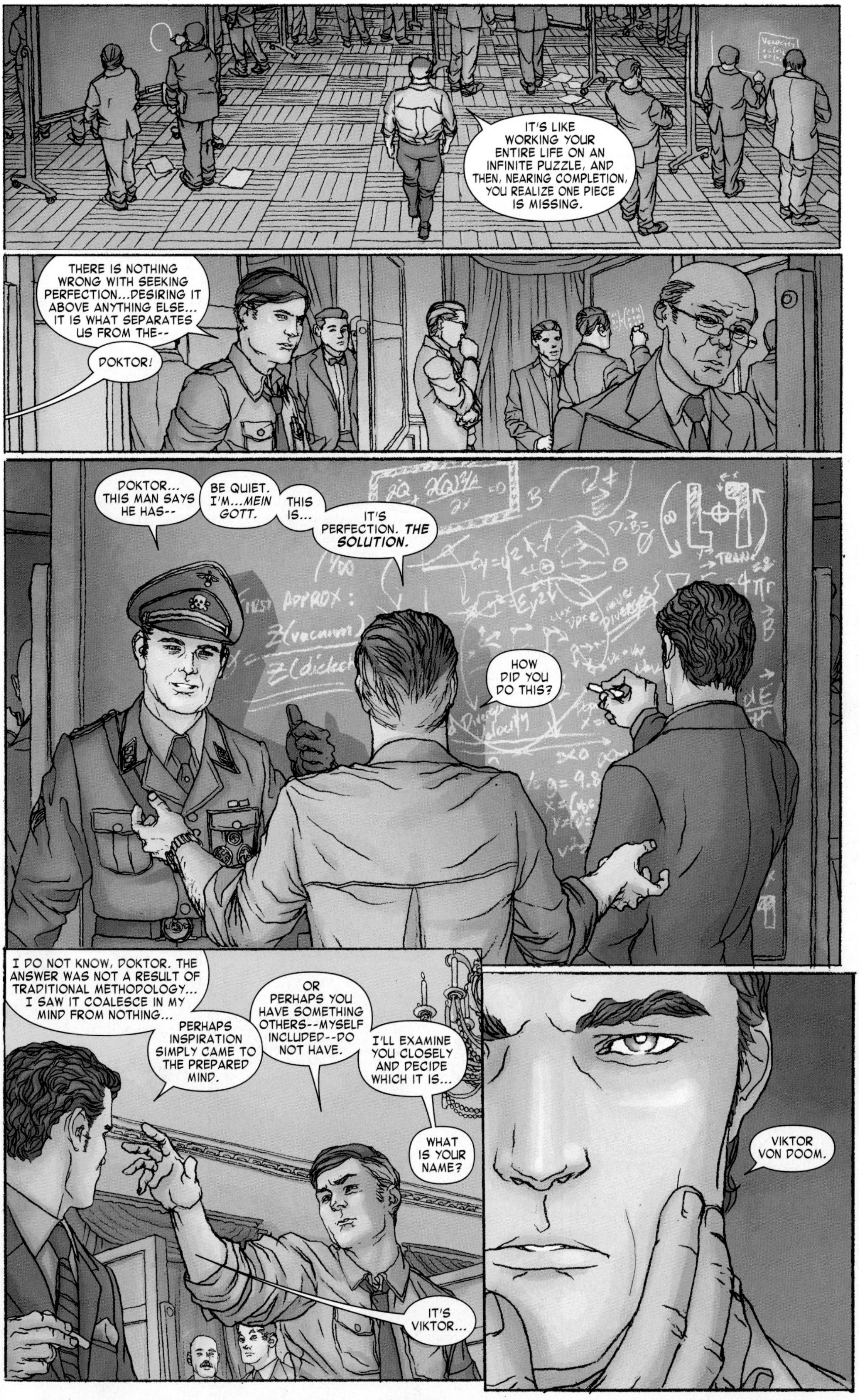
IT'S LIKE WORKING YOUR ENTIRE LIFE ON AN INFINITE PUZZLE, AND THEN, NEARING COMPLETION, YOU REALIZE ONE PIECE IS MISSING.
THERE IS NOTHING WRONG WITH SEEKING PERFECTION...DESIRING IT ABOVE ANYTHING ELSE... IT IS WHAT SEPARATES US FROM THE--
DOKTOR!
DOKTOR... THIS MAN SAYS HE HAS--
BE QUIET. I'M...MEIN GOTT.
THIS IS...
IT'S PERFECTION. THE SOLUTION.
HOW DID YOU DO THIS?
I DO NOT KNOW, DOKTOR. THE ANSWER WAS NOT A RESULT OF TRADITIONAL METHODOLOGY... I SAW IT COALESCE IN MY MIND FROM NOTHING...
PERHAPS INSPIRATION SIMPLY CAME TO THE PREPARED MIND.
OR PERHAPS YOU HAVE SOMETHING OTHERS--MYSELF INCLUDED--DO NOT HAVE.
I'LL EXAMINE YOU CLOSELY AND DECIDE WHICH IT IS...
WHAT IS YOUR NAME?
IT'S VIKTOR...
VIKTOR VON DOOM.

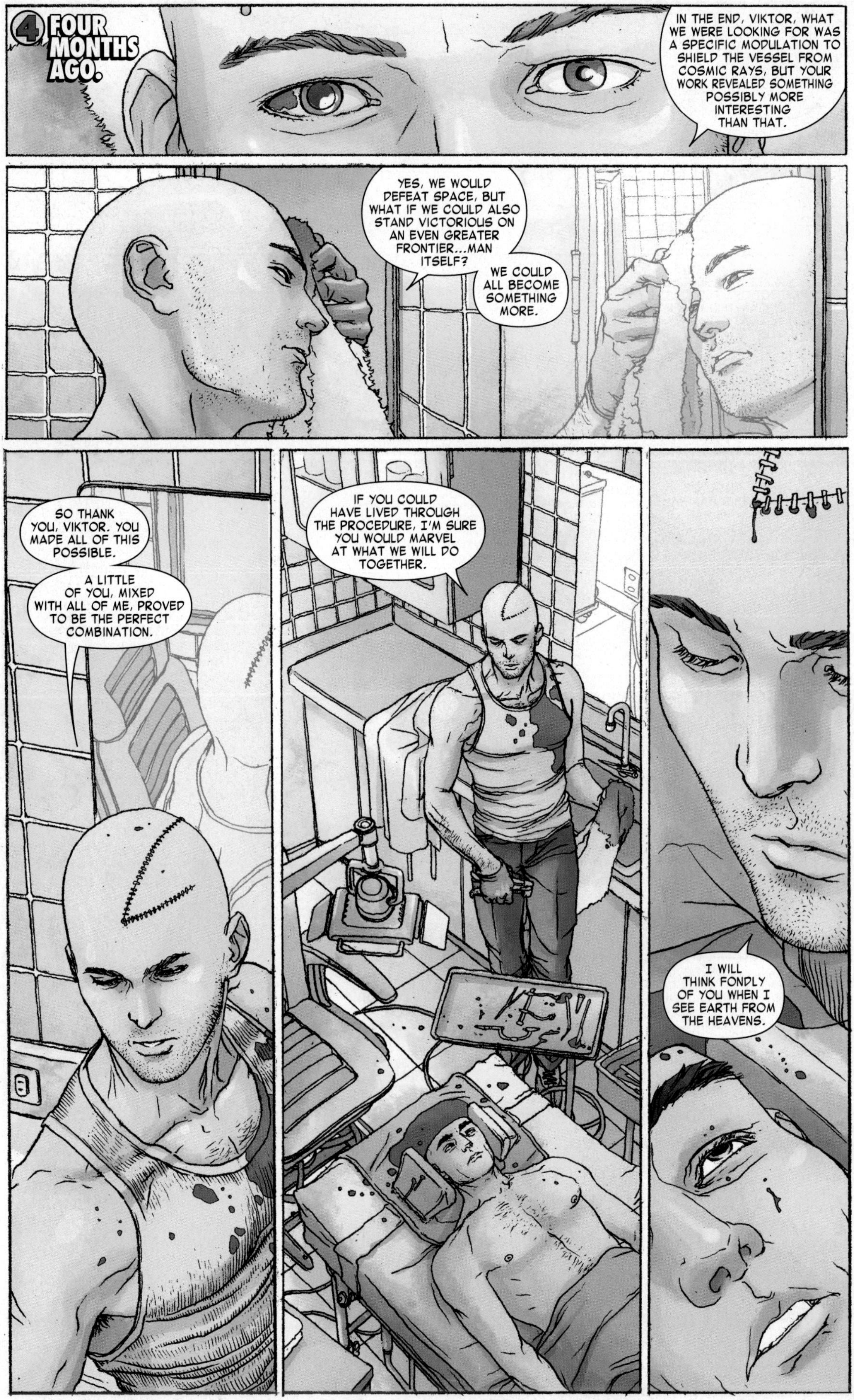
FOUR MONTHS AGO.
IN THE END, VIKTOR, WHAT WE WERE LOOKING FOR WAS A SPECIFIC MODULATION TO SHIELD THE VESSEL FROM COSMIC RAYS, BUT YOUR WORK REVEALED SOMETHING POSSIBLY MORE INTERESTING THAN THAT.
YES, WE WOULD DEFEAT SPACE, BUT WHAT IF WE COULD ALSO STAND VICTORIOUS ON AN EVEN GREATER FRONTIER...MAN ITSELF?
WE COULD ALL BECOME SOMETHING MORE.
SO THANK YOU, VIKTOR. YOU MADE ALL OF THIS POSSIBLE.
A LITTLE OF YOU, MIXED WITH ALL OF ME, PROVED TO BE THE PERFECT COMBINATION.
IF YOU COULD HAVE LIVED THROUGH THE PROCEDURE, I'M SURE YOU WOULD MARVEL AT WHAT WE WILL DO TOGETHER.
I WILL THINK FONDLY OF YOU WHEN I SEE EARTH FROM THE HEAVENS.

REACHING THE RADIATION BELT, DOKTOR.

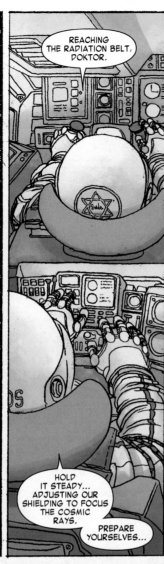

HOLD IT STEADY... ADJUSTING OUR SHIELDING TO FOCUS THE COSMIC RAYS.

PREPARE YOURSELVES...

THIS COULD HURT A BIT.

AARGGHH!

SKIN... TURNING ICE COLD. FREEZING.

I CAN'T FEEL MY HANDS... MY ARMS...

LOSING CONTROL.

WE'RE GOING TO CR-CRASH.

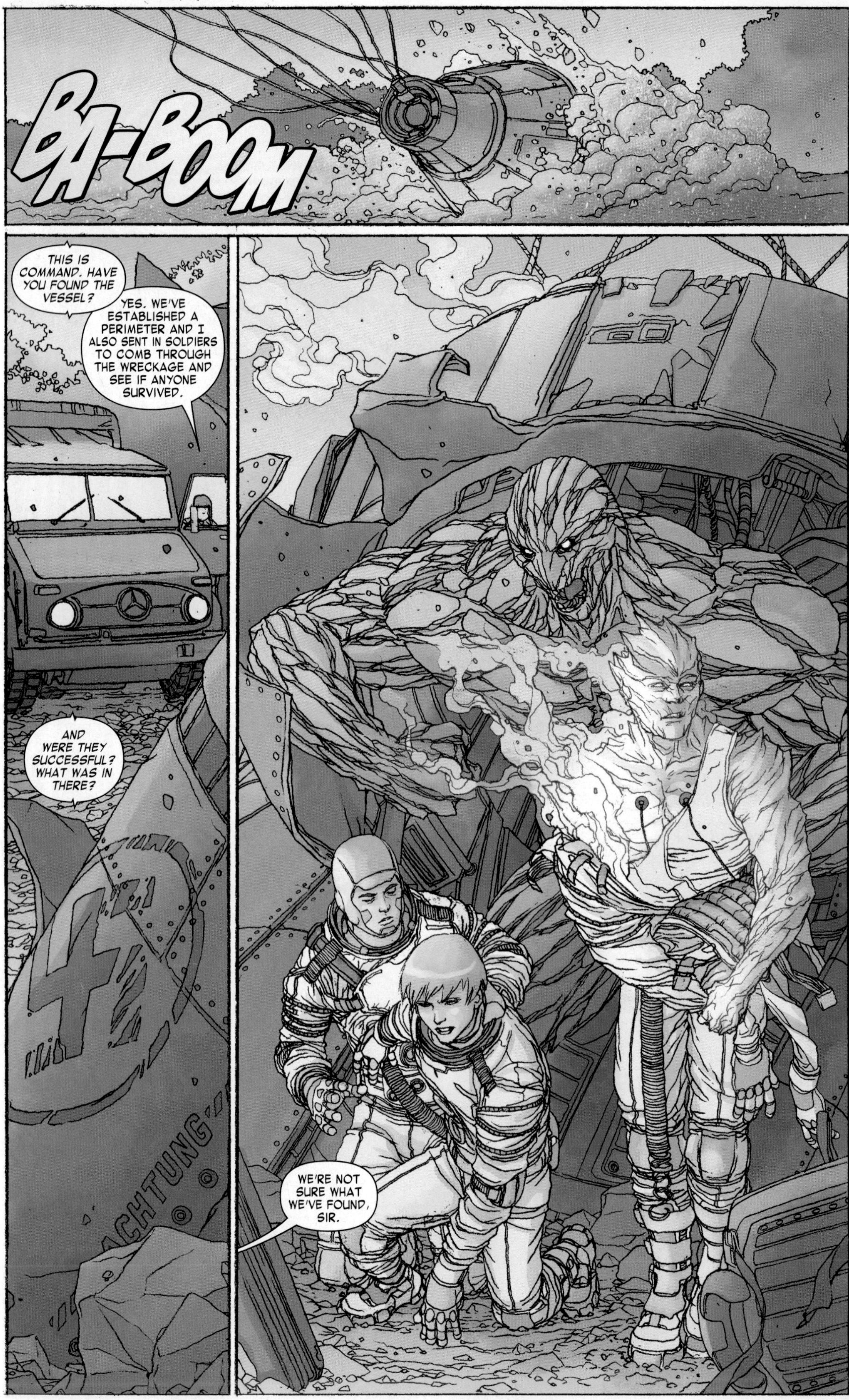
BA-BOOM
THIS IS COMMAND. HAVE YOU FOUND THE VESSEL?
YES. WE'VE ESTABLISHED A PERIMETER AND I ALSO SENT IN SOLDIERS TO COMB THROUGH THE WRECKAGE AND SEE IF ANYONE SURVIVED.
AND WERE THEY SUCCESSFUL? WHAT WAS IN THERE?
WE'RE NOT SURE WHAT WE'VE FOUND, SIR.
ACHTUNG

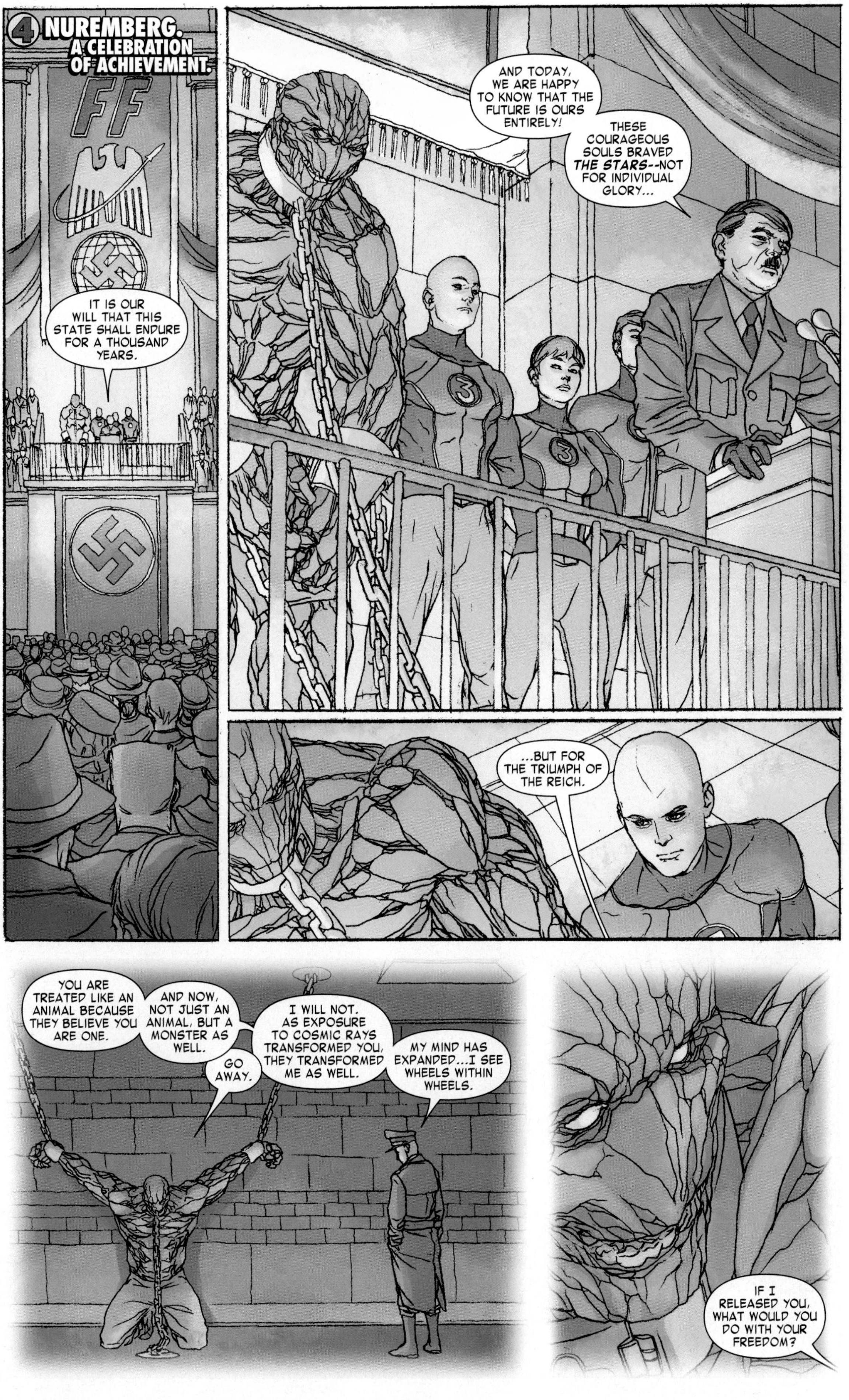

4 NUREMBERG. A CELEBRATION OF ACHIEVEMENT.
FF
IT IS OUR WILL THAT THIS STATE SHALL ENDURE FOR A THOUSAND YEARS.
AND TODAY, WE ARE HAPPY TO KNOW THAT THE FUTURE IS OURS ENTIRELY!
THESE COURAGEOUS SOULS BRAVED THE STARS--NOT FOR INDIVIDUAL GLORY...
...BUT FOR THE TRIUMPH OF THE REICH.
YOU ARE TREATED LIKE AN ANIMAL BECAUSE THEY BELIEVE YOU ARE ONE.
AND NOW, NOT JUST AN ANIMAL, BUT A MONSTER AS WELL.
GO AWAY.
I WILL NOT. AS EXPOSURE TO COSMIC RAYS TRANSFORMED YOU, THEY TRANSFORMED ME AS WELL.
MY MIND HAS EXPANDED...I SEE WHEELS WITHIN WHEELS.
IF I RELEASED YOU, WHAT WOULD YOU DO WITH YOUR FREEDOM?

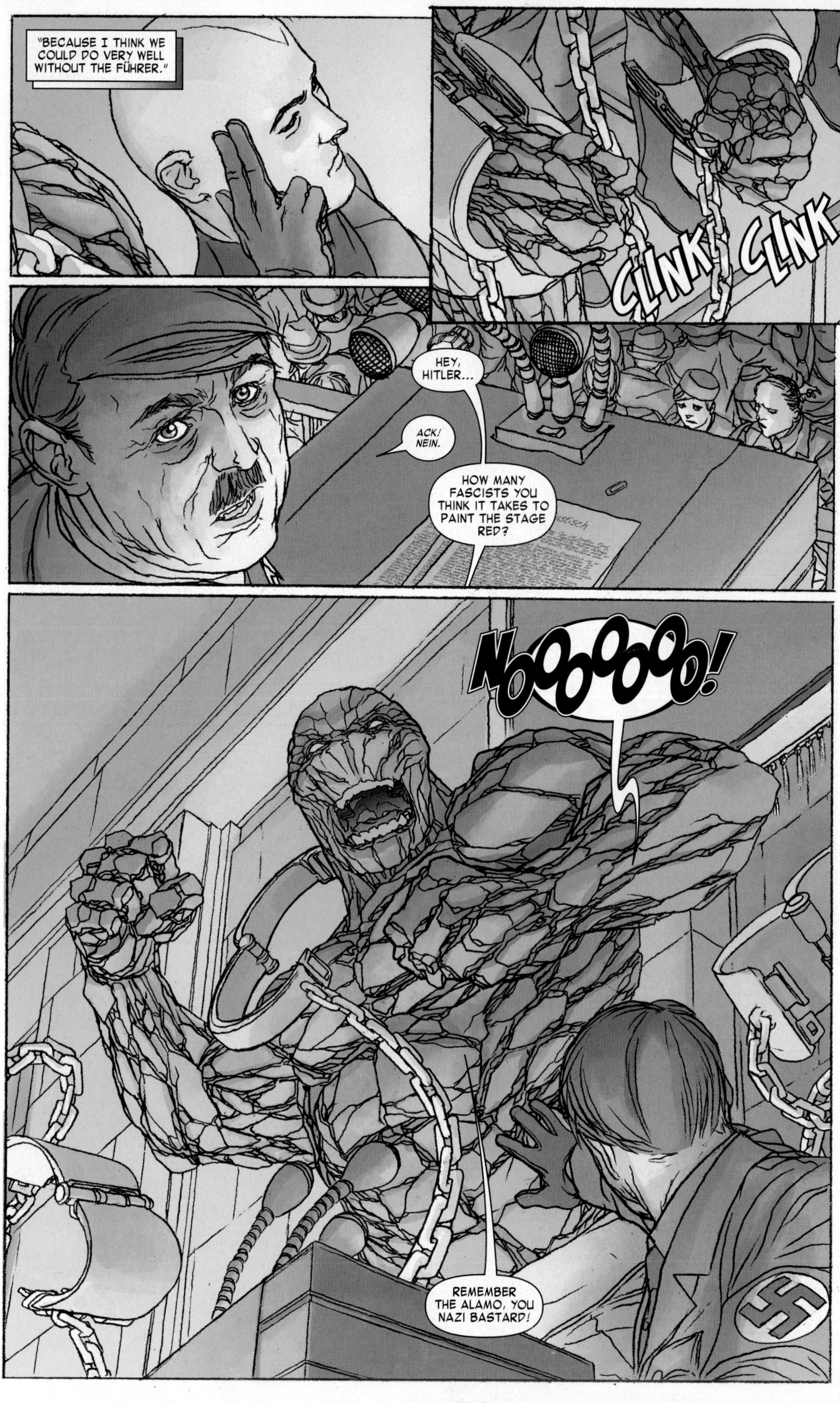
"BECAUSE I THINK WE COULD DO VERY WELL WITHOUT THE FÜHRER."
CLINK CLINK
HEY, HITLER...
ACK! NEIN.
HOW MANY FASCISTS YOU THINK IT TAKES TO PAINT THE STAGE RED?
NOOOOOOO!
REMEMBER THE ALAMO, YOU NAZI BASTARD!

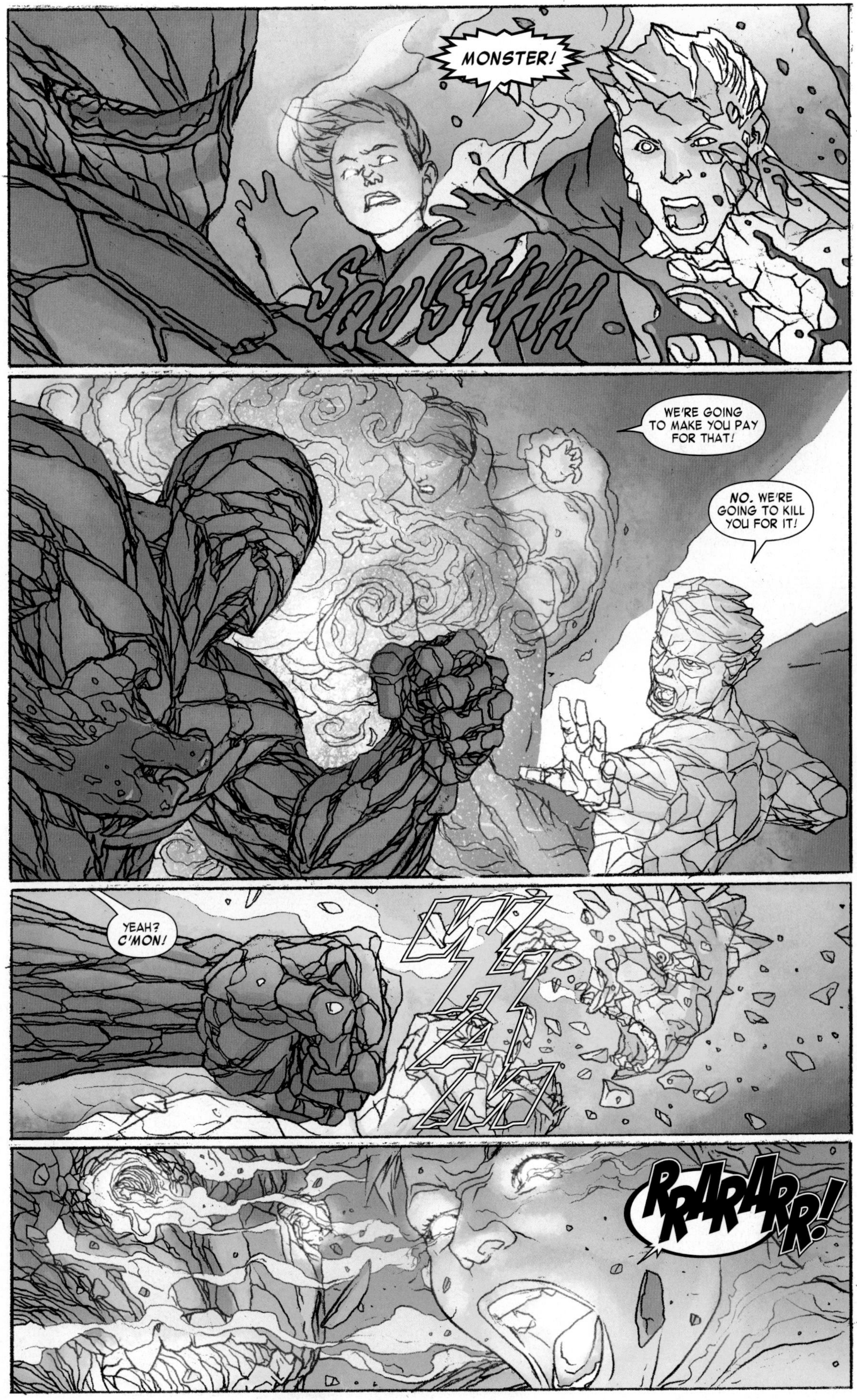
MONSTER!
SQUSHHH
WE'RE GOING TO MAKE YOU PAY FOR THAT!
NO. WE'RE GOING TO KILL YOU FOR IT!
YEAH? C'MON!
RRARARRR!

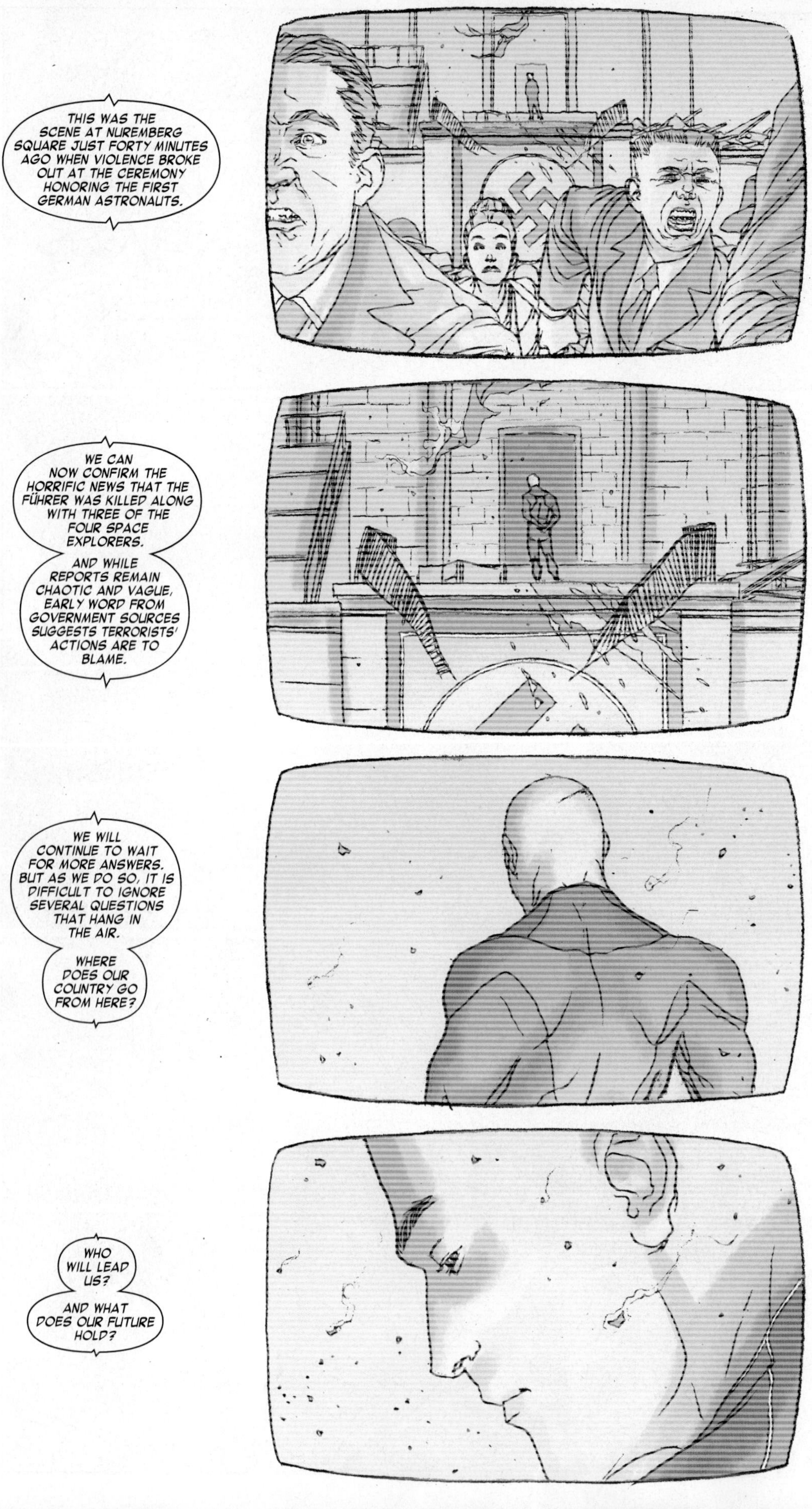
THIS WAS THE SCENE AT NUREMBERG SQUARE JUST FORTY MINUTES AGO WHEN VIOLENCE BROKE OUT AT THE CEREMONY HONORING THE FIRST GERMAN ASTRONAUTS.
WE CAN NOW CONFIRM THE HORRIFIC NEWS THAT THE FÜHRER WAS KILLED ALONG WITH THREE OF THE FOUR SPACE EXPLORERS.
AND WHILE REPORTS REMAIN CHAOTIC AND VAGUE, EARLY WORD FROM GOVERNMENT SOURCES SUGGESTS TERRORISTS' ACTIONS ARE TO BLAME.
WE WILL CONTINUE TO WAIT FOR MORE ANSWERS. BUT AS WE DO SO, IT IS DIFFICULT TO IGNORE SEVERAL QUESTIONS THAT HANG IN THE AIR.
WHERE DOES OUR COUNTRY GO FROM HERE?
WHO WILL LEAD US?
AND WHAT DOES OUR FUTURE HOLD?

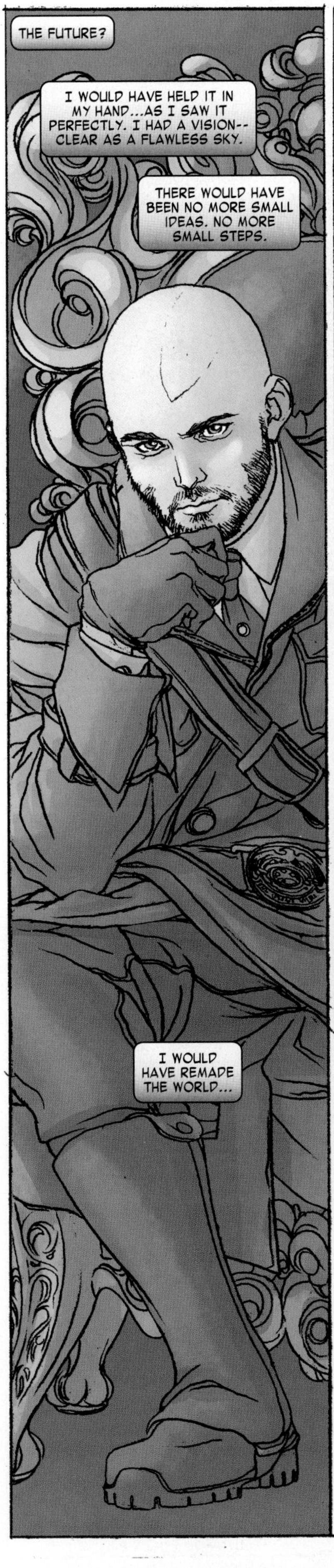
THE FUTURE?
I WOULD HAVE HELD IT IN MY HAND...AS I SAW IT PERFECTLY. I HAD A VISION--CLEAR AS A FLAWLESS SKY.
THERE WOULD HAVE BEEN NO MORE SMALL IDEAS. NO MORE SMALL STEPS.
I WOULD HAVE REMADE THE WORLD...

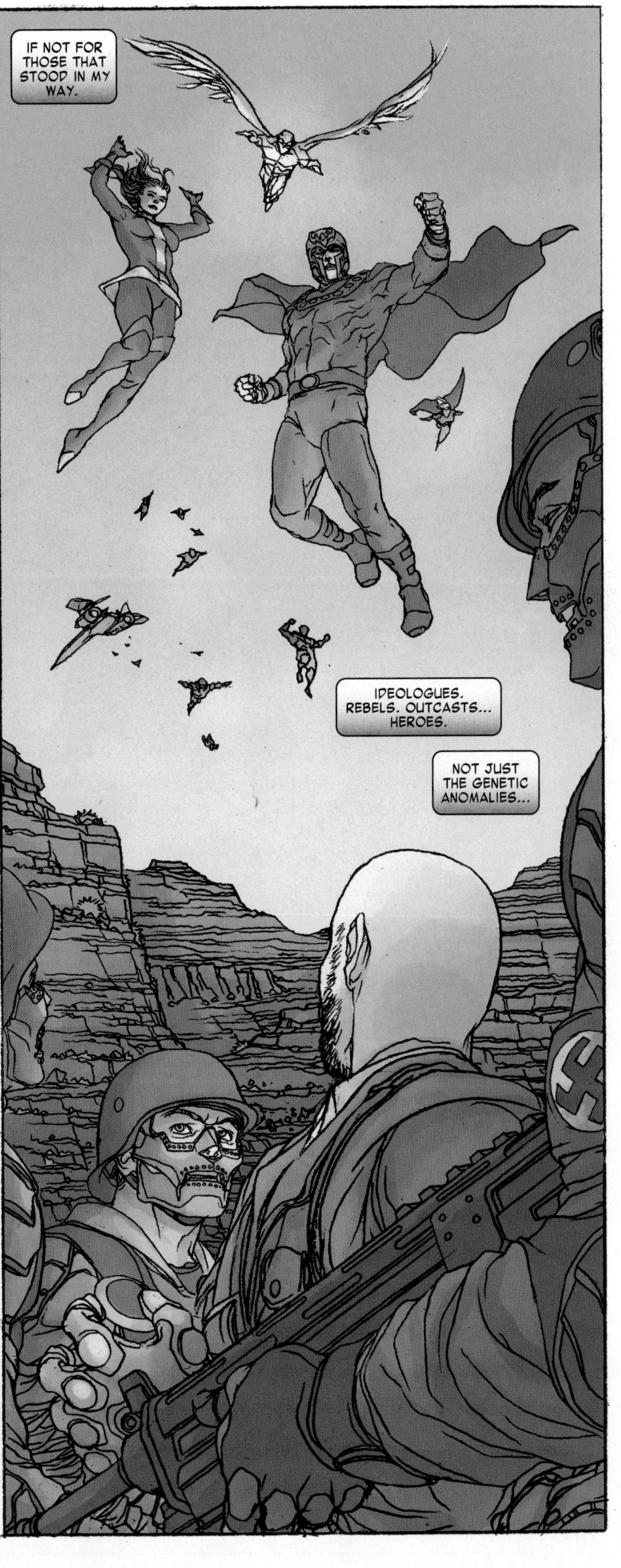
IF NOT FOR THOSE THAT STOOD IN MY WAY.
IDEOLOGUES. REBELS. OUTCASTS... HEROES.
NOT JUST THE GENETIC ANOMALIES...

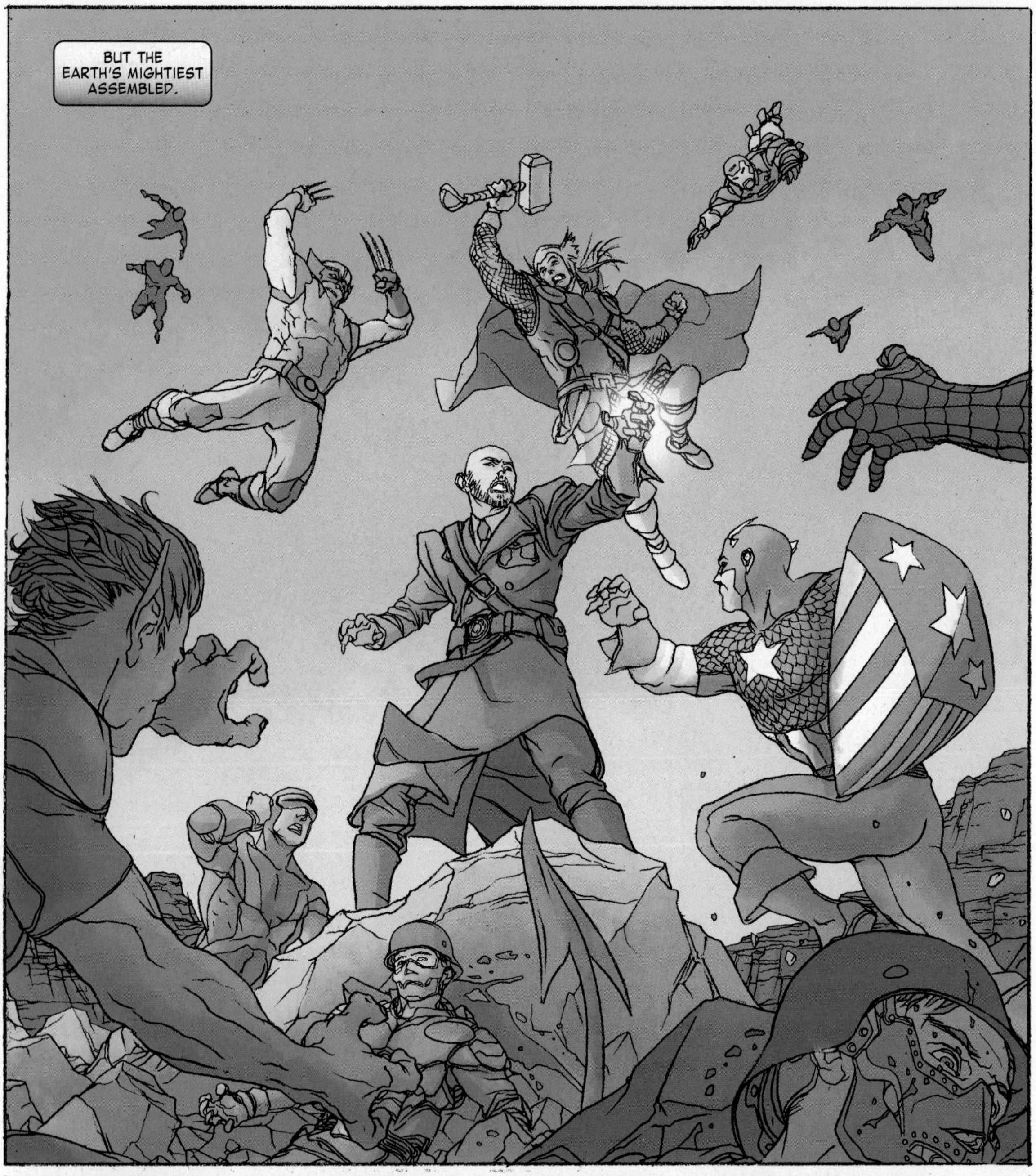
BUT THE EARTH'S MIGHTIEST ASSEMBLED.

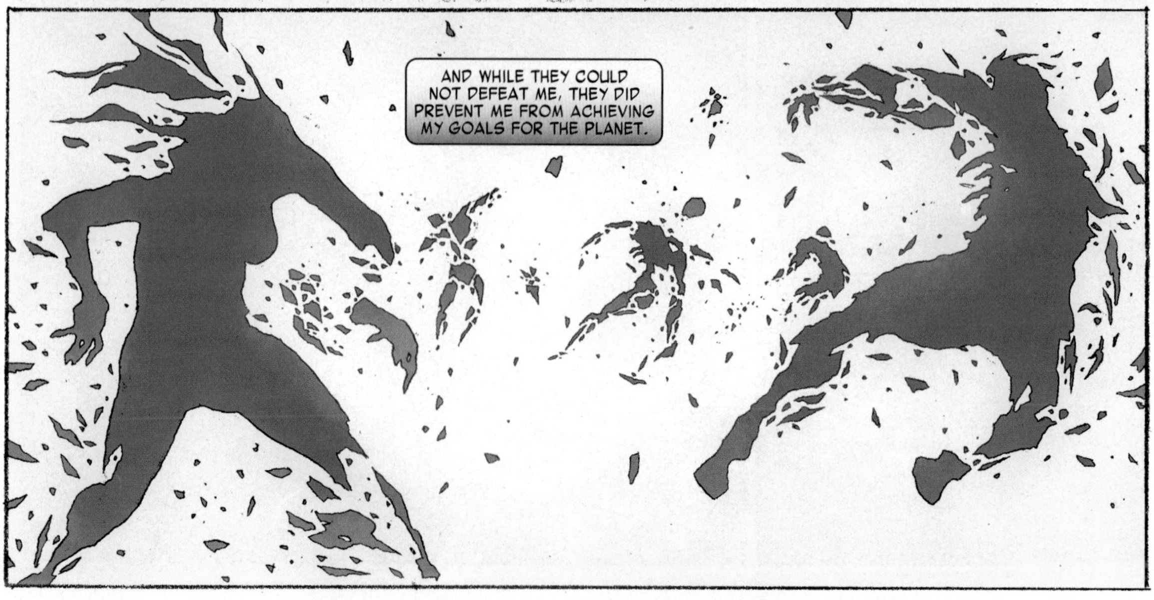
AND WHILE THEY COULD NOT DEFEAT ME, THEY DID PREVENT ME FROM ACHIEVING MY GOALS FOR THE PLANET.

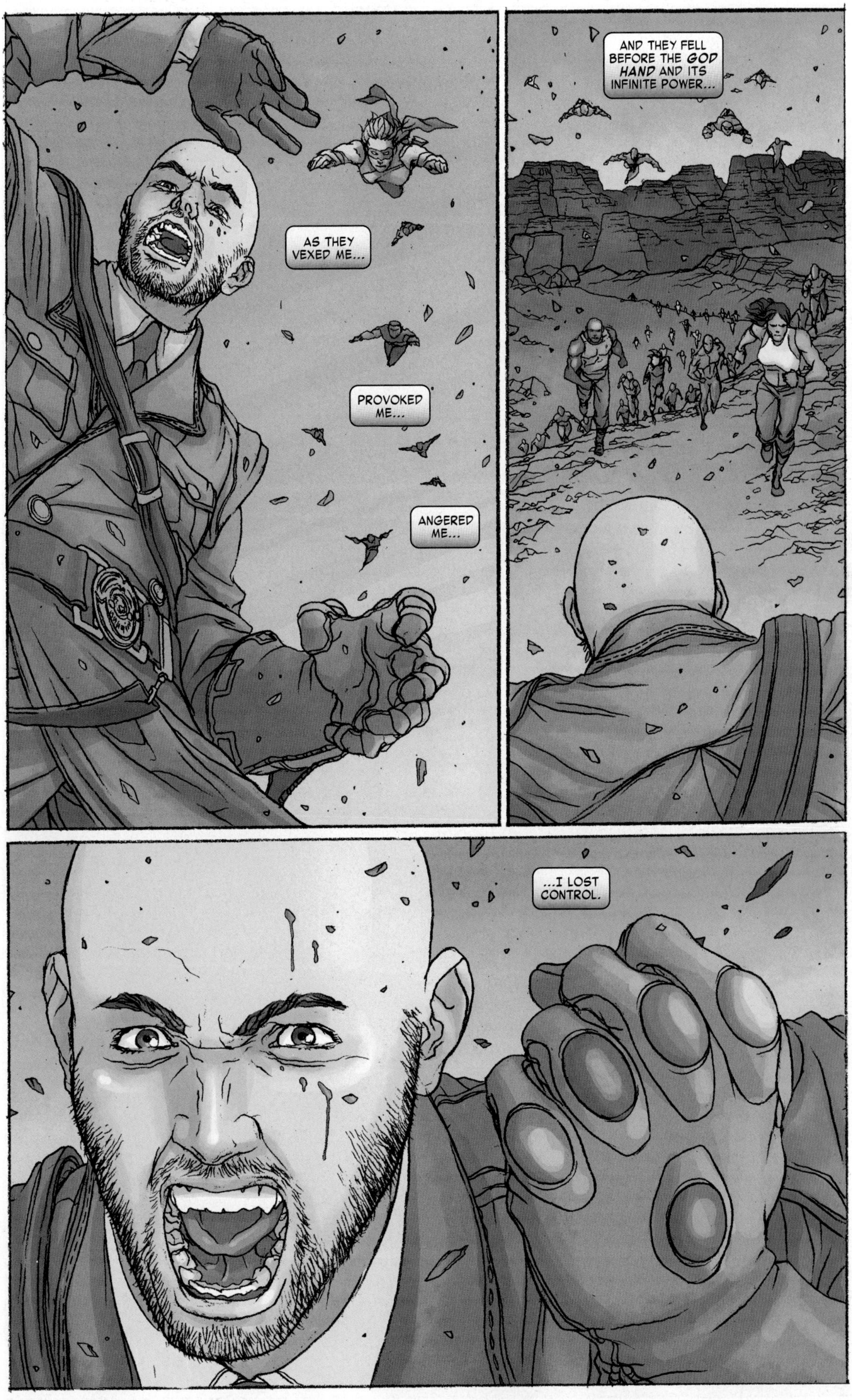
AS THEY VEXED ME...
PROVOKED ME...
ANGERED ME...
AND THEY FELL BEFORE THE GOD HAND AND ITS INFINITE POWER...
...I LOST CONTROL.

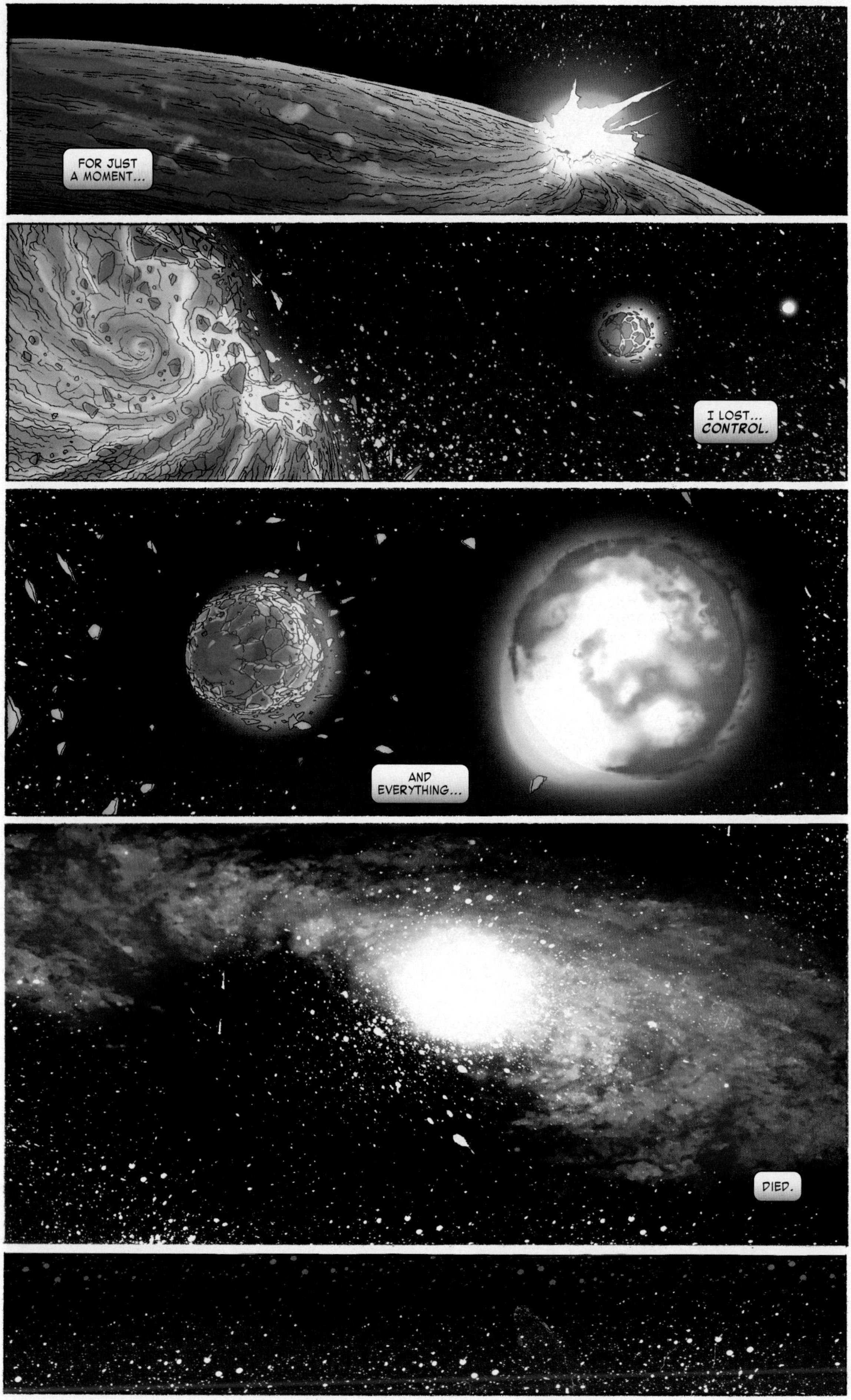
FOR JUST A MOMENT...
I LOST... CONTROL.
AND EVERYTHING...
DIED.

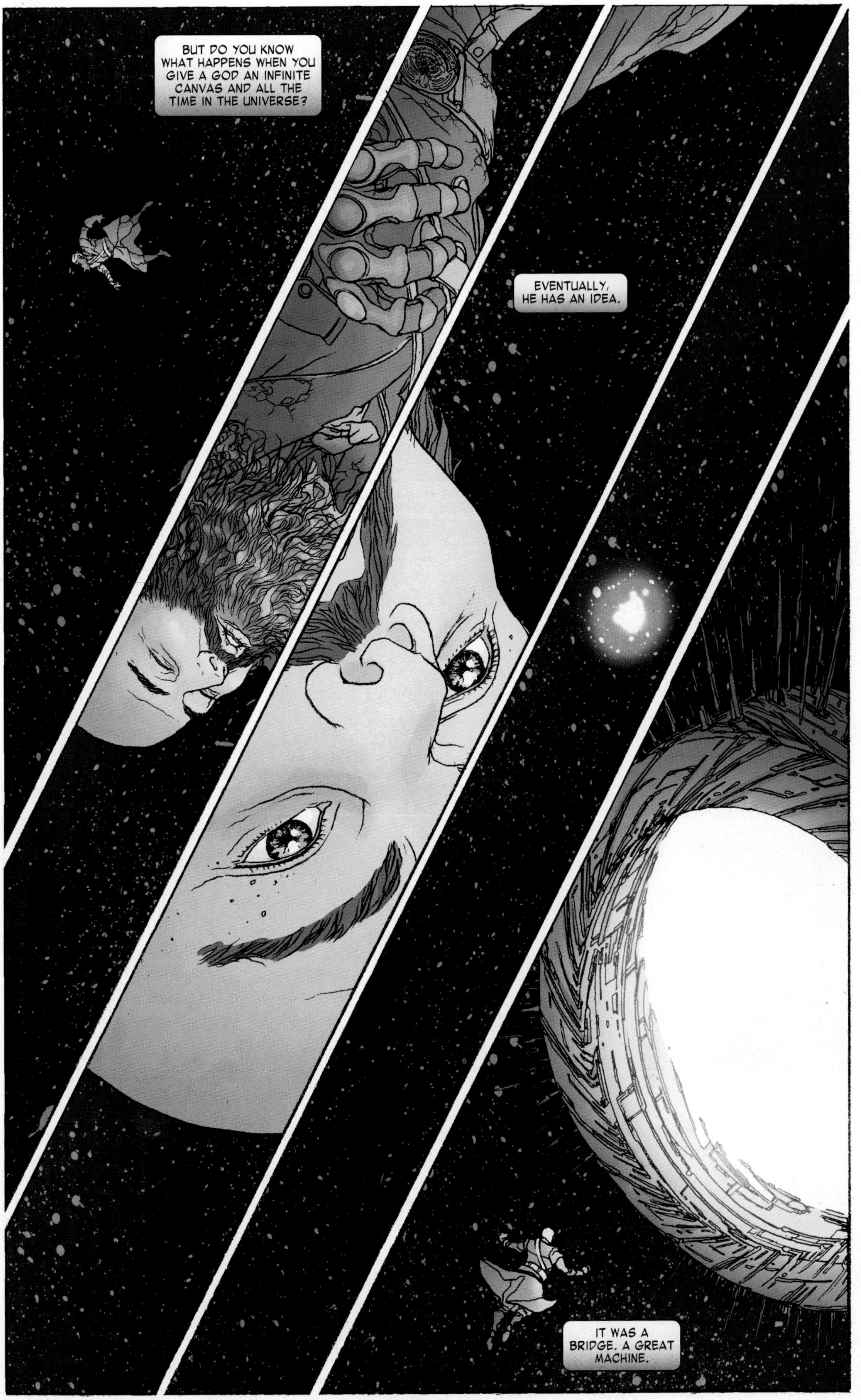
BUT DO YOU KNOW WHAT HAPPENS WHEN YOU GIVE A GOD AN INFINITE CANVAS AND ALL THE TIME IN THE UNIVERSE?
EVENTUALLY, HE HAS AN IDEA.
IT WAS A BRIDGE. A GREAT MACHINE.

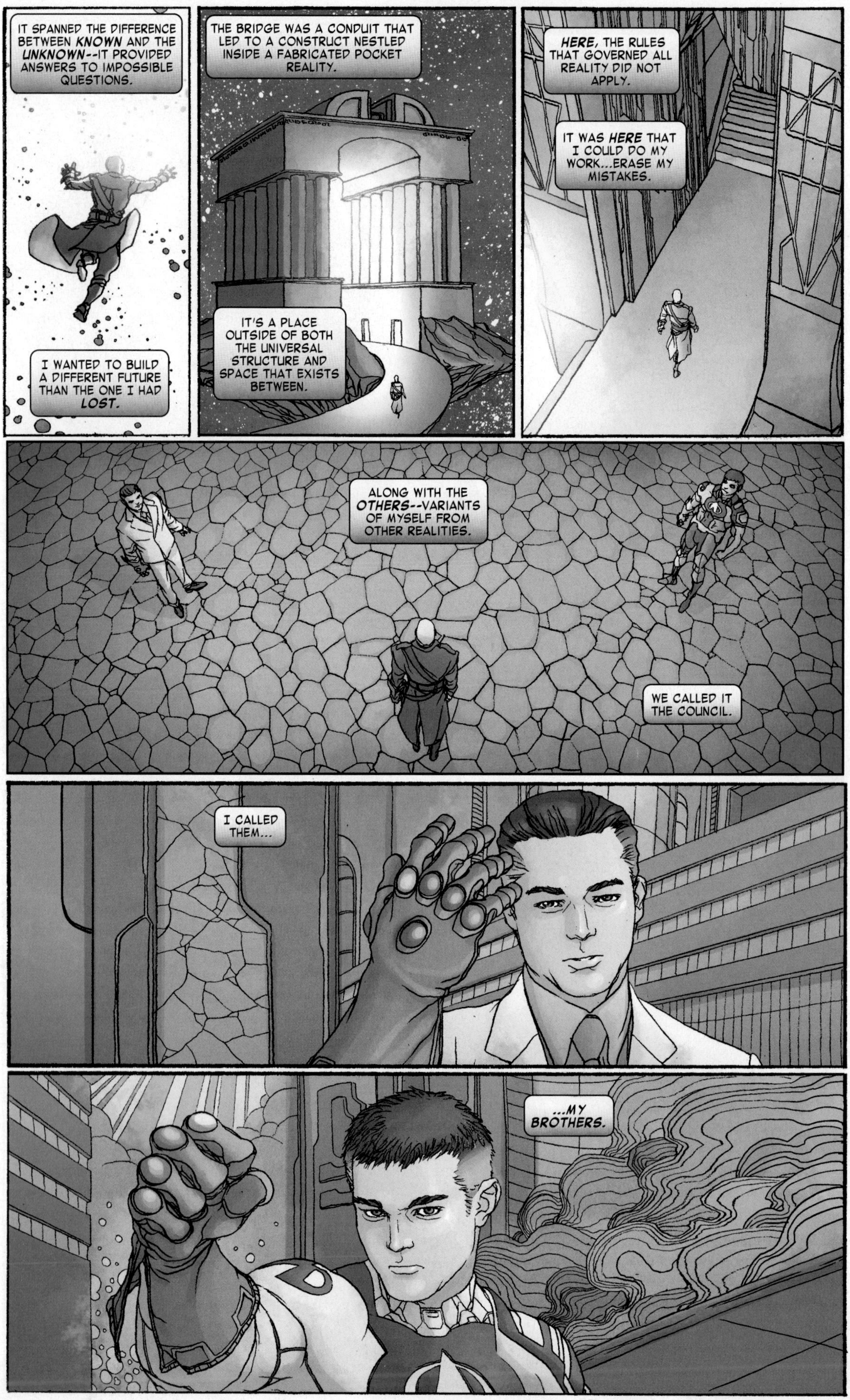
IT SPANNED THE DIFFERENCE BETWEEN KNOWN AND THE UNKNOWN--IT PROVIDED ANSWERS TO IMPOSSIBLE QUESTIONS.
I WANTED TO BUILD A DIFFERENT FUTURE THAN THE ONE I HAD LOST.
THE BRIDGE WAS A CONDUIT THAT LED TO A CONSTRUCT NESTLED INSIDE A FABRICATED POCKET REALITY.
IT'S A PLACE OUTSIDE OF BOTH THE UNIVERSAL STRUCTURE AND SPACE THAT EXISTS BETWEEN.
HERE, THE RULES THAT GOVERNED ALL REALITY DID NOT APPLY.
IT WAS HERE THAT I COULD DO MY WORK...ERASE MY MISTAKES.
ALONG WITH THE OTHERS--VARIANTS OF MYSELF FROM OTHER REALITIES.
WE CALLED IT THE COUNCIL.
I CALLED THEM...
...MY BROTHERS.

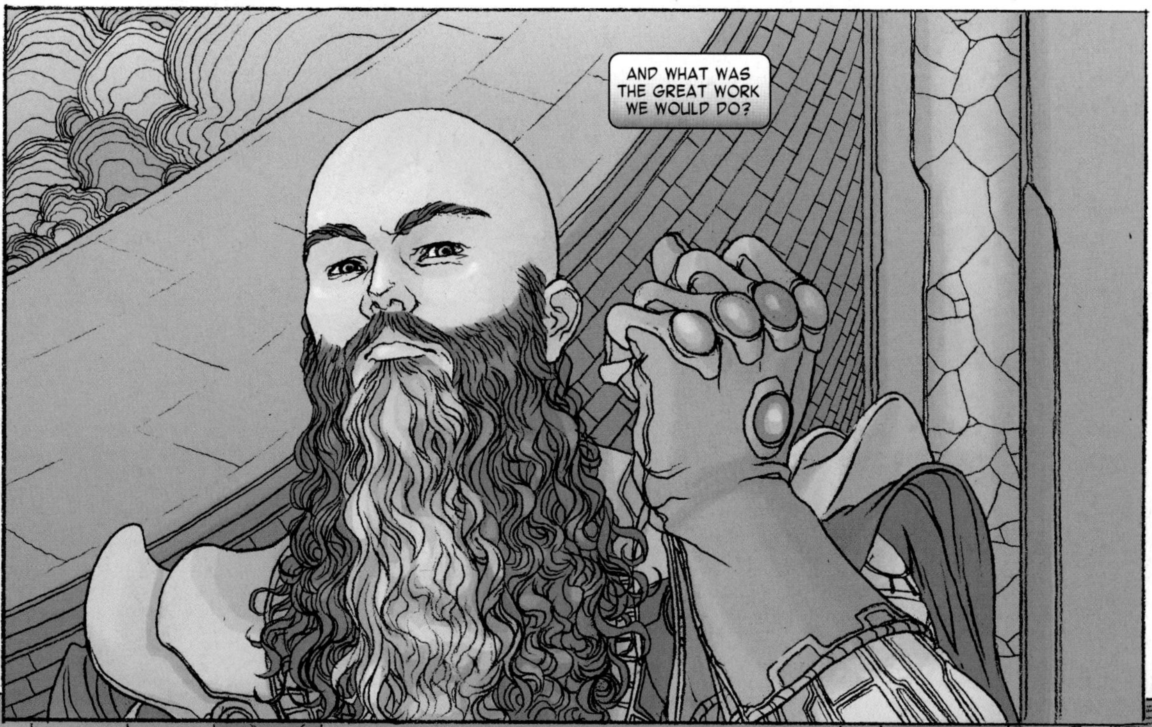
AND WHAT WAS THE GREAT WORK WE WOULD DO?

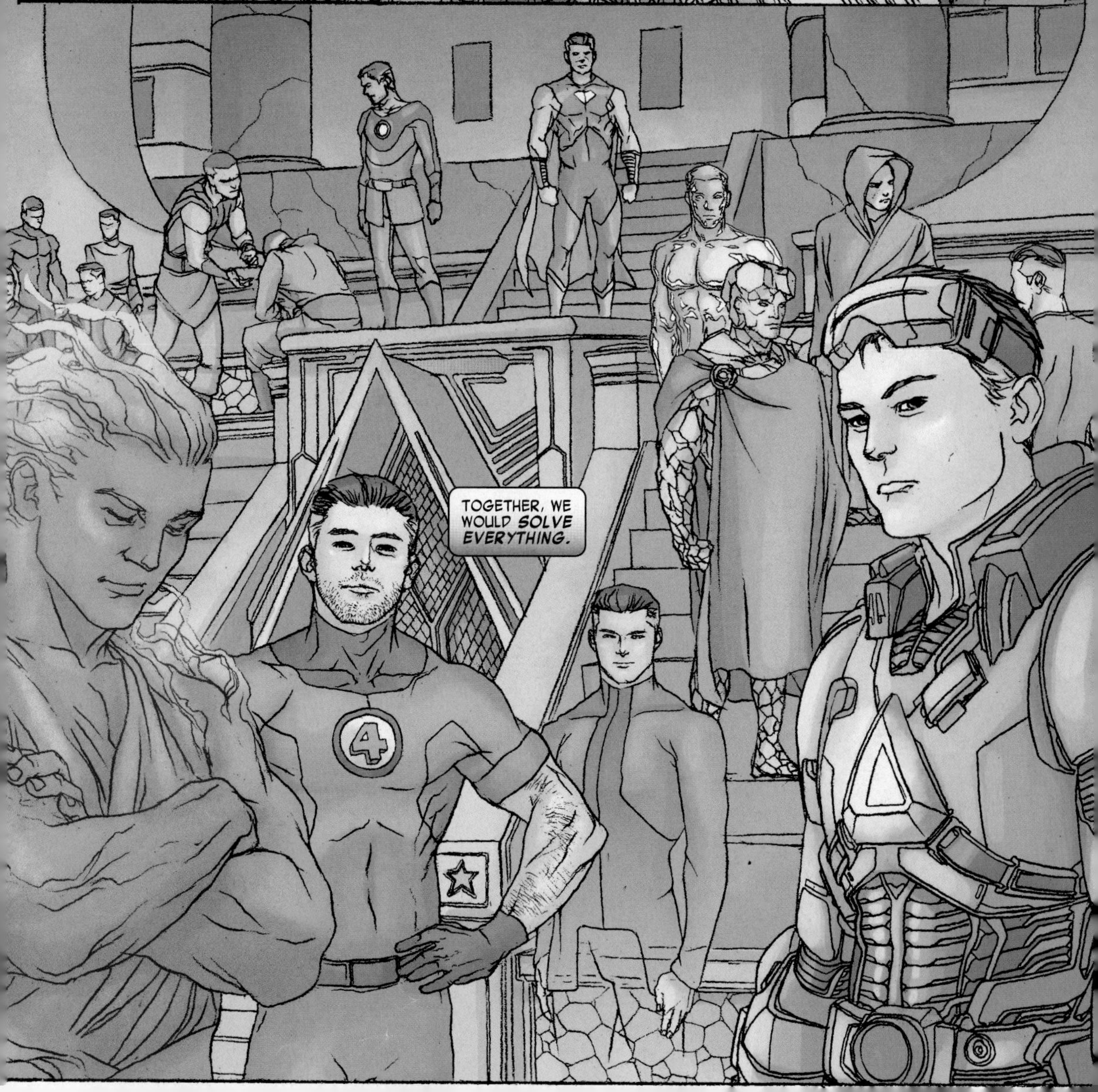
TOGETHER, WE WOULD SOLVE EVERYTHING.

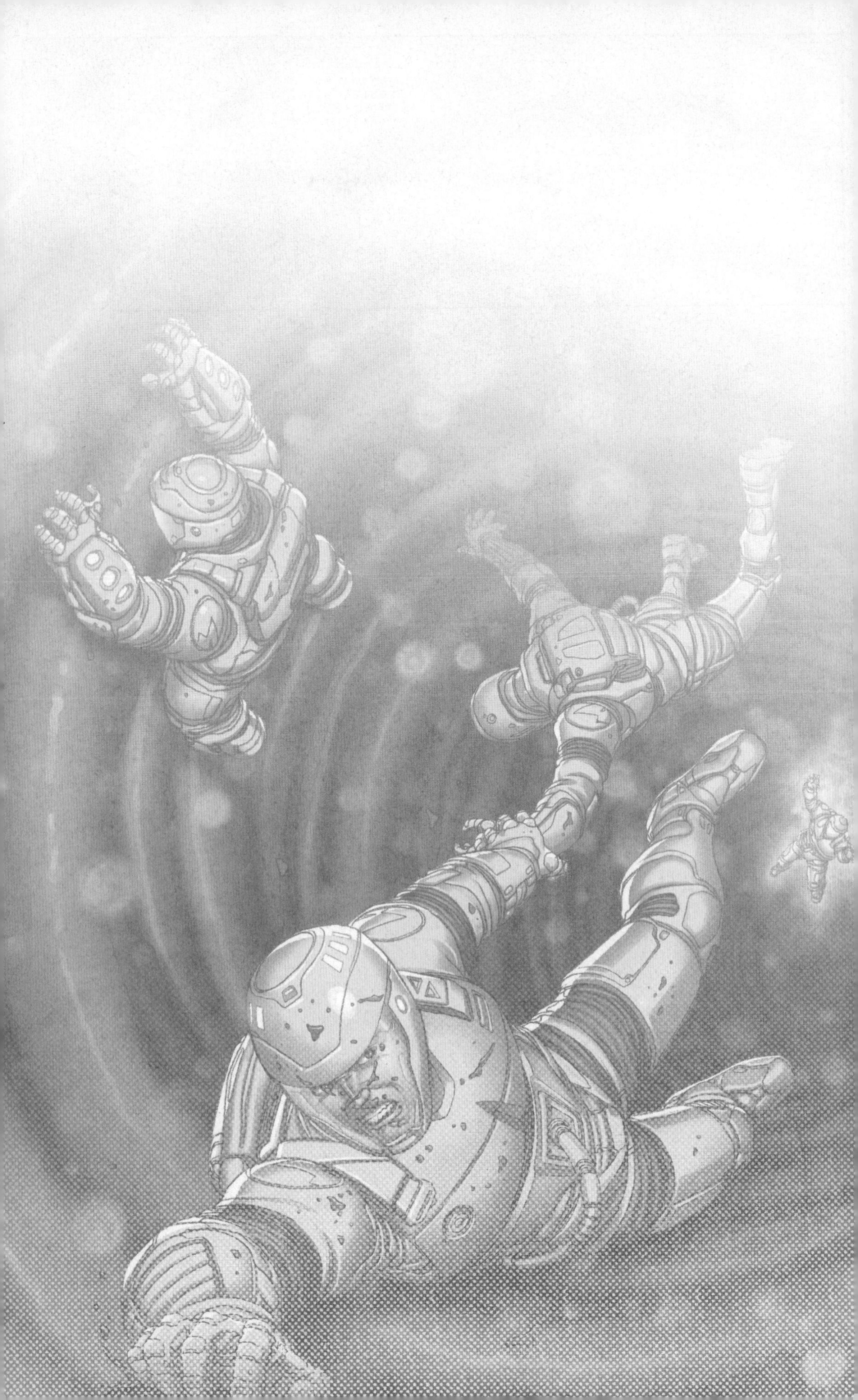

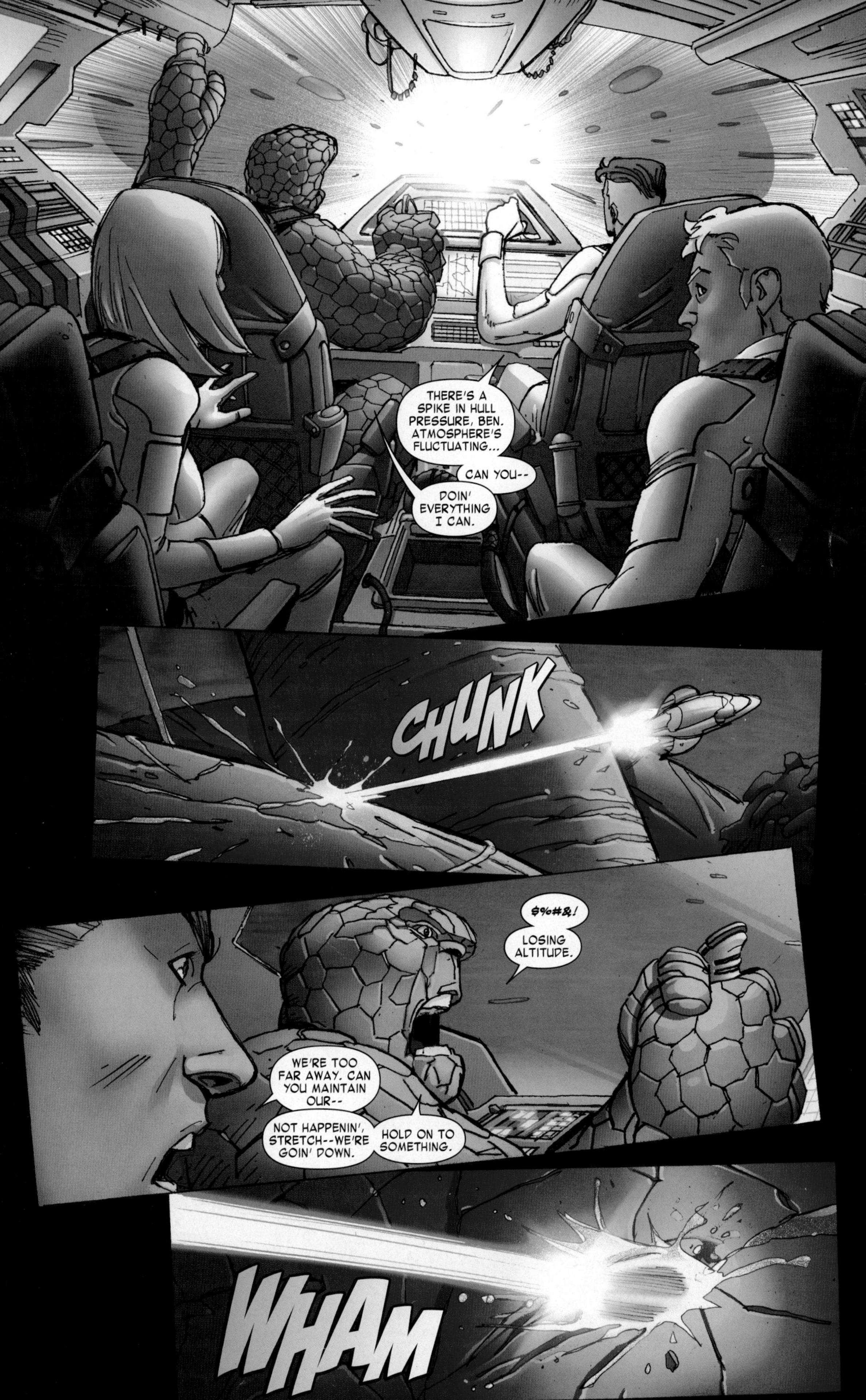
THERE'S A SPIKE IN HULL PRESSURE, BEN. ATMOSPHERE'S FLUCTUATING...
CAN YOU--
DOIN' EVERYTHING I CAN.
CHUNK
$%#&!
LOSING ALTITUDE.
WE'RE TOO FAR AWAY. CAN YOU MAINTAIN OUR--
NOT HAPPENIN', STRETCH--WE'RE GOIN' DOWN.
HOLD ON TO SOMETHING.
WHAM

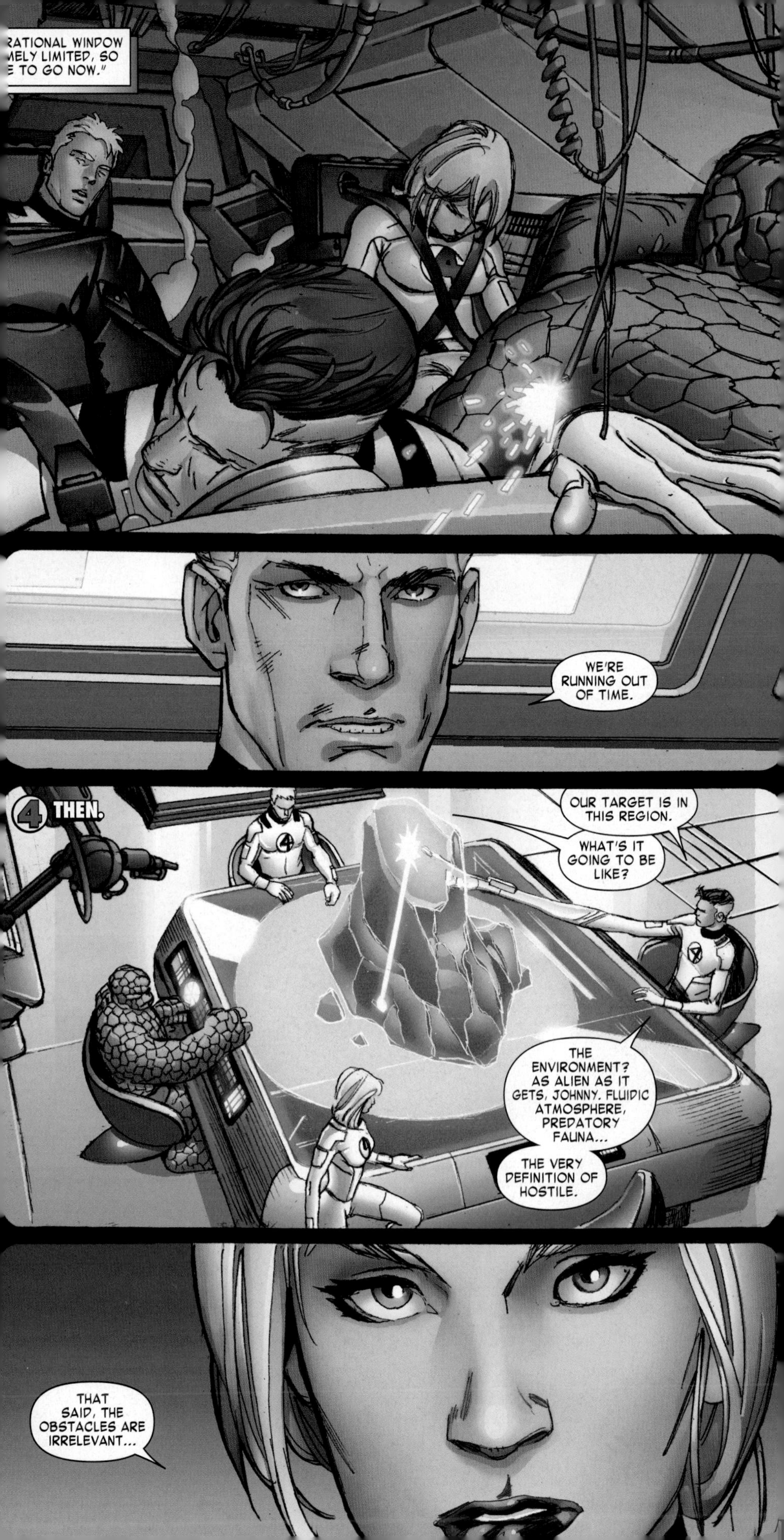

RATIONAL WINDOW
MELY LIMITED, SO
E TO GO NOW."
WE'RE RUNNING OUT OF TIME.
4 THEN.
OUR TARGET IS IN THIS REGION.
WHAT'S IT GOING TO BE LIKE?
THE ENVIRONMENT? AS ALIEN AS IT GETS, JOHNNY. FLUIDIC ATMOSPHERE, PREDATORY FAUNA...
THE VERY DEFINITION OF HOSTILE.
THAT SAID, THE OBSTACLES ARE IRRELEVANT...

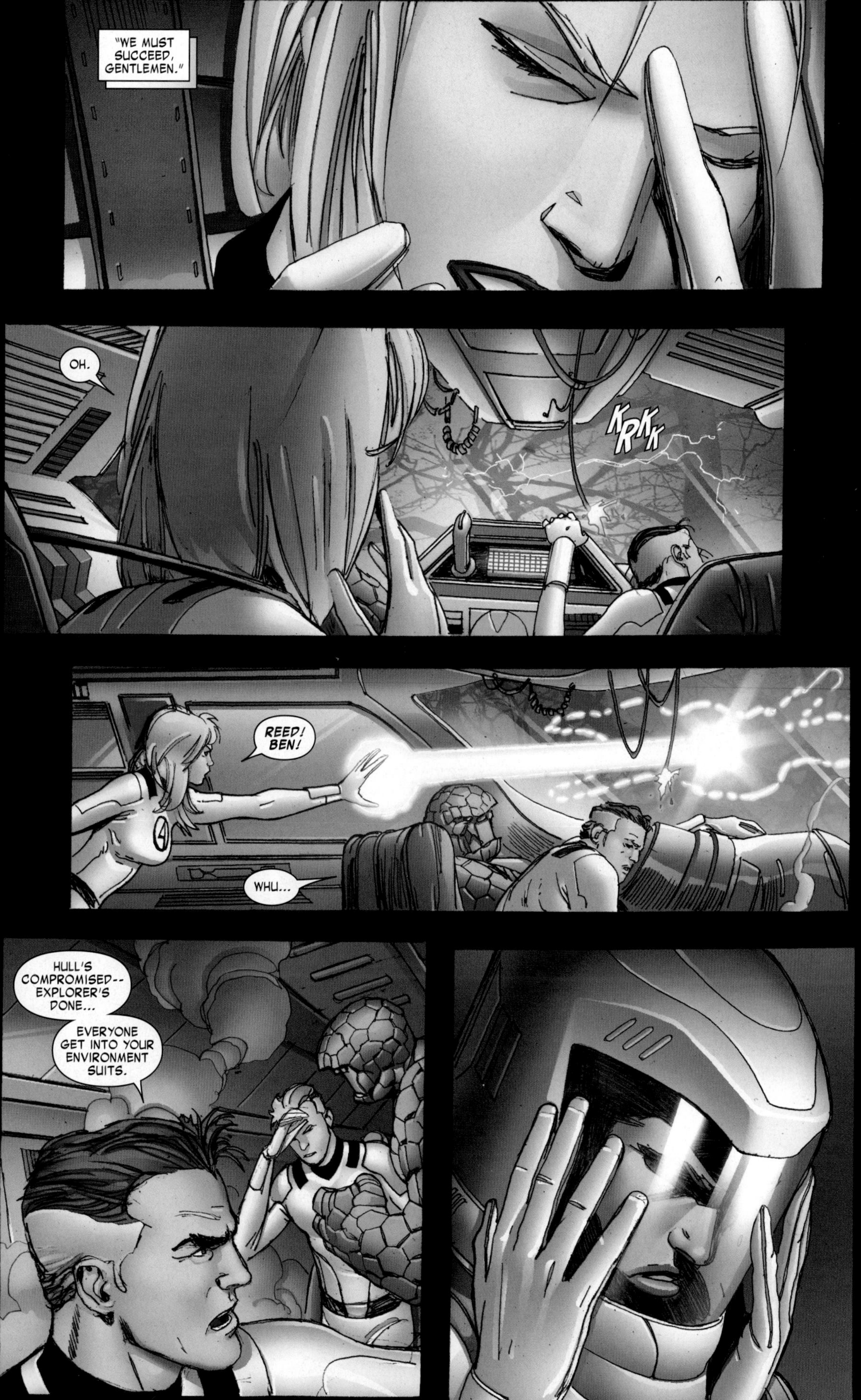
"WE MUST SUCCEED, GENTLEMEN."
OH.
KRKK
REED! BEN!
WHU...
HULL'S COMPROMISED-- EXPLORER'S DONE...
EVERYONE GET INTO YOUR ENVIRONMENT SUITS.

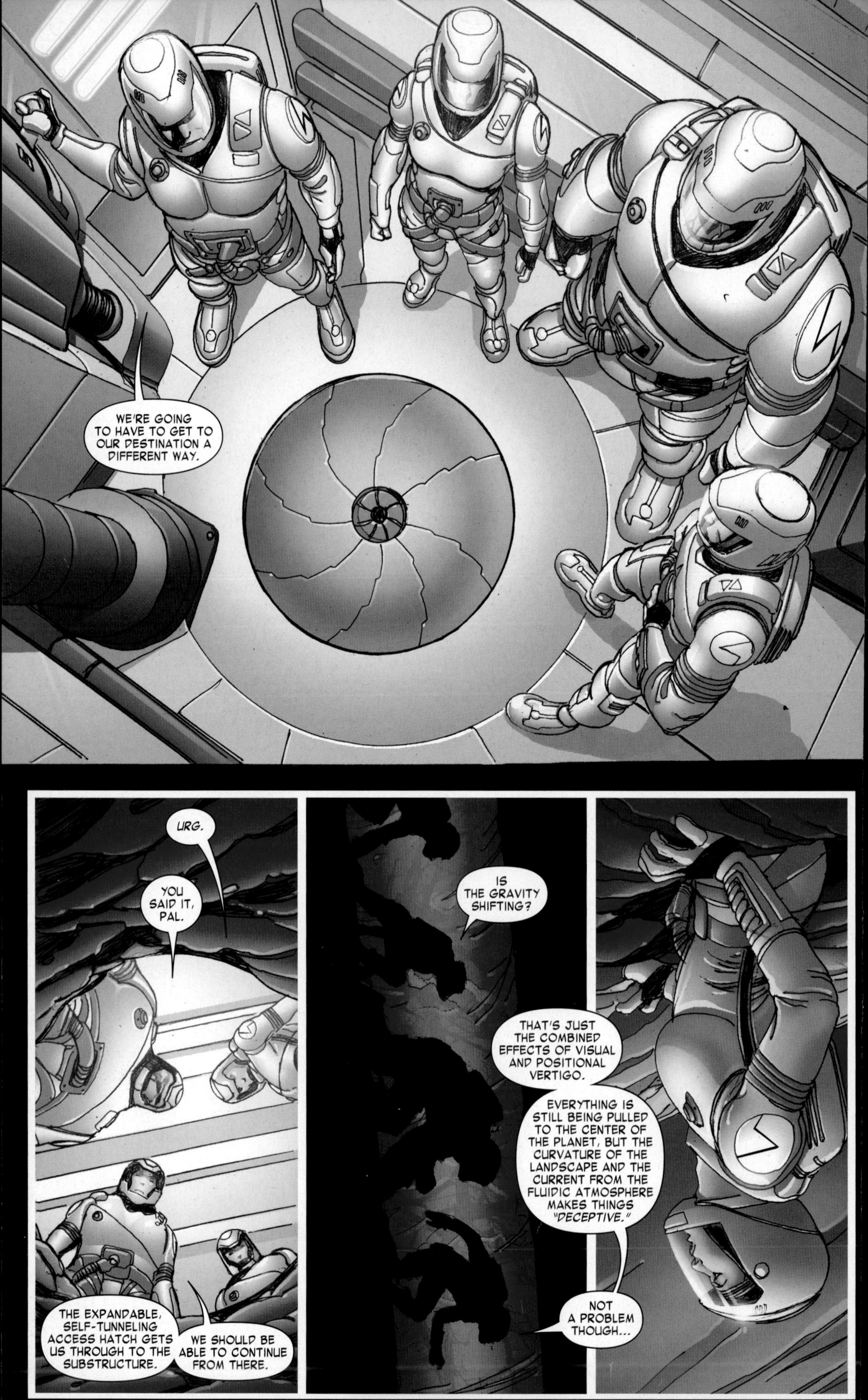
WE'RE GOING TO HAVE TO GET TO OUR DESTINATION A DIFFERENT WAY.
URG.
YOU SAID IT, PAL.
THE EXPANDABLE, SELF-TUNNELING ACCESS HATCH GETS US THROUGH TO THE SUBSTRUCTURE.
WE SHOULD BE ABLE TO CONTINUE FROM THERE.
IS THE GRAVITY SHIFTING?
THAT'S JUST THE COMBINED EFFECTS OF VISUAL AND POSITIONAL VERTIGO.
EVERYTHING IS STILL BEING PULLED TO THE CENTER OF THE PLANET, BUT THE CURVATURE OF THE LANDSCAPE AND THE CURRENT FROM THE FLUIDIC ATMOSPHERE MAKES THINGS "DECEPTIVE."
NOT A PROBLEM THOUGH...

THE BOOTS AND GLOVES OF OUR ENVIRONMENT SUITS ARE CAPABLE OF TEMPORARILY BONDING TO THE NATIVE TERRAIN.
WHOA. WOULD YOU LOOK AT THAT.
OKAY. LET'S GET MOVING.
OUR SUITS HAVE A LIMITED OXYGEN SUPPLY, AND WITHOUT THE SHIP, THIS IS GOING TO TAKE A GOOD BIT LONGER.

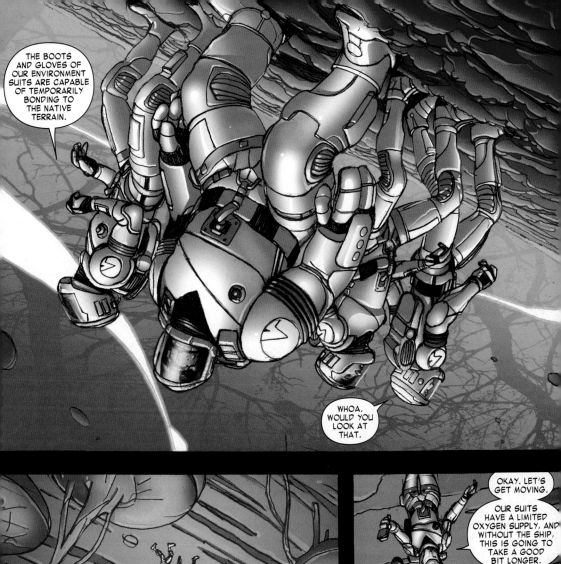

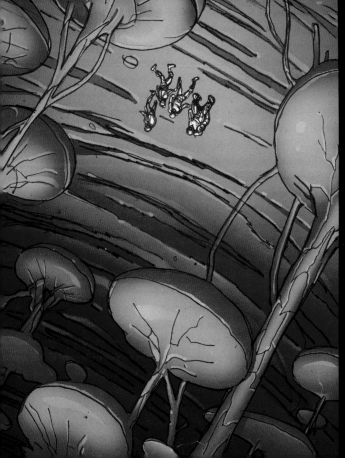

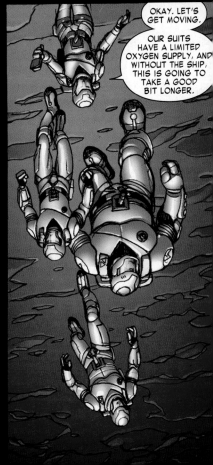

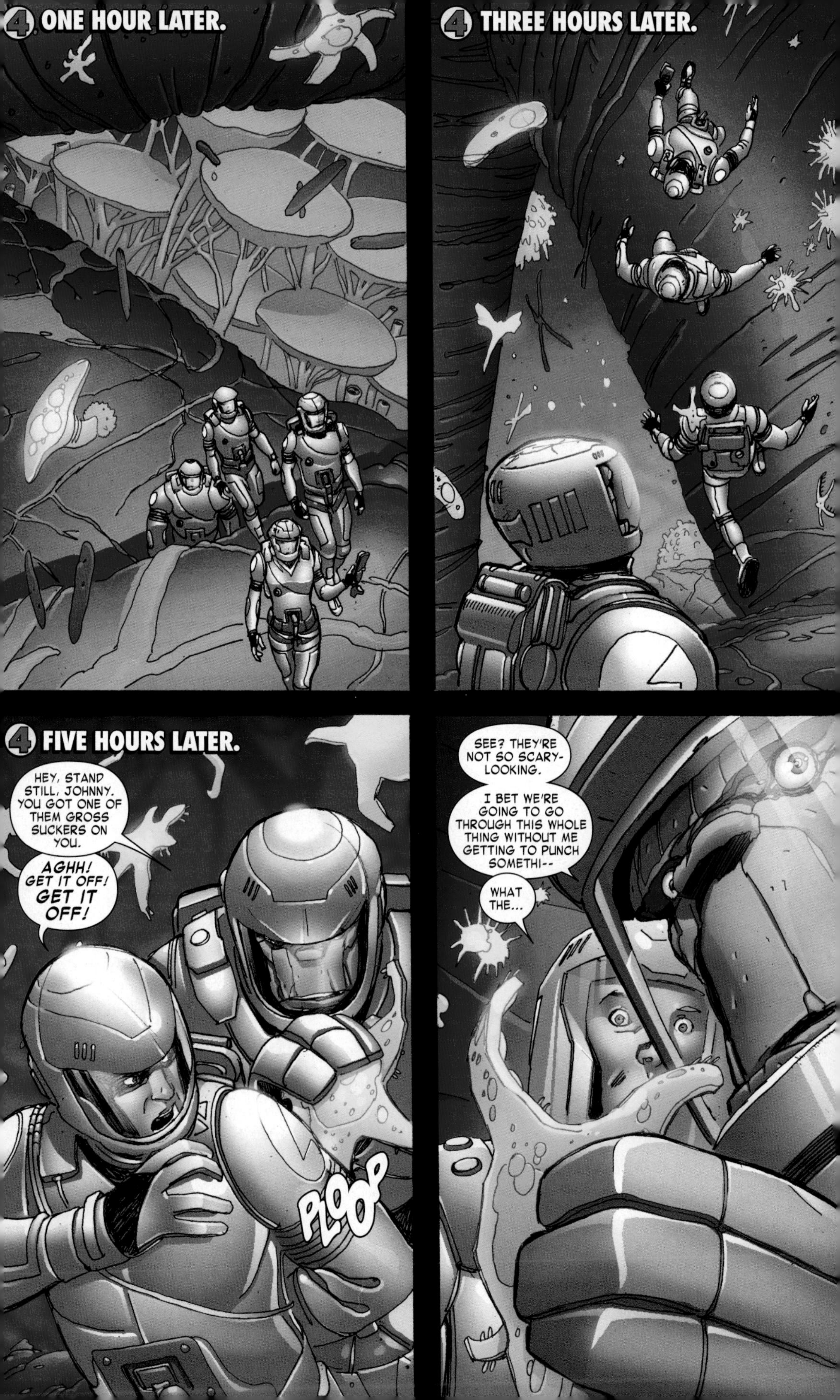
ONE HOUR LATER.
THREE HOURS LATER.
FIVE HOURS LATER.
HEY, STAND STILL, JOHNNY. YOU GOT ONE OF THEM GROSS SUCKERS ON YOU.
AGHH! GET IT OFF! GET IT OFF!
PLOOP
SEE? THEY'RE NOT SO SCARY-LOOKING.
I BET WE'RE GOING TO GO THROUGH THIS WHOLE THING WITHOUT ME GETTING TO PUNCH SOMETHI--
WHAT THE...

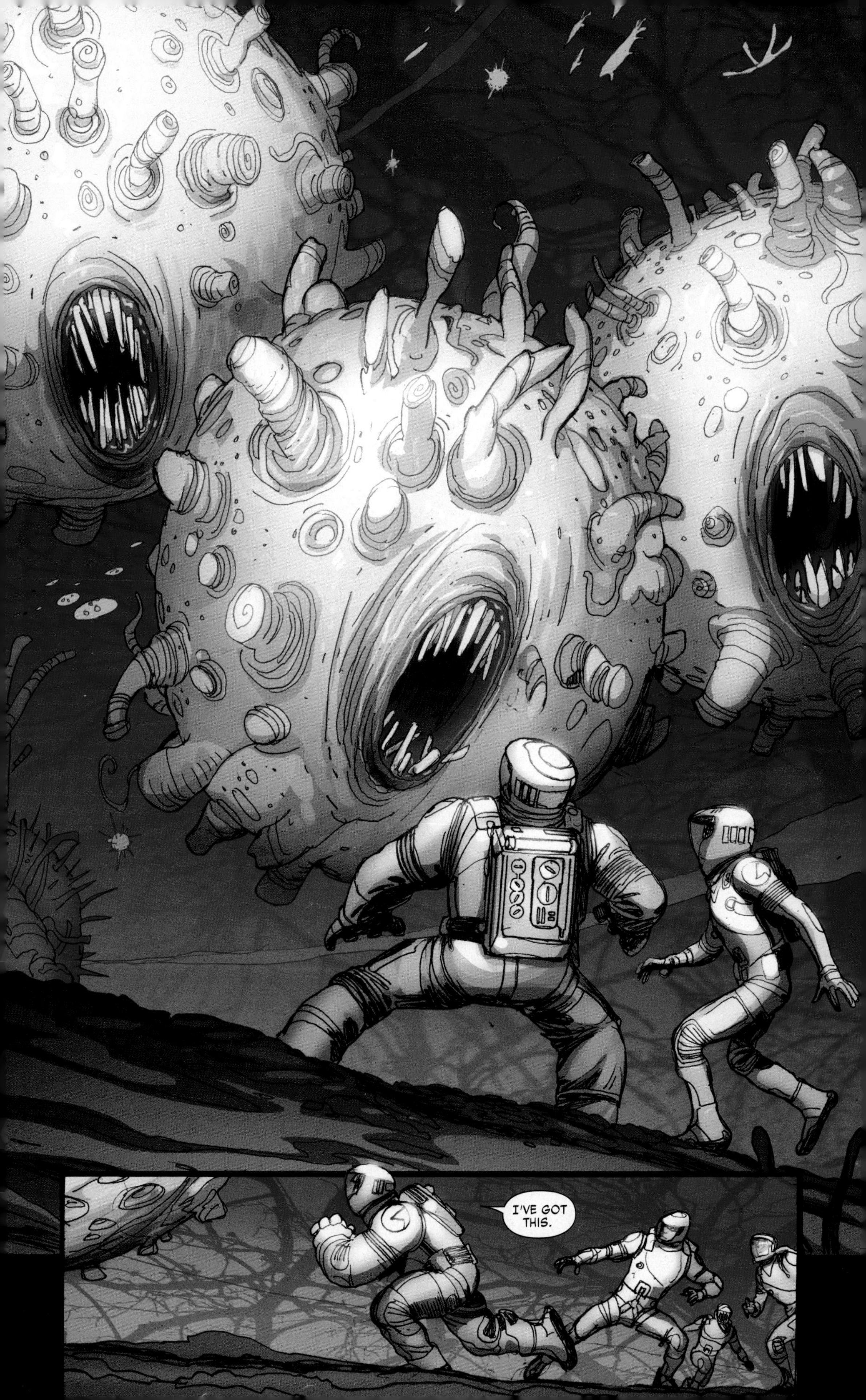
I'VE GOT THIS.

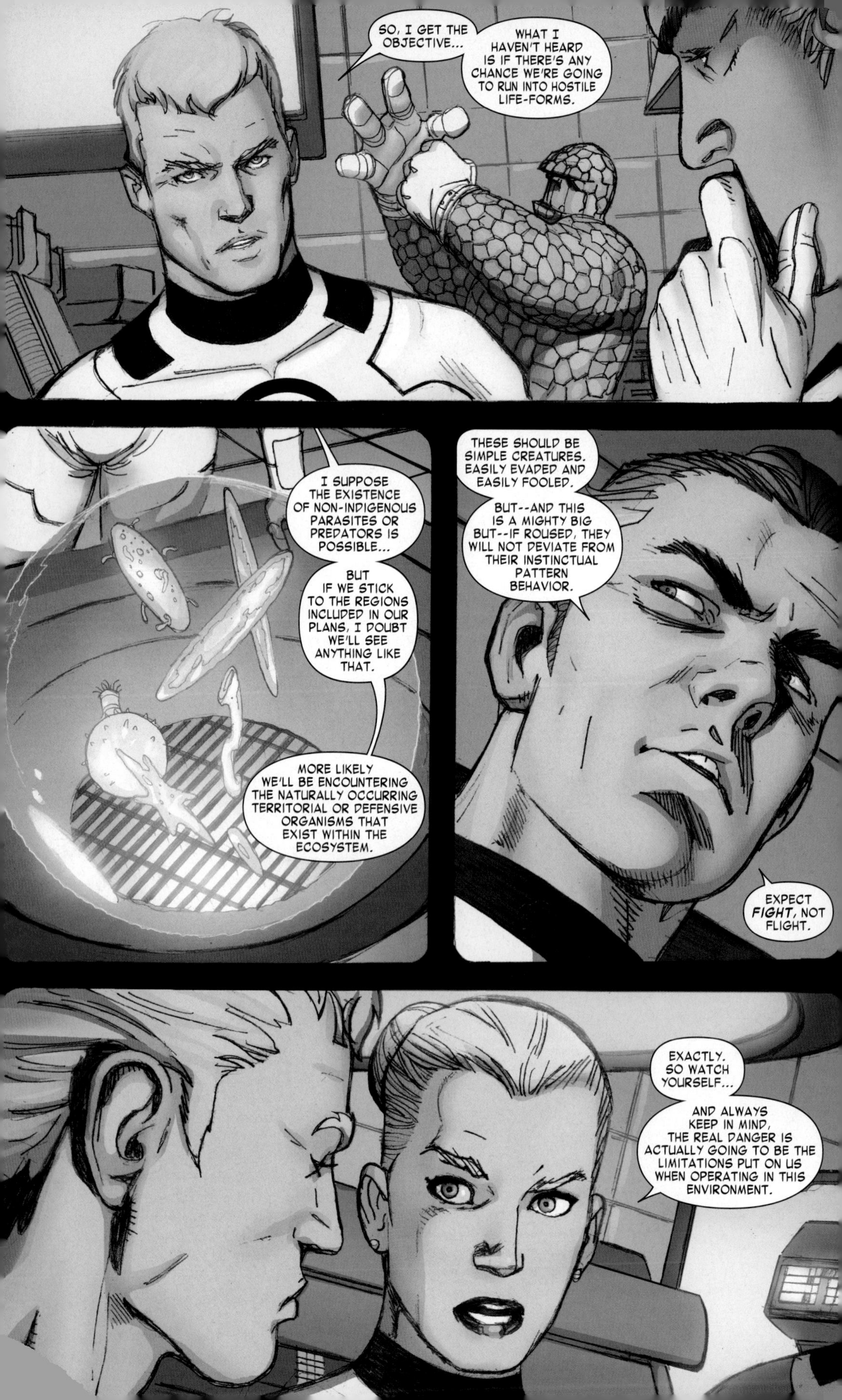
SO, I GET THE OBJECTIVE...
WHAT I HAVEN'T HEARD IS IF THERE'S ANY CHANCE WE'RE GOING TO RUN INTO HOSTILE LIFE-FORMS.
I SUPPOSE THE EXISTENCE OF NON-INDIGENOUS PARASITES OR PREDATORS IS POSSIBLE...
BUT IF WE STICK TO THE REGIONS INCLUDED IN OUR PLANS, I DOUBT WE'LL SEE ANYTHING LIKE THAT.
MORE LIKELY WE'LL BE ENCOUNTERING THE NATURALLY OCCURRING TERRITORIAL OR DEFENSIVE ORGANISMS THAT EXIST WITHIN THE ECOSYSTEM.
THESE SHOULD BE SIMPLE CREATURES. EASILY EVADED AND EASILY FOOLED.
BUT--AND THIS IS A MIGHTY BIG BUT--IF ROUSED, THEY WILL NOT DEVIATE FROM THEIR INSTINCTUAL PATTERN BEHAVIOR.
EXPECT *FIGHT*, NOT FLIGHT.
EXACTLY. SO WATCH YOURSELF...
AND ALWAYS KEEP IN MIND, THE REAL DANGER IS ACTUALLY GOING TO BE THE LIMITATIONS PUT ON US WHEN OPERATING IN THIS ENVIRONMENT.

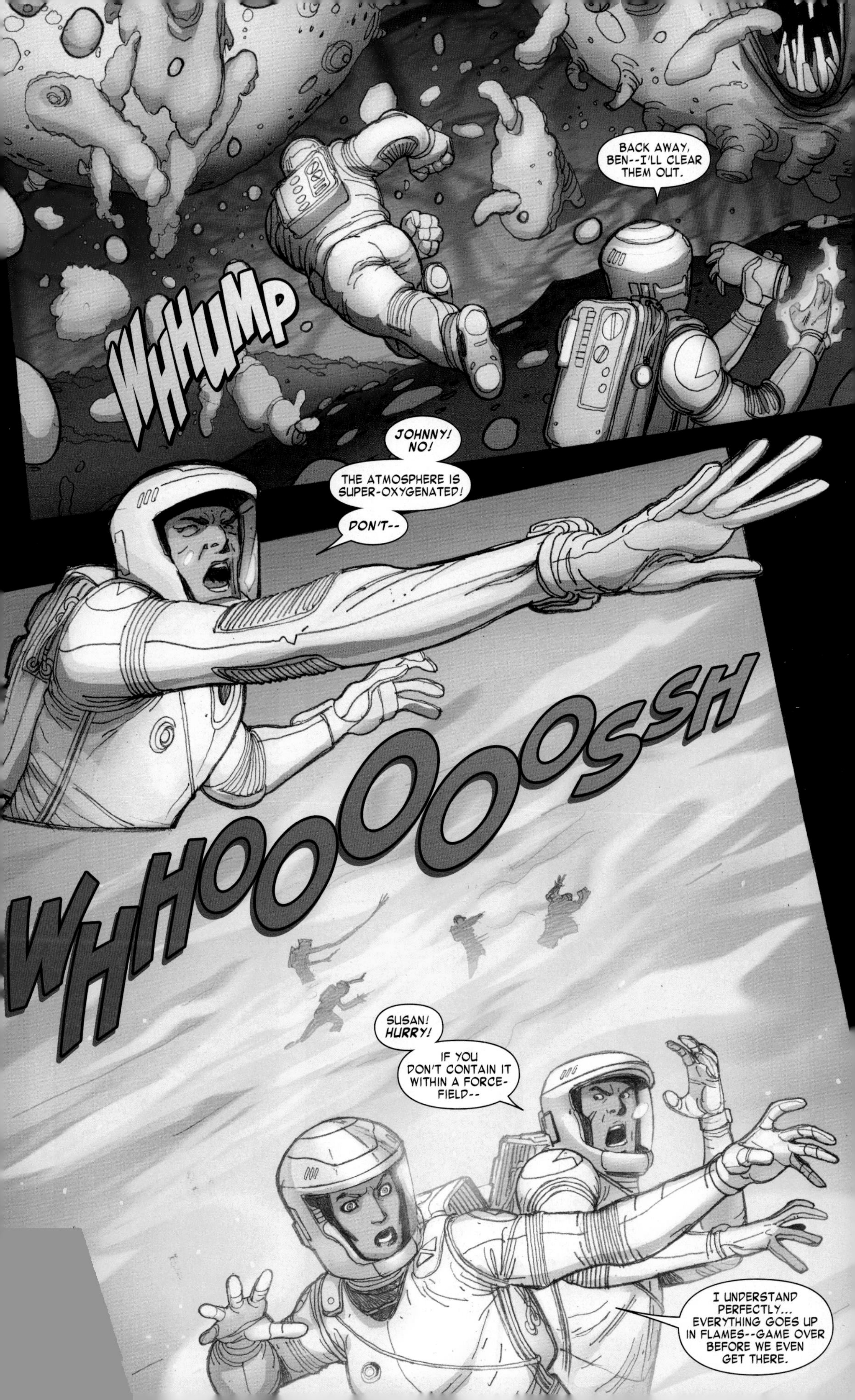
BACK AWAY, BEN--I'LL CLEAR THEM OUT.
WHHUMP
JOHNNY! NO!
THE ATMOSPHERE IS SUPER-OXYGENATED!
DON'T--
WHHOOOOOOSSH
SUSAN! HURRY!
IF YOU DON'T CONTAIN IT WITHIN A FORCE-FIELD--
I UNDERSTAND PERFECTLY... EVERYTHING GOES UP IN FLAMES--GAME OVER BEFORE WE EVEN GET THERE.

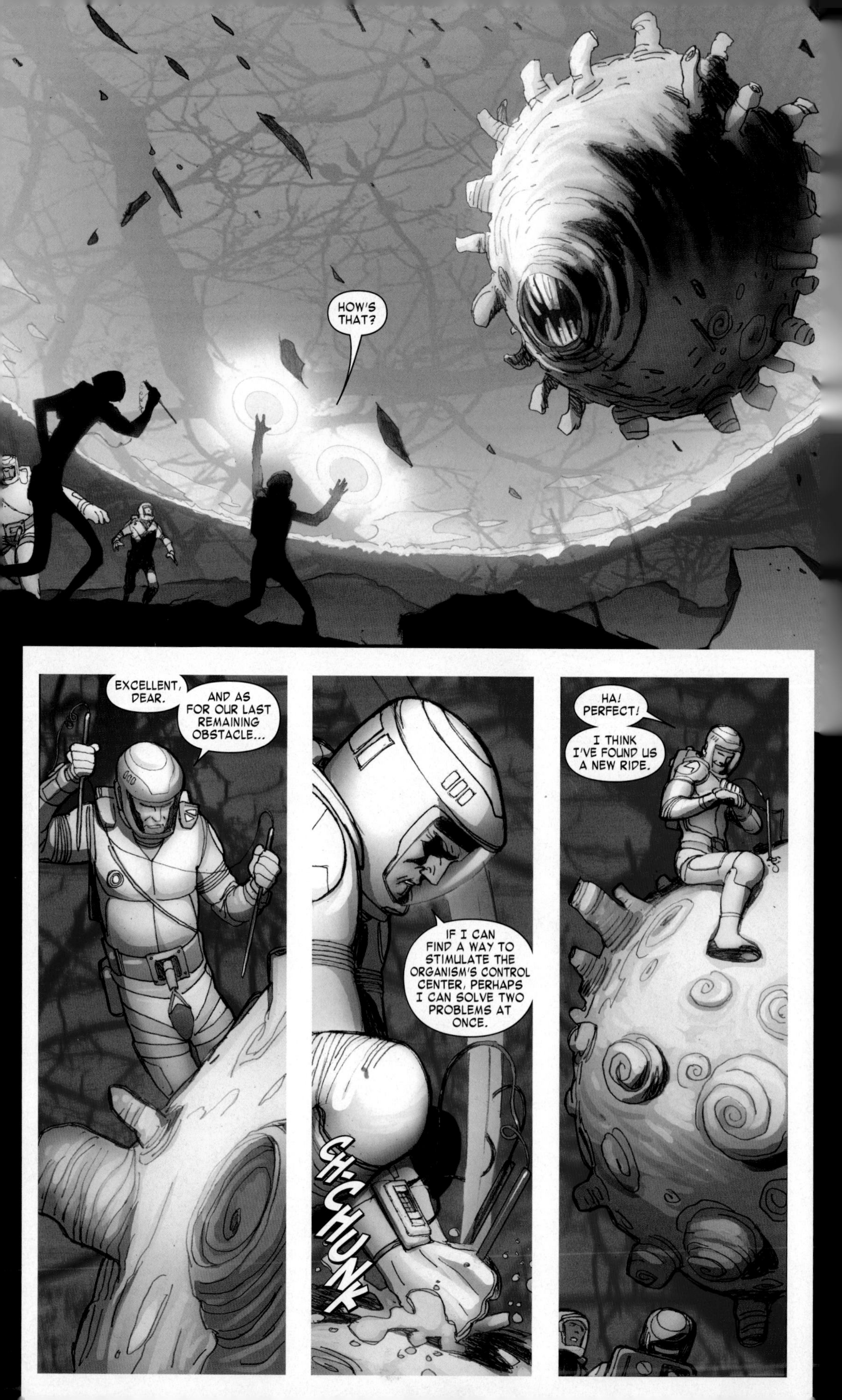
HOW'S THAT?
EXCELLENT, DEAR.
AND AS FOR OUR LAST REMAINING OBSTACLE...
IF I CAN FIND A WAY TO STIMULATE THE ORGANISM'S CONTROL CENTER, PERHAPS I CAN SOLVE TWO PROBLEMS AT ONCE.
CH-CHUNK
HA! PERFECT!
I THINK I'VE FOUND US A NEW RIDE.

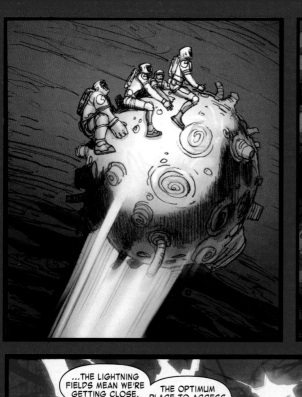

EVERYONE HOLD ON...

...THE LIGHTNING FIELDS MEAN WE'RE GETTING CLOSE.

THE OPTIMUM PLACE TO ACCESS THE STRATUM IS TWO CLICKS IN.

THIS IS GOING TO GET HAIRY.

ALMOST THER--

KRAK-A-THOOM

WHOA!

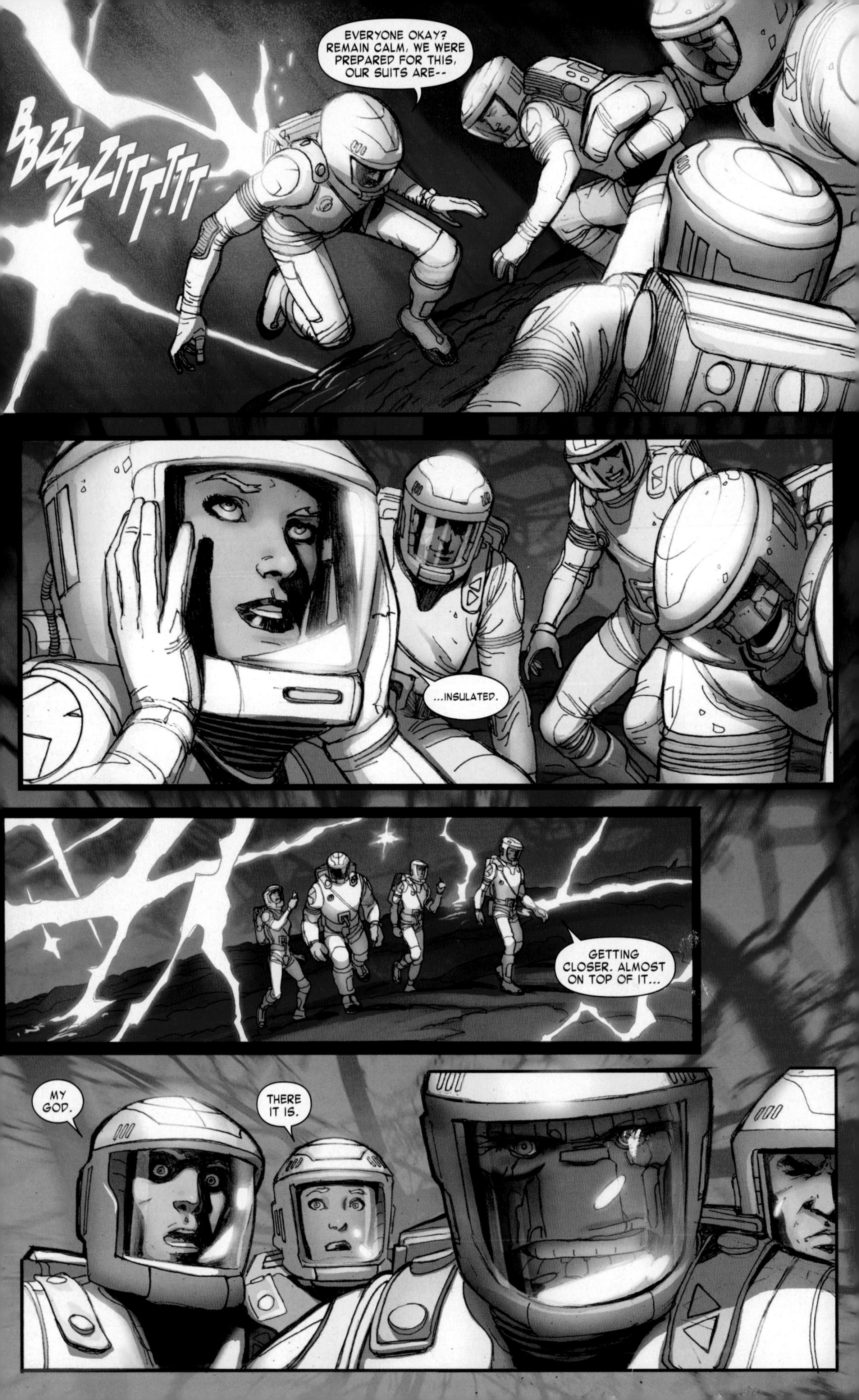
EVERYONE OKAY? REMAIN CALM, WE WERE PREPARED FOR THIS, OUR SUITS ARE--
BBZZZZTTTTTTT
...INSULATED.
GETTING CLOSER. ALMOST ON TOP OF IT...
MY GOD.
THERE IT IS.

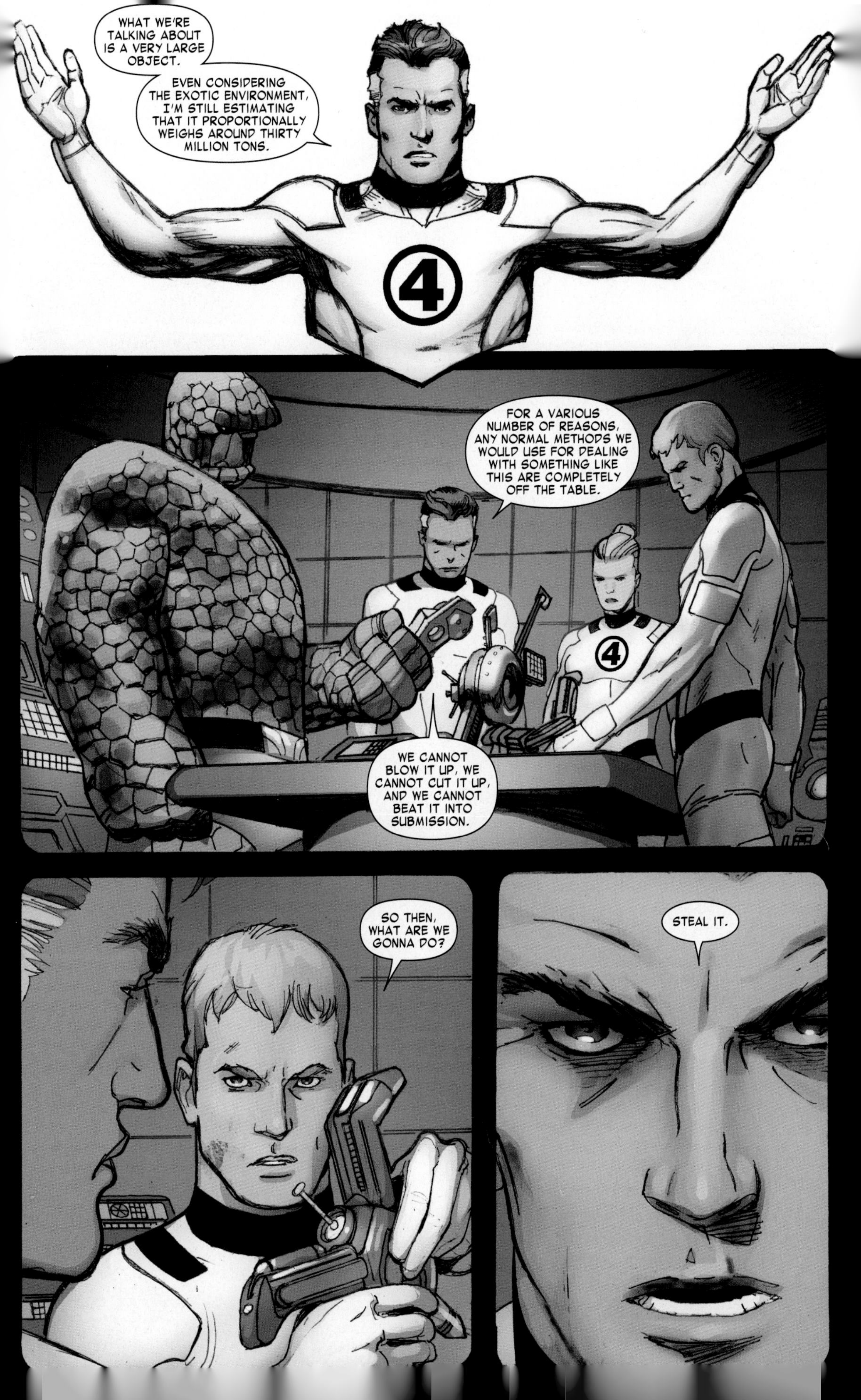
WHAT WE'RE TALKING ABOUT IS A VERY LARGE OBJECT.
EVEN CONSIDERING THE EXOTIC ENVIRONMENT, I'M STILL ESTIMATING THAT IT PROPORTIONALLY WEIGHS AROUND THIRTY MILLION TONS.
FOR A VARIOUS NUMBER OF REASONS, ANY NORMAL METHODS WE WOULD USE FOR DEALING WITH SOMETHING LIKE THIS ARE COMPLETELY OFF THE TABLE.
WE CANNOT BLOW IT UP, WE CANNOT CUT IT UP, AND WE CANNOT BEAT IT INTO SUBMISSION.
SO THEN, WHAT ARE WE GONNA DO?
STEAL IT.

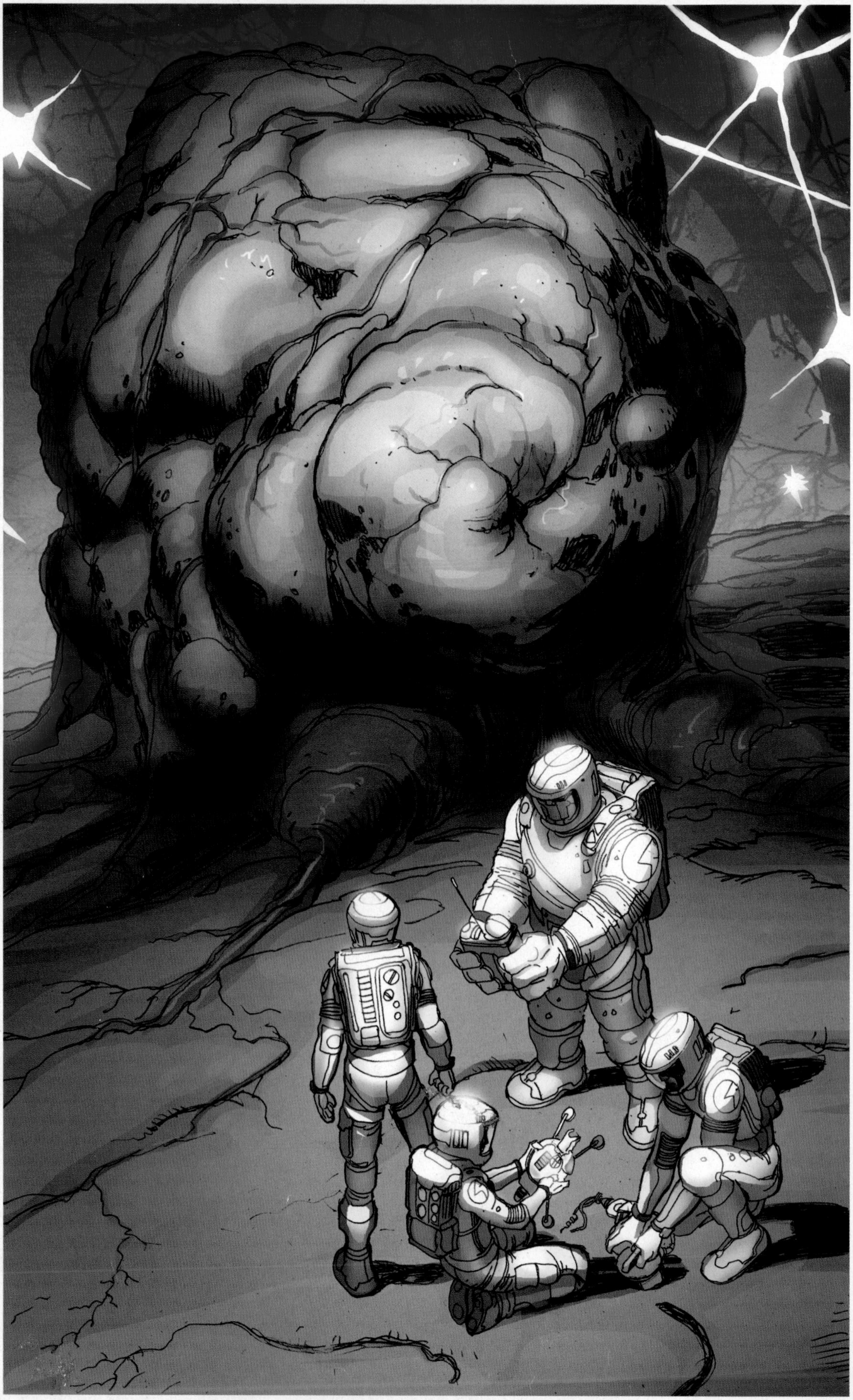

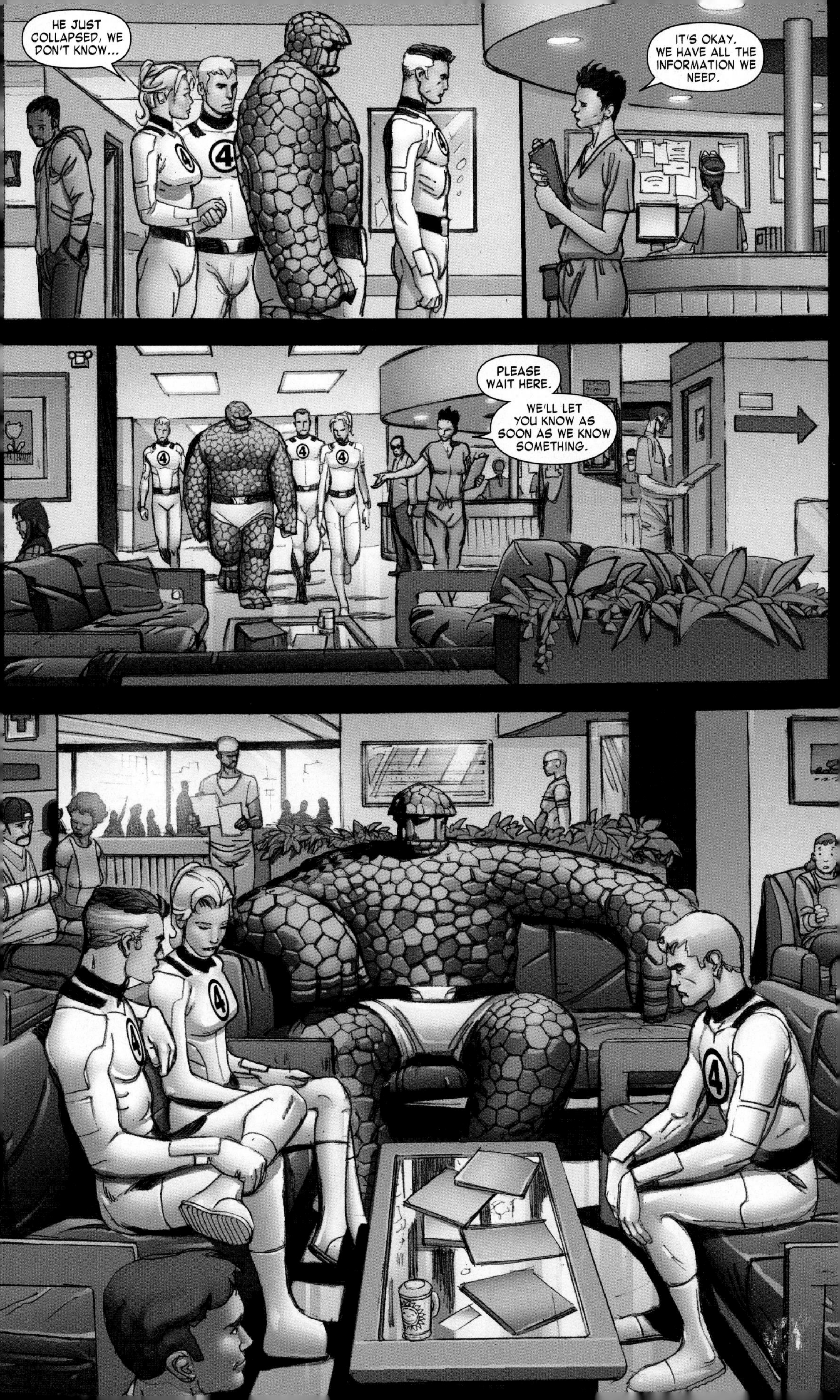
HE JUST COLLAPSED, WE DON'T KNOW...
IT'S OKAY. WE HAVE ALL THE INFORMATION WE NEED.
PLEASE WAIT HERE.
WE'LL LET YOU KNOW AS SOON AS WE KNOW SOMETHING.

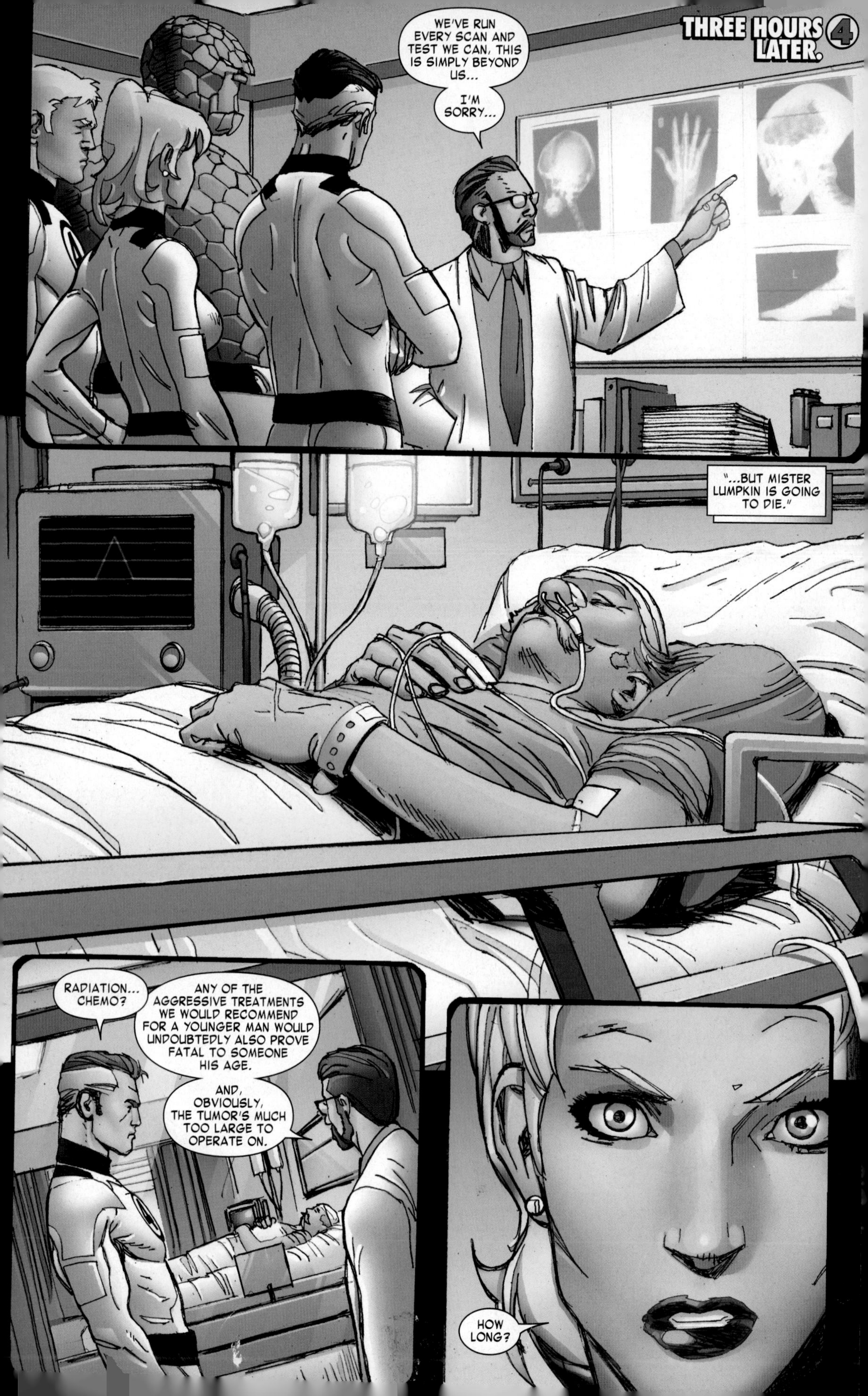
THREE HOURS LATER.
4
WE'VE RUN EVERY SCAN AND TEST WE CAN, THIS IS SIMPLY BEYOND US...
I'M SORRY...
"...BUT MISTER LUMPKIN IS GOING TO DIE."
RADIATION... CHEMO?
ANY OF THE AGGRESSIVE TREATMENTS WE WOULD RECOMMEND FOR A YOUNGER MAN WOULD UNDOUBTEDLY ALSO PROVE FATAL TO SOMEONE HIS AGE.
AND, OBVIOUSLY, THE TUMOR'S MUCH TOO LARGE TO OPERATE ON.
HOW LONG?

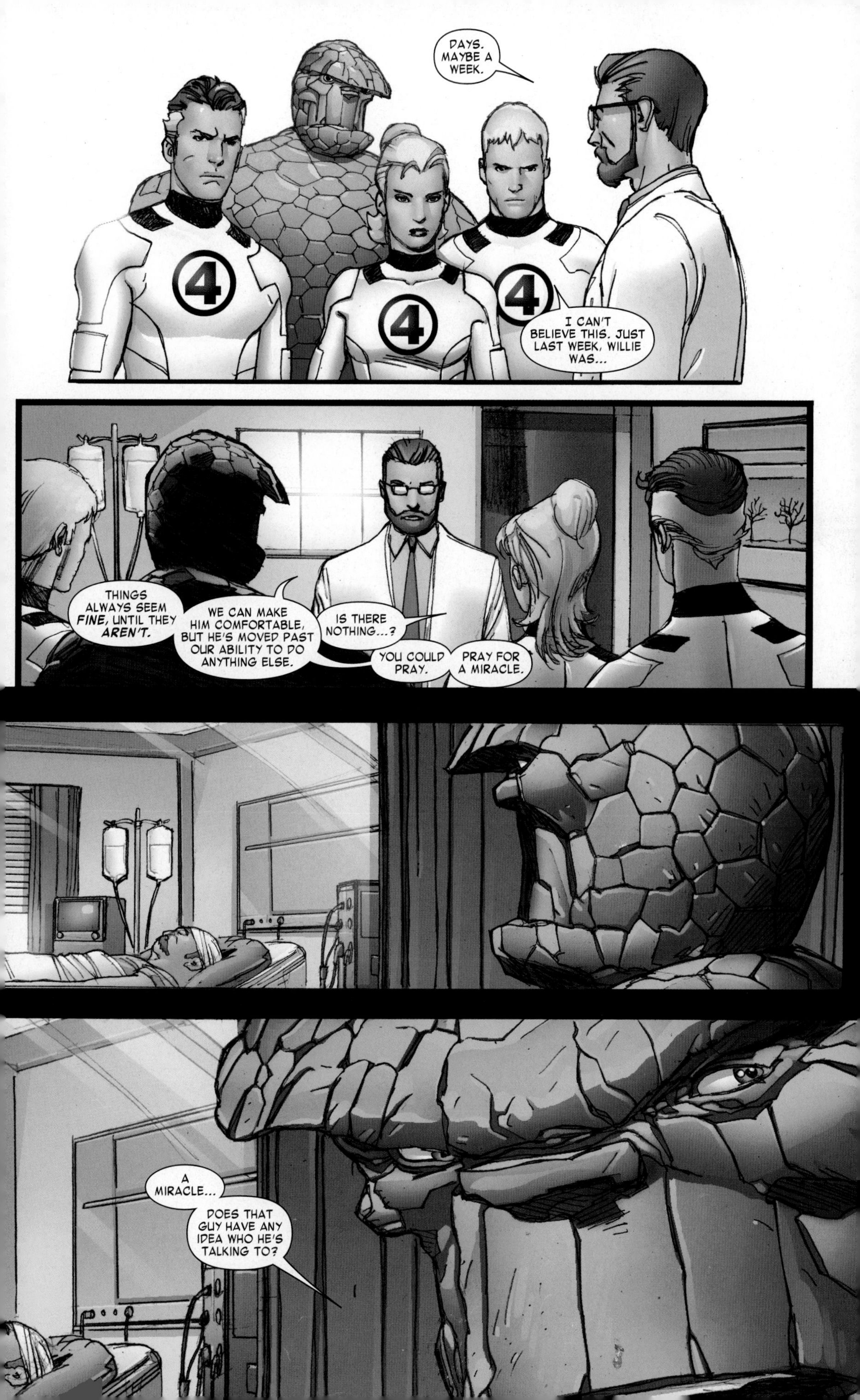
DAYS. MAYBE A WEEK.
I CAN'T BELIEVE THIS. JUST LAST WEEK, WILLIE WAS...
THINGS ALWAYS SEEM *FINE*, UNTIL THEY *AREN'T.*
WE CAN MAKE HIM COMFORTABLE, BUT HE'S MOVED PAST OUR ABILITY TO DO ANYTHING ELSE.
IS THERE NOTHING...?
YOU COULD PRAY.
PRAY FOR A MIRACLE.
A MIRACLE...
DOES THAT GUY HAVE ANY IDEA WHO HE'S TALKING TO?

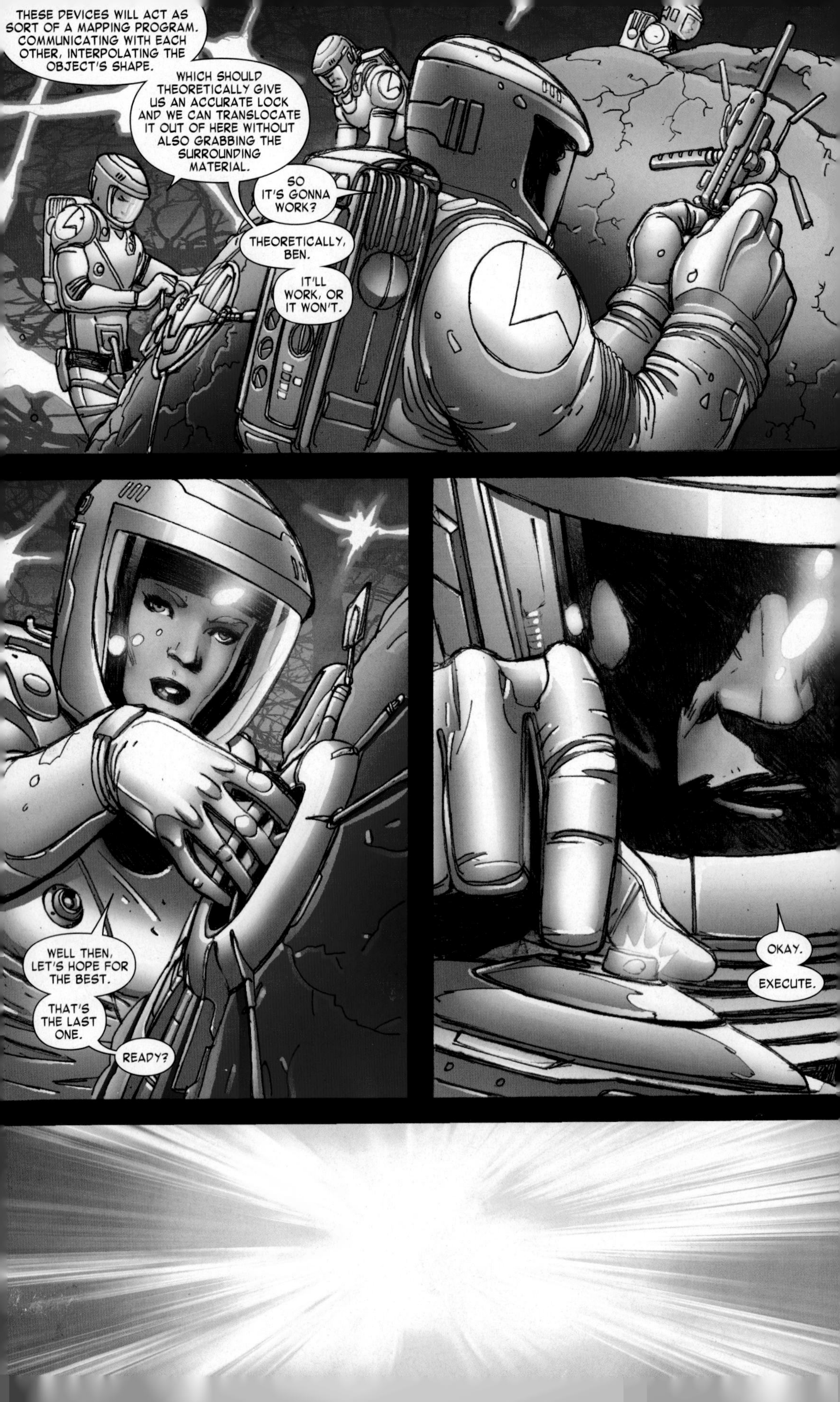
THESE DEVICES WILL ACT AS SORT OF A MAPPING PROGRAM. COMMUNICATING WITH EACH OTHER, INTERPOLATING THE OBJECT'S SHAPE.
WHICH SHOULD THEORETICALLY GIVE US AN ACCURATE LOCK AND WE CAN TRANSLOCATE IT OUT OF HERE WITHOUT ALSO GRABBING THE SURROUNDING MATERIAL.
SO IT'S GONNA WORK?
THEORETICALLY, BEN.
IT'LL WORK, OR IT WON'T.
WELL THEN, LET'S HOPE FOR THE BEST.
THAT'S THE LAST ONE.
READY?
OKAY.
EXECUTE.

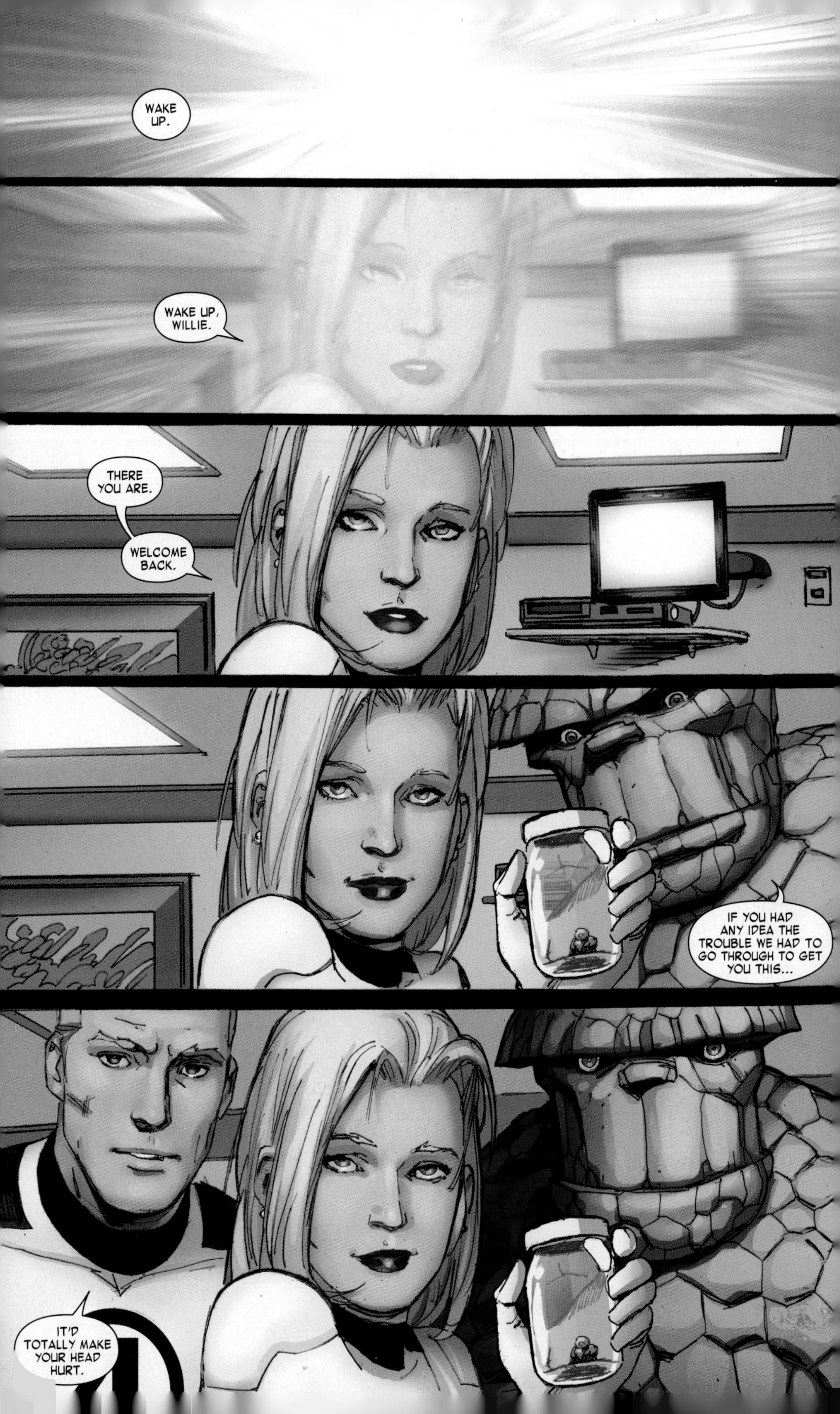
WAKE UP.
WAKE UP, WILLIE.
THERE YOU ARE.
WELCOME BACK.
IF YOU HAD ANY IDEA THE TROUBLE WE HAD TO GO THROUGH TO GET YOU THIS...
IT'D TOTALLY MAKE YOUR HEAD HURT.

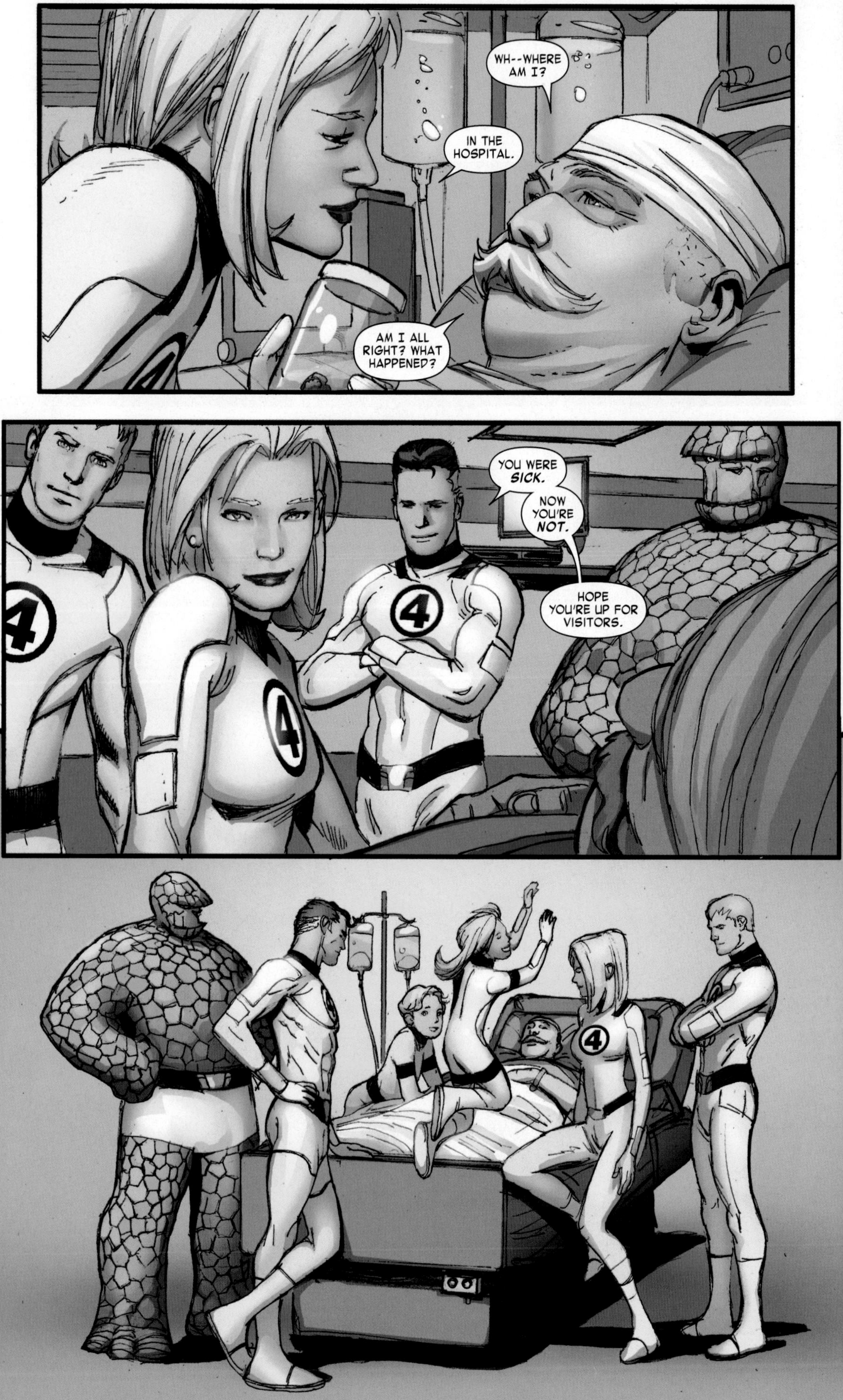
WH--WHERE AM I?
IN THE HOSPITAL.
AM I ALL RIGHT? WHAT HAPPENED?
YOU WERE SICK.
NOW YOU'RE NOT.
HOPE YOU'RE UP FOR VISITORS.

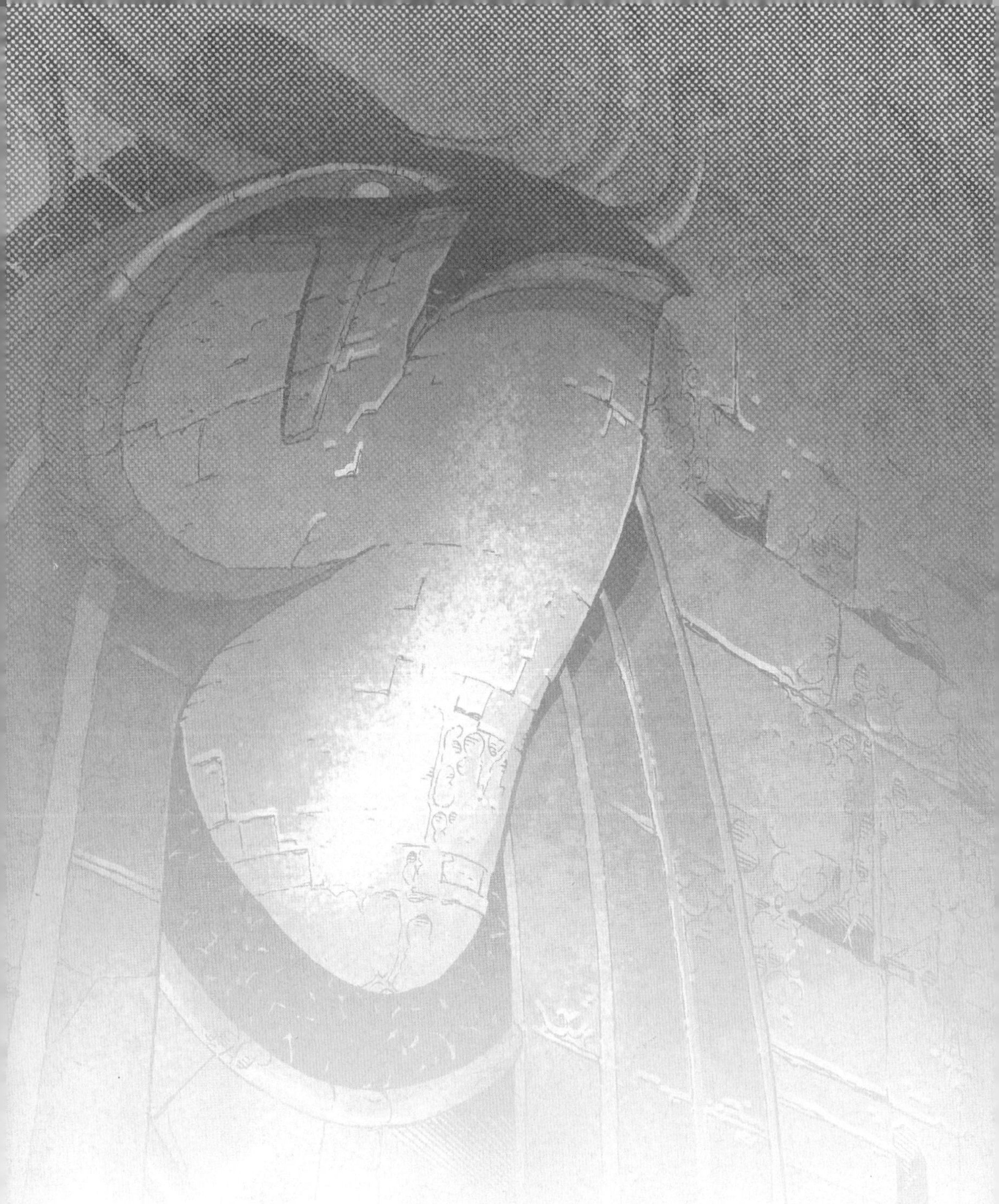

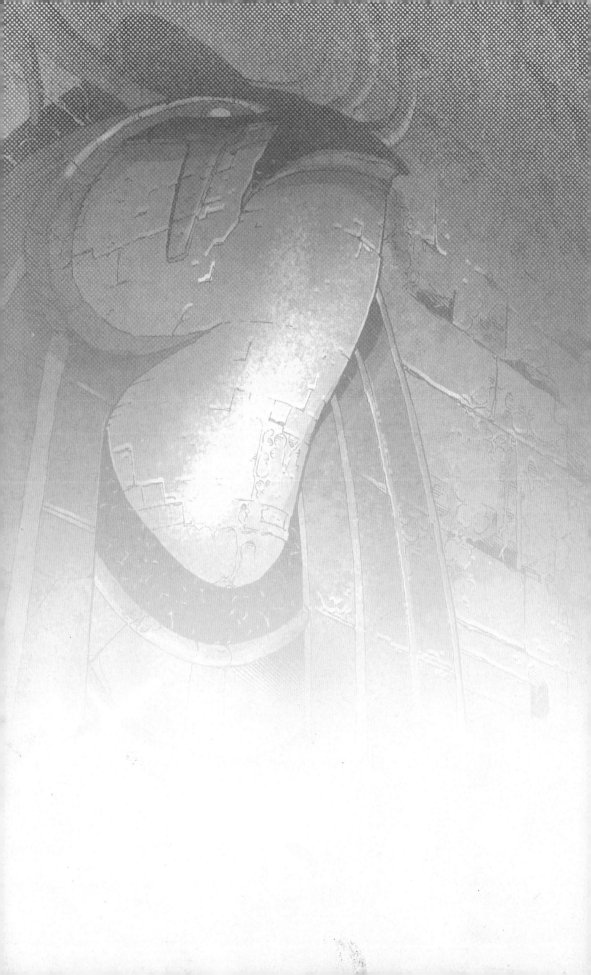

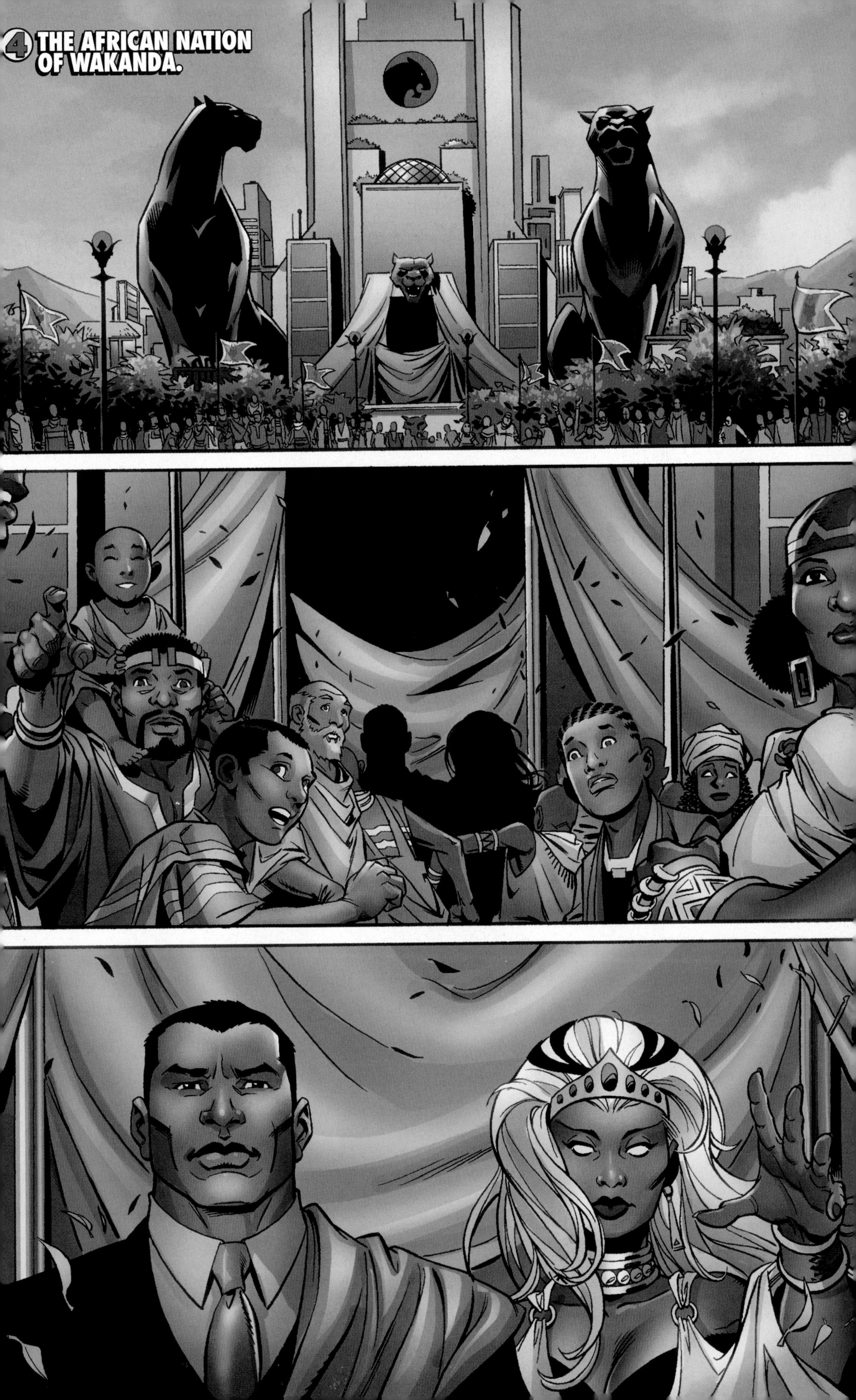
4 THE AFRICAN NATION OF WAKANDA.

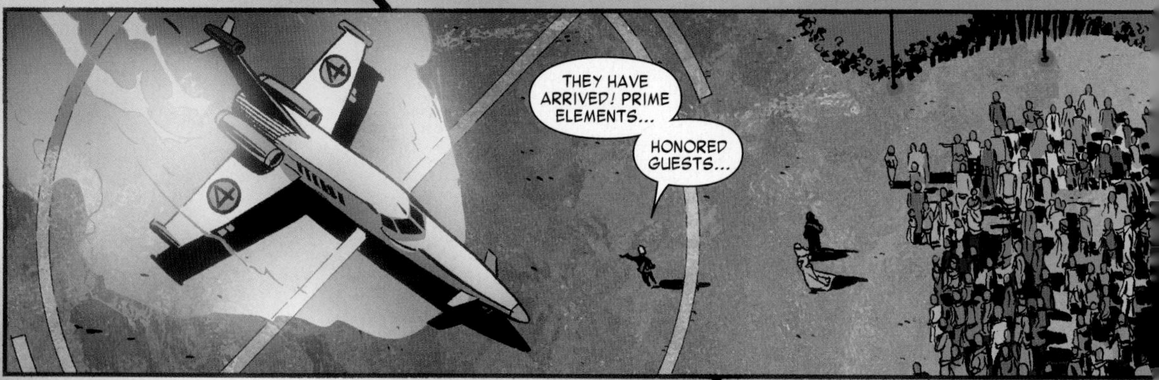
THEY HAVE ARRIVED! PRIME ELEMENTS...
HONORED GUESTS...

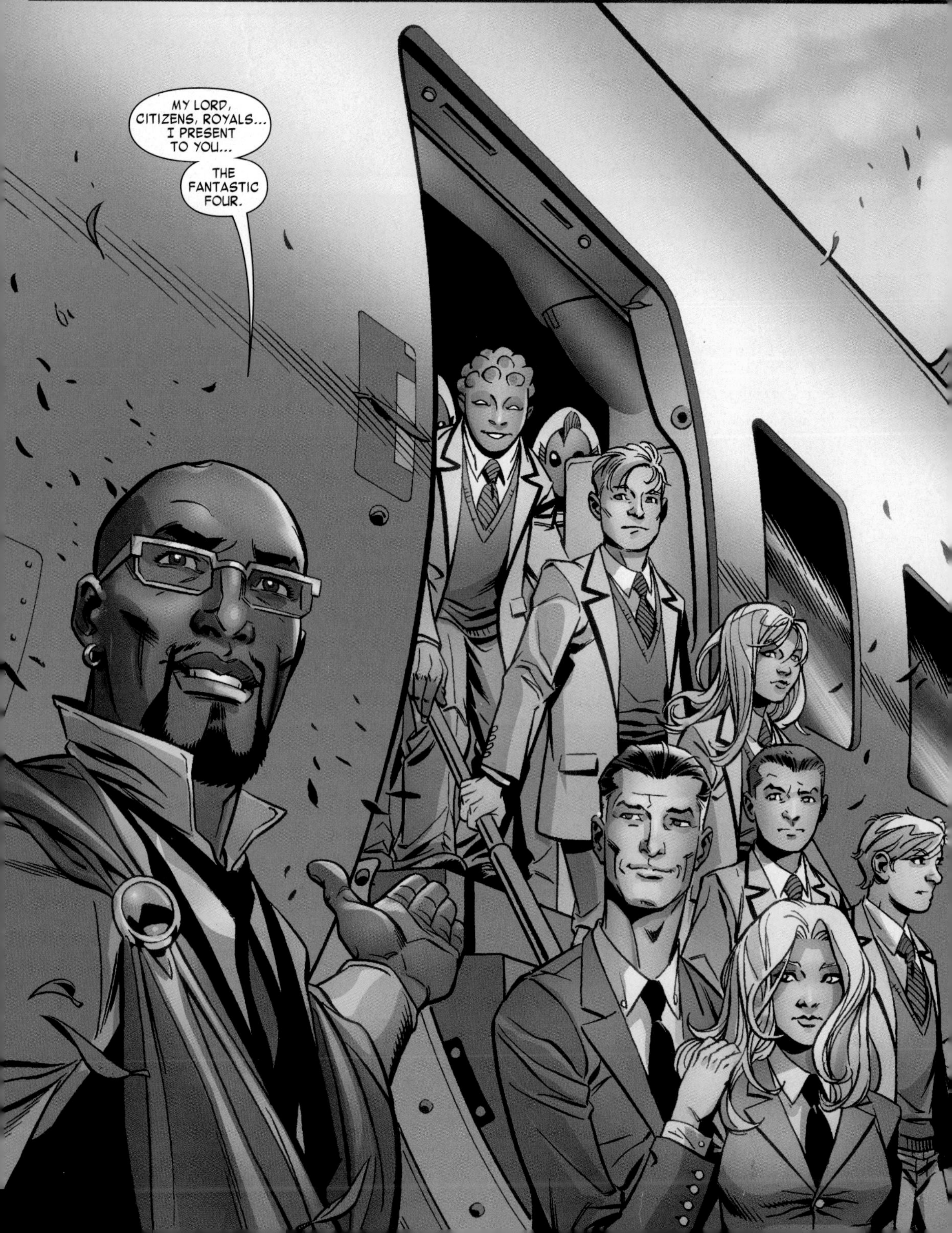
MY LORD, CITIZENS, ROYALS... I PRESENT TO YOU...
THE FANTASTIC FOUR.

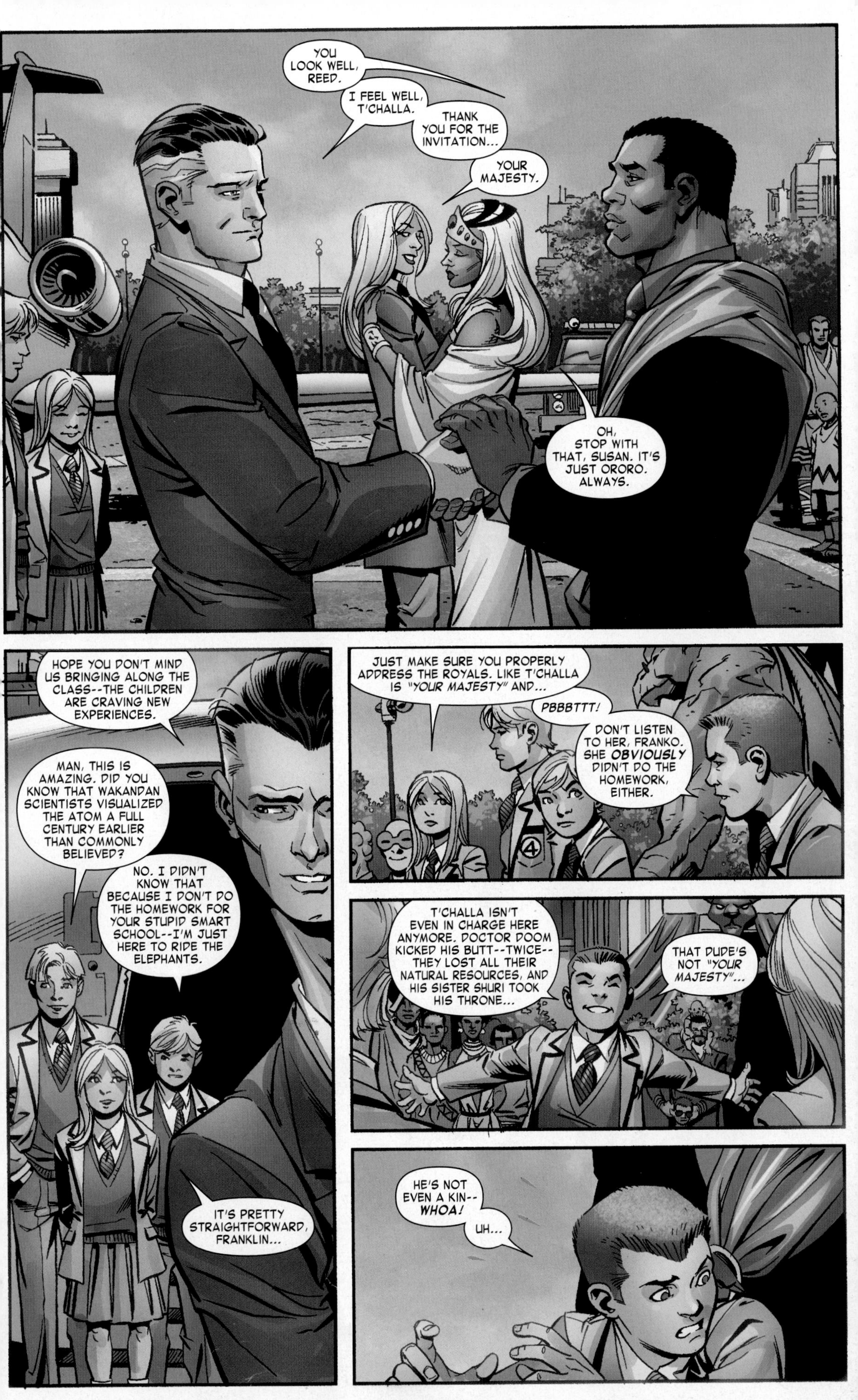
YOU LOOK WELL, REED.
I FEEL WELL, T'CHALLA.
THANK YOU FOR THE INVITATION...
YOUR MAJESTY.
OH, STOP WITH THAT, SUSAN. IT'S JUST ORORO. ALWAYS.
HOPE YOU DON'T MIND US BRINGING ALONG THE CLASS--THE CHILDREN ARE CRAVING NEW EXPERIENCES.
MAN, THIS IS AMAZING. DID YOU KNOW THAT WAKANDAN SCIENTISTS VISUALIZED THE ATOM A FULL CENTURY EARLIER THAN COMMONLY BELIEVED?
NO. I DIDN'T KNOW THAT BECAUSE I DON'T DO THE HOMEWORK FOR YOUR STUPID SMART SCHOOL--I'M JUST HERE TO RIDE THE ELEPHANTS.
IT'S PRETTY STRAIGHTFORWARD, FRANKLIN...
JUST MAKE SURE YOU PROPERLY ADDRESS THE ROYALS. LIKE T'CHALLA IS "YOUR MAJESTY" AND...
PBBBTTT!
DON'T LISTEN TO HER, FRANKO. SHE OBVIOUSLY DIDN'T DO THE HOMEWORK, EITHER.
T'CHALLA ISN'T EVEN IN CHARGE HERE ANYMORE. DOCTOR DOOM KICKED HIS BUTT--TWICE--THEY LOST ALL THEIR NATURAL RESOURCES, AND HIS SISTER SHURI TOOK HIS THRONE...
THAT DUDE'S NOT "YOUR MAJESTY"...
HE'S NOT EVEN A KIN--WHOA!
UH...

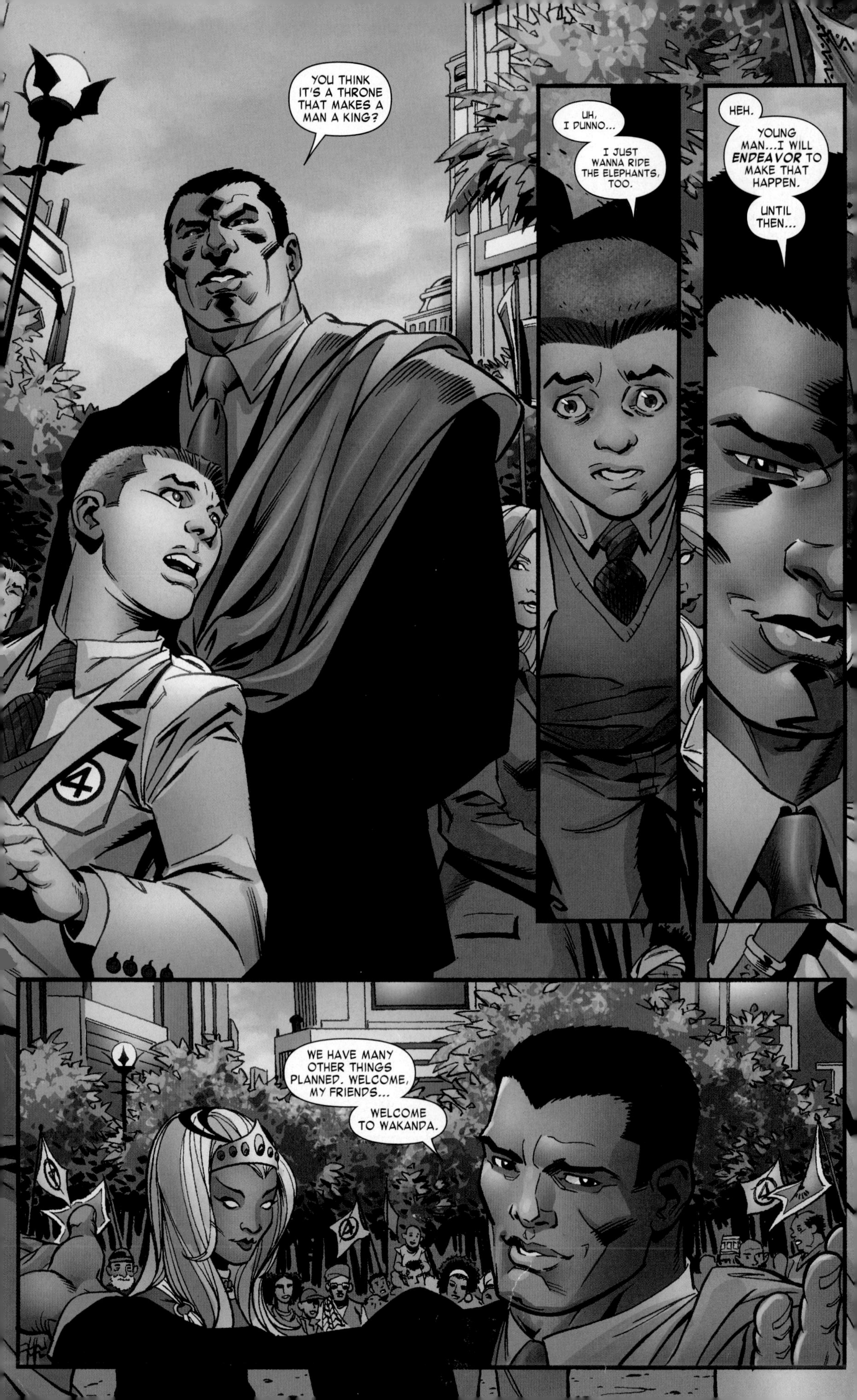
YOU THINK IT'S A THRONE THAT MAKES A MAN A KING?
UH, I DUNNO...
I JUST WANNA RIDE THE ELEPHANTS, TOO.
HEH.
YOUNG MAN...I WILL ENDEAVOR TO MAKE THAT HAPPEN.
UNTIL THEN...
WE HAVE MANY OTHER THINGS PLANNED. WELCOME, MY FRIENDS...
WELCOME TO WAKANDA.

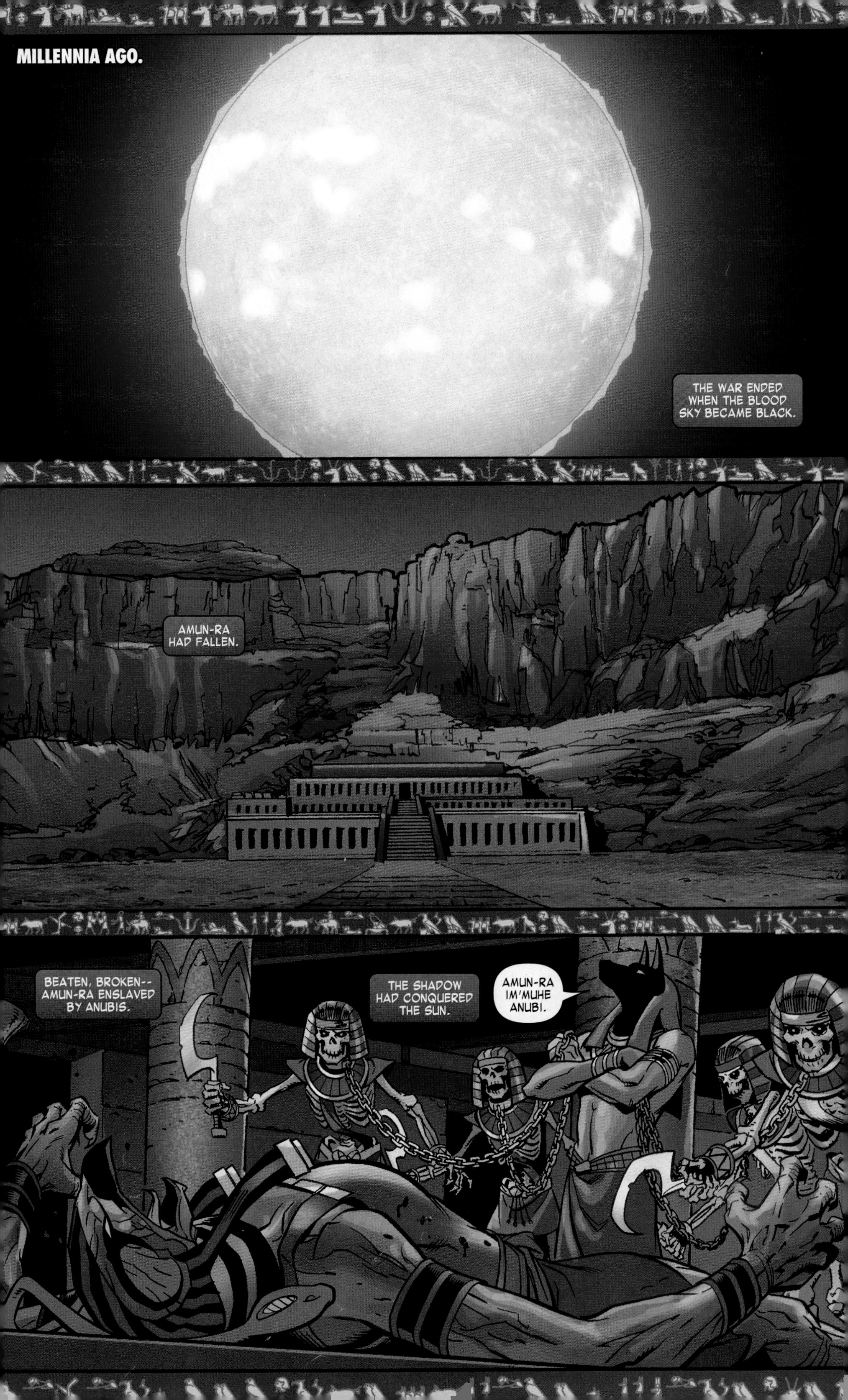
MILLENNIA AGO.
THE WAR ENDED WHEN THE BLOOD SKY BECAME BLACK.
AMUN-RA HAD FALLEN.
BEATEN, BROKEN-- AMUN-RA ENSLAVED BY ANUBIS.
THE SHADOW HAD CONQUERED THE SUN.
AMUN-RA IM'MUHE ANUBI.

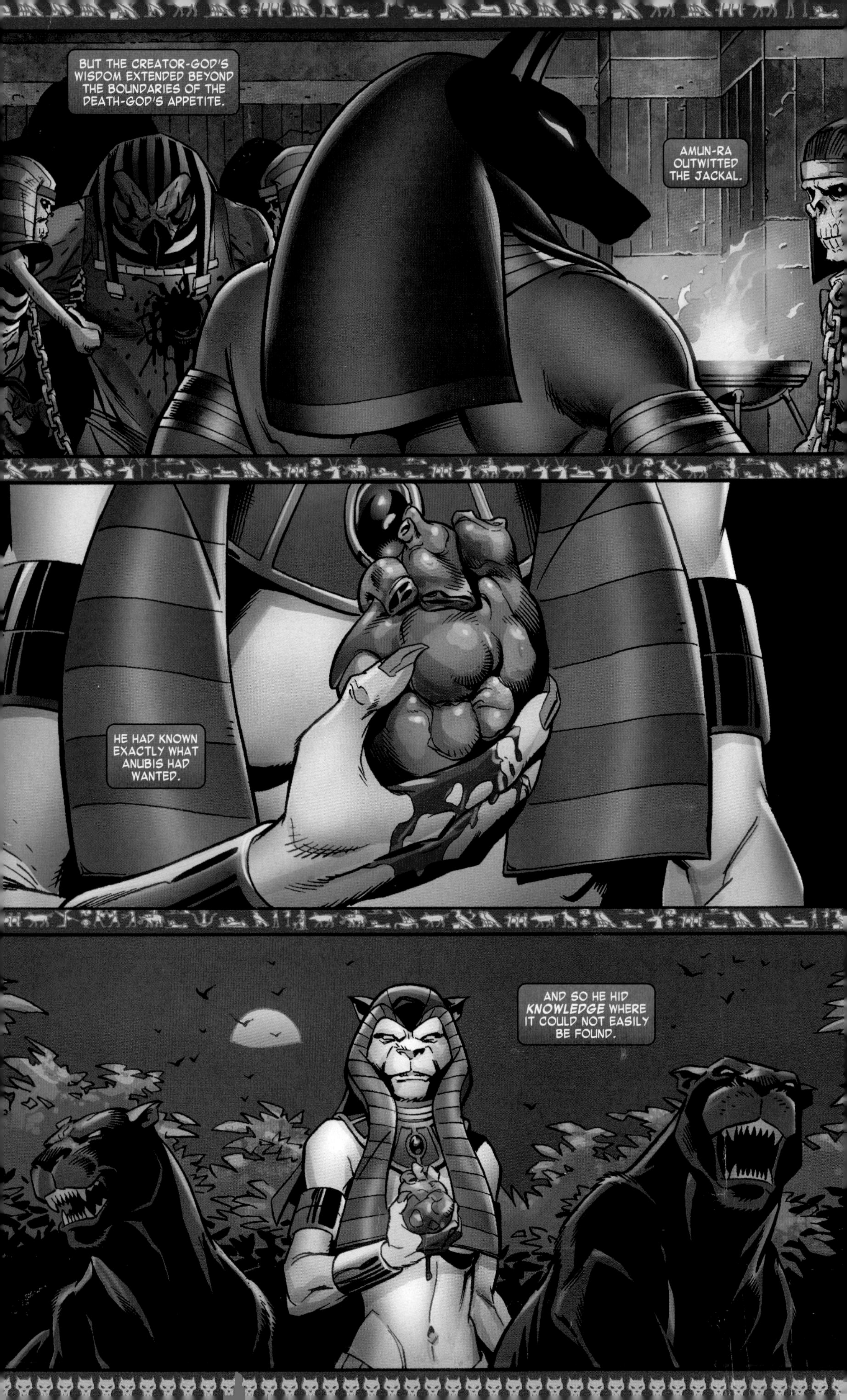

BUT THE CREATOR-GOD'S WISDOM EXTENDED BEYOND THE BOUNDARIES OF THE DEATH-GOD'S APPETITE.
AMUN-RA OUTWITTED THE JACKAL.
HE HAD KNOWN EXACTLY WHAT ANUBIS HAD WANTED.
AND SO HE HID *KNOWLEDGE* WHERE IT COULD NOT EASILY BE FOUND.

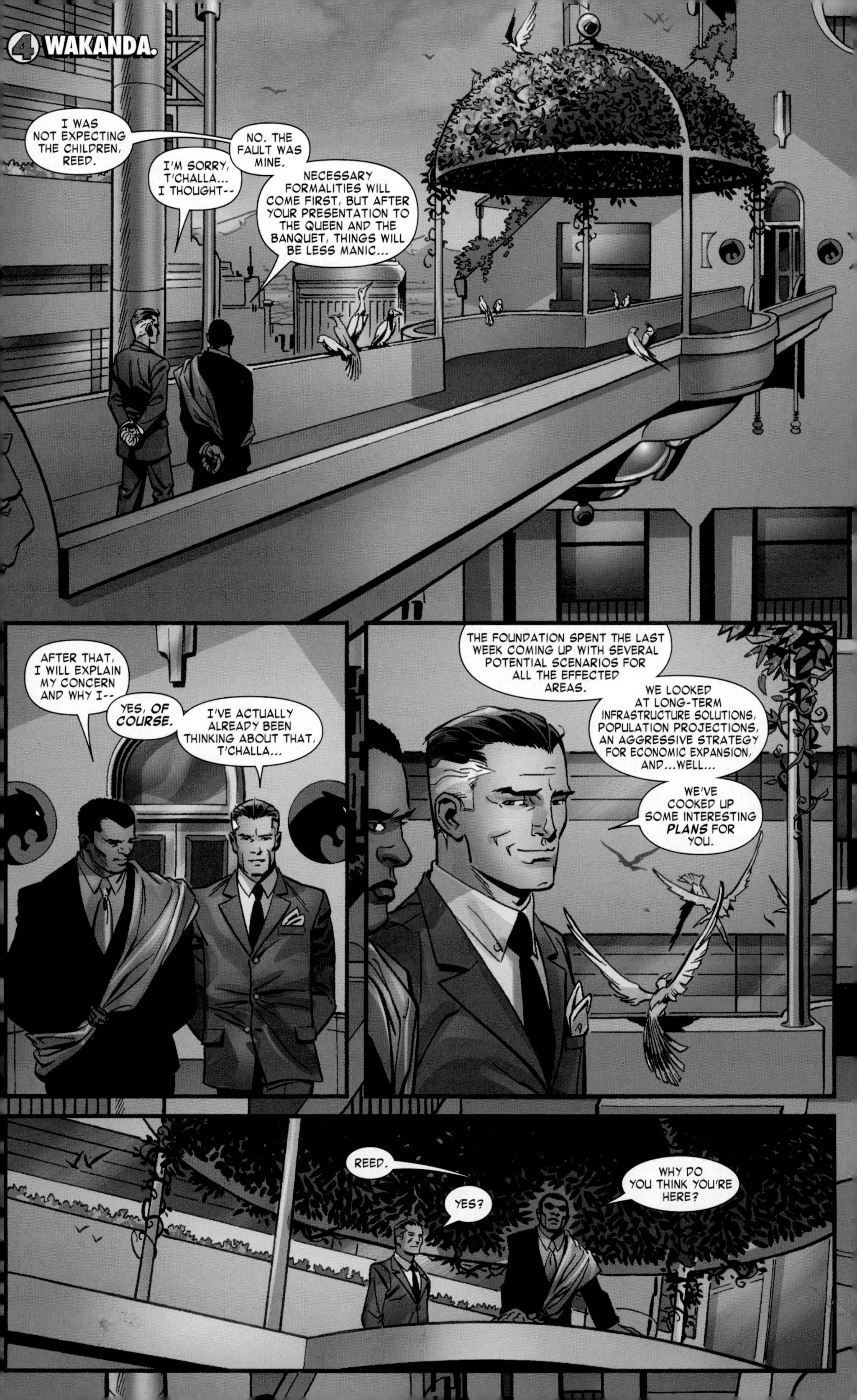
4 WAKANDA.
I WAS NOT EXPECTING THE CHILDREN, REED.
I'M SORRY, T'CHALLA... I THOUGHT--
NO. THE FAULT WAS MINE.
NECESSARY FORMALITIES WILL COME FIRST, BUT AFTER YOUR PRESENTATION TO THE QUEEN AND THE BANQUET, THINGS WILL BE LESS MANIC...
AFTER THAT, I WILL EXPLAIN MY CONCERN AND WHY I--
YES, OF COURSE.
I'VE ACTUALLY ALREADY BEEN THINKING ABOUT THAT, T'CHALLA...
THE FOUNDATION SPENT THE LAST WEEK COMING UP WITH SEVERAL POTENTIAL SCENARIOS FOR ALL THE EFFECTED AREAS.
WE LOOKED AT LONG-TERM INFRASTRUCTURE SOLUTIONS, POPULATION PROJECTIONS, AN AGGRESSIVE STRATEGY FOR ECONOMIC EXPANSION, AND...WELL...
WE'VE COOKED UP SOME INTERESTING PLANS FOR YOU.
REED.
YES?
WHY DO YOU THINK YOU'RE HERE?

VIBRANIUM.

YOUR NUMBER ONE EXPORT BECAME INERT OVERNIGHT. AS A RESULT, YOUR NATION HAS UNDOUBTEDLY LOST ITS MAIN ABILITY TO GENERATE REVENUE...

THIS WOULD NATURALLY RESULT IN SEVERE REPERCUSSIONS-- FINANCIAL HARDSHIP, TRADE IMBALANCE...EVERYTHING RELATED TO THE WELL-BEING OF A COUNTRY.

WE CAN HELP.

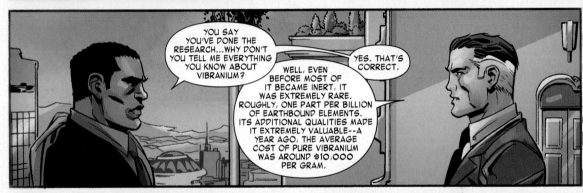

YOU SAY YOU'VE DONE THE RESEARCH...WHY DON'T YOU TELL ME EVERYTHING YOU KNOW ABOUT VIBRANIUM?

YES. THAT'S CORRECT.

WELL, EVEN BEFORE MOST OF IT BECAME INERT, IT WAS EXTREMELY RARE. ROUGHLY, ONE PART PER BILLION OF EARTHBOUND ELEMENTS. ITS ADDITIONAL QUALITIES MADE IT EXTREMELY VALUABLE--A YEAR AGO, THE AVERAGE COST OF PURE VIBRANIUM WAS AROUND $10,000 PER GRAM.

SO WHAT DOES--

WE ARE NOT PEASANTS WHO FELL BACKWARDS INTO WEALTH, REED.

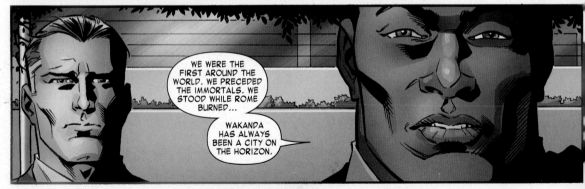

WE WERE THE FIRST AROUND THE WORLD. WE PRECEDED THE IMMORTALS. WE STOOD WHILE ROME BURNED...

WAKANDA HAS ALWAYS BEEN A CITY ON THE HORIZON.

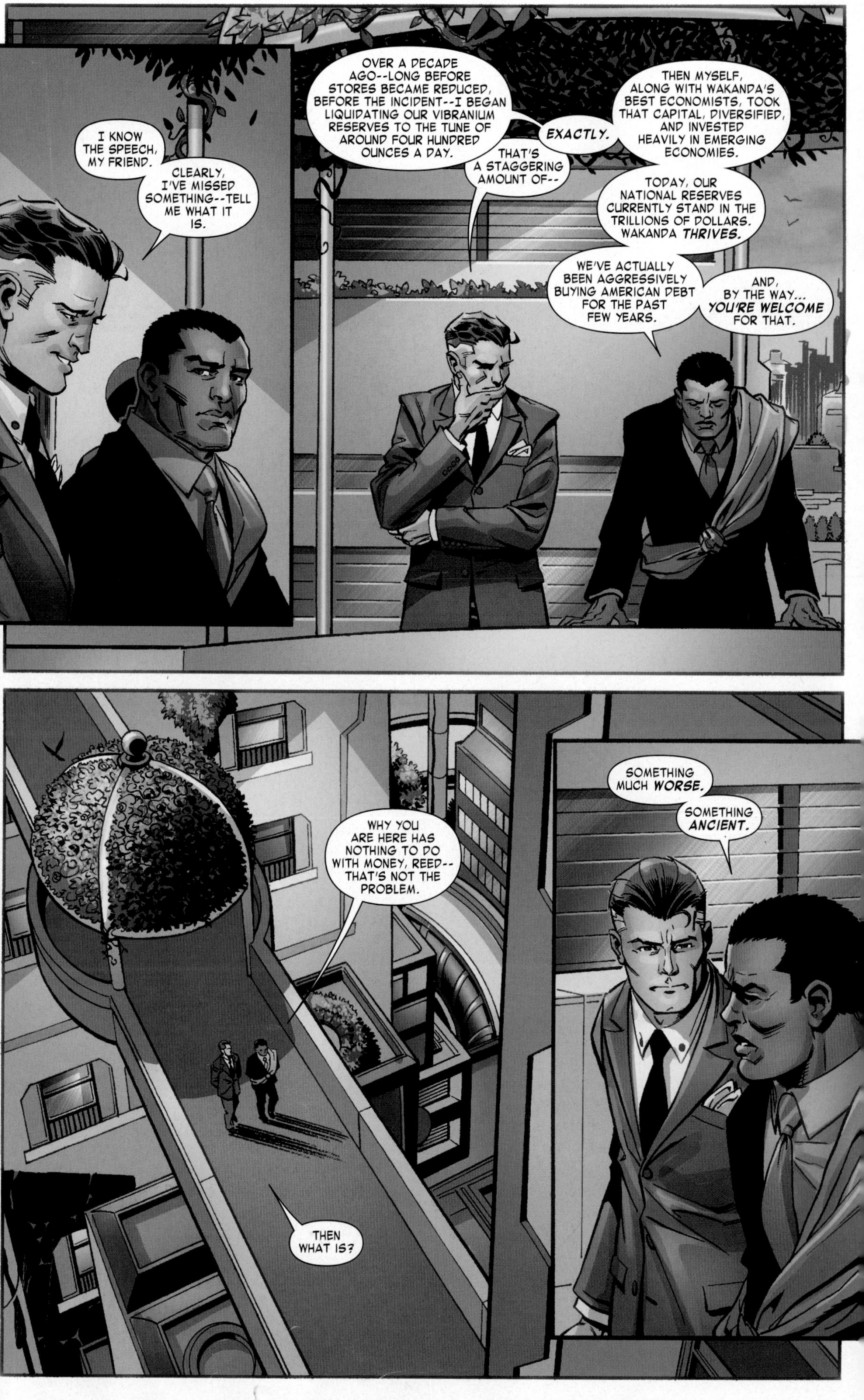
I KNOW THE SPEECH, MY FRIEND.
CLEARLY, I'VE MISSED SOMETHING--TELL ME WHAT IT IS.
OVER A DECADE AGO--LONG BEFORE STORES BECAME REDUCED, BEFORE THE INCIDENT--I BEGAN LIQUIDATING OUR VIBRANIUM RESERVES TO THE TUNE OF AROUND FOUR HUNDRED OUNCES A DAY.
THAT'S A STAGGERING AMOUNT OF--
EXACTLY.
THEN MYSELF, ALONG WITH WAKANDA'S BEST ECONOMISTS, TOOK THAT CAPITAL, DIVERSIFIED, AND INVESTED HEAVILY IN EMERGING ECONOMIES.
TODAY, OUR NATIONAL RESERVES CURRENTLY STAND IN THE TRILLIONS OF DOLLARS. WAKANDA THRIVES.
WE'VE ACTUALLY BEEN AGGRESSIVELY BUYING AMERICAN DEBT FOR THE PAST FEW YEARS.
AND, BY THE WAY... YOU'RE WELCOME FOR THAT.
WHY YOU ARE HERE HAS NOTHING TO DO WITH MONEY, REED--THAT'S NOT THE PROBLEM.
THEN WHAT IS?
SOMETHING MUCH WORSE.
SOMETHING ANCIENT.

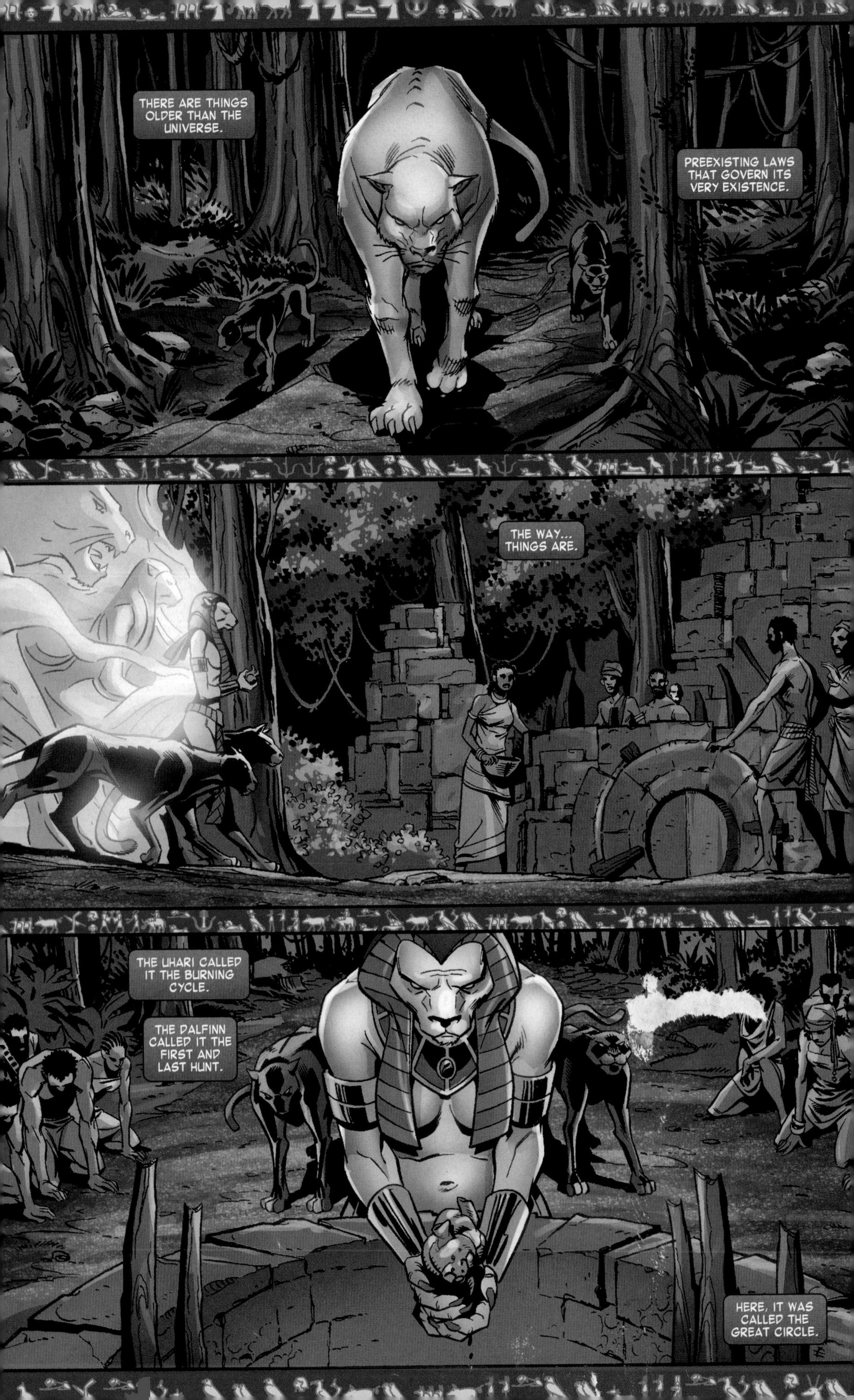
THERE ARE THINGS OLDER THAN THE UNIVERSE.
PREEXISTING LAWS THAT GOVERN ITS VERY EXISTENCE.
THE WAY... THINGS ARE.
THE UHARI CALLED IT THE BURNING CYCLE.
THE DALFINN CALLED IT THE FIRST AND LAST HUNT.
HERE, IT WAS CALLED THE GREAT CIRCLE.

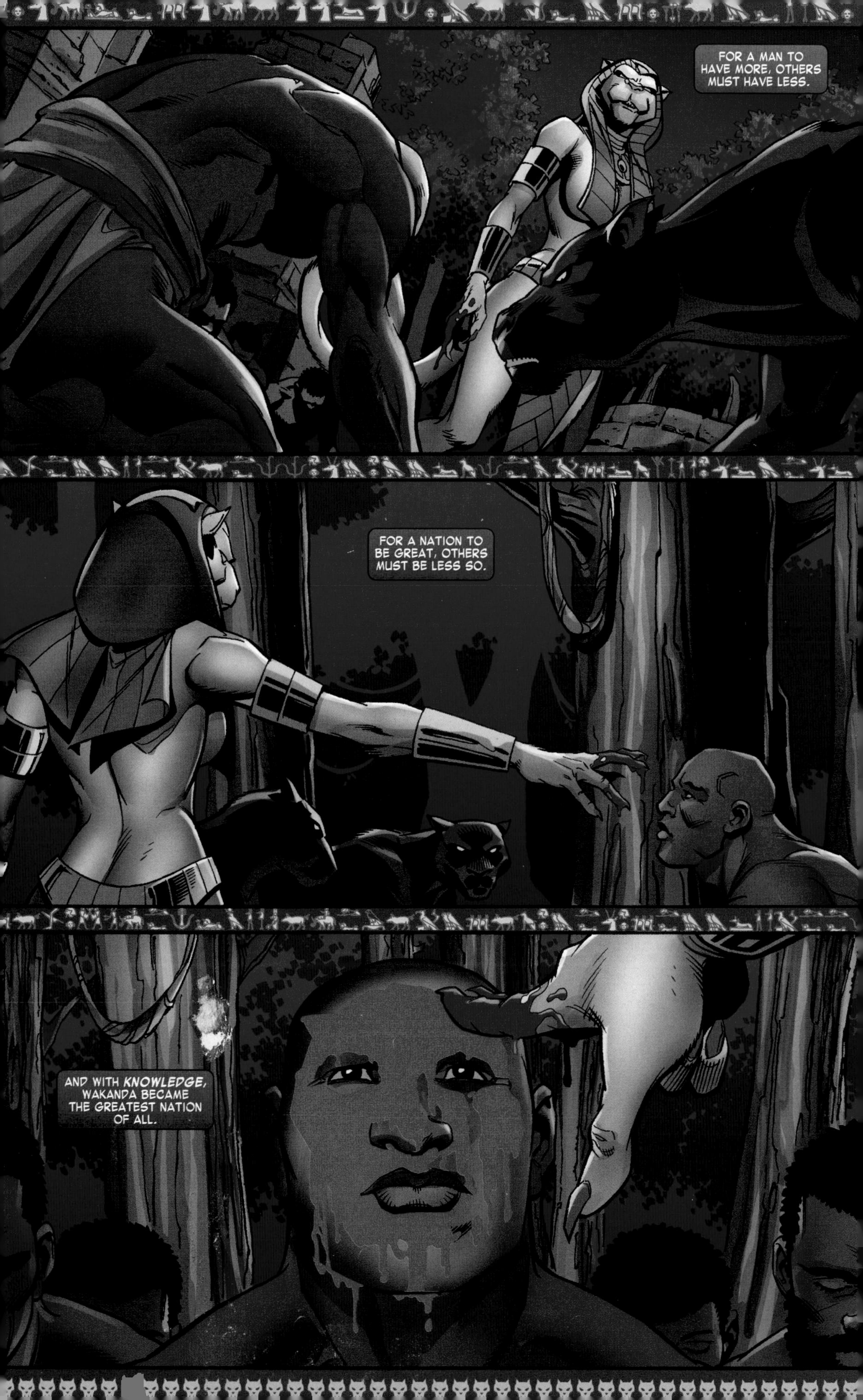
FOR A MAN TO HAVE MORE, OTHERS MUST HAVE LESS.
FOR A NATION TO BE GREAT, OTHERS MUST BE LESS SO.
AND WITH *KNOWLEDGE*, WAKANDA BECAME THE GREATEST NATION OF ALL.

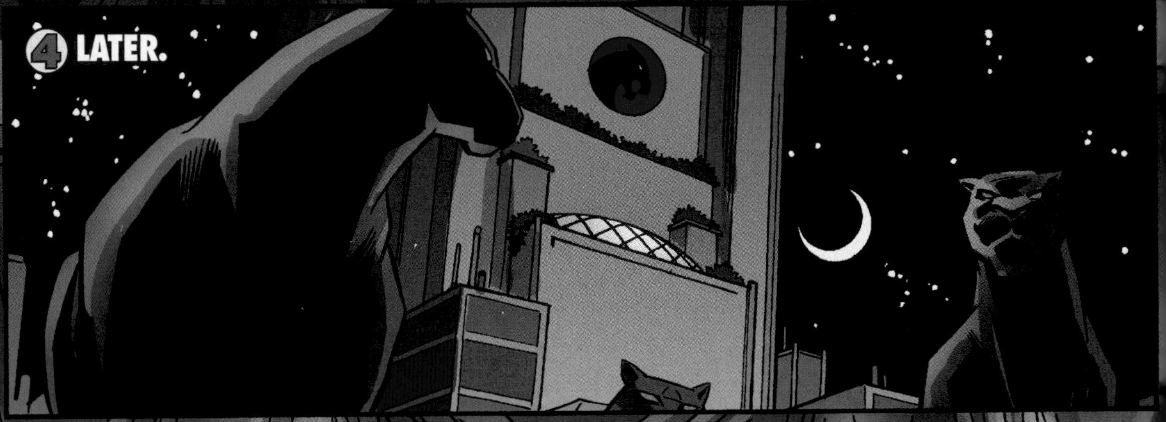
LATER.

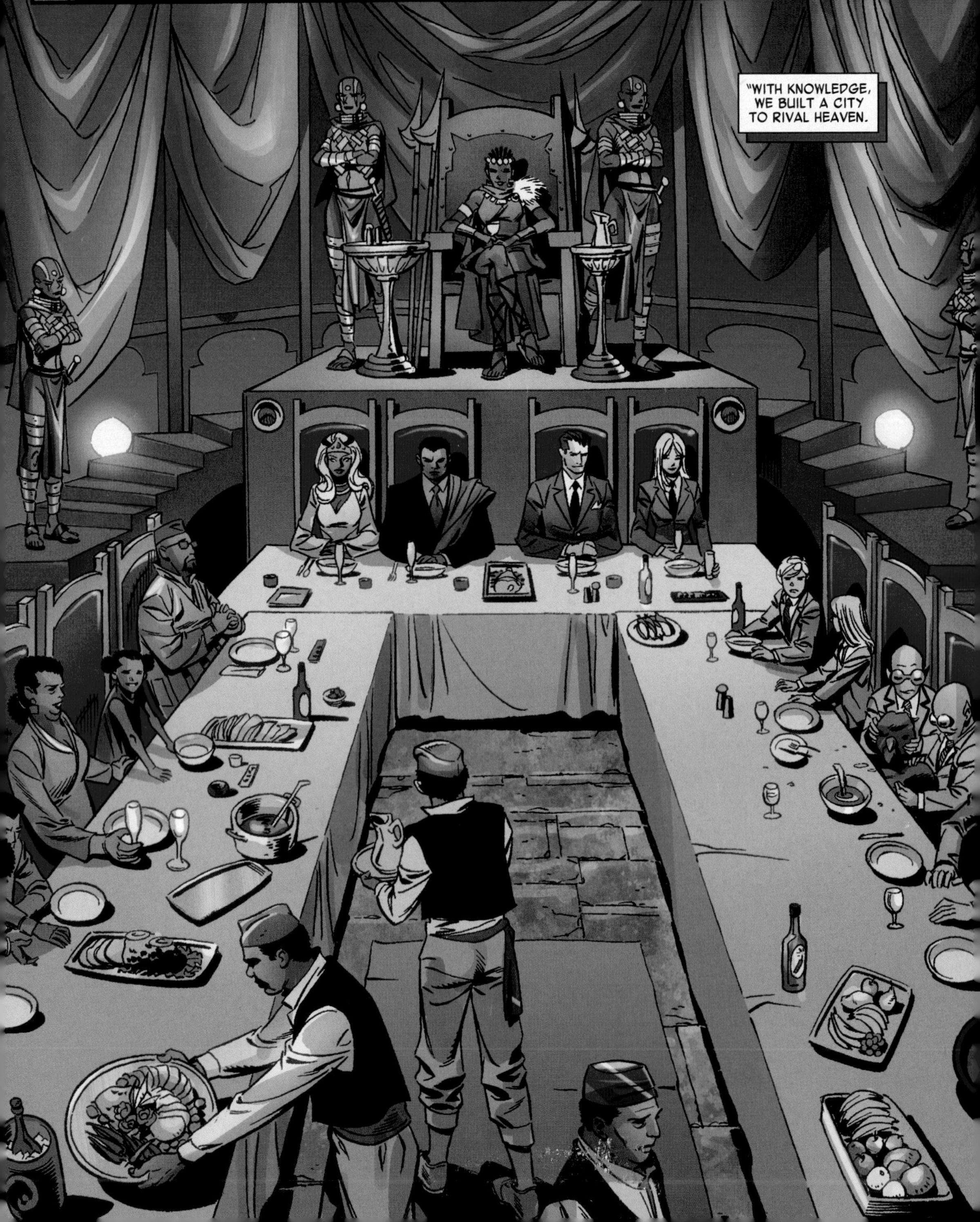
"WITH KNOWLEDGE, WE BUILT A CITY TO RIVAL HEAVEN.

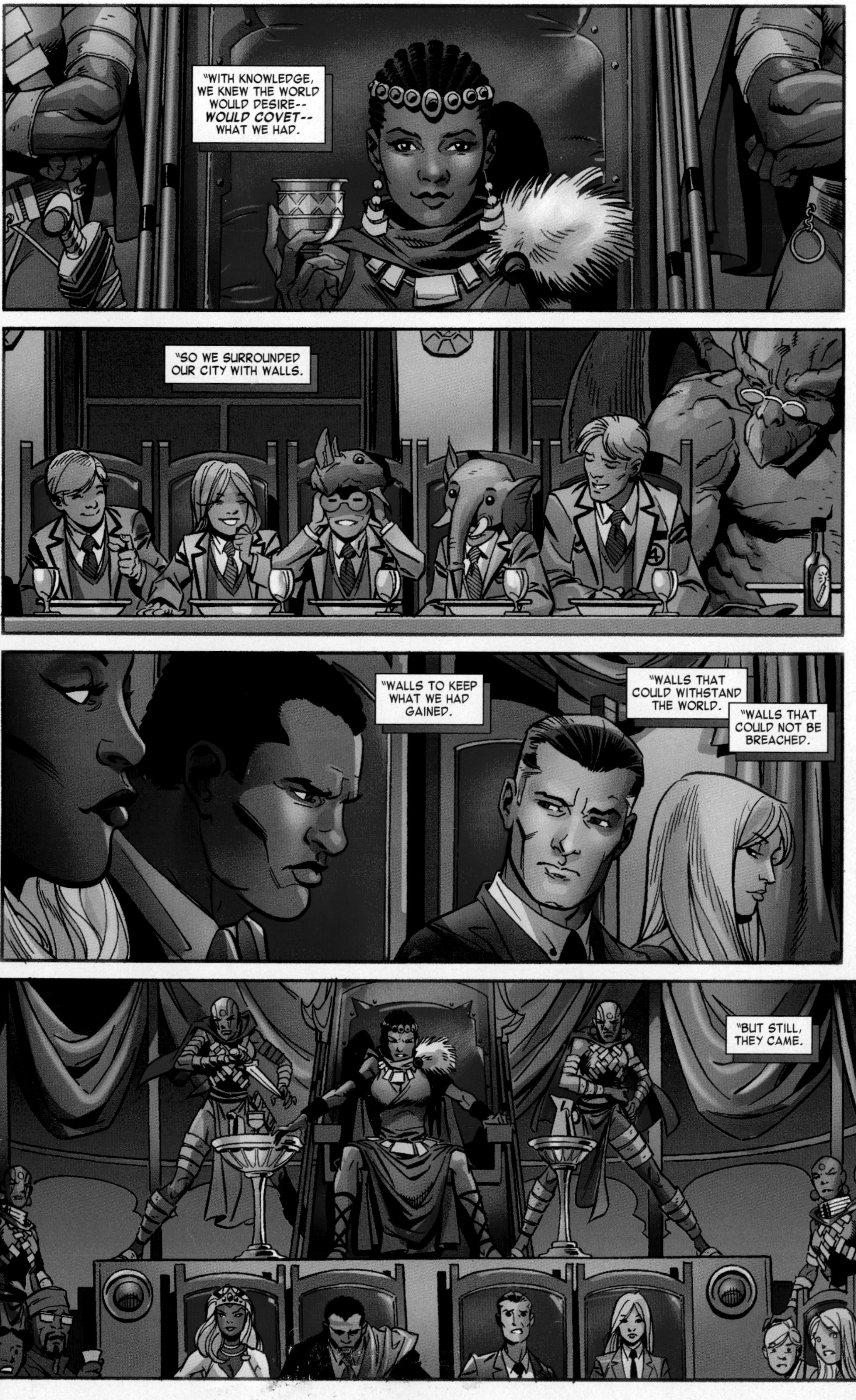
"WITH KNOWLEDGE, WE KNEW THE WORLD WOULD DESIRE-- WOULD COVET-- WHAT WE HAD.
"SO WE SURROUNDED OUR CITY WITH WALLS.
"WALLS TO KEEP WHAT WE HAD GAINED.
"WALLS THAT COULD WITHSTAND THE WORLD.
"WALLS THAT COULD NOT BE BREACHED.
"BUT STILL, THEY CAME.

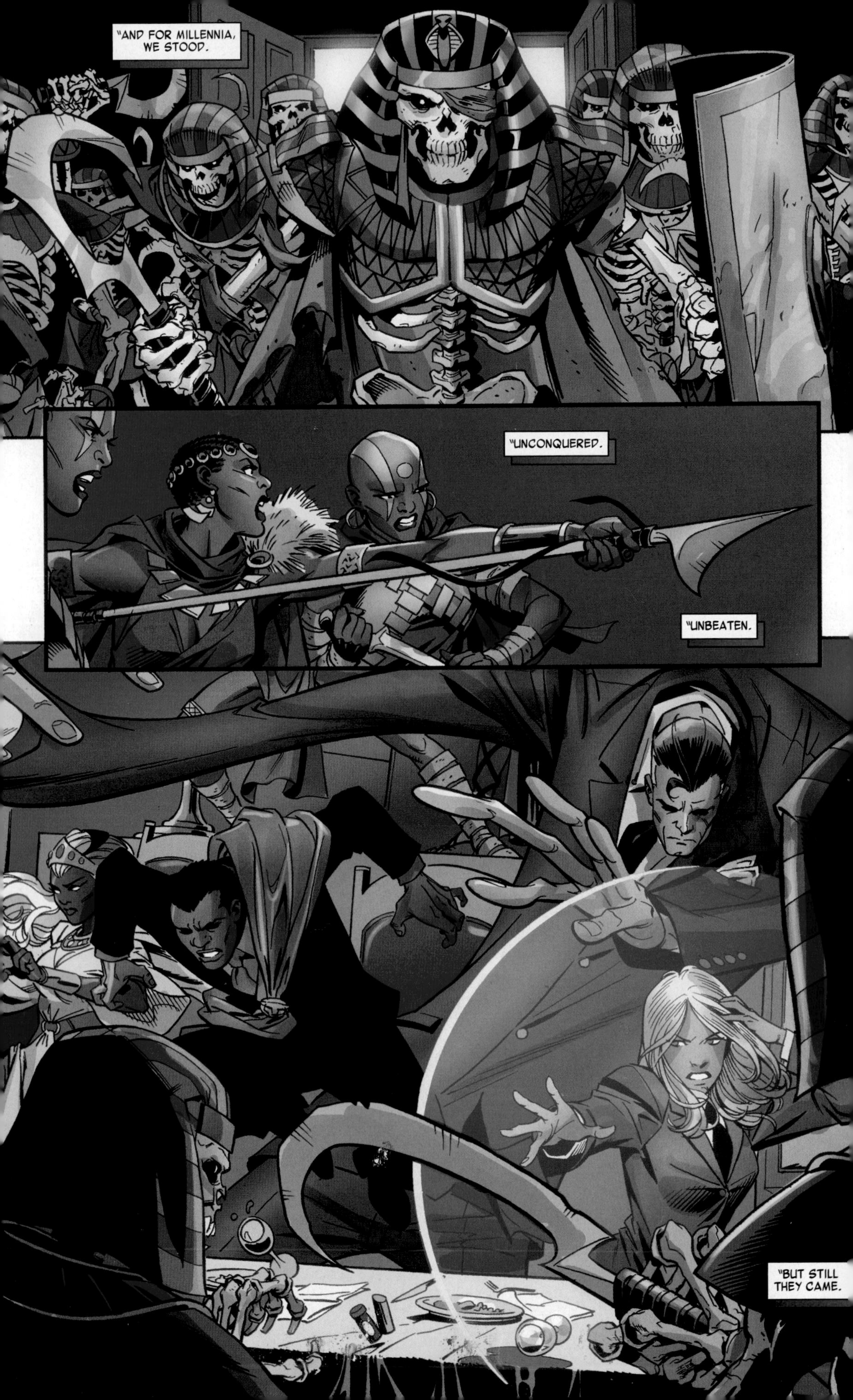
"AND FOR MILLENNIA, WE STOOD.
"UNCONQUERED.
"UNBEATEN.
"BUT STILL THEY CAME.

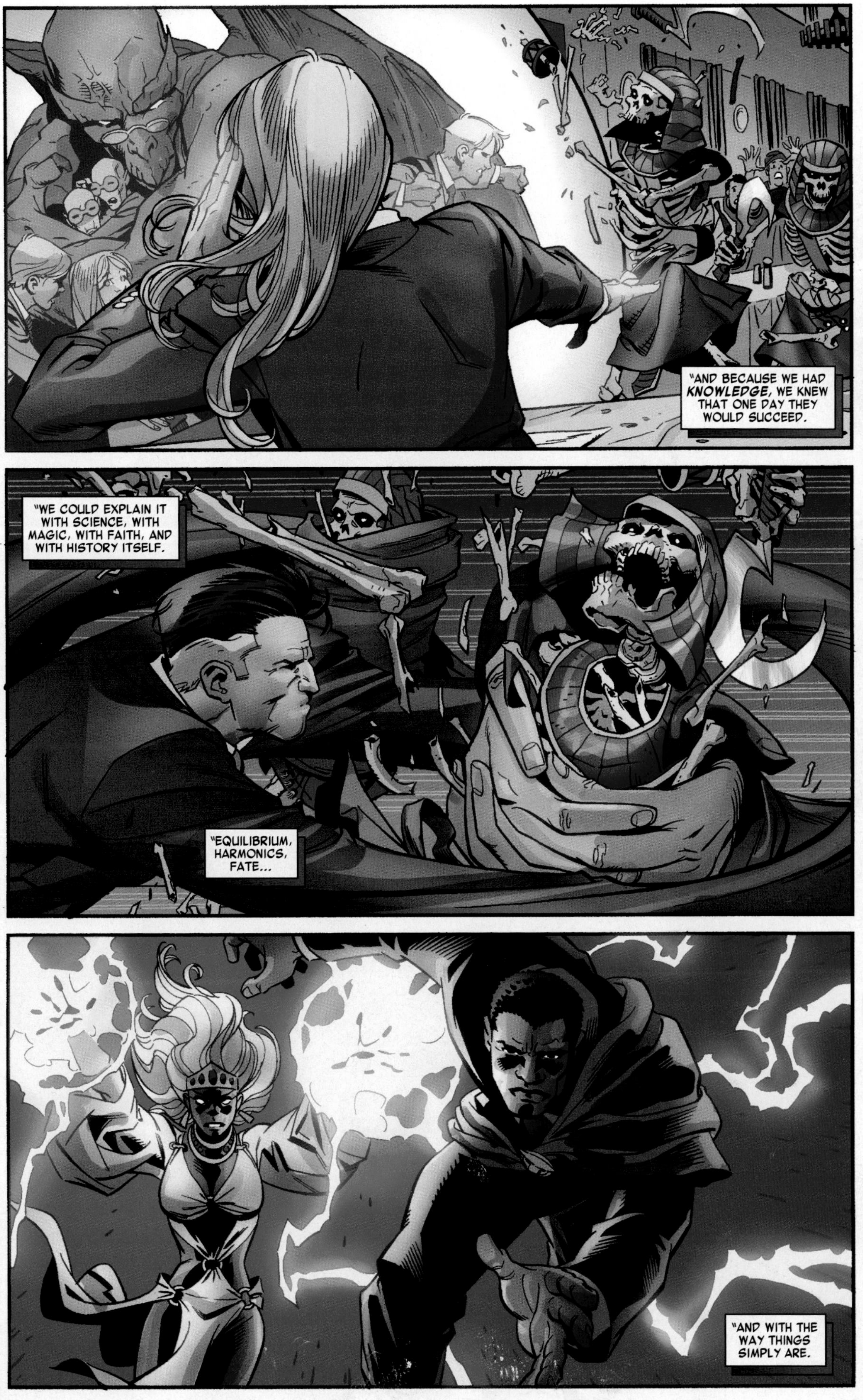
"AND BECAUSE WE HAD KNOWLEDGE, WE KNEW THAT ONE DAY THEY WOULD SUCCEED.
"WE COULD EXPLAIN IT WITH SCIENCE, WITH MAGIC, WITH FAITH, AND WITH HISTORY ITSELF.
"EQUILIBRIUM, HARMONICS, FATE...
"AND WITH THE WAY THINGS SIMPLY ARE.

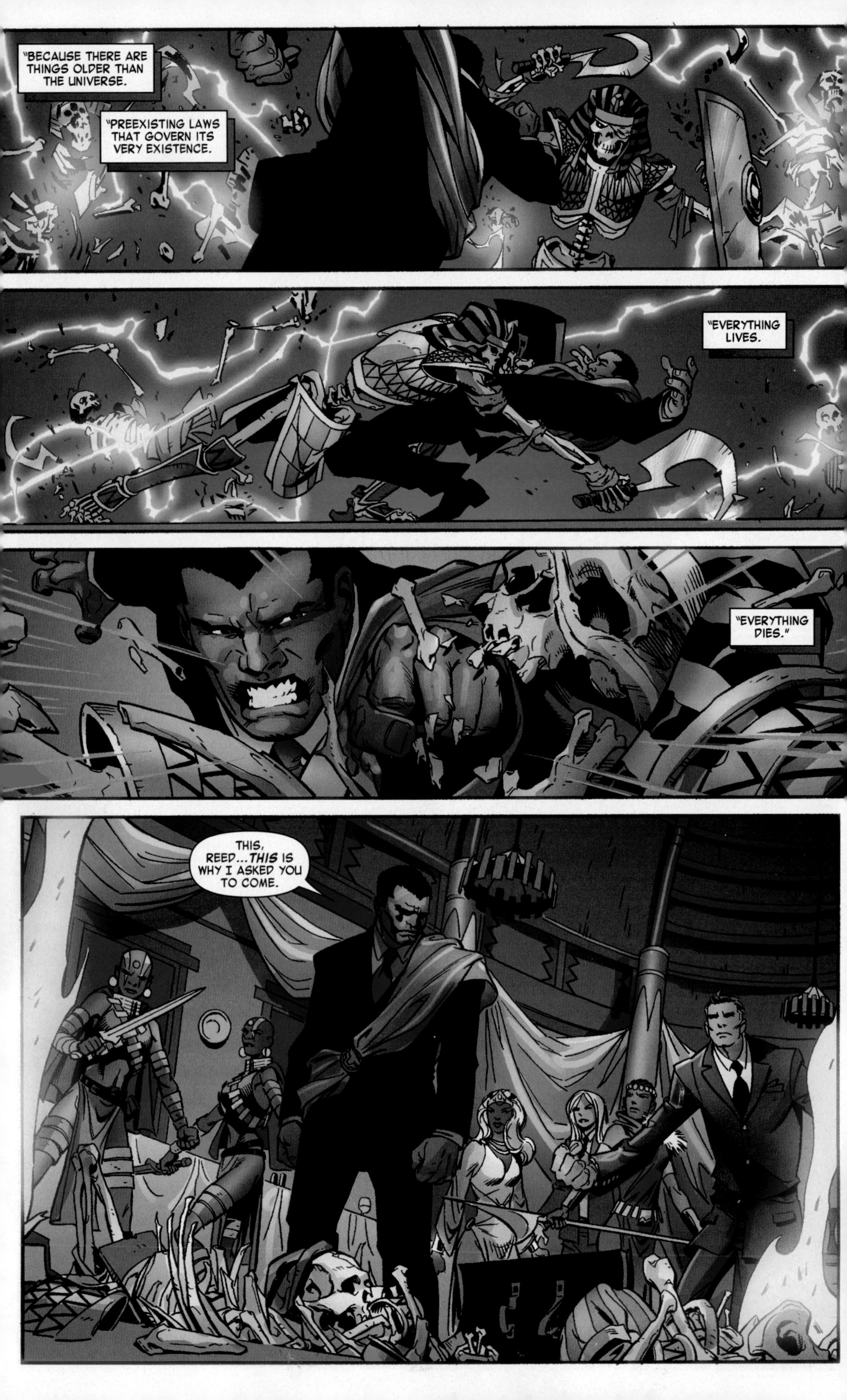
"BECAUSE THERE ARE THINGS OLDER THAN THE UNIVERSE.
"PREEXISTING LAWS THAT GOVERN ITS VERY EXISTENCE.
"EVERYTHING LIVES.
"EVERYTHING DIES."
THIS, REED...THIS IS WHY I ASKED YOU TO COME.

THAT WAS THE THIRD ATTACK THIS MONTH. TWO IN THE LAST WEEK...

THEY ARE INCREASING IN FREQUENCY.

OUR TIME GROWS SHORT.

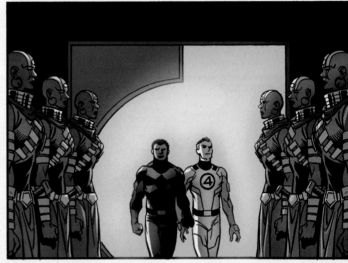

SAFE JOURNEY, BELOVED.

WISDOM AND LIGHT ILLUMINATE YOUR PATH.

COME BACK SAFELY, MY LORD.

MAY YOU BE WHAT HE NEEDS YOU TO BE.

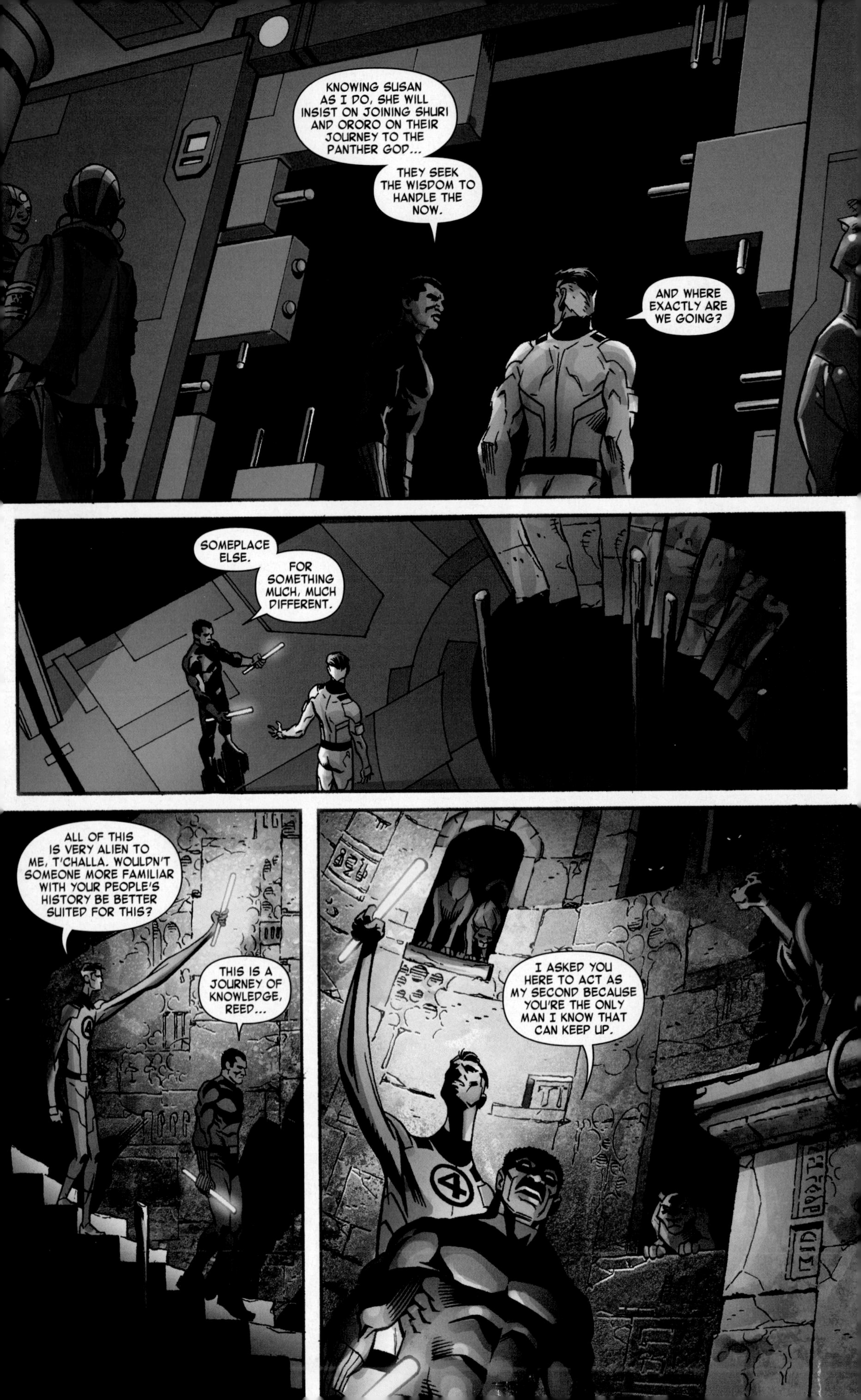
KNOWING SUSAN AS I DO, SHE WILL INSIST ON JOINING SHURI AND ORORO ON THEIR JOURNEY TO THE PANTHER GOD...
THEY SEEK THE WISDOM TO HANDLE THE NOW.
AND WHERE EXACTLY ARE WE GOING?
SOMEPLACE ELSE.
FOR SOMETHING MUCH, MUCH DIFFERENT.
ALL OF THIS IS VERY ALIEN TO ME, T'CHALLA. WOULDN'T SOMEONE MORE FAMILIAR WITH YOUR PEOPLE'S HISTORY BE BETTER SUITED FOR THIS?
THIS IS A JOURNEY OF KNOWLEDGE, REED...
I ASKED YOU HERE TO ACT AS MY SECOND BECAUSE YOU'RE THE ONLY MAN I KNOW THAT CAN KEEP UP.

WE'VE REACHED THE BOTTOM.

PERFECTLY PRESERVED... THOSE DESIGNS PREDATE DEMOTIC SYMBOLS...

WHAT IS THIS?

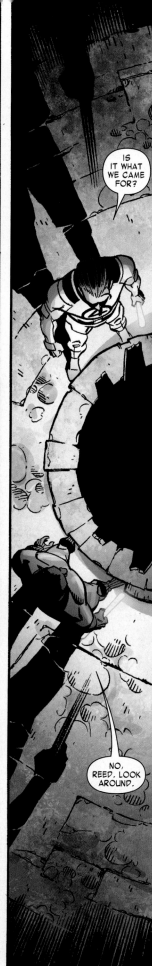

IS IT WHAT WE CAME FOR?

NO, REED. LOOK AROUND.

THIS IS NOT OUR DESTINATION...

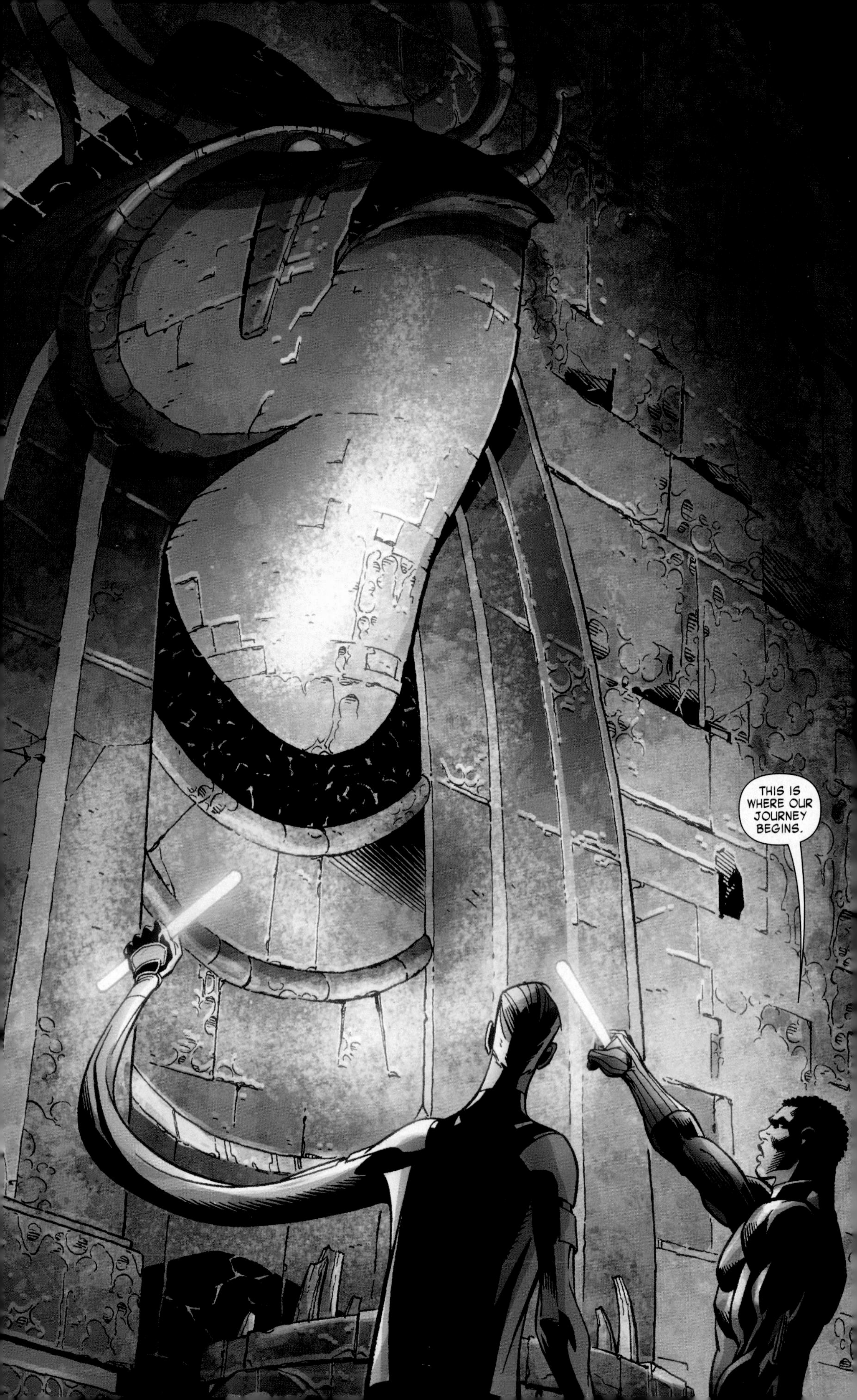
THIS IS WHERE OUR JOURNEY BEGINS.

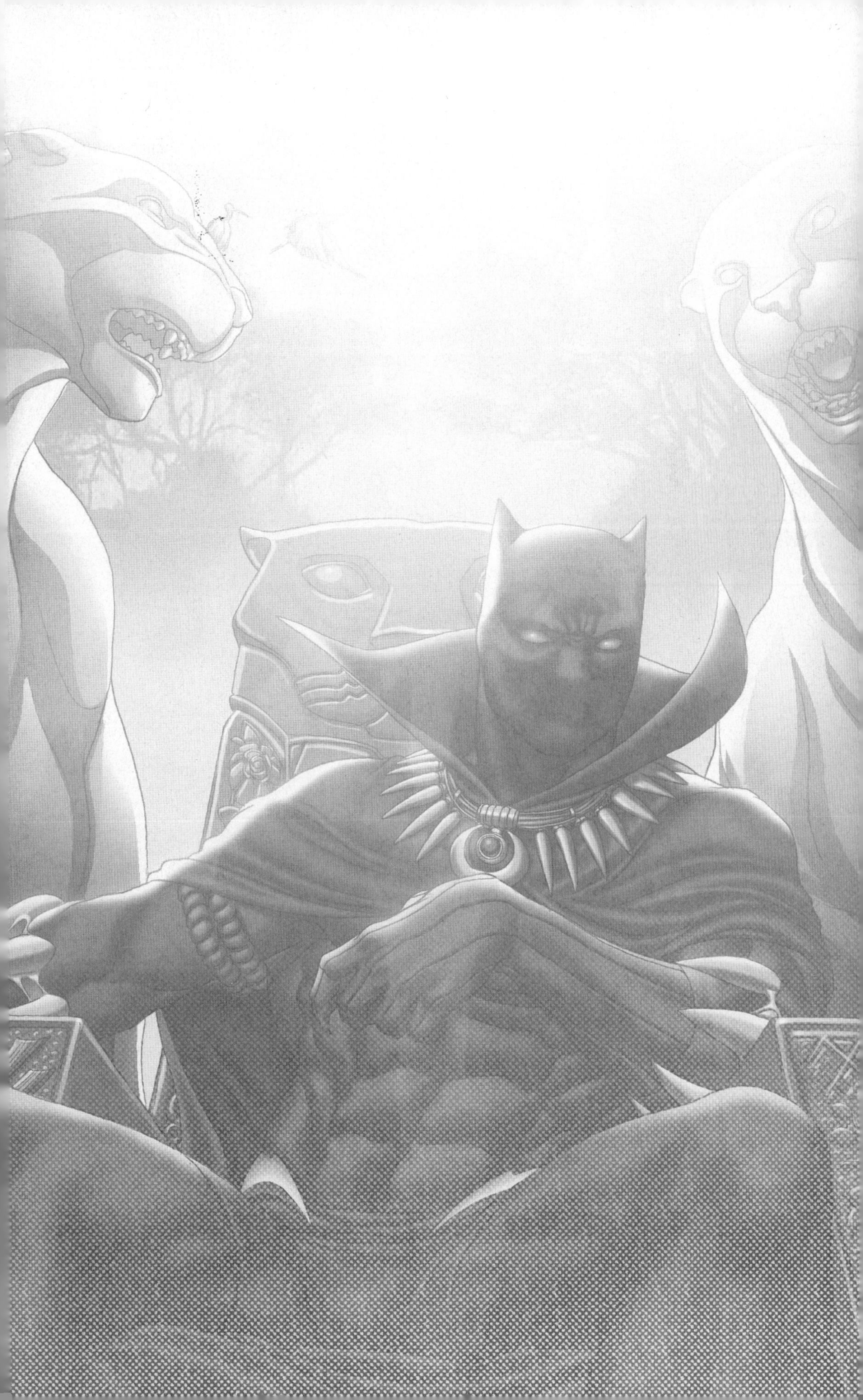

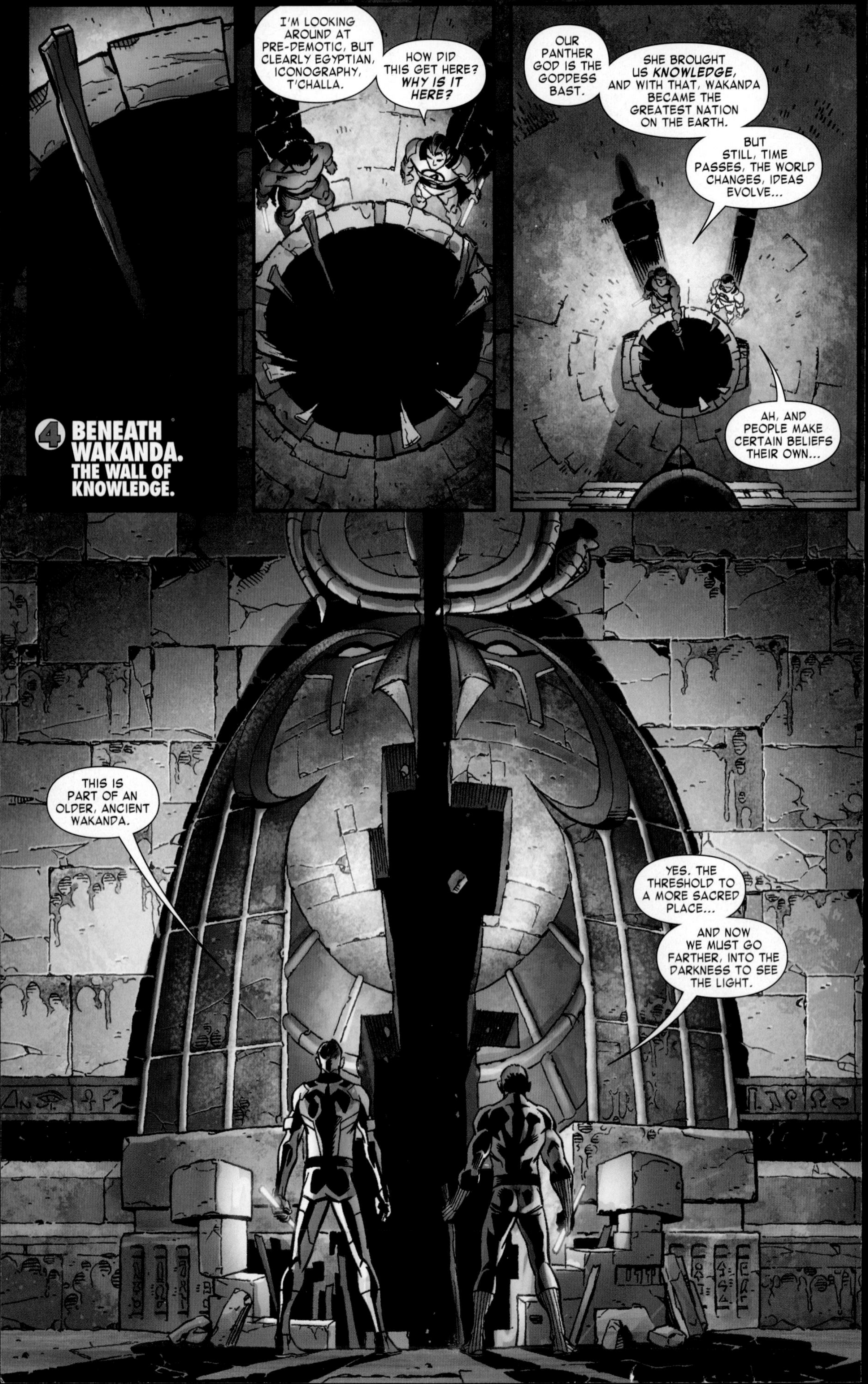
BENEATH WAKANDA. THE WALL OF KNOWLEDGE.
I'M LOOKING AROUND AT PRE-DEMOTIC, BUT CLEARLY EGYPTIAN, ICONOGRAPHY, T'CHALLA.
HOW DID THIS GET HERE? WHY IS IT HERE?
OUR PANTHER GOD IS THE GODDESS BAST.
SHE BROUGHT US KNOWLEDGE, AND WITH THAT, WAKANDA BECAME THE GREATEST NATION ON THE EARTH.
BUT STILL, TIME PASSES, THE WORLD CHANGES, IDEAS EVOLVE...
AH, AND PEOPLE MAKE CERTAIN BELIEFS THEIR OWN...
THIS IS PART OF AN OLDER, ANCIENT WAKANDA.
YES. THE THRESHOLD TO A MORE SACRED PLACE...
AND NOW WE MUST GO FARTHER, INTO THE DARKNESS TO SEE THE LIGHT.

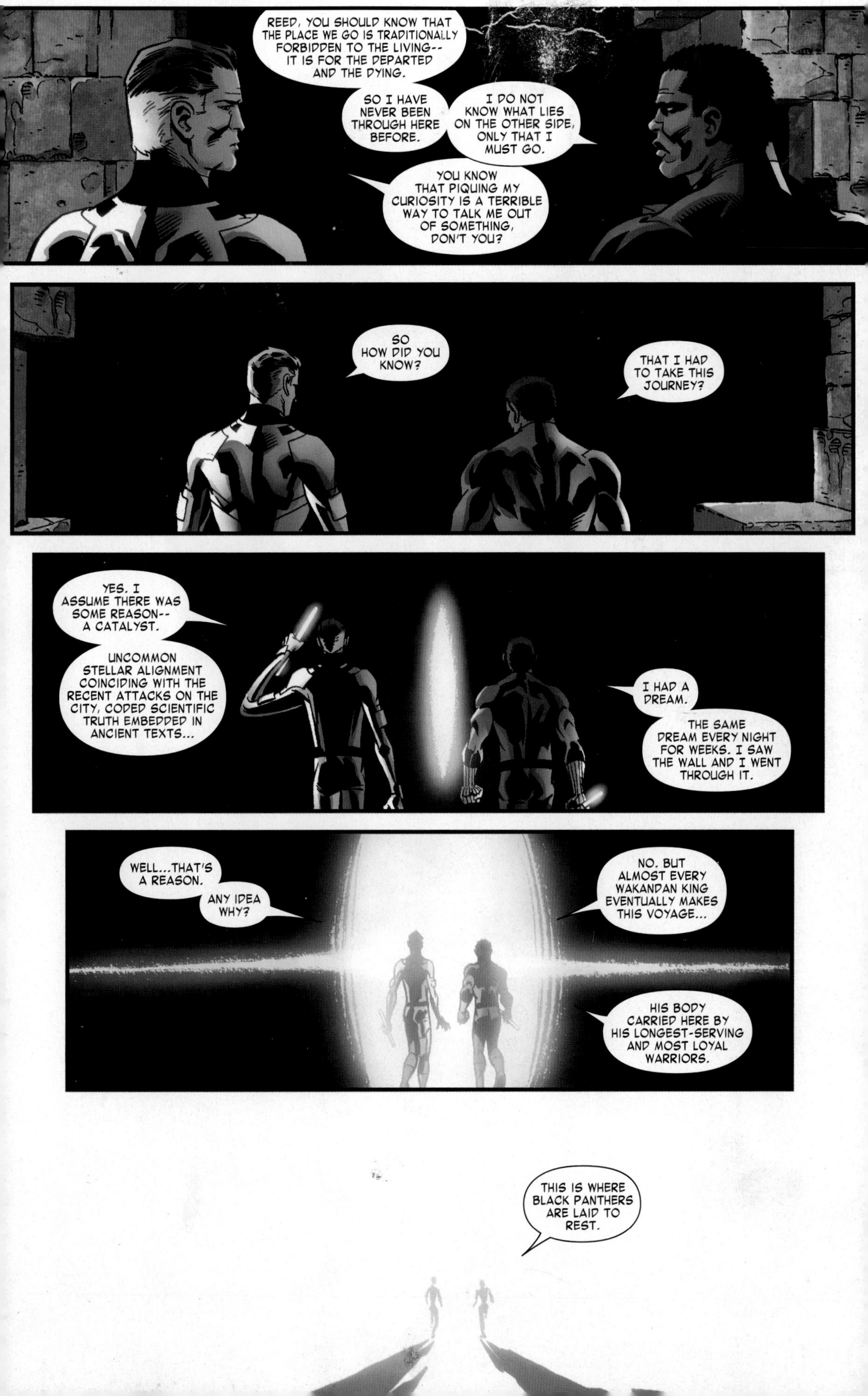
REED, YOU SHOULD KNOW THAT THE PLACE WE GO IS TRADITIONALLY FORBIDDEN TO THE LIVING-- IT IS FOR THE DEPARTED AND THE DYING.
SO I HAVE NEVER BEEN THROUGH HERE BEFORE.
I DO NOT KNOW WHAT LIES ON THE OTHER SIDE, ONLY THAT I MUST GO.
YOU KNOW THAT PIQUING MY CURIOSITY IS A TERRIBLE WAY TO TALK ME OUT OF SOMETHING, DON'T YOU?
SO HOW DID YOU KNOW?
THAT I HAD TO TAKE THIS JOURNEY?
YES. I ASSUME THERE WAS SOME REASON-- A CATALYST.
UNCOMMON STELLAR ALIGNMENT COINCIDING WITH THE RECENT ATTACKS ON THE CITY, CODED SCIENTIFIC TRUTH EMBEDDED IN ANCIENT TEXTS...
I HAD A DREAM.
THE SAME DREAM EVERY NIGHT FOR WEEKS. I SAW THE WALL AND I WENT THROUGH IT.
WELL...THAT'S A REASON.
ANY IDEA WHY?
NO. BUT ALMOST EVERY WAKANDAN KING EVENTUALLY MAKES THIS VOYAGE...
HIS BODY CARRIED HERE BY HIS LONGEST-SERVING AND MOST LOYAL WARRIORS.
THIS IS WHERE BLACK PANTHERS ARE LAID TO REST.

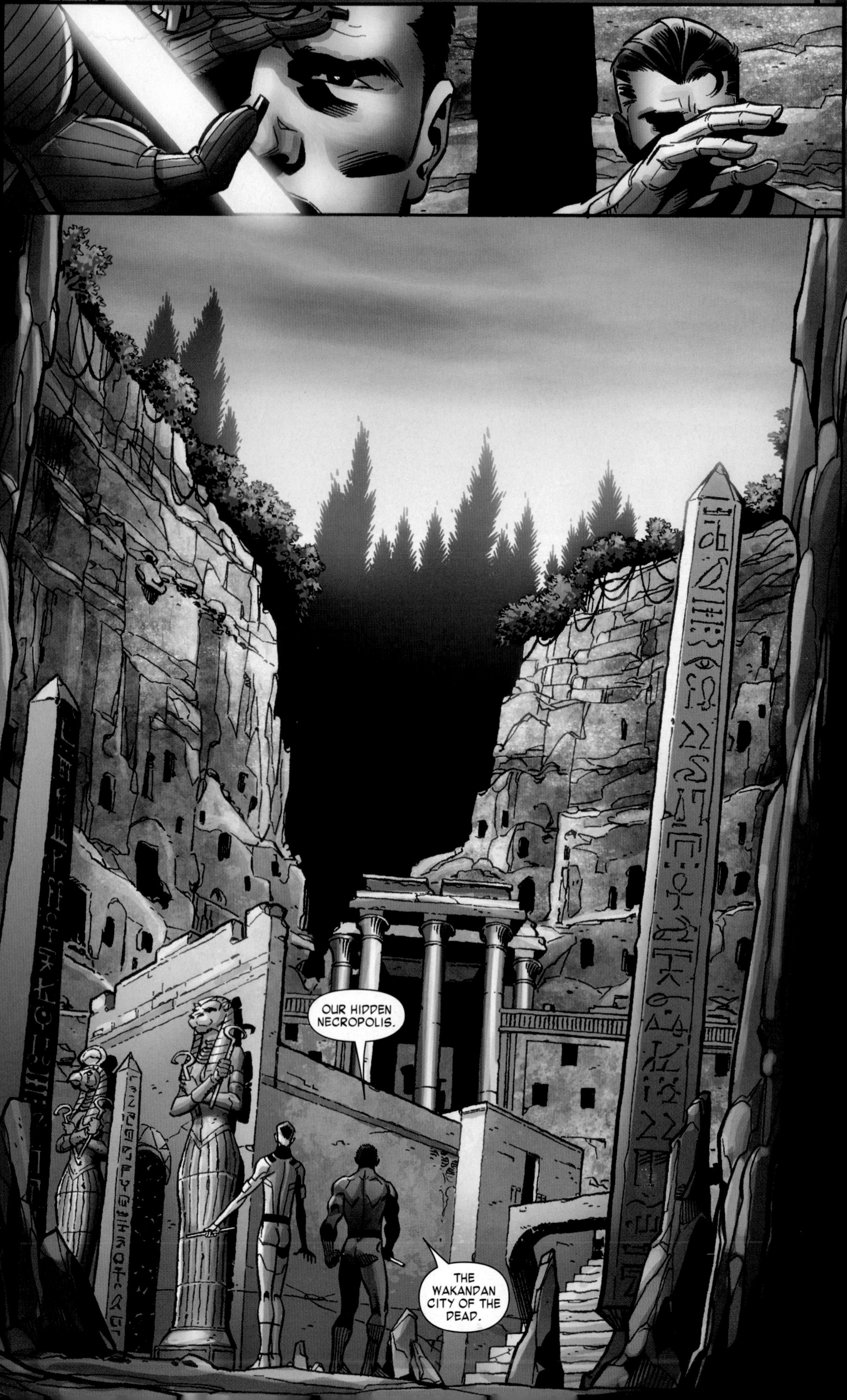
OUR HIDDEN NECROPOLIS.
THE WAKANDAN CITY OF THE DEAD.

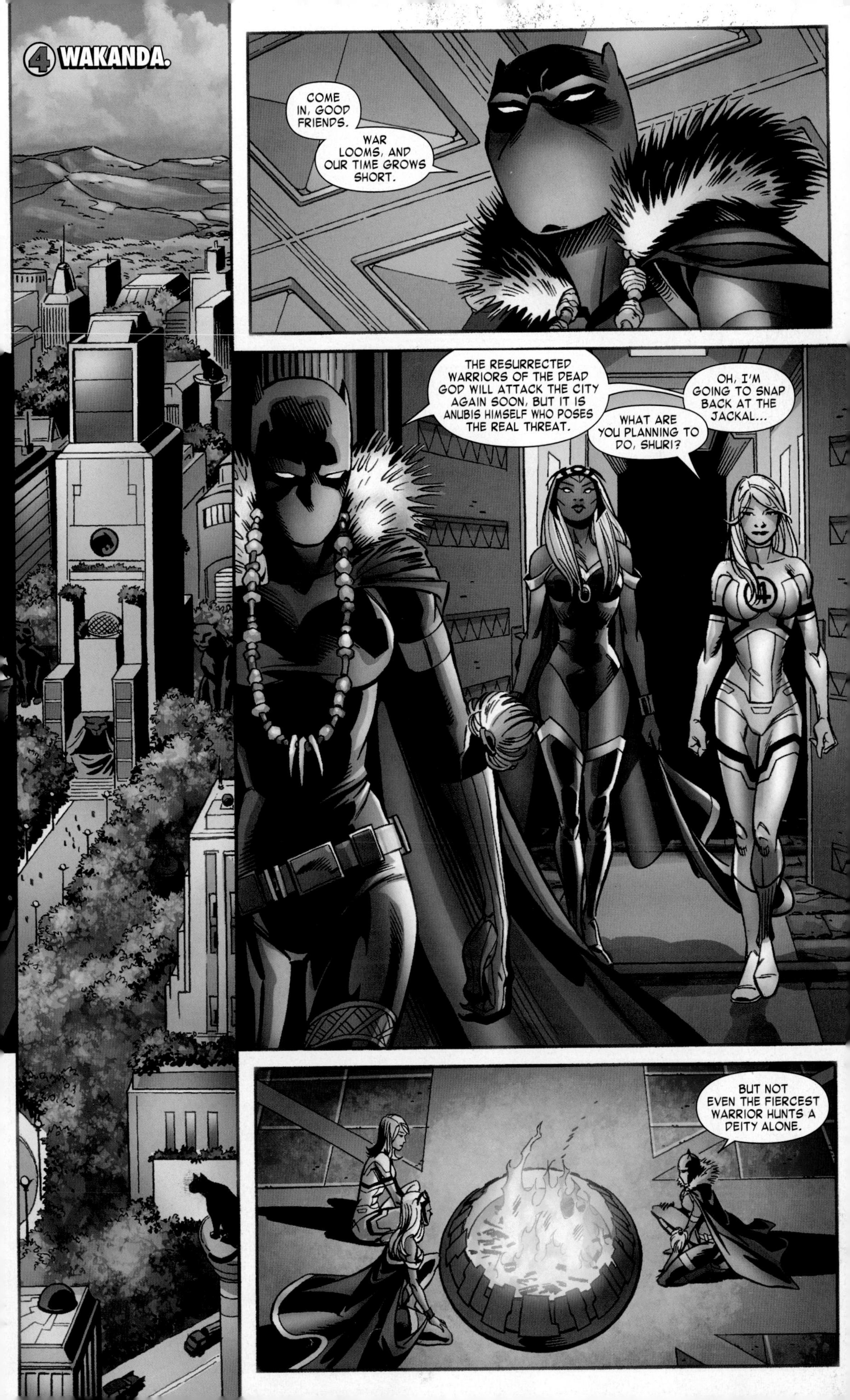
WAKANDA.
COME IN, GOOD FRIENDS.
WAR LOOMS, AND OUR TIME GROWS SHORT.
THE RESURRECTED WARRIORS OF THE DEAD GOD WILL ATTACK THE CITY AGAIN SOON, BUT IT IS ANUBIS HIMSELF WHO POSES THE REAL THREAT.
WHAT ARE YOU PLANNING TO DO, SHURI?
OH, I'M GOING TO SNAP BACK AT THE JACKAL...
BUT NOT EVEN THE FIERCEST WARRIOR HUNTS A DEITY ALONE.

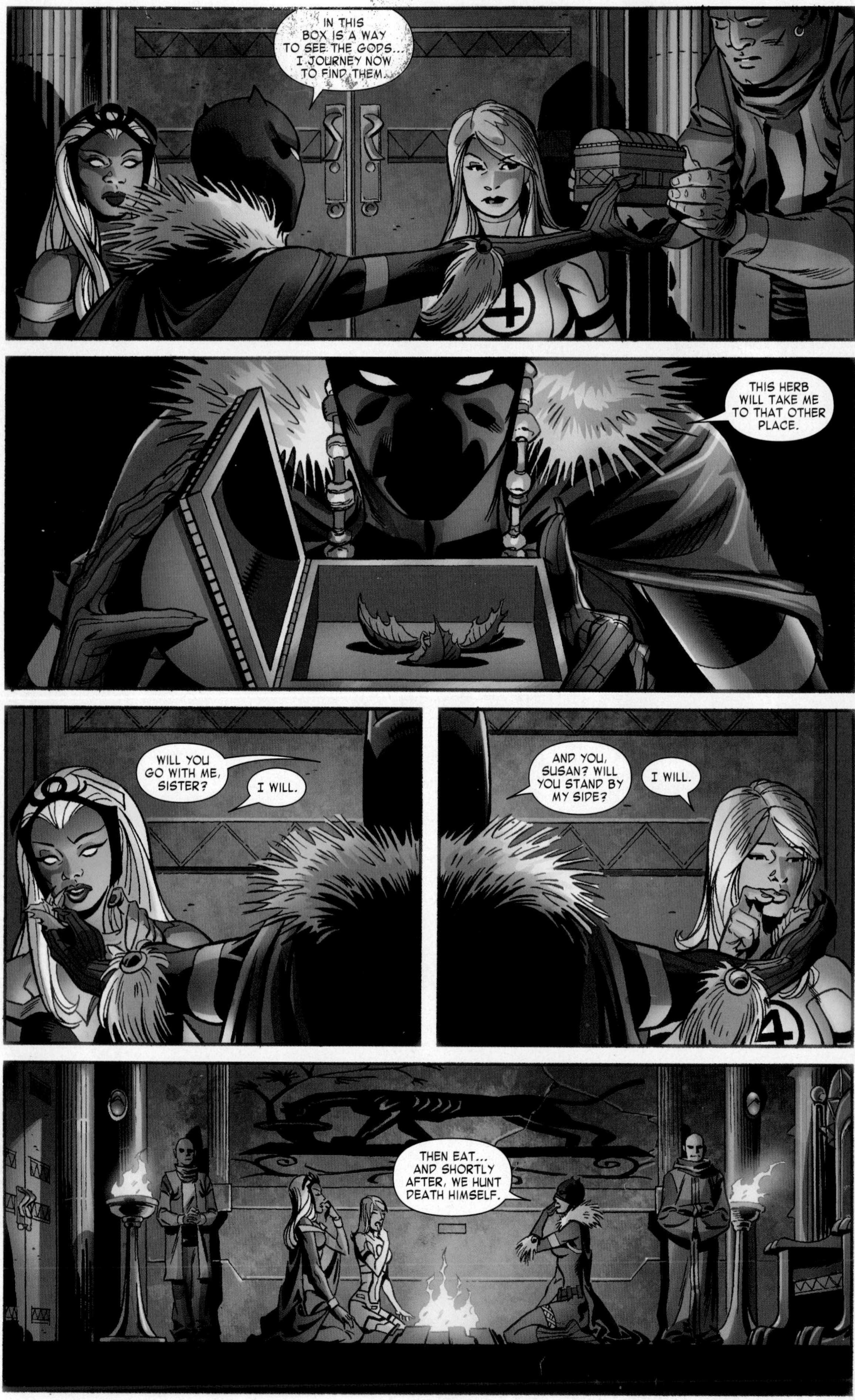
IN THIS BOX IS A WAY TO SEE THE GODS... I JOURNEY NOW TO FIND THEM.
THIS HERB WILL TAKE ME TO THAT OTHER PLACE.
WILL YOU GO WITH ME, SISTER?
I WILL.
AND YOU, SUSAN? WILL YOU STAND BY MY SIDE?
I WILL.
THEN EAT... AND SHORTLY AFTER, WE HUNT DEATH HIMSELF.

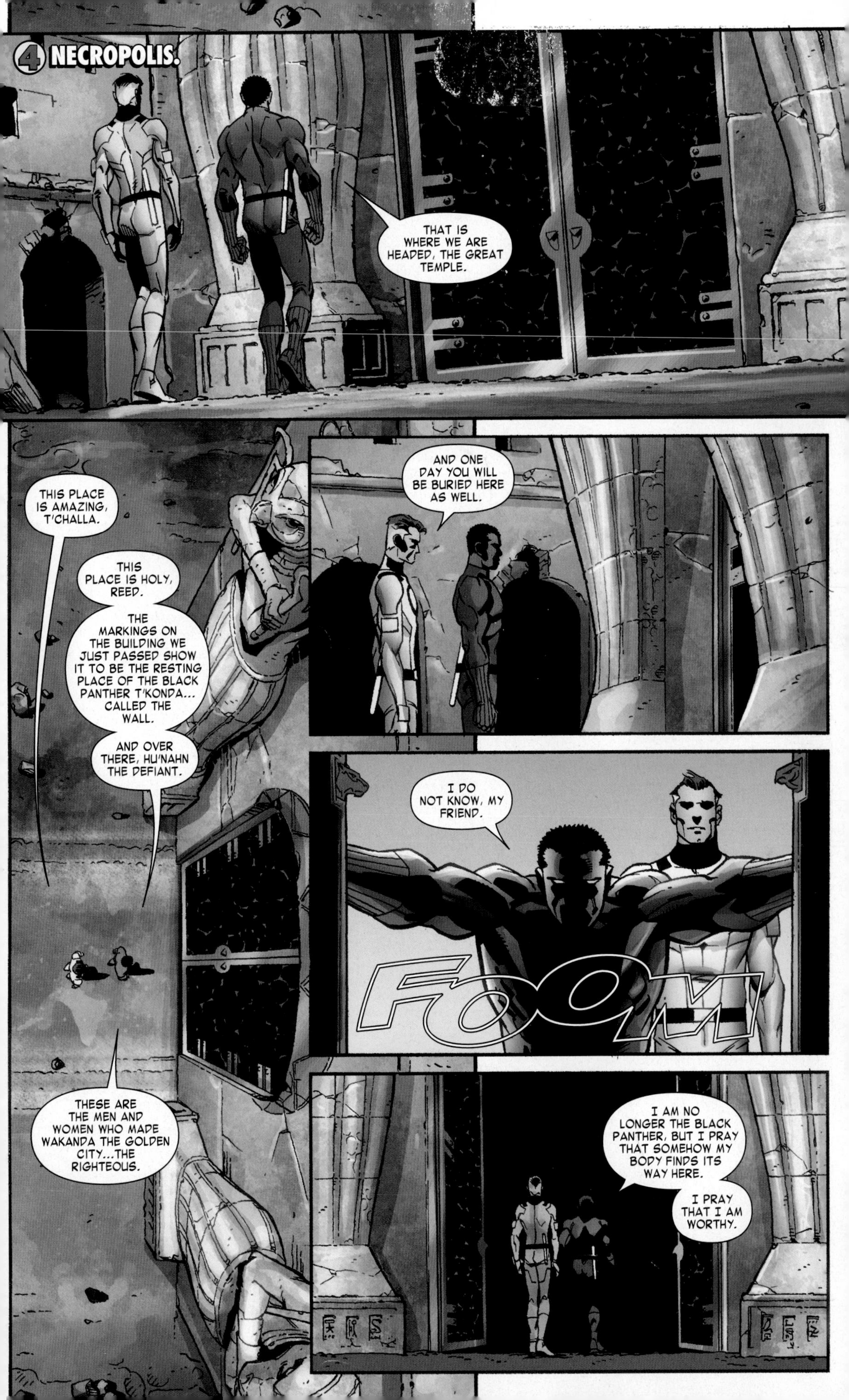

4 NECROPOLIS.
THAT IS WHERE WE ARE HEADED, THE GREAT TEMPLE.
THIS PLACE IS AMAZING, T'CHALLA.
THIS PLACE IS HOLY, REED.
THE MARKINGS ON THE BUILDING WE JUST PASSED SHOW IT TO BE THE RESTING PLACE OF THE BLACK PANTHER T'KONDA... CALLED THE WALL.
AND OVER THERE, HU'NAHN THE DEFIANT.
THESE ARE THE MEN AND WOMEN WHO MADE WAKANDA THE GOLDEN CITY...THE RIGHTEOUS.
AND ONE DAY YOU WILL BE BURIED HERE AS WELL.
I DO NOT KNOW, MY FRIEND.
FOOM
I AM NO LONGER THE BLACK PANTHER, BUT I PRAY THAT SOMEHOW MY BODY FINDS ITS WAY HERE.
I PRAY THAT I AM WORTHY.

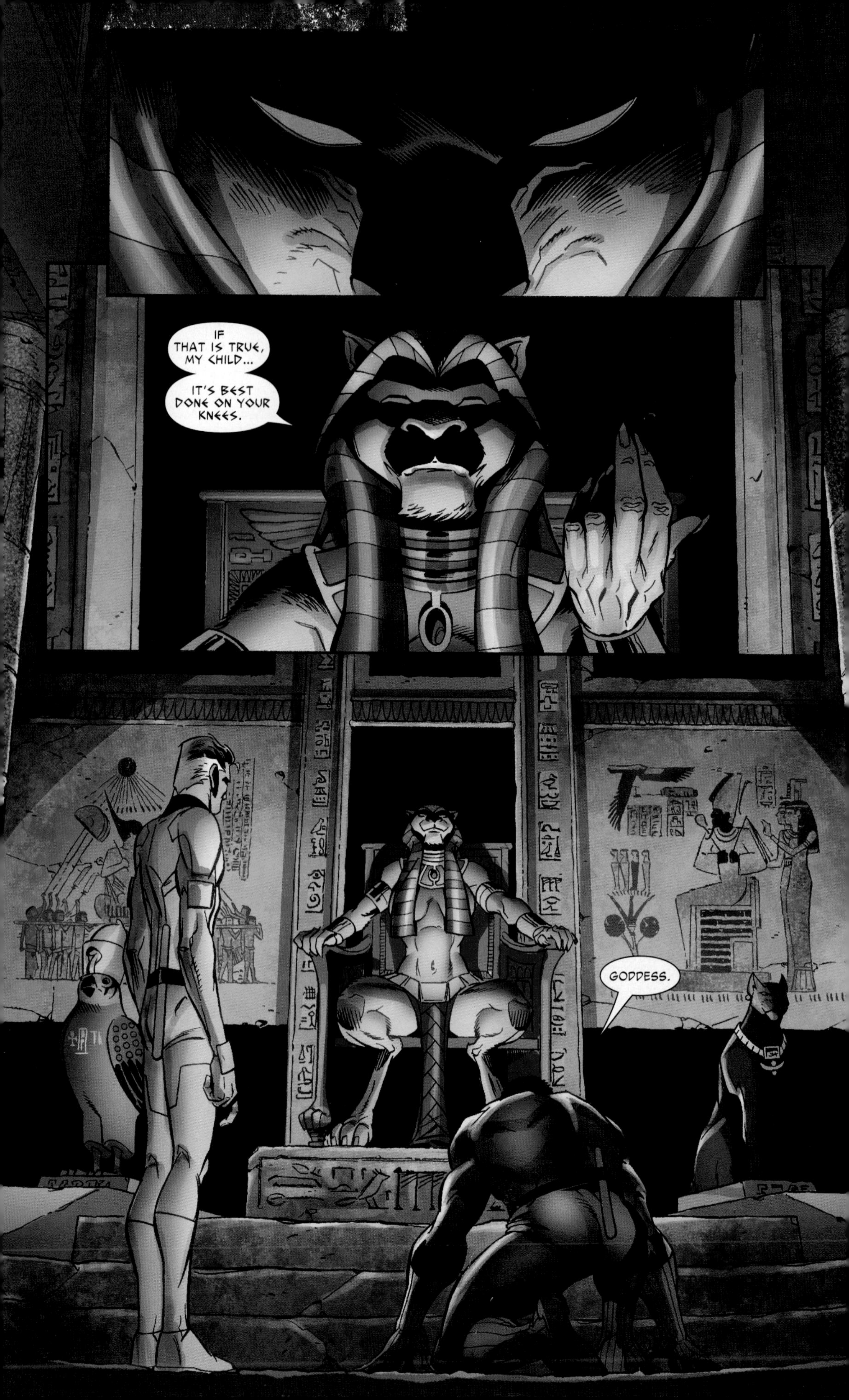
IF THAT IS TRUE, MY CHILD...
IT'S BEST DONE ON YOUR KNEES.
GODDESS.

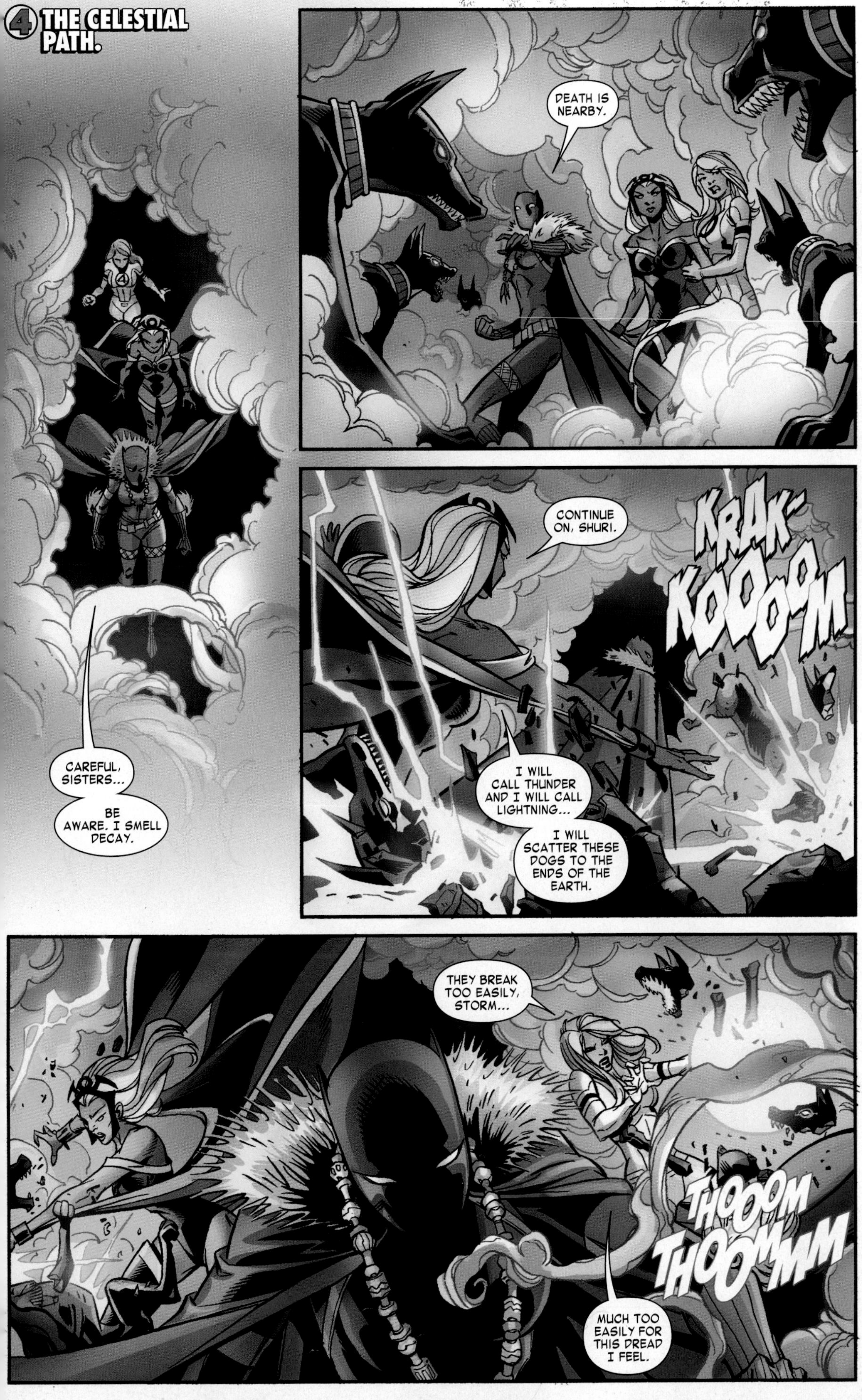
4 THE CELESTIAL PATH.
CAREFUL, SISTERS...
BE AWARE. I SMELL DECAY.
DEATH IS NEARBY.
CONTINUE ON, SHURI.
I WILL CALL THUNDER AND I WILL CALL LIGHTNING...
I WILL SCATTER THESE DOGS TO THE ENDS OF THE EARTH.
KRAK-KOOOOOM
THEY BREAK TOO EASILY, STORM...
THOOOM THOOMMM
MUCH TOO EASILY FOR THIS DREAD I FEEL.

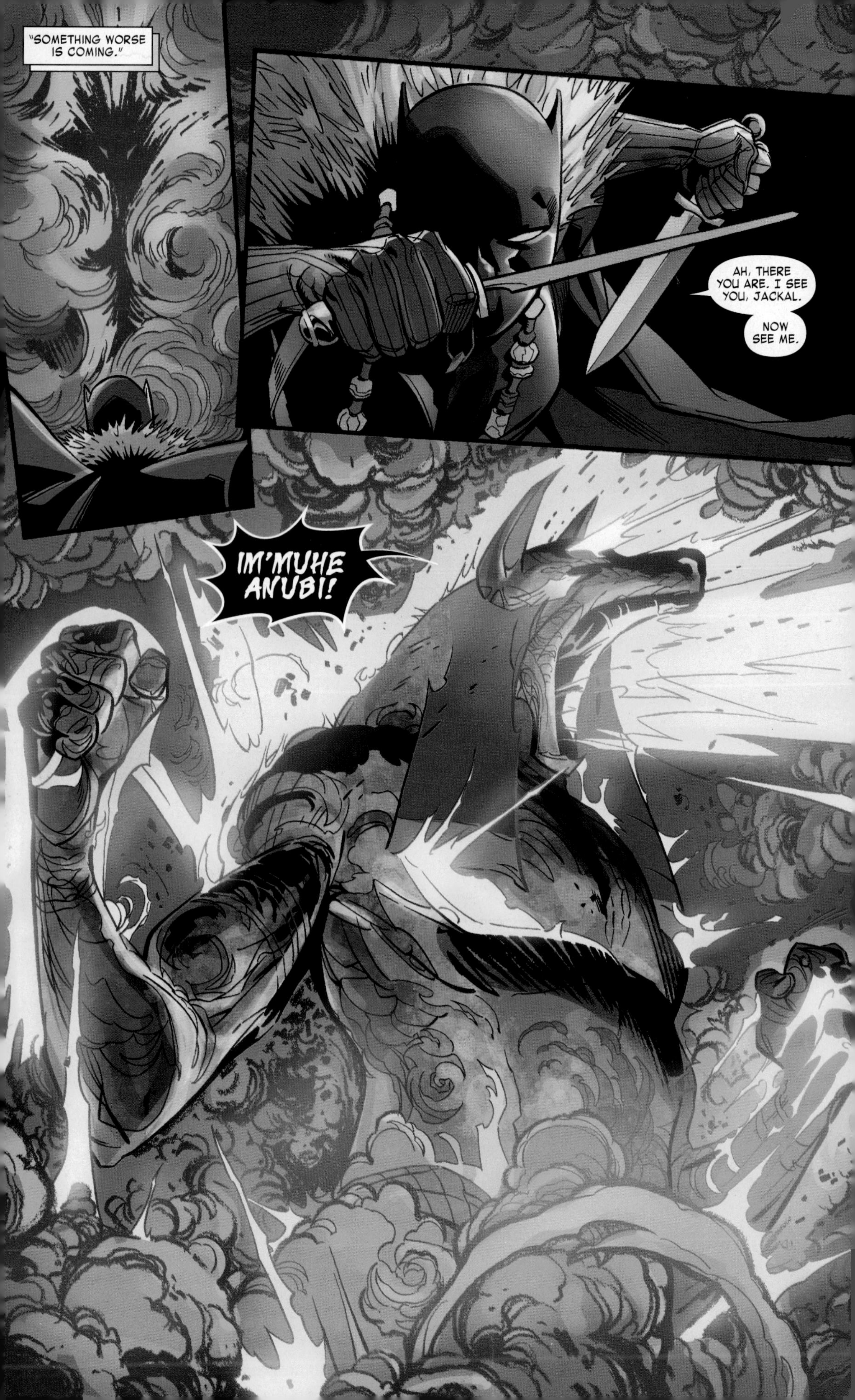
"SOMETHING WORSE IS COMING."
AH, THERE YOU ARE. I SEE YOU, JACKAL.
NOW SEE ME.
IM'MUHE ANUBI!

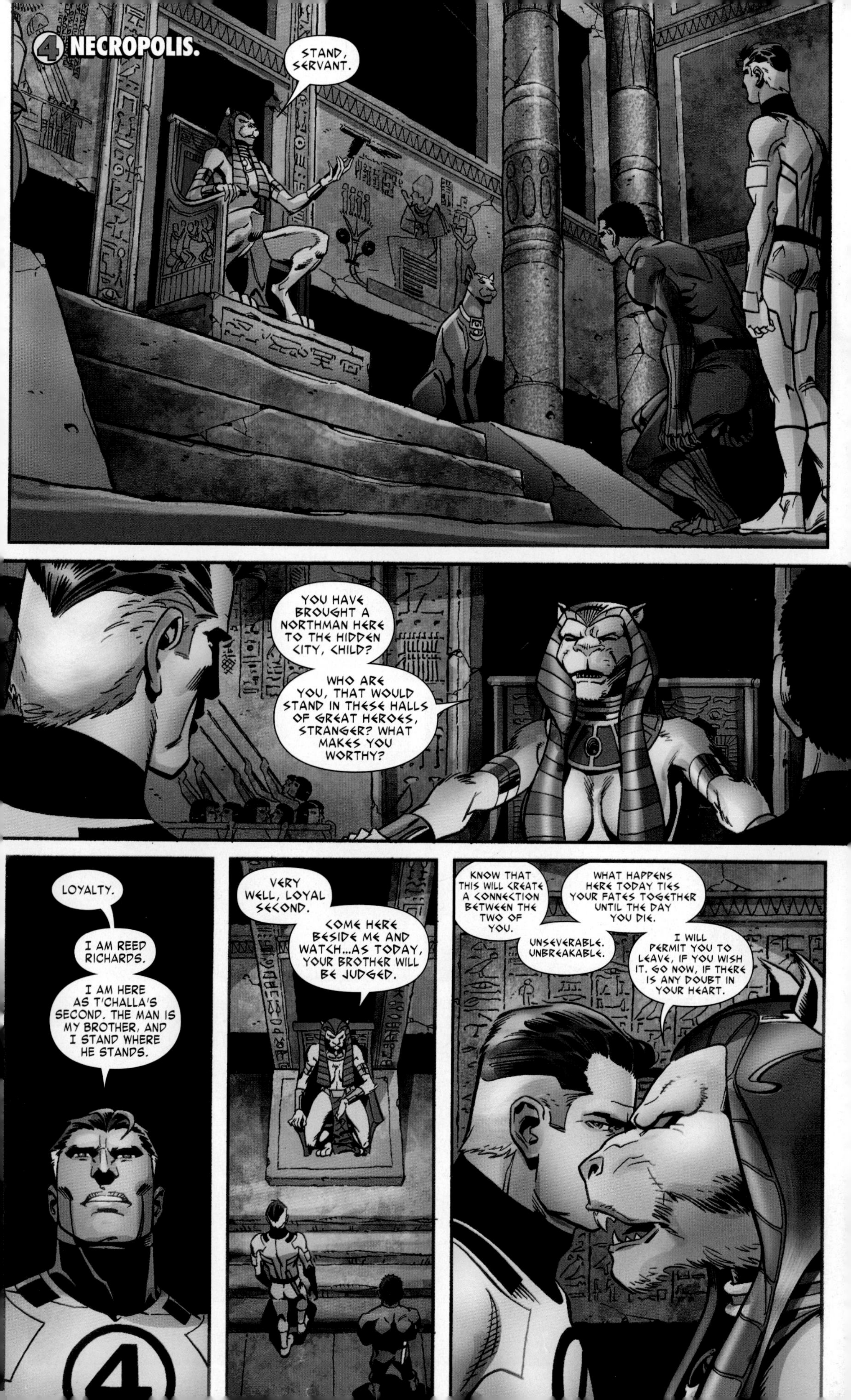

NECROPOLIS.
STAND, SERVANT.
YOU HAVE BROUGHT A NORTHMAN HERE TO THE HIDDEN CITY, CHILD?
WHO ARE YOU, THAT WOULD STAND IN THESE HALLS OF GREAT HEROES, STRANGER? WHAT MAKES YOU WORTHY?
LOYALTY.
I AM REED RICHARDS.
I AM HERE AS T'CHALLA'S SECOND. THE MAN IS MY BROTHER, AND I STAND WHERE HE STANDS.
VERY WELL, LOYAL SECOND.
COME HERE BESIDE ME AND WATCH...AS TODAY, YOUR BROTHER WILL BE JUDGED.
KNOW THAT THIS WILL CREATE A CONNECTION BETWEEN THE TWO OF YOU.
WHAT HAPPENS HERE TODAY TIES YOUR FATES TOGETHER UNTIL THE DAY YOU DIE.
UNSEVERABLE. UNBREAKABLE.
I WILL PERMIT YOU TO LEAVE, IF YOU WISH IT. GO NOW, IF THERE IS ANY DOUBT IN YOUR HEART.

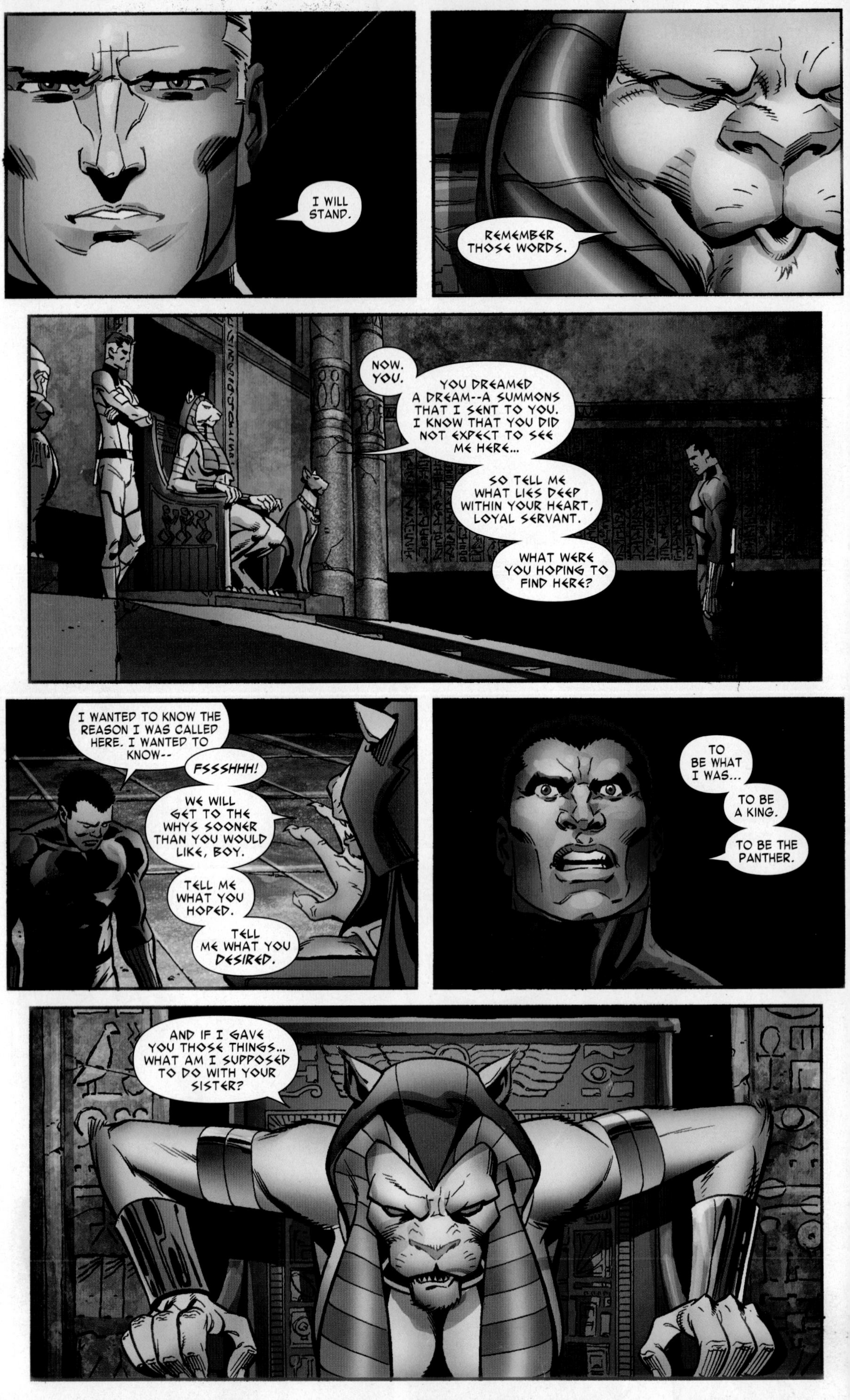

I WILL STAND.
REMEMBER THOSE WORDS.
NOW. YOU.
YOU DREAMED A DREAM--A SUMMONS THAT I SENT TO YOU. I KNOW THAT YOU DID NOT EXPECT TO SEE ME HERE...
SO TELL ME WHAT LIES DEEP WITHIN YOUR HEART, LOYAL SERVANT.
WHAT WERE YOU HOPING TO FIND HERE?
I WANTED TO KNOW THE REASON I WAS CALLED HERE. I WANTED TO KNOW--
FSSSHHH!
WE WILL GET TO THE WHYS SOONER THAN YOU WOULD LIKE, BOY.
TELL ME WHAT YOU HOPED.
TELL ME WHAT YOU DESIRED.
TO BE WHAT I WAS...
TO BE A KING.
TO BE THE PANTHER.
AND IF I GAVE YOU THOSE THINGS... WHAT AM I SUPPOSED TO DO WITH YOUR SISTER?

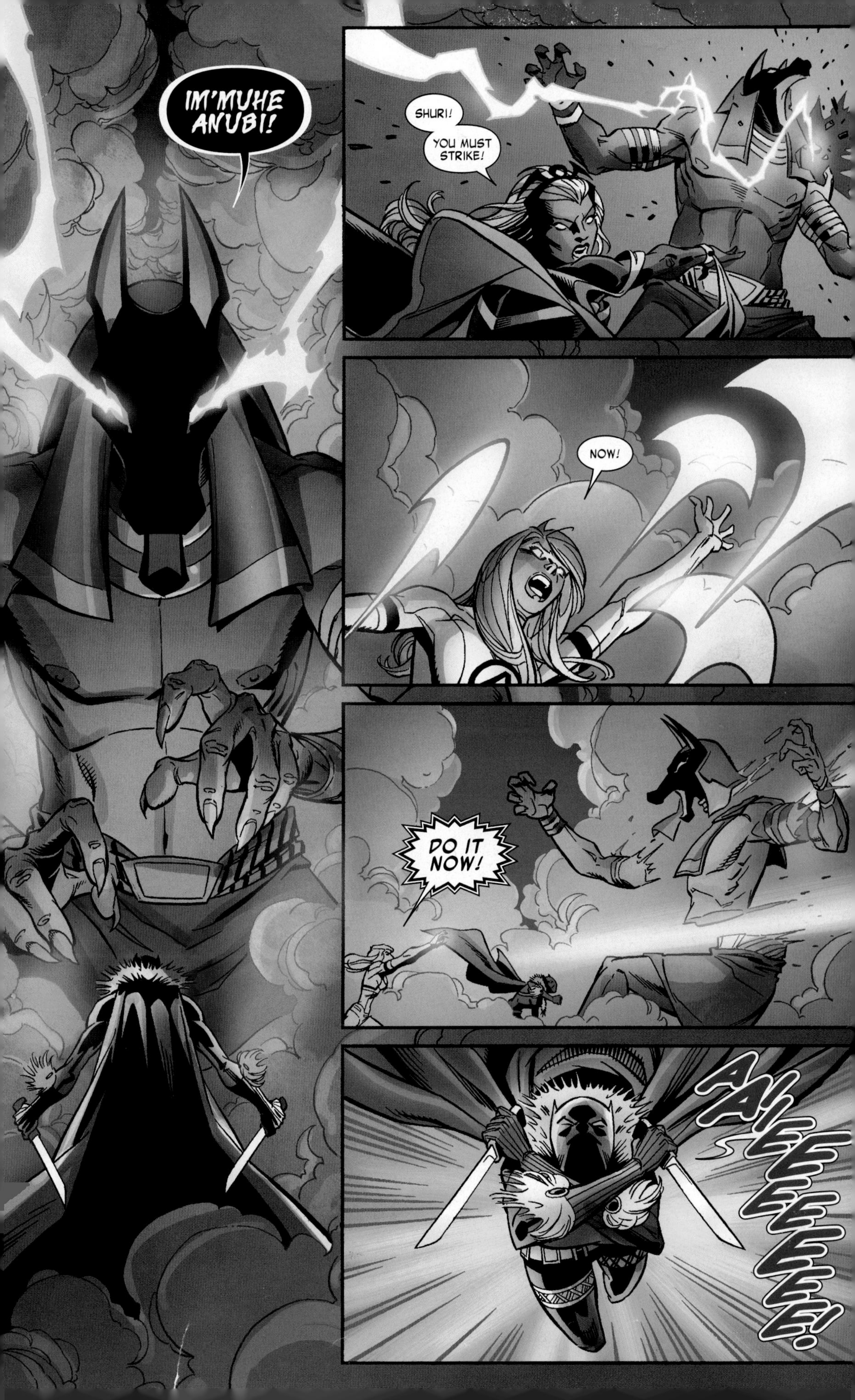
IM'MUHE ANUBI!
SHURI!
YOU MUST STRIKE!
NOW!
DO IT NOW!
AAIEEEEEEEEE!

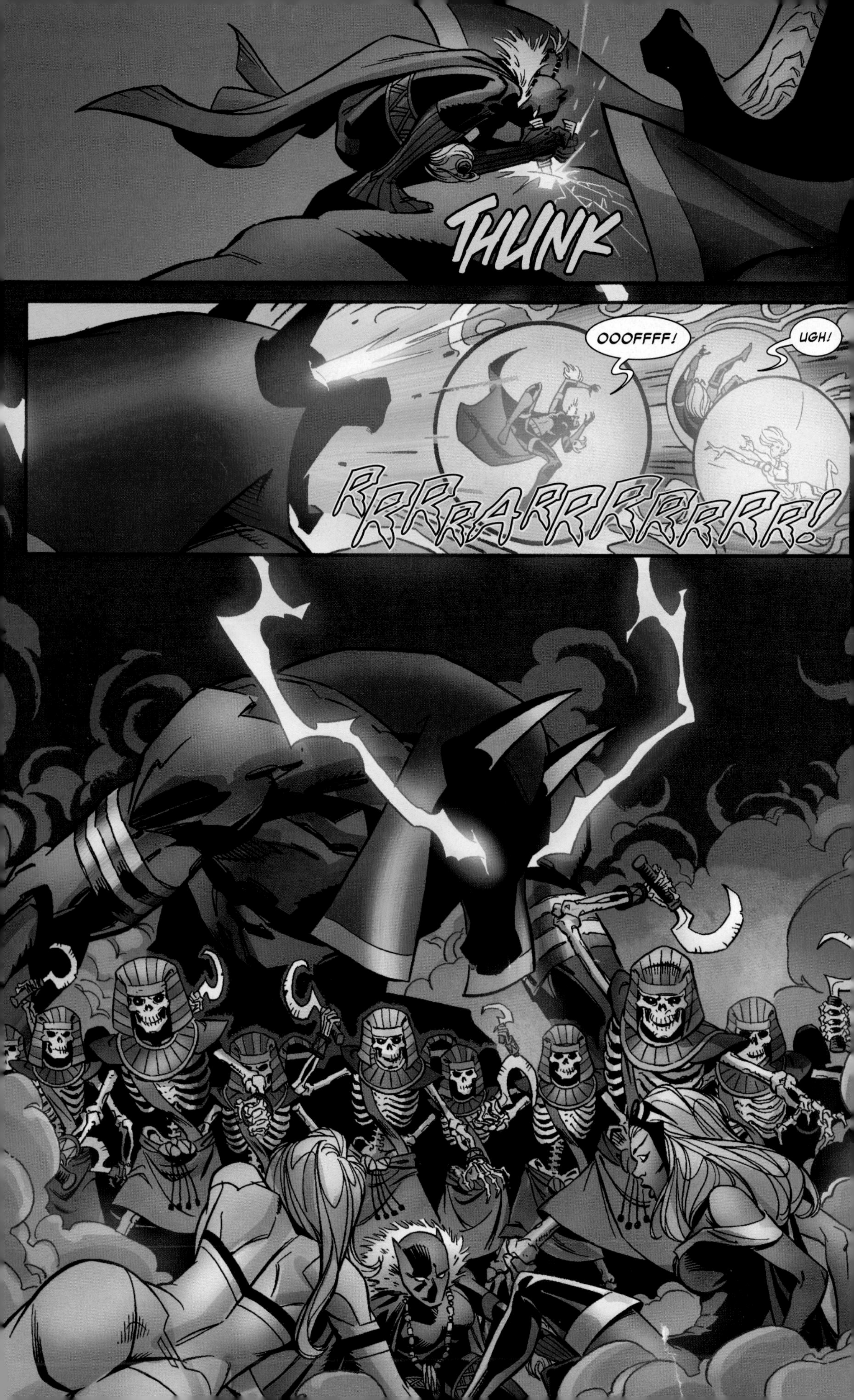
THUNK
OOOFFFF!
UGH!
RRRRARRRRRRRR!

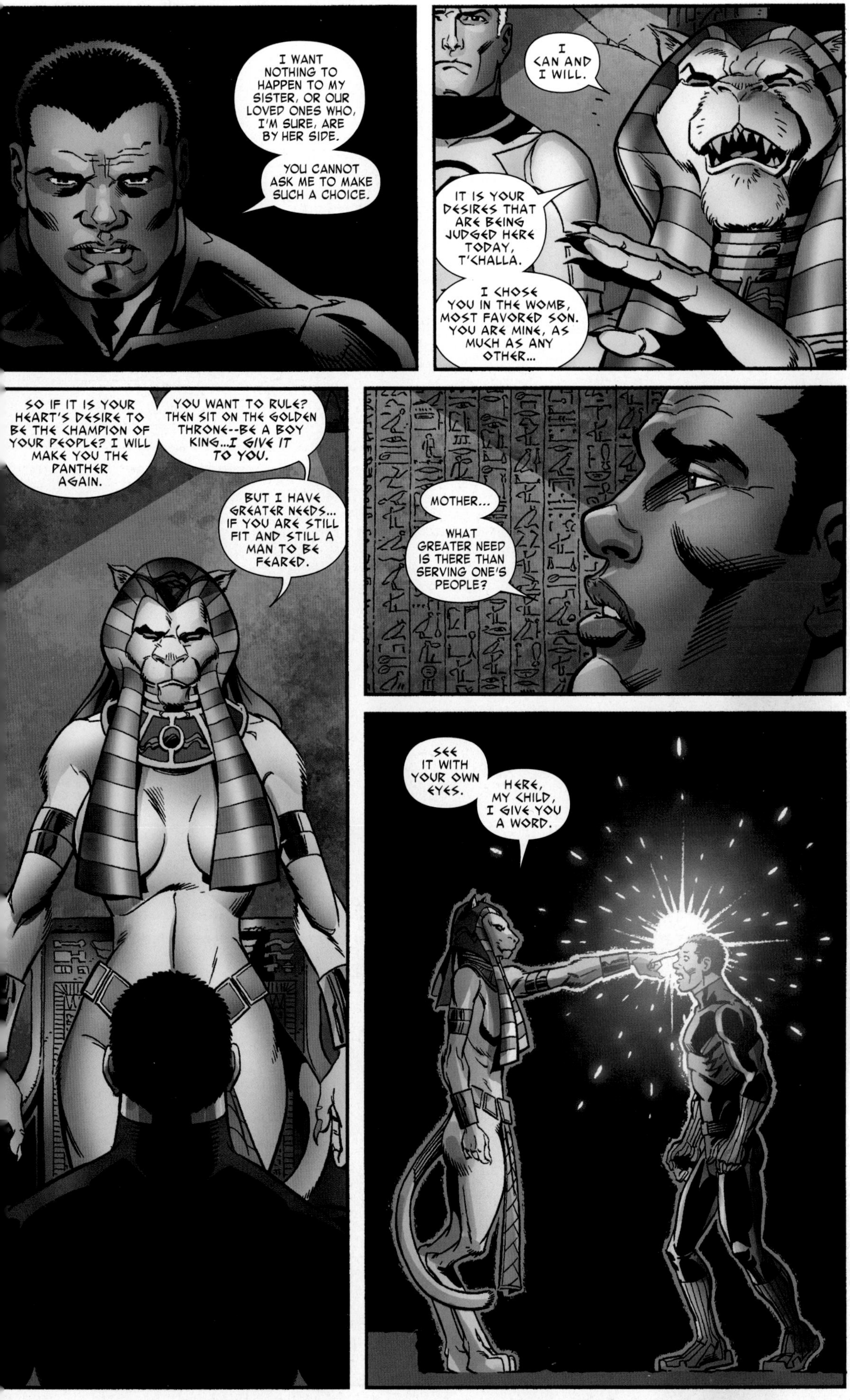
I WANT NOTHING TO HAPPEN TO MY SISTER, OR OUR LOVED ONES WHO, I'M SURE, ARE BY HER SIDE.
YOU CANNOT ASK ME TO MAKE SUCH A CHOICE.
I CAN AND I WILL.
IT IS YOUR DESIRES THAT ARE BEING JUDGED HERE TODAY, T'CHALLA.
I CHOSE YOU IN THE WOMB, MOST FAVORED SON. YOU ARE MINE, AS MUCH AS ANY OTHER...
SO IF IT IS YOUR HEART'S DESIRE TO BE THE CHAMPION OF YOUR PEOPLE? I WILL MAKE YOU THE PANTHER AGAIN.
YOU WANT TO RULE? THEN SIT ON THE GOLDEN THRONE--BE A BOY KING...I GIVE IT TO YOU.
BUT I HAVE GREATER NEEDS... IF YOU ARE STILL FIT AND STILL A MAN TO BE FEARED.
MOTHER...
WHAT GREATER NEED IS THERE THAN SERVING ONE'S PEOPLE?
SEE IT WITH YOUR OWN EYES.
HERE, MY CHILD, I GIVE YOU A WORD.

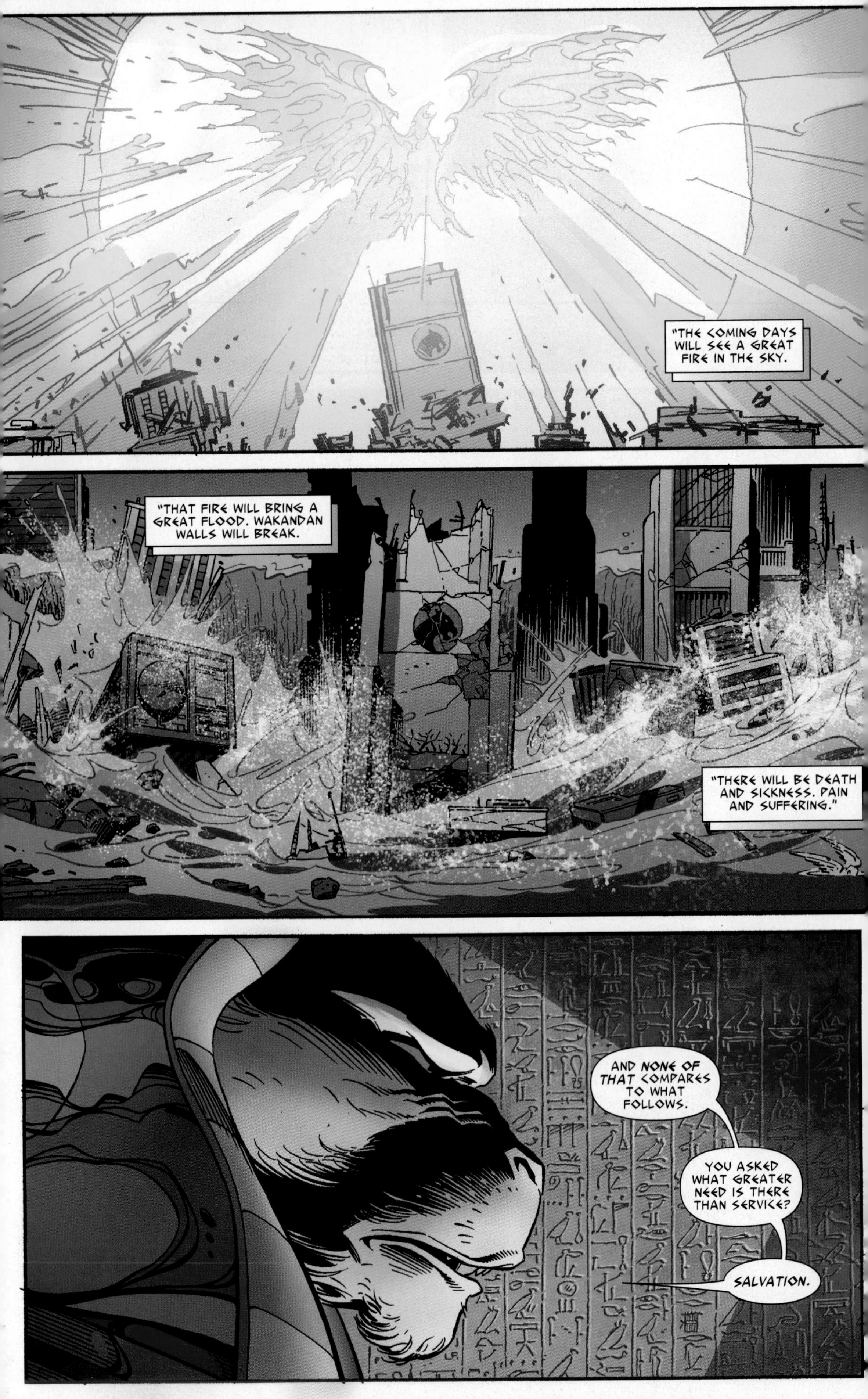
"THE COMING DAYS WILL SEE A GREAT FIRE IN THE SKY.
"THAT FIRE WILL BRING A GREAT FLOOD. WAKANDAN WALLS WILL BREAK.
"THERE WILL BE DEATH AND SICKNESS. PAIN AND SUFFERING."
AND NONE OF THAT COMPARES TO WHAT FOLLOWS.
YOU ASKED WHAT GREATER NEED IS THERE THAN SERVICE?
SALVATION.

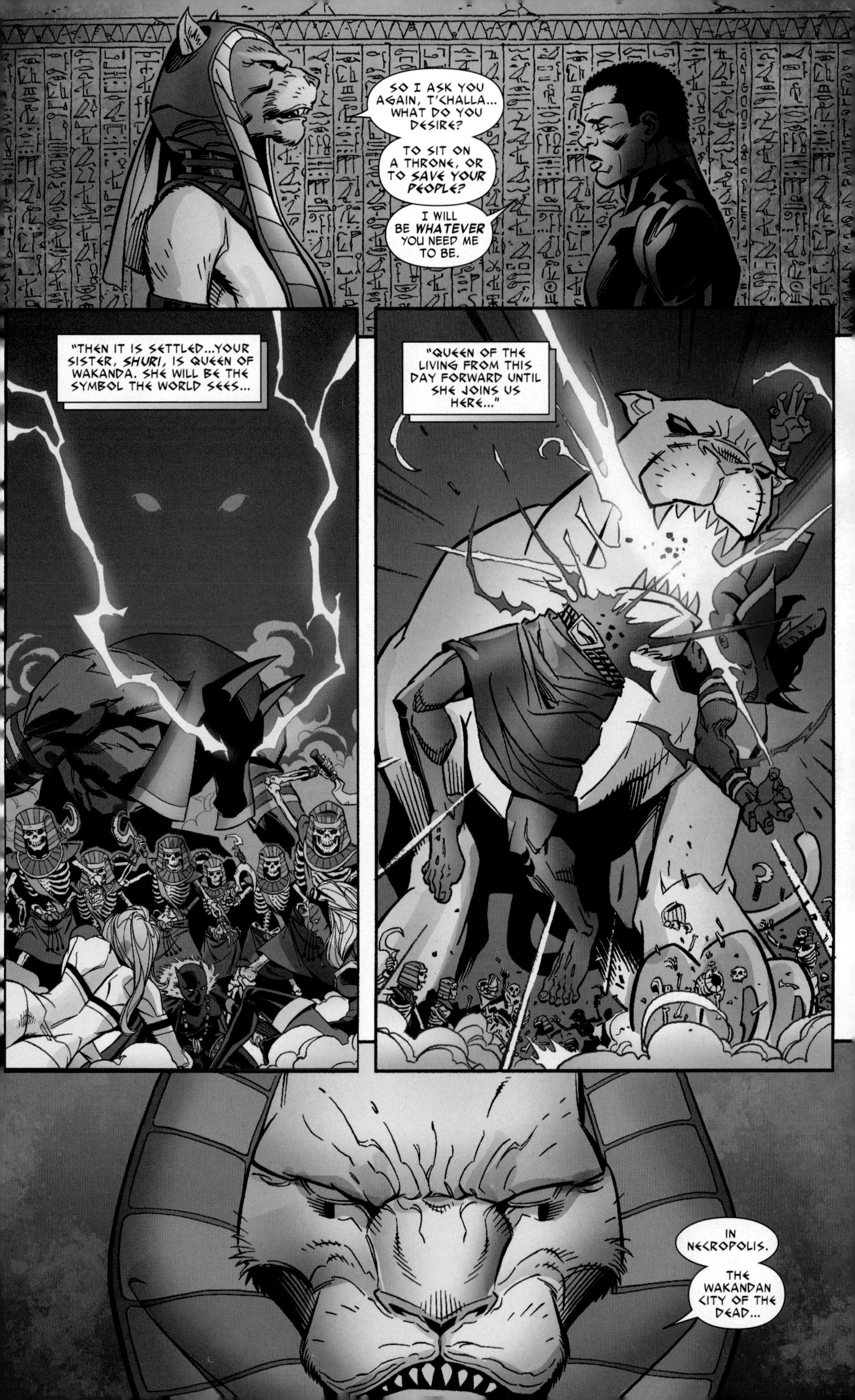
SO I ASK YOU AGAIN, T'CHALLA... WHAT DO YOU DESIRE?
TO SIT ON A THRONE, OR TO SAVE YOUR PEOPLE?
I WILL BE WHATEVER YOU NEED ME TO BE.
"THEN IT IS SETTLED...YOUR SISTER, SHURI, IS QUEEN OF WAKANDA. SHE WILL BE THE SYMBOL THE WORLD SEES...
"QUEEN OF THE LIVING FROM THIS DAY FORWARD UNTIL SHE JOINS US HERE..."
IN NECROPOLIS.
THE WAKANDAN CITY OF THE DEAD...

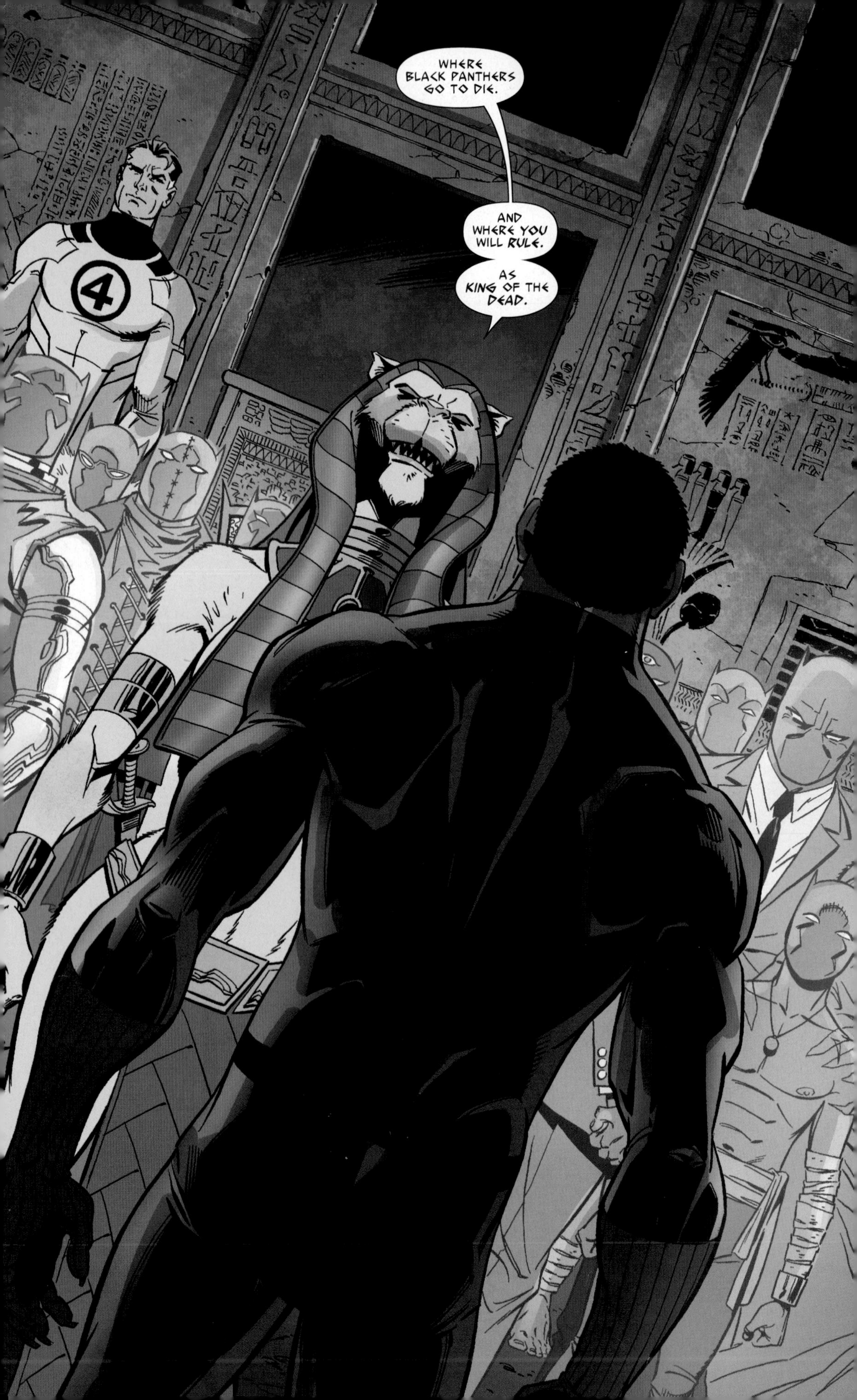
WHERE BLACK PANTHERS GO TO DIE.
AND WHERE YOU WILL RULE.
AS KING OF THE DEAD.

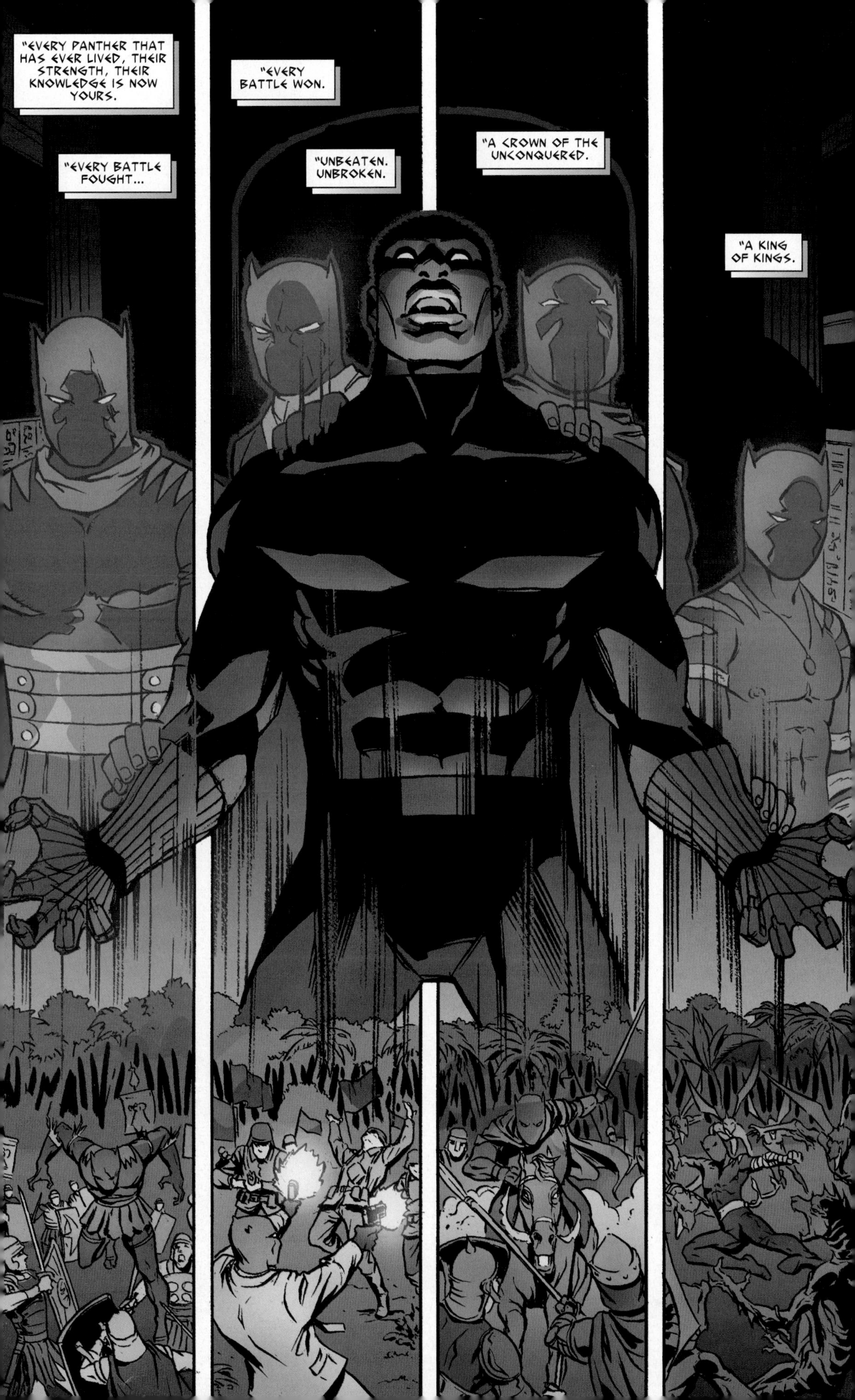
"EVERY PANTHER THAT HAS EVER LIVED, THEIR STRENGTH, THEIR KNOWLEDGE IS NOW YOURS.
"EVERY BATTLE FOUGHT...
"EVERY BATTLE WON.
"UNBEATEN. UNBROKEN.
"A CROWN OF THE UNCONQUERED.
"A KING OF KINGS.

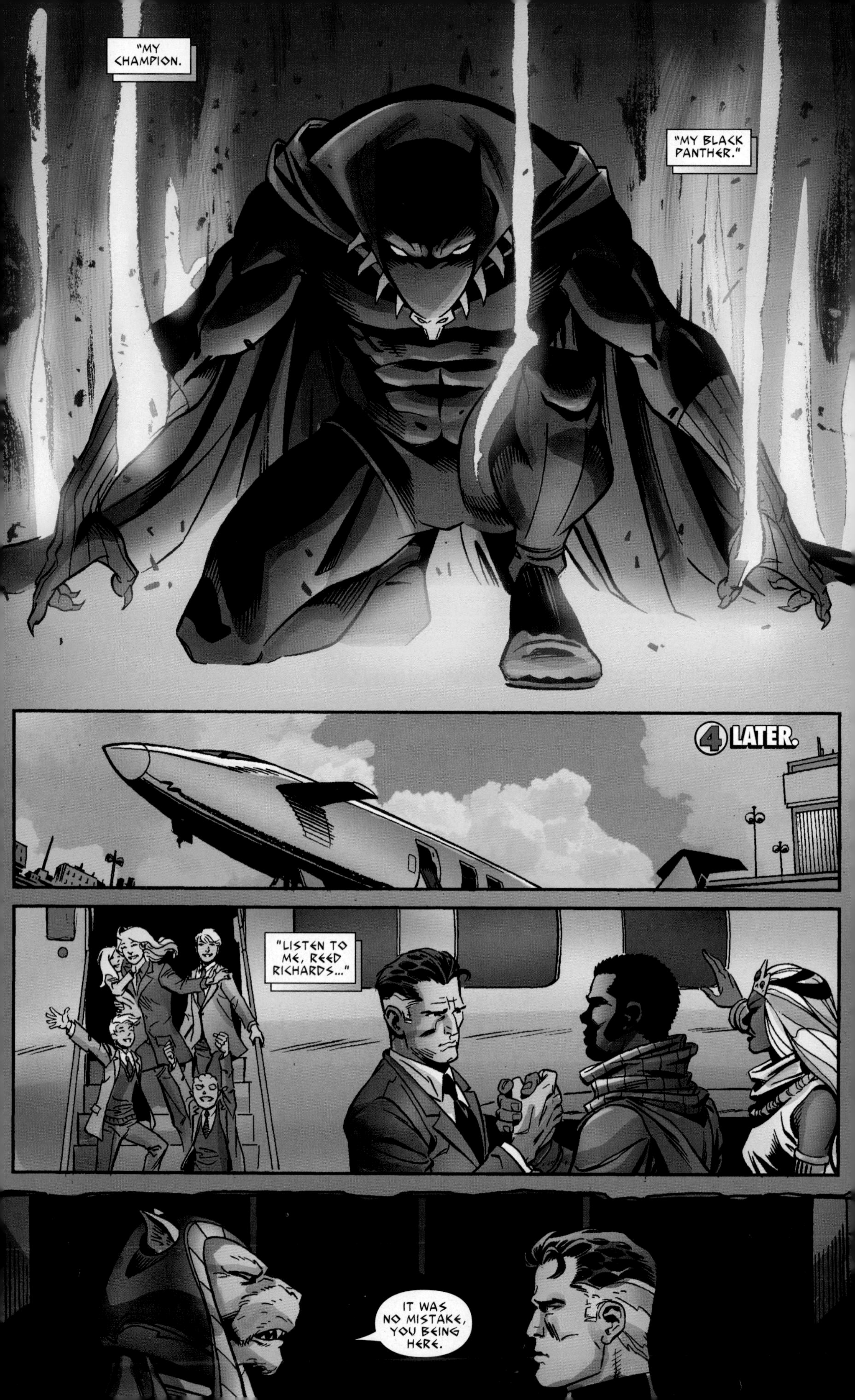
"MY CHAMPION.
"MY BLACK PANTHER."
4 LATER.
"LISTEN TO ME, REED RICHARDS..."
IT WAS NO MISTAKE, YOU BEING HERE.

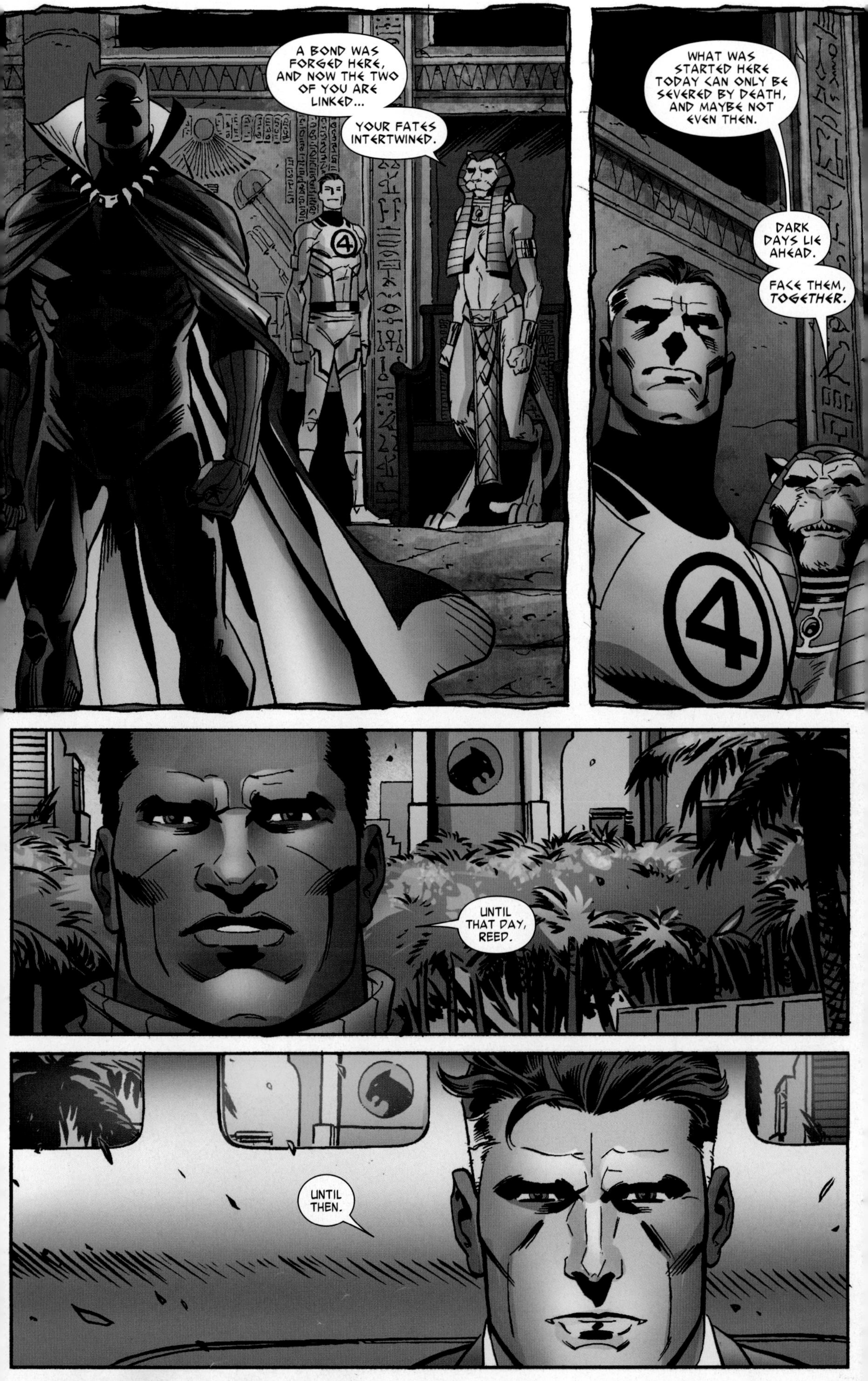
A BOND WAS FORGED HERE, AND NOW THE TWO OF YOU ARE LINKED...
YOUR FATES INTERTWINED.
WHAT WAS STARTED HERE TODAY CAN ONLY BE SEVERED BY DEATH, AND MAYBE NOT EVEN THEN.
DARK DAYS LIE AHEAD.
FACE THEM, *TOGETHER.*
UNTIL THAT DAY, REED.
UNTIL THEN.

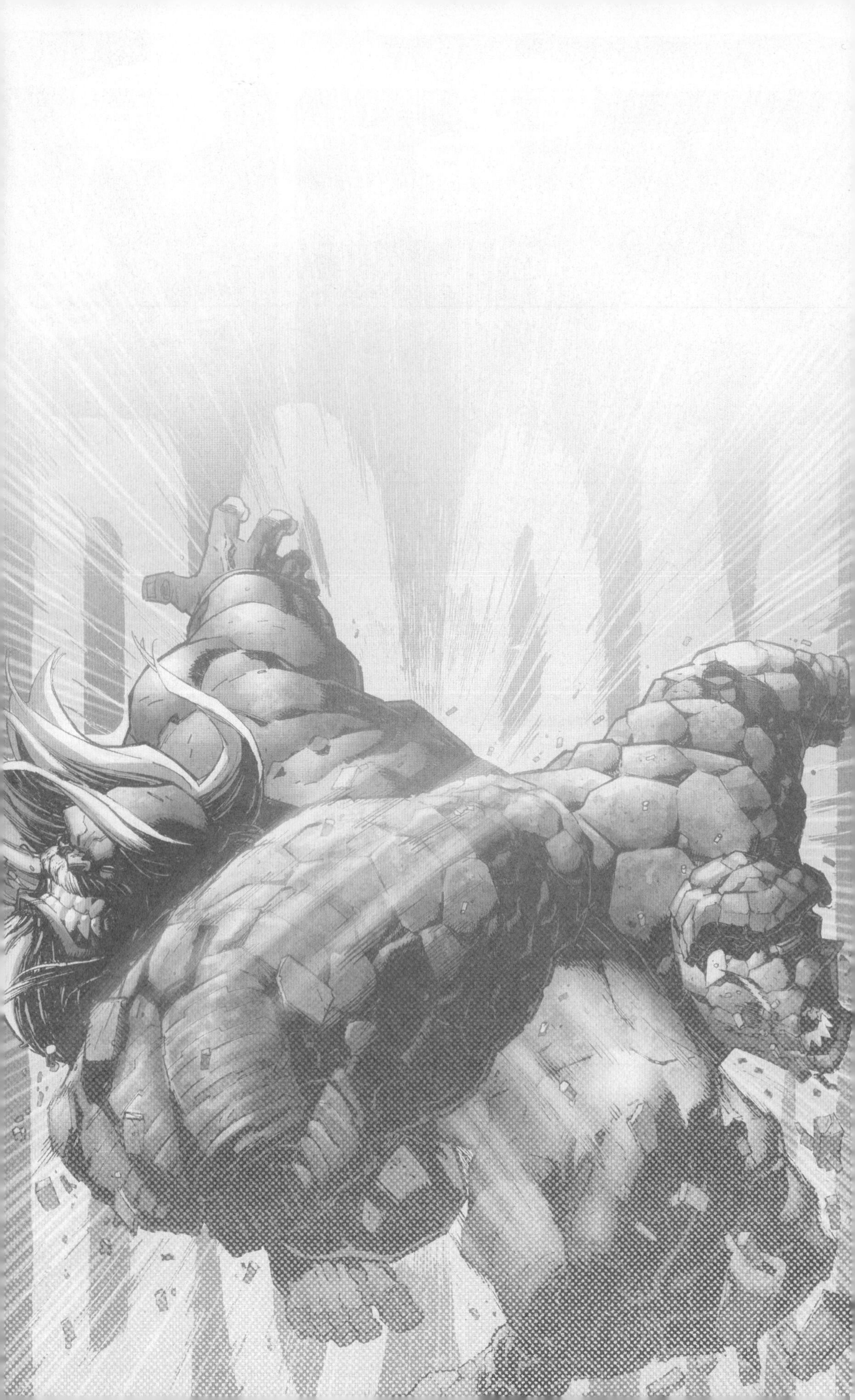

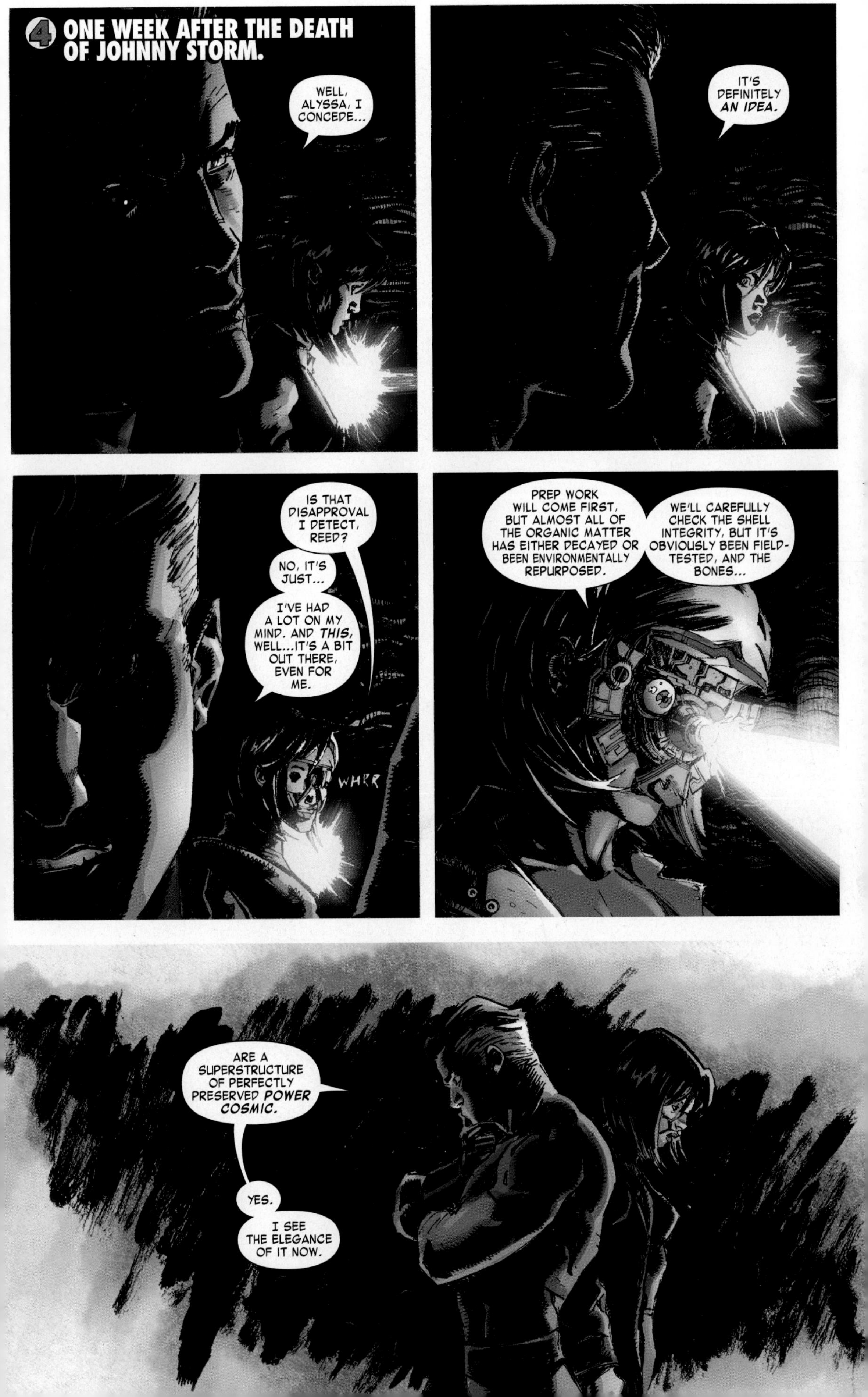
ONE WEEK AFTER THE DEATH OF JOHNNY STORM.
WELL, ALYSSA, I CONCEDE...
IT'S DEFINITELY AN IDEA.
IS THAT DISAPPROVAL I DETECT, REED?
NO, IT'S JUST...
I'VE HAD A LOT ON MY MIND. AND THIS, WELL...IT'S A BIT OUT THERE, EVEN FOR ME.
WHRR
PREP WORK WILL COME FIRST, BUT ALMOST ALL OF THE ORGANIC MATTER HAS EITHER DECAYED OR BEEN ENVIRONMENTALLY REPURPOSED.
WE'LL CAREFULLY CHECK THE SHELL INTEGRITY, BUT IT'S OBVIOUSLY BEEN FIELD-TESTED, AND THE BONES...
ARE A SUPERSTRUCTURE OF PERFECTLY PRESERVED POWER COSMIC.
YES.
I SEE THE ELEGANCE OF IT NOW.

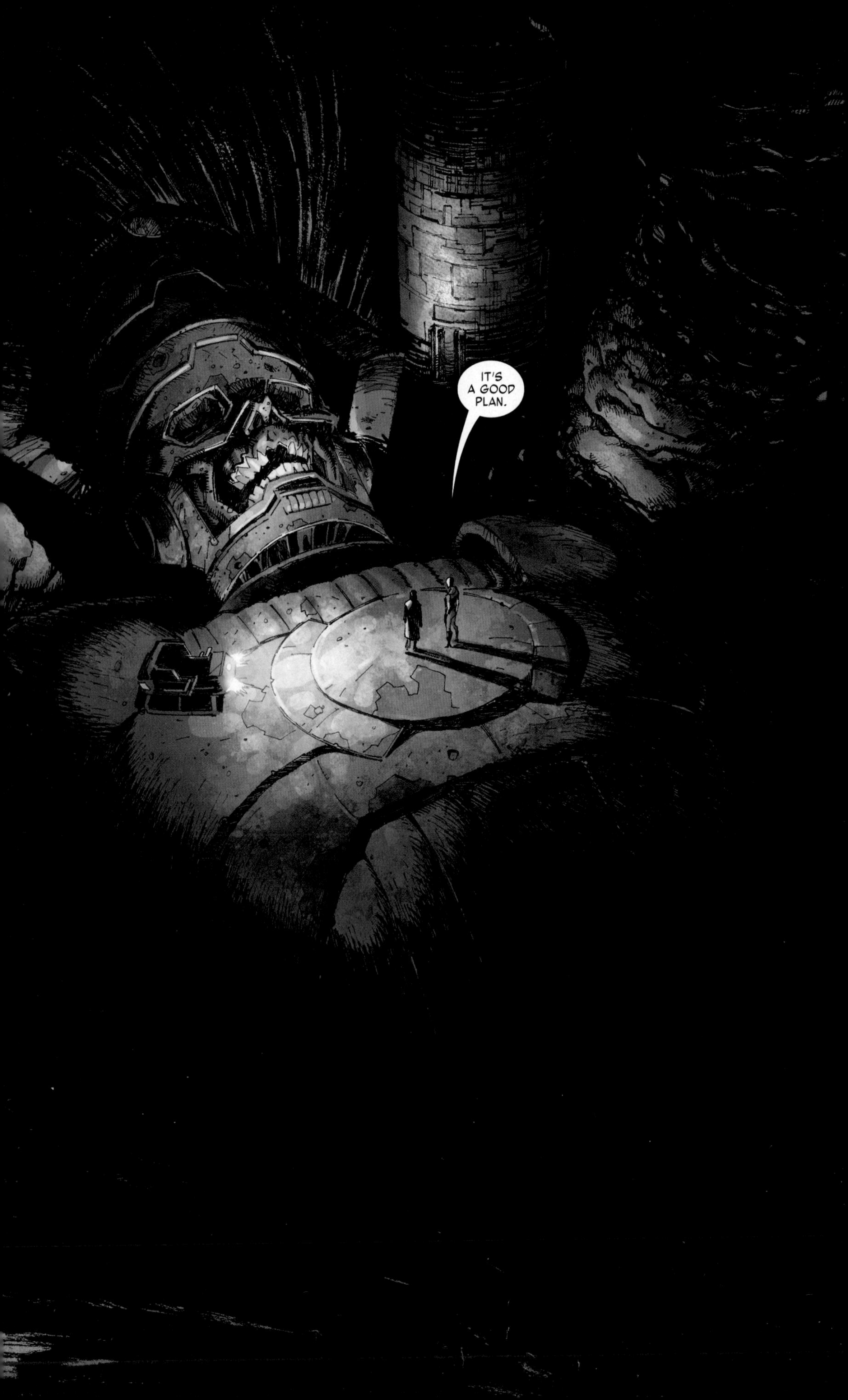
IT'S A GOOD PLAN.

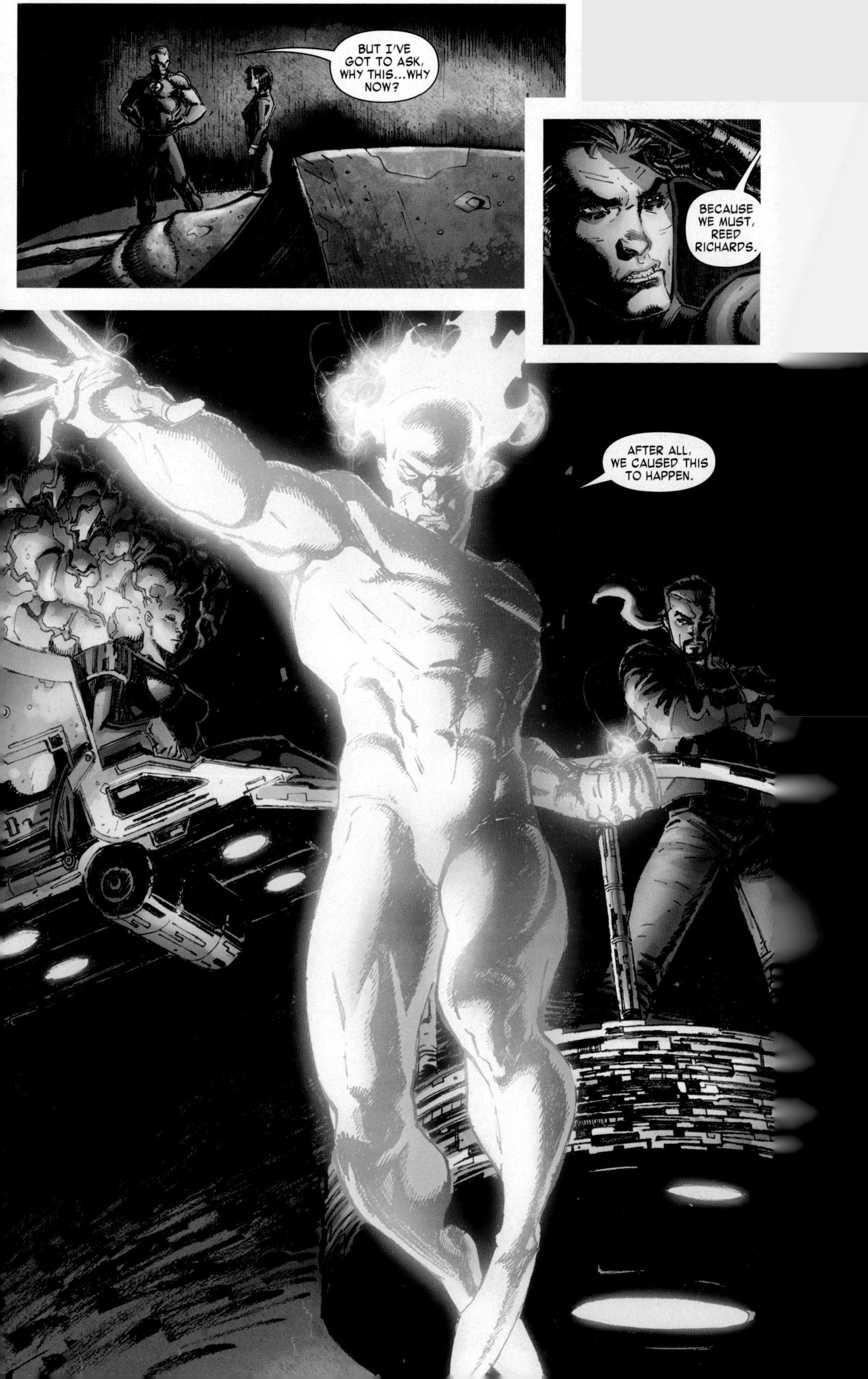
BUT I'VE GOT TO ASK, WHY THIS...WHY NOW?
BECAUSE WE MUST, REED RICHARDS.
AFTER ALL, WE CAUSED THIS TO HAPPEN.

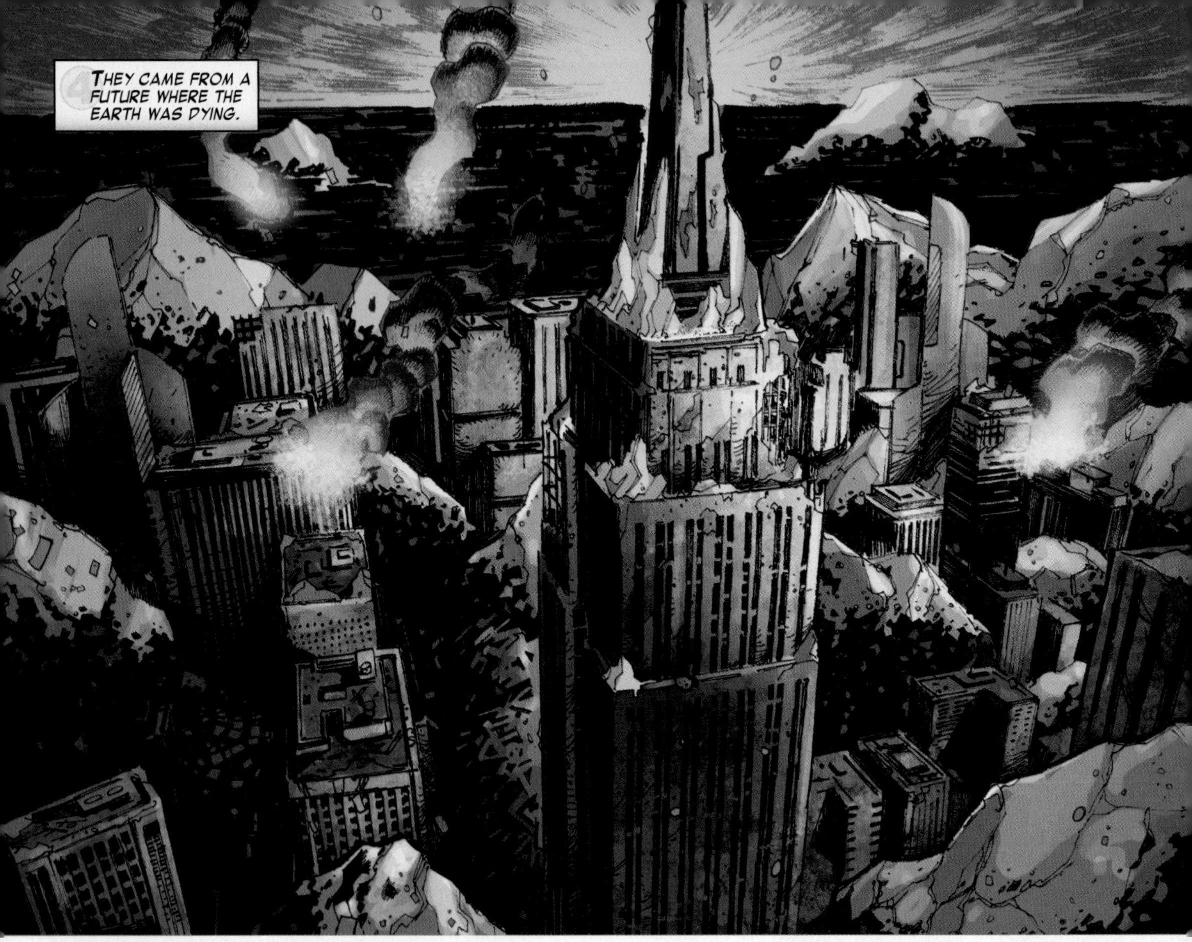
THEY CAME FROM A FUTURE WHERE THE EARTH WAS DYING.

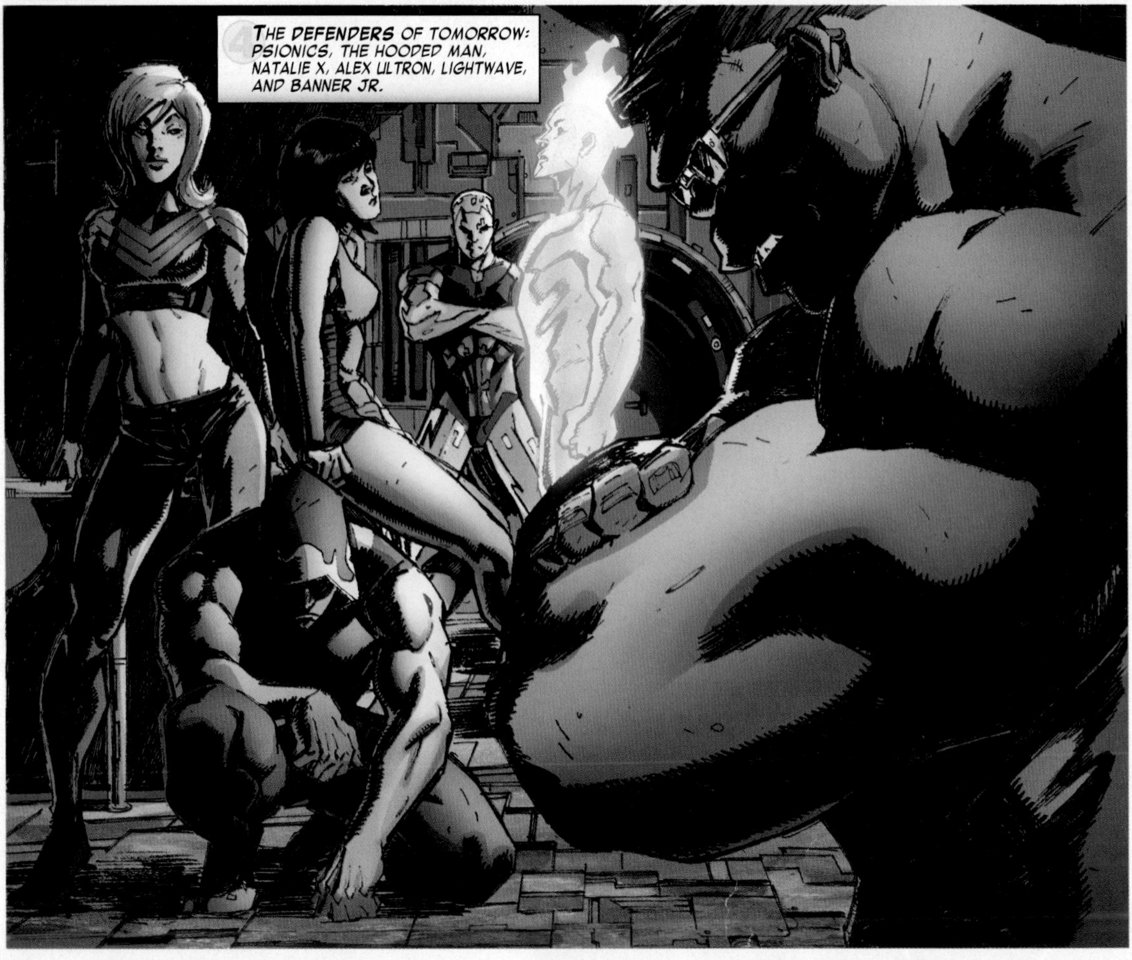
THE DEFENDERS OF TOMORROW: PSIONICS, THE HOODED MAN, NATALIE X, ALEX ULTRON, LIGHTWAVE, AND BANNER JR.

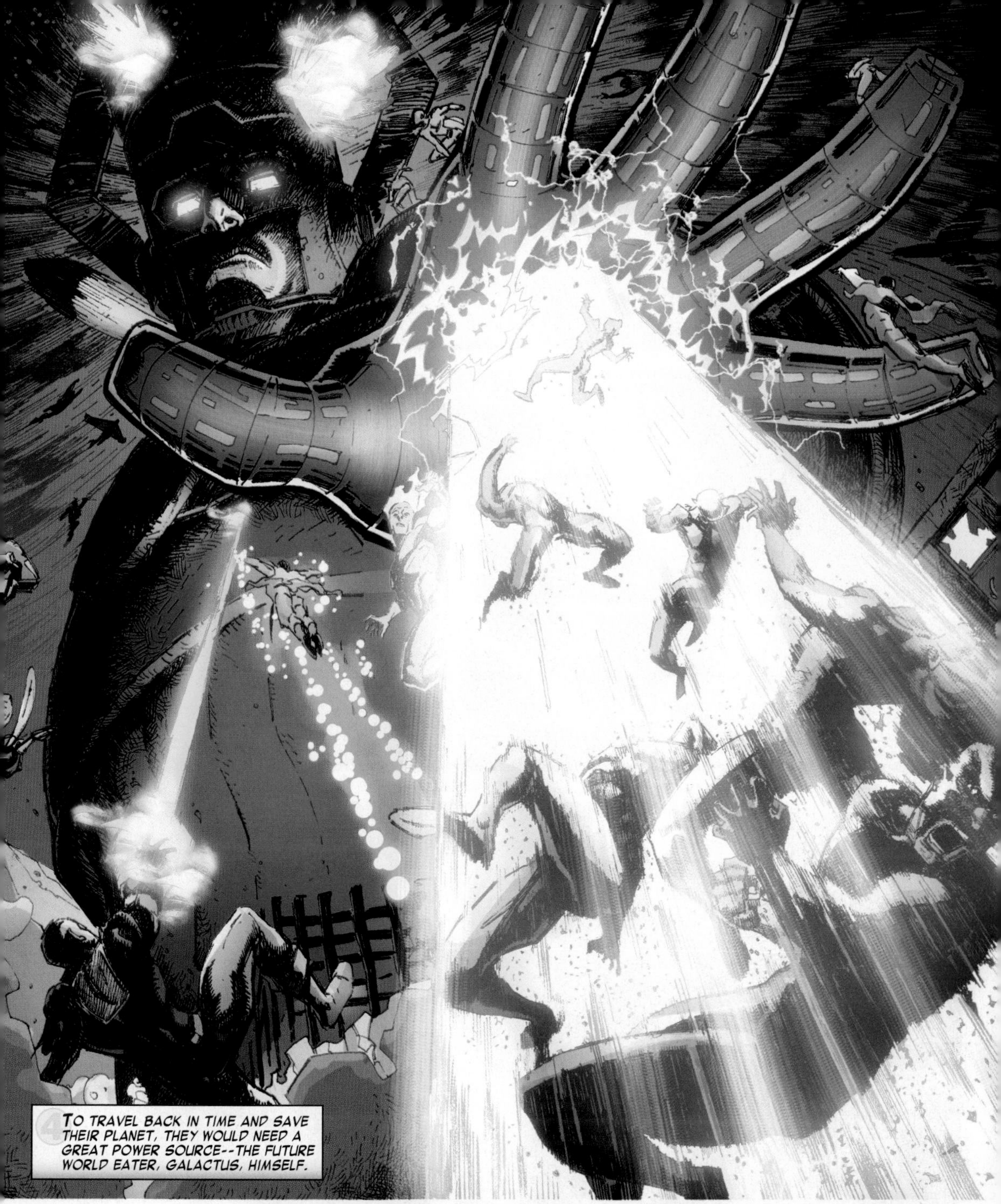
TO TRAVEL BACK IN TIME AND SAVE THEIR PLANET, THEY WOULD NEED A GREAT POWER SOURCE--THE FUTURE WORLD EATER, GALACTUS, HIMSELF.

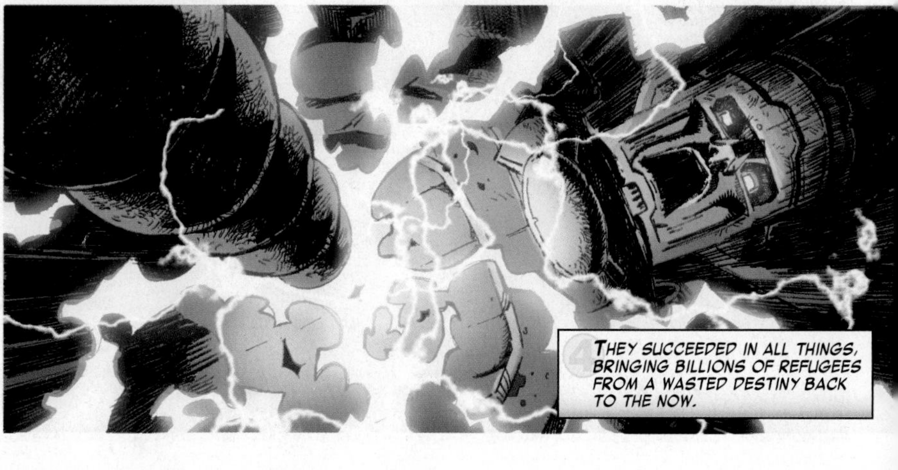
THEY SUCCEEDED IN ALL THINGS, BRINGING BILLIONS OF REFUGEES FROM A WASTED DESTINY BACK TO THE NOW.

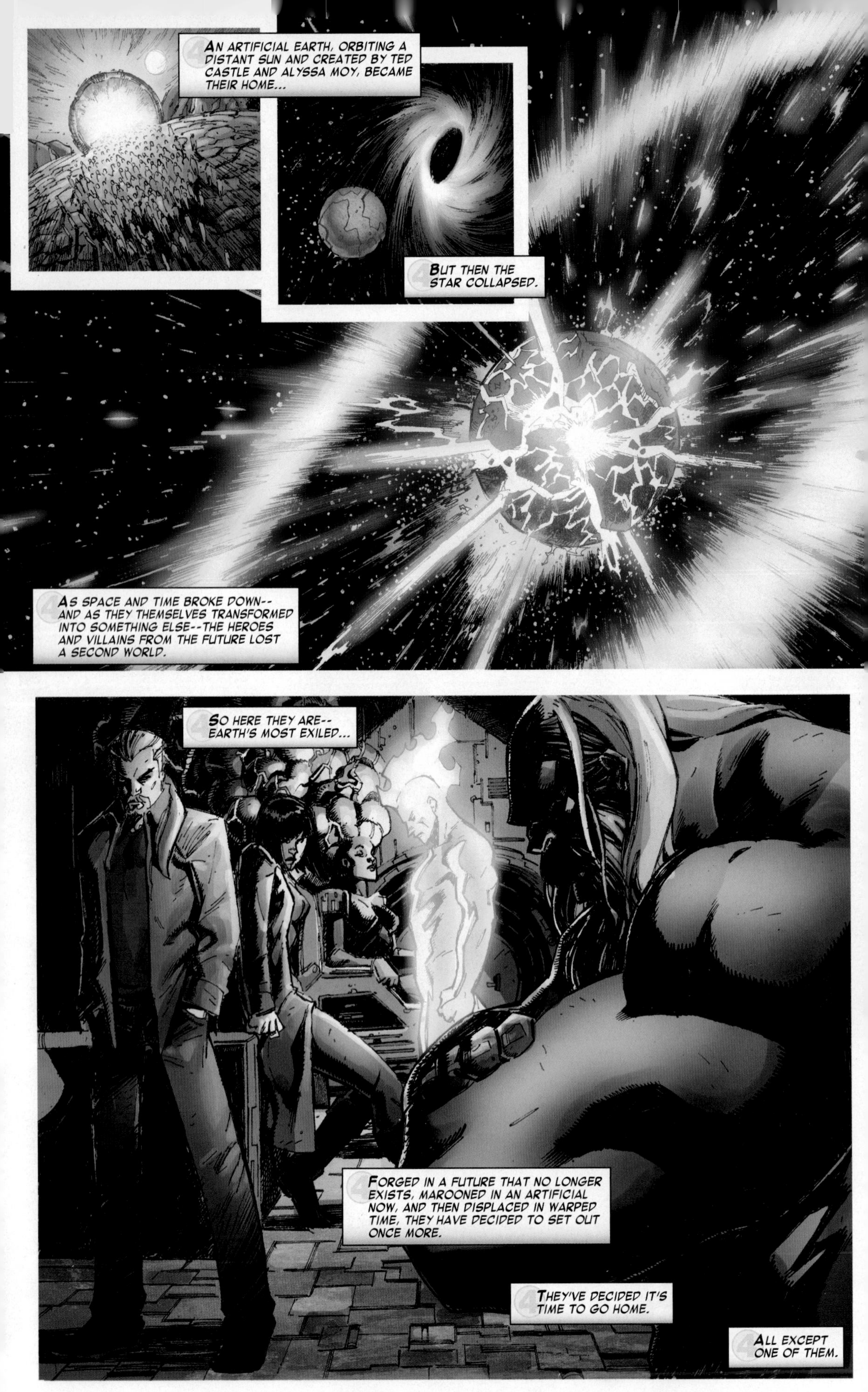
AN ARTIFICIAL EARTH, ORBITING A DISTANT SUN AND CREATED BY TED CASTLE AND ALYSSA MOY, BECAME THEIR HOME...
BUT THEN THE STAR COLLAPSED.
AS SPACE AND TIME BROKE DOWN--AND AS THEY THEMSELVES TRANSFORMED INTO SOMETHING ELSE--THE HEROES AND VILLAINS FROM THE FUTURE LOST A SECOND WORLD.
SO HERE THEY ARE--EARTH'S MOST EXILED...
FORGED IN A FUTURE THAT NO LONGER EXISTS, MAROONED IN AN ARTIFICIAL NOW, AND THEN DISPLACED IN WARPED TIME, THEY HAVE DECIDED TO SET OUT ONCE MORE.
THEY'VE DECIDED IT'S TIME TO GO HOME.
ALL EXCEPT ONE OF THEM.

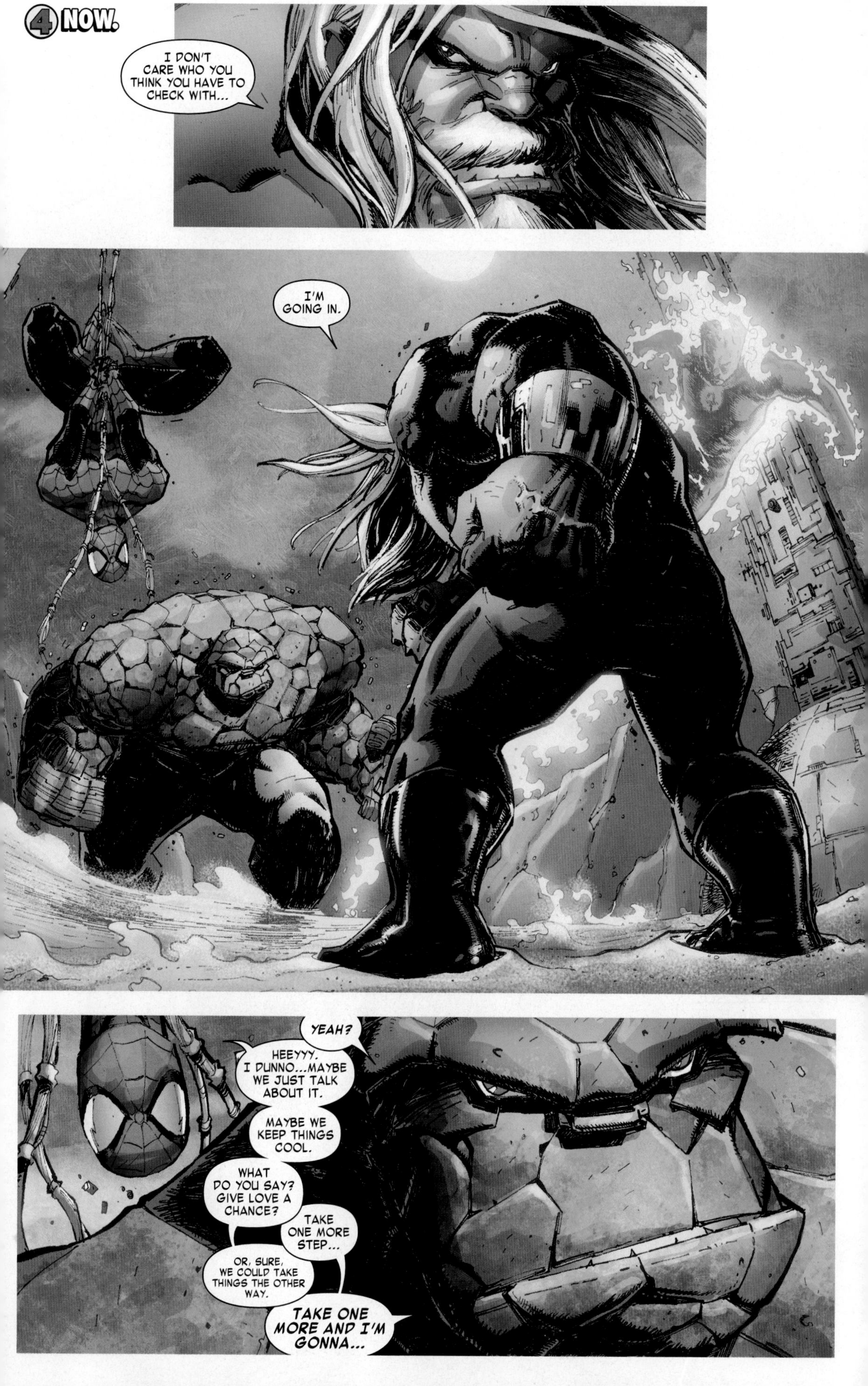

I DON'T CARE WHO YOU THINK YOU HAVE TO CHECK WITH...
I'M GOING IN.
YEAH?
HEEYYY. I DUNNO...MAYBE WE JUST TALK ABOUT IT.
MAYBE WE KEEP THINGS COOL.
WHAT DO YOU SAY? GIVE LOVE A CHANCE?
TAKE ONE MORE STEP...
OR, SURE, WE COULD TAKE THINGS THE OTHER WAY.
TAKE ONE MORE AND I'M GONNA...

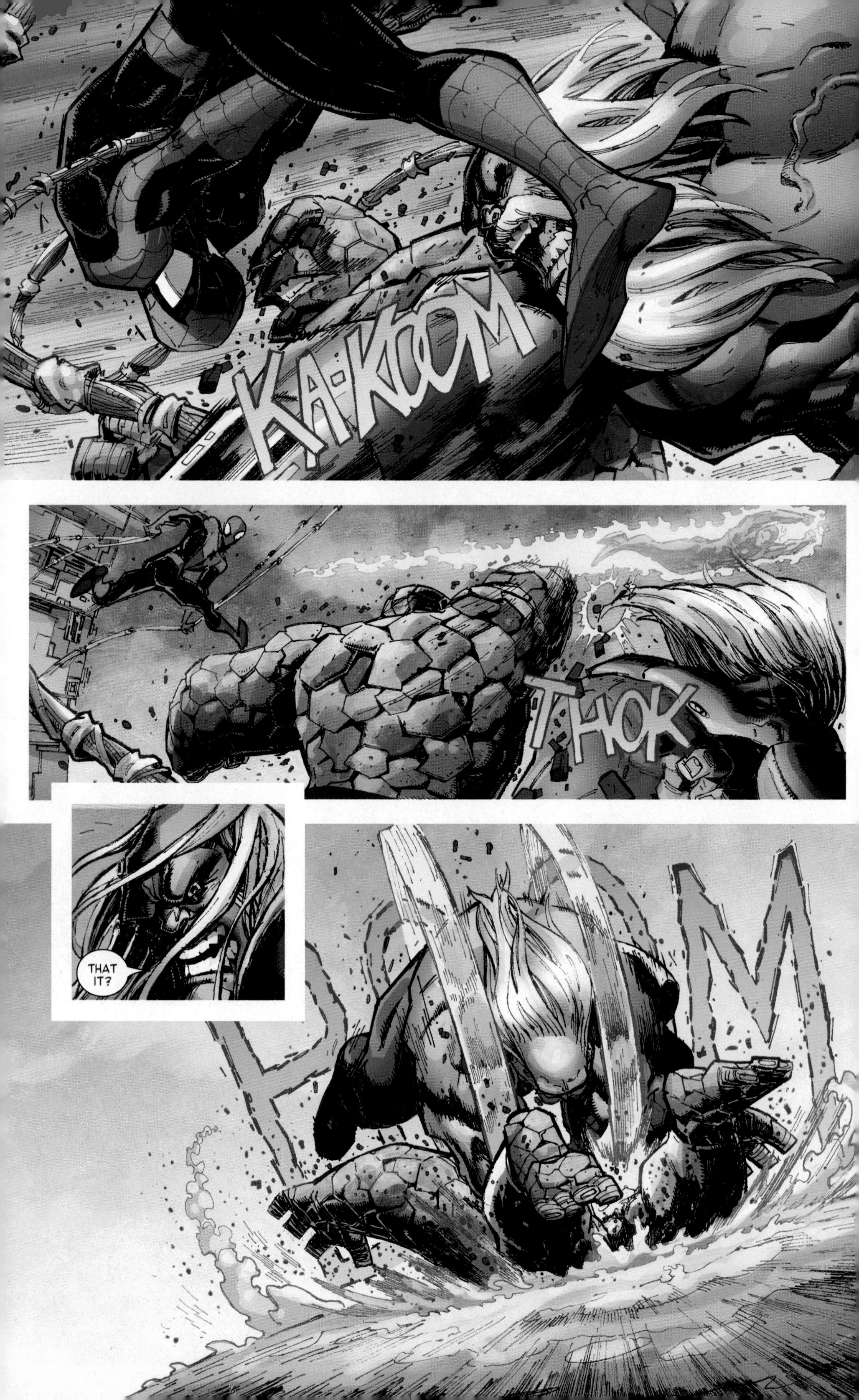
KA-KOOM
THOK
THAT IT?

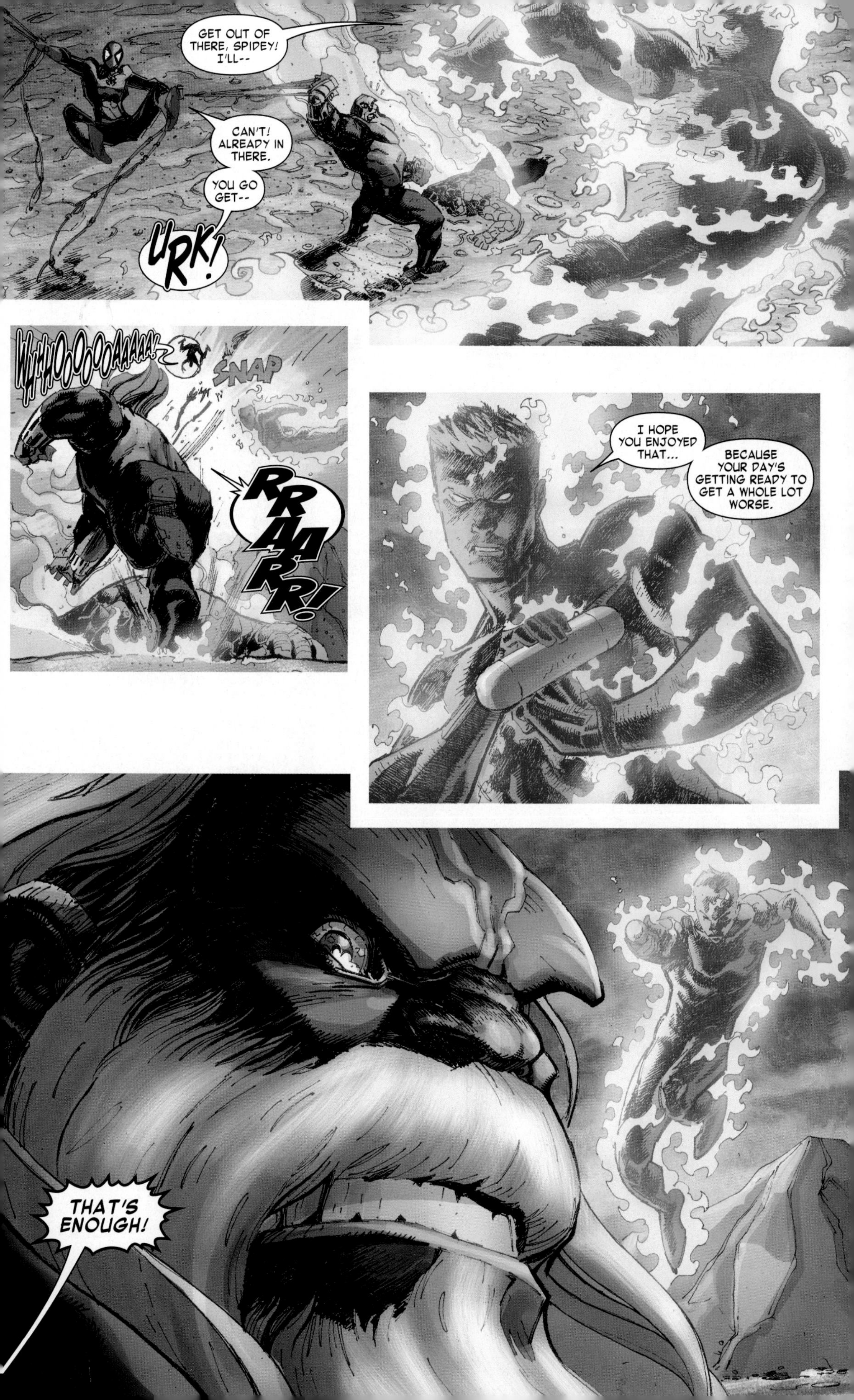

GET OUT OF THERE, SPIDEY! I'LL--
CAN'T! ALREADY IN THERE.
YOU GO GET--
URK!
SNAP
RRAARR!
I HOPE YOU ENJOYED THAT...
BECAUSE YOUR DAY'S GETTING READY TO GET A WHOLE LOT WORSE.
THAT'S ENOUGH!

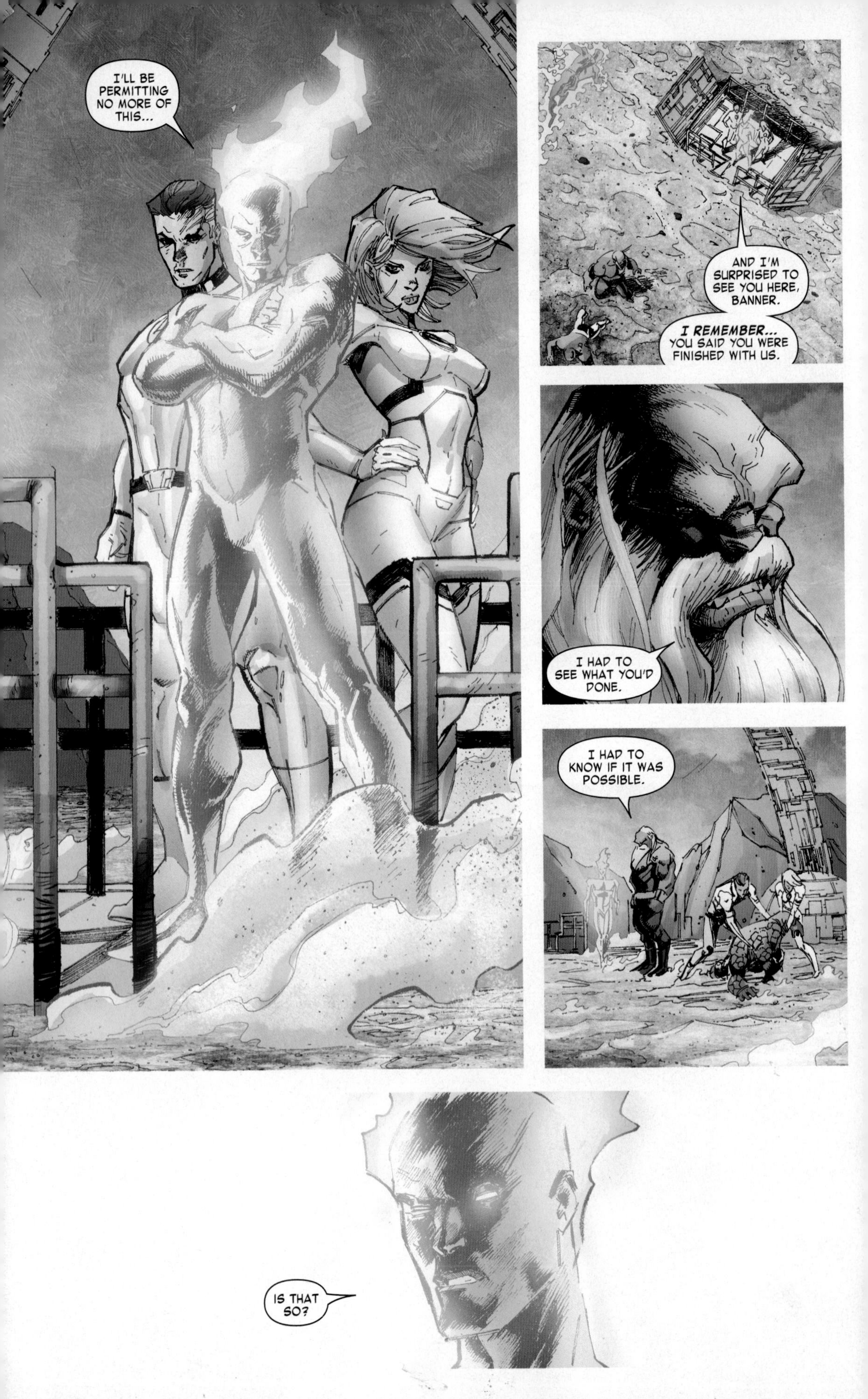
I'LL BE PERMITTING NO MORE OF THIS...
AND I'M SURPRISED TO SEE YOU HERE, BANNER.
I REMEMBER... YOU SAID YOU WERE FINISHED WITH US.
I HAD TO SEE WHAT YOU'D DONE.
I HAD TO KNOW IF IT WAS POSSIBLE.
IS THAT SO?

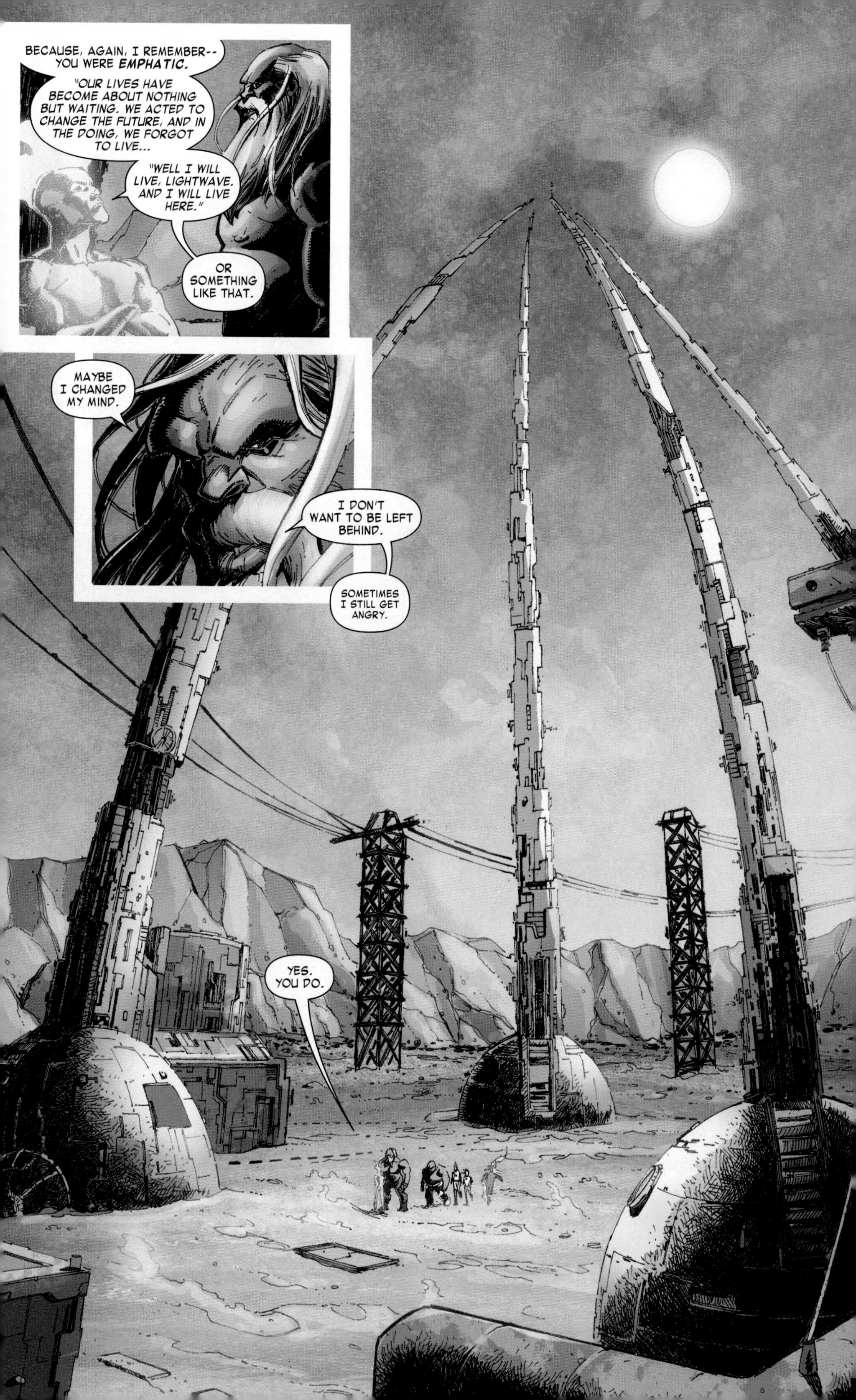
BECAUSE, AGAIN, I REMEMBER-- YOU WERE EMPHATIC.
"OUR LIVES HAVE BECOME ABOUT NOTHING BUT WAITING. WE ACTED TO CHANGE THE FUTURE, AND IN THE DOING, WE FORGOT TO LIVE...
"WELL I WILL LIVE, LIGHTWAVE. AND I WILL LIVE HERE."
OR SOMETHING LIKE THAT.
MAYBE I CHANGED MY MIND.
I DON'T WANT TO BE LEFT BEHIND.
SOMETIMES I STILL GET ANGRY.
YES. YOU DO.

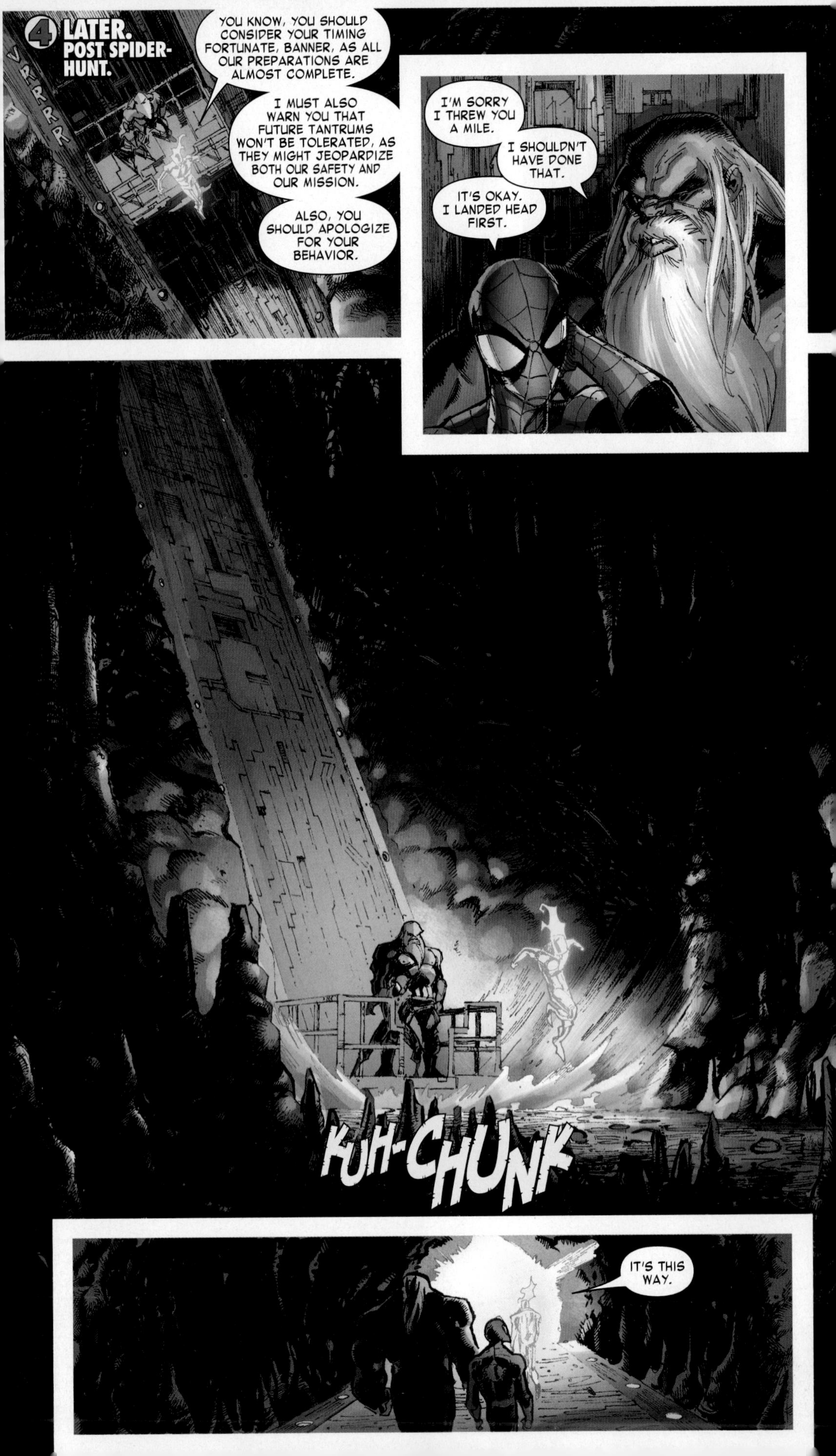
4 LATER. POST SPIDER-HUNT.
VRRRR
YOU KNOW, YOU SHOULD CONSIDER YOUR TIMING FORTUNATE, BANNER, AS ALL OUR PREPARATIONS ARE ALMOST COMPLETE.
I MUST ALSO WARN YOU THAT FUTURE TANTRUMS WON'T BE TOLERATED, AS THEY MIGHT JEOPARDIZE BOTH OUR SAFETY AND OUR MISSION.
ALSO, YOU SHOULD APOLOGIZE FOR YOUR BEHAVIOR.
I'M SORRY I THREW YOU A MILE.
I SHOULDN'T HAVE DONE THAT.
IT'S OKAY. I LANDED HEAD FIRST.
KUH-CHUNK
IT'S THIS WAY.

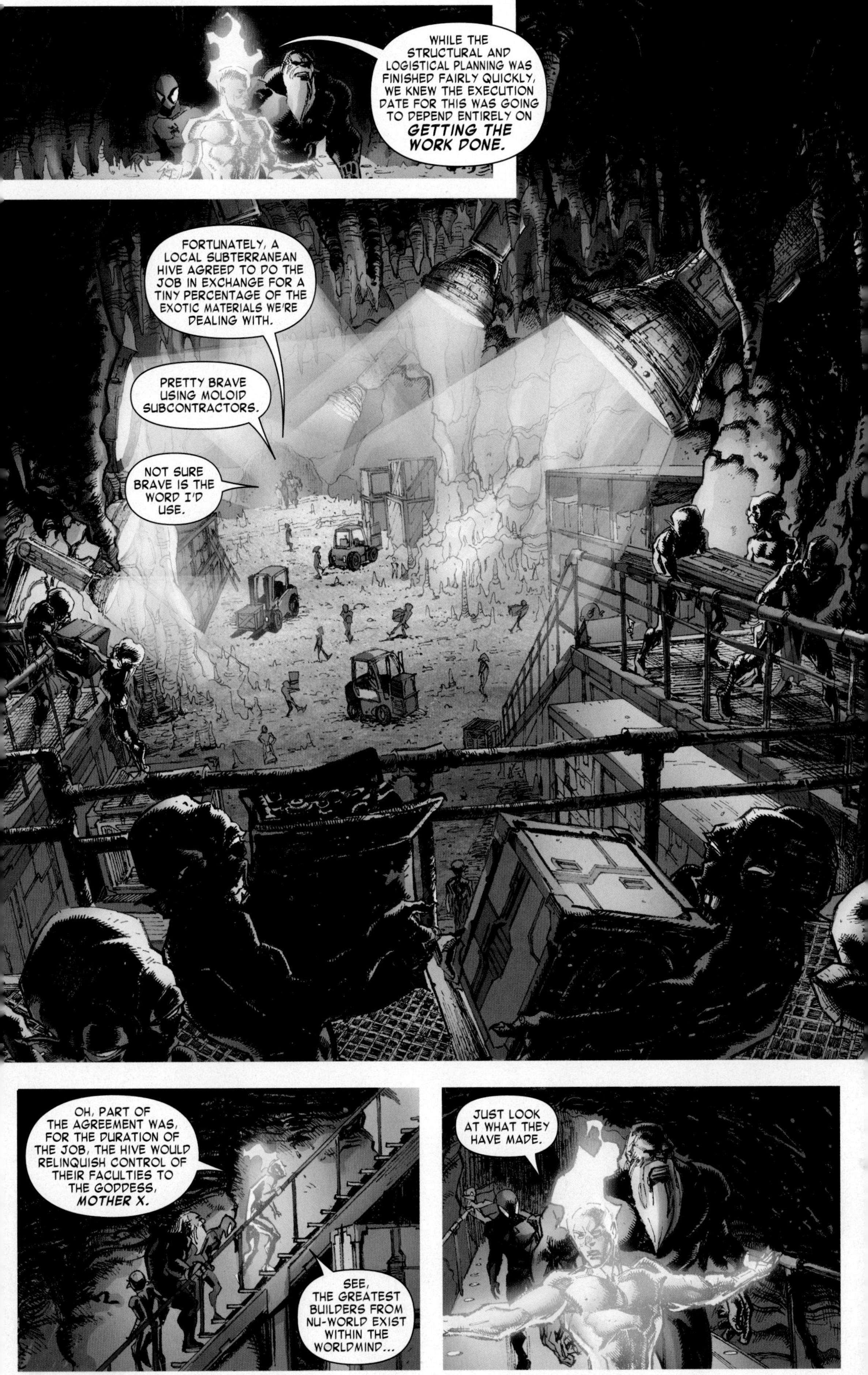
WHILE THE STRUCTURAL AND LOGISTICAL PLANNING WAS FINISHED FAIRLY QUICKLY, WE KNEW THE EXECUTION DATE FOR THIS WAS GOING TO DEPEND ENTIRELY ON GETTING THE WORK DONE.
FORTUNATELY, A LOCAL SUBTERRANEAN HIVE AGREED TO DO THE JOB IN EXCHANGE FOR A TINY PERCENTAGE OF THE EXOTIC MATERIALS WE'RE DEALING WITH.
PRETTY BRAVE USING MOLOID SUBCONTRACTORS.
NOT SURE BRAVE IS THE WORD I'D USE.
OH, PART OF THE AGREEMENT WAS, FOR THE DURATION OF THE JOB, THE HIVE WOULD RELINQUISH CONTROL OF THEIR FACULTIES TO THE GODDESS, MOTHER X.
SEE, THE GREATEST BUILDERS FROM NU-WORLD EXIST WITHIN THE WORLDMIND...
JUST LOOK AT WHAT THEY HAVE MADE.

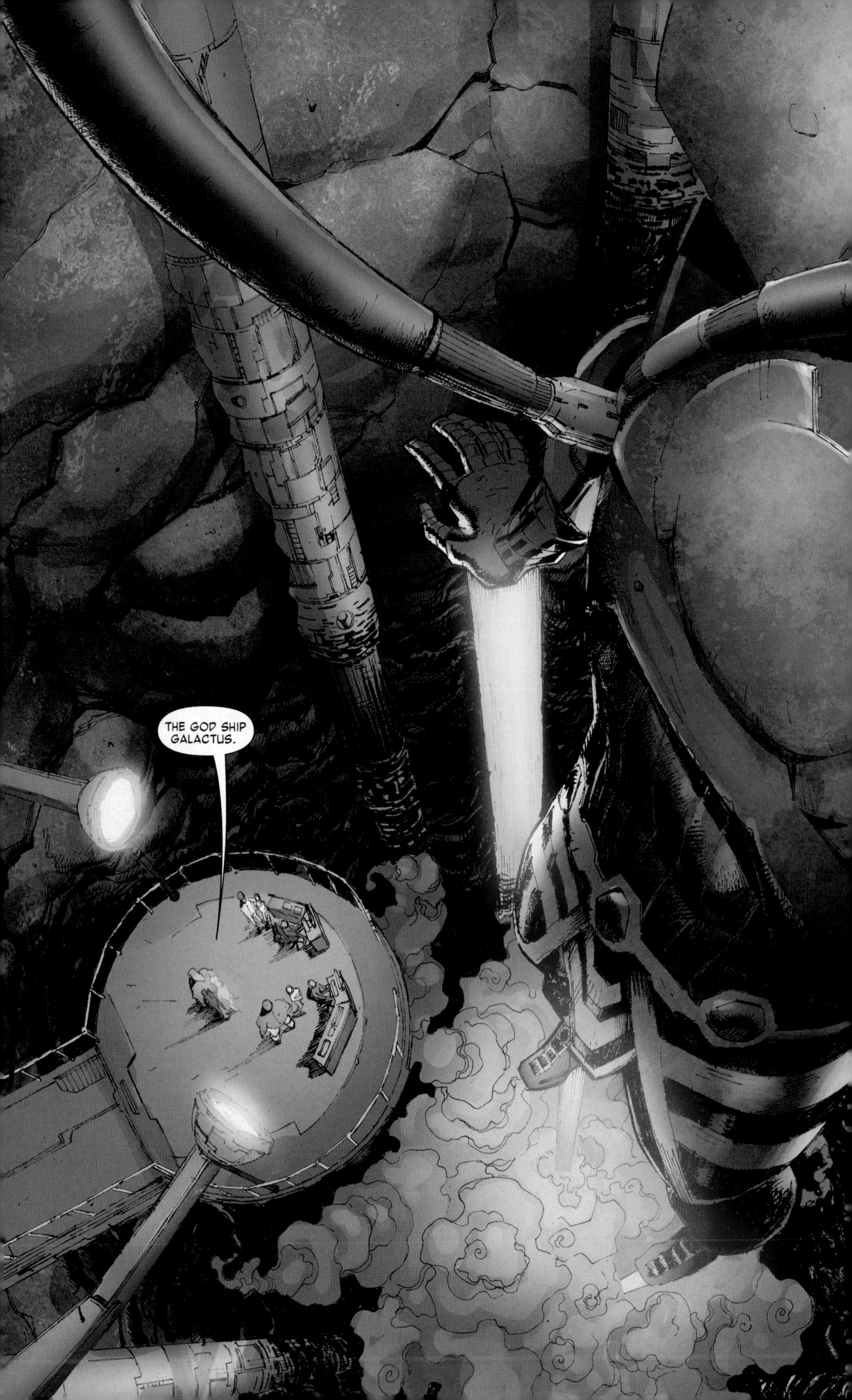
THE GOD SHIP GALACTUS.

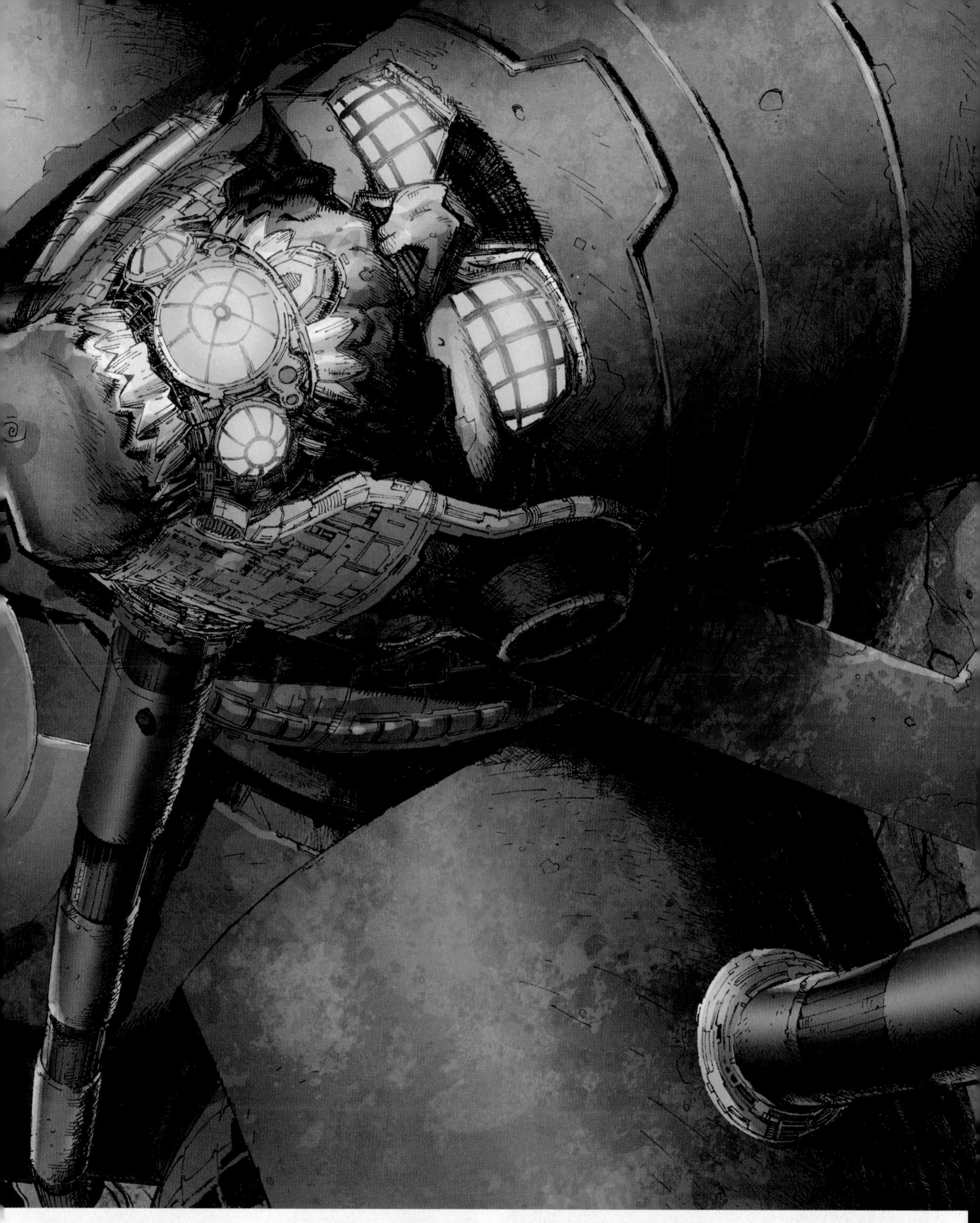

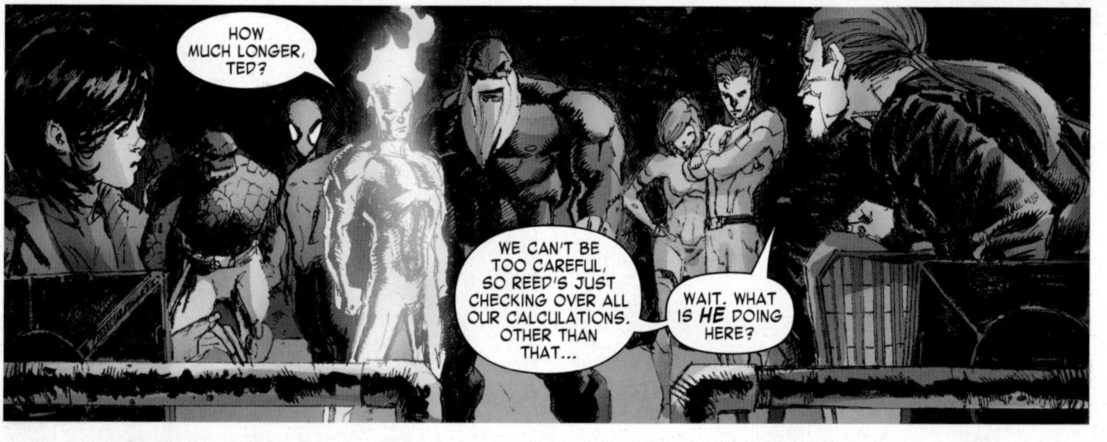
HOW MUCH LONGER, TED?
WE CAN'T BE TOO CAREFUL, SO REED'S JUST CHECKING OVER ALL OUR CALCULATIONS. OTHER THAN THAT...
WAIT. WHAT IS HE DOING HERE?

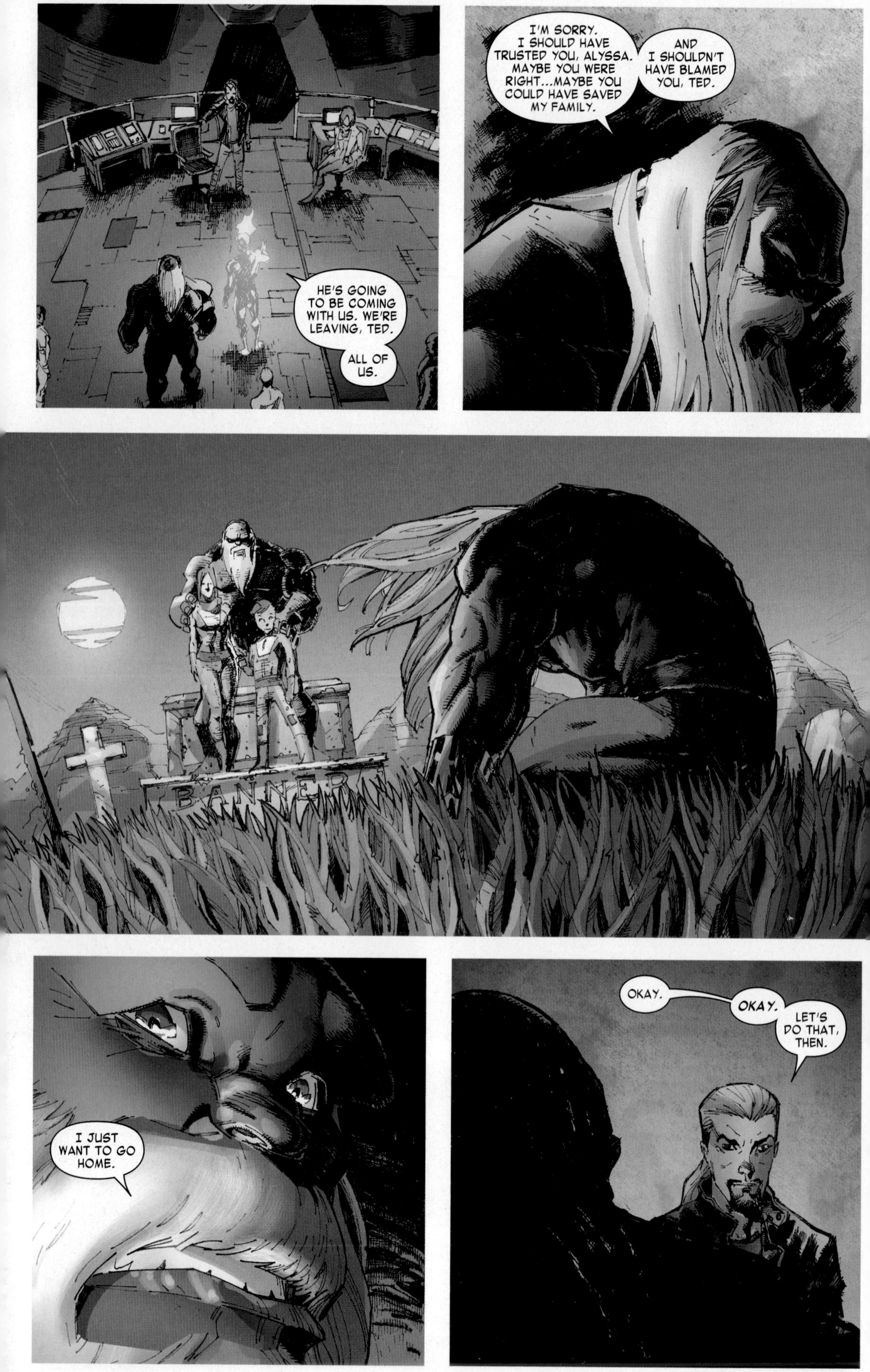
HE'S GOING TO BE COMING WITH US. WE'RE LEAVING, TED.
ALL OF US.
I'M SORRY. I SHOULD HAVE TRUSTED YOU, ALYSSA. MAYBE YOU WERE RIGHT...MAYBE YOU COULD HAVE SAVED MY FAMILY.
AND I SHOULDN'T HAVE BLAMED YOU, TED.
BANNER
I JUST WANT TO GO HOME.
OKAY.
OKAY.
LET'S DO THAT, THEN.

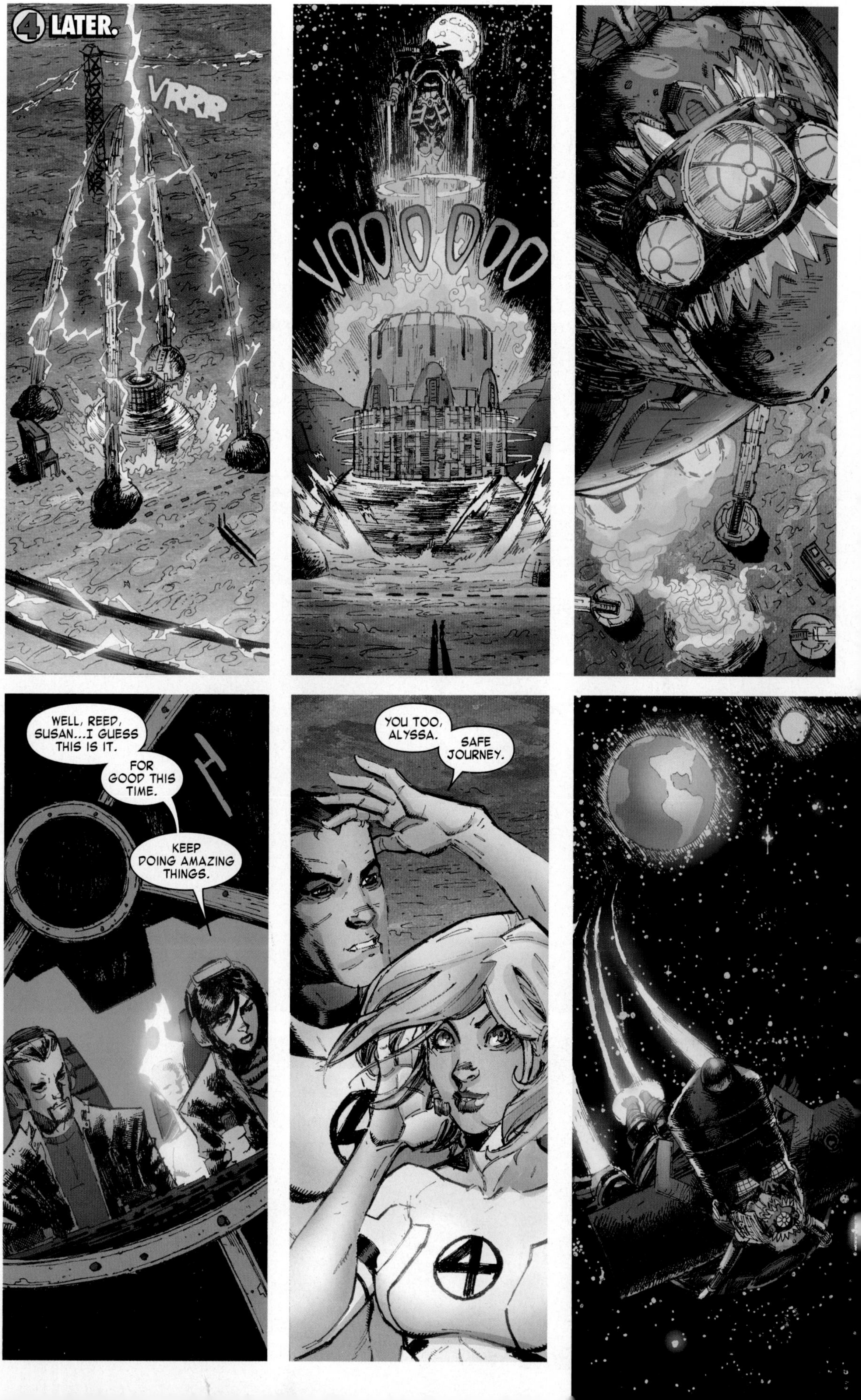
LATER.
VRRRR
VOOOOOO
WELL, REED, SUSAN...I GUESS THIS IS IT.
FOR GOOD THIS TIME.
KEEP DOING AMAZING THINGS.
YOU TOO, ALYSSA.
SAFE JOURNEY.

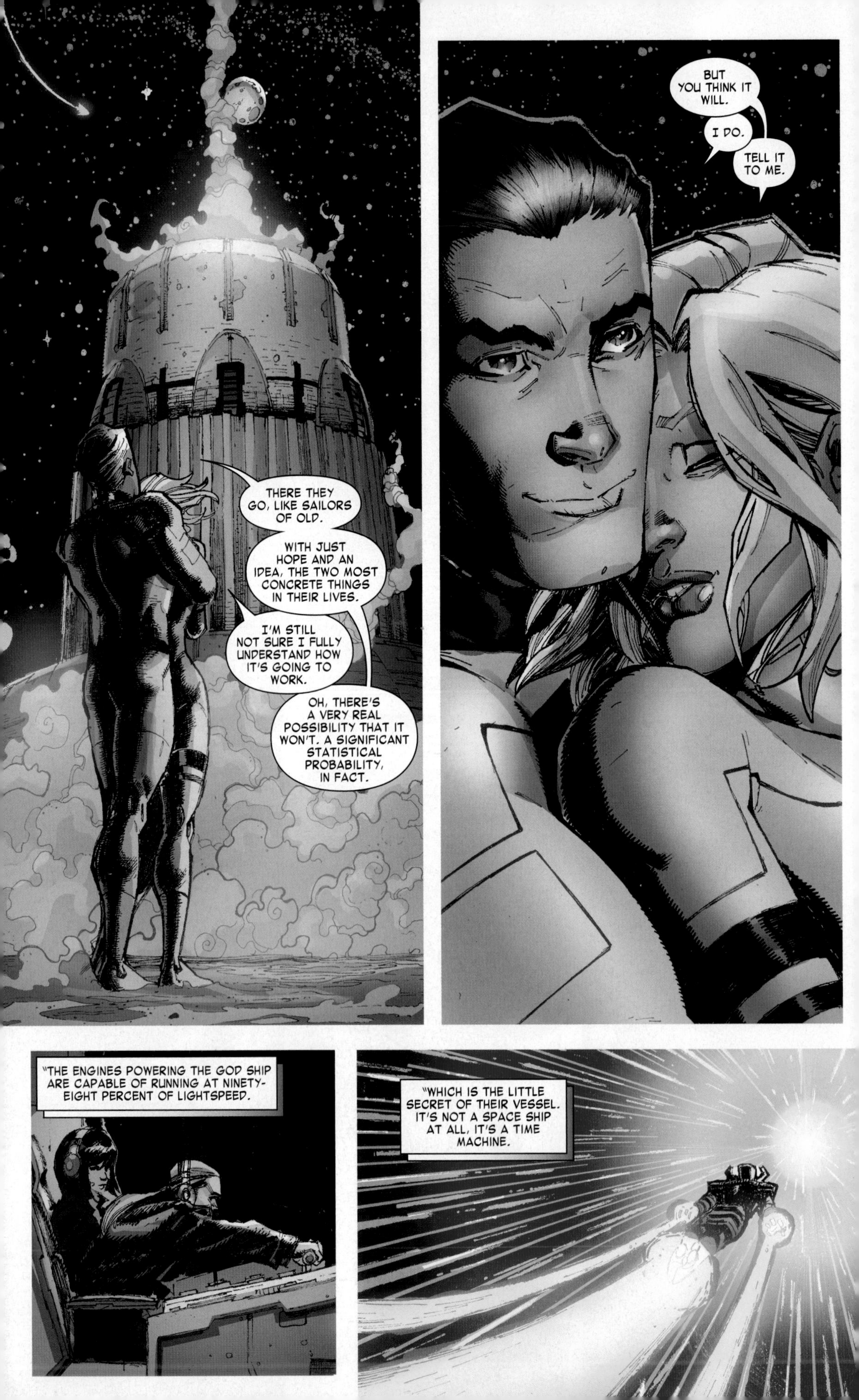
THERE THEY GO, LIKE SAILORS OF OLD.
WITH JUST HOPE AND AN IDEA, THE TWO MOST CONCRETE THINGS IN THEIR LIVES.
I'M STILL NOT SURE I FULLY UNDERSTAND HOW IT'S GOING TO WORK.
OH, THERE'S A VERY REAL POSSIBILITY THAT IT WON'T. A SIGNIFICANT STATISTICAL PROBABILITY, IN FACT.
BUT YOU THINK IT WILL.
I DO.
TELL IT TO ME.
"THE ENGINES POWERING THE GOD SHIP ARE CAPABLE OF RUNNING AT NINETY-EIGHT PERCENT OF LIGHTSPEED.
"WHICH IS THE LITTLE SECRET OF THEIR VESSEL. IT'S NOT A SPACE SHIP AT ALL, IT'S A TIME MACHINE.

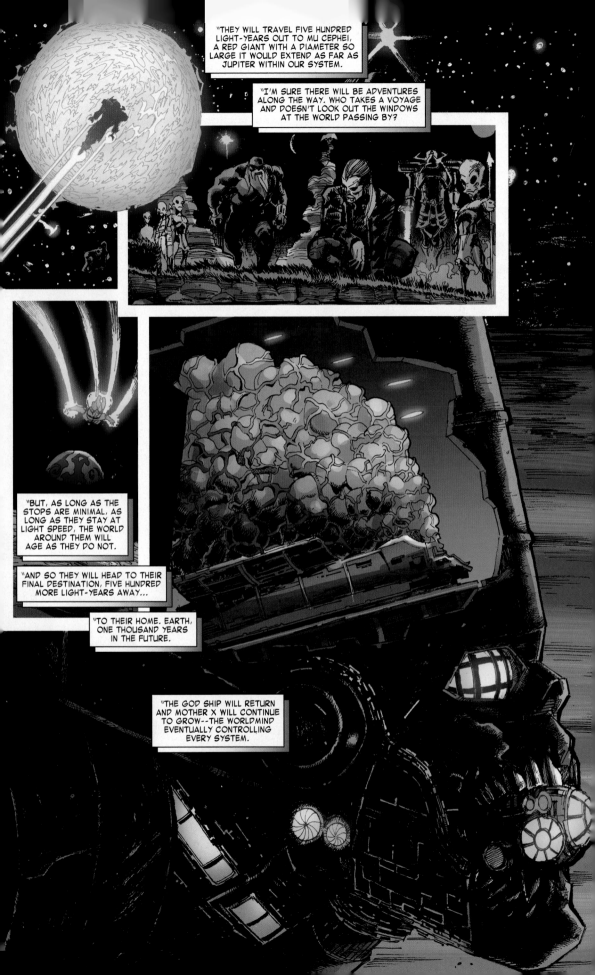

"THEY WILL TRAVEL FIVE HUNDRED LIGHT-YEARS OUT TO MU CEPHEI, A RED GIANT WITH A DIAMETER SO LARGE IT WOULD EXTEND AS FAR AS JUPITER WITHIN OUR SYSTEM.

"I'M SURE THERE WILL BE ADVENTURES ALONG THE WAY. WHO TAKES A VOYAGE AND DOESN'T LOOK OUT THE WINDOWS AT THE WORLD PASSING BY?

"BUT, AS LONG AS THE STOPS ARE MINIMAL, AS LONG AS THEY STAY AT LIGHT SPEED, THE WORLD AROUND THEM WILL AGE AS THEY DO NOT.

"AND SO THEY WILL HEAD TO THEIR FINAL DESTINATION, FIVE HUNDRED MORE LIGHT-YEARS AWAY...

"TO THEIR HOME. EARTH, ONE THOUSAND YEARS IN THE FUTURE.

"THE GOD SHIP WILL RETURN AND MOTHER X WILL CONTINUE TO GROW--THE WORLDMIND EVENTUALLY CONTROLLING EVERY SYSTEM.

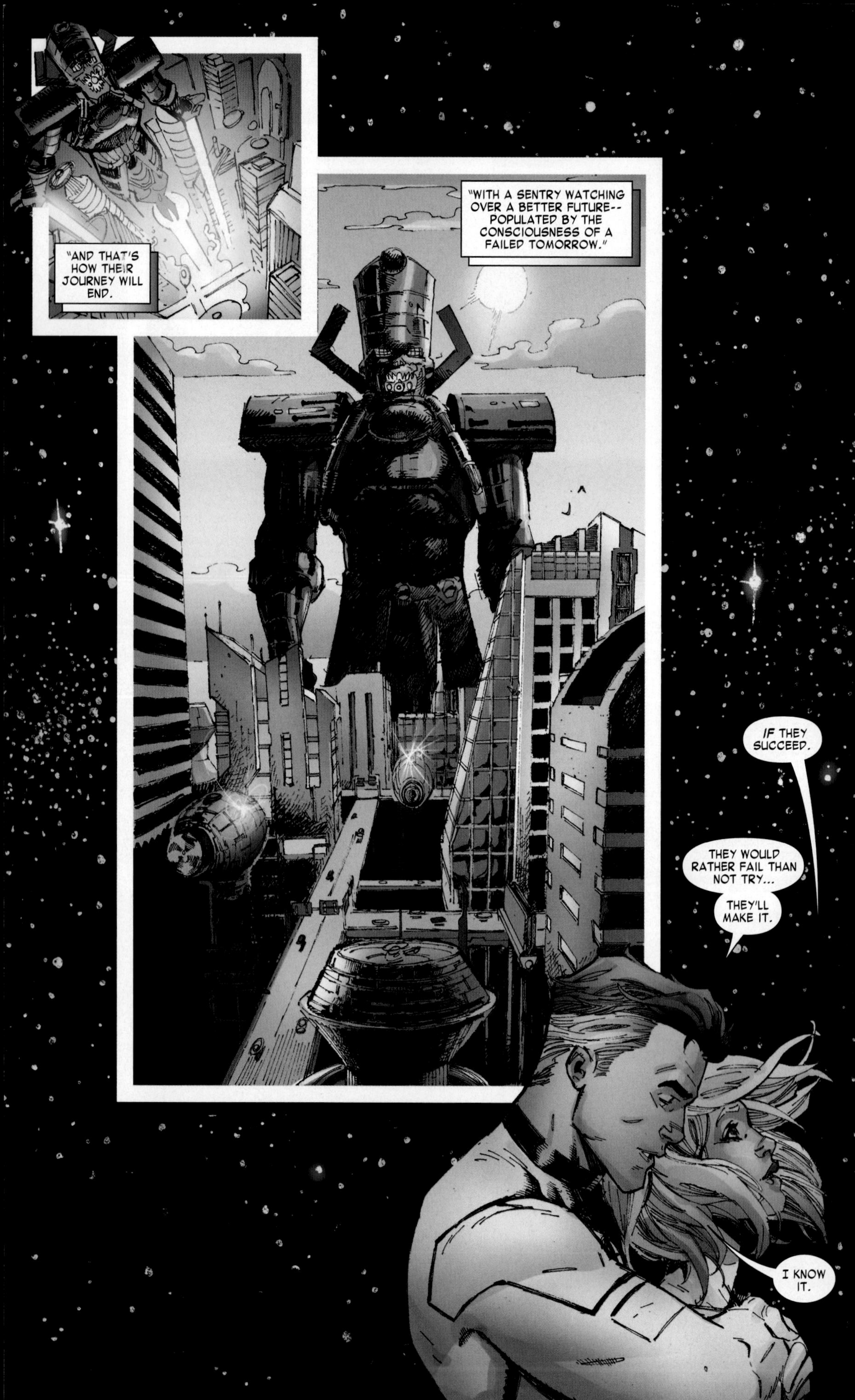
"AND THAT'S HOW THEIR JOURNEY WILL END.
"WITH A SENTRY WATCHING OVER A BETTER FUTURE--POPULATED BY THE CONSCIOUSNESS OF A FAILED TOMORROW."
IF THEY SUCCEED.
THEY WOULD RATHER FAIL THAN NOT TRY...
THEY'LL MAKE IT.
I KNOW IT.

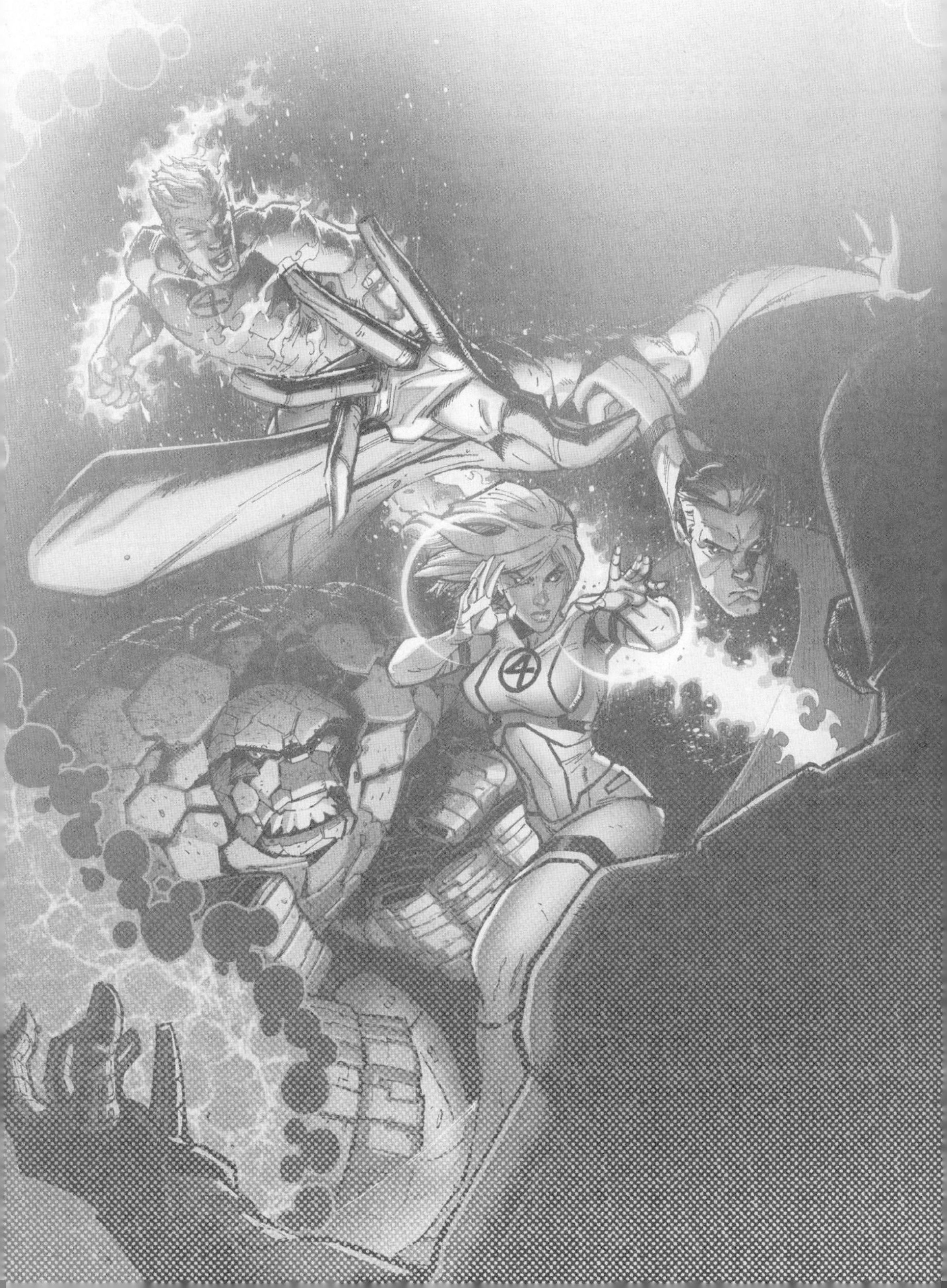

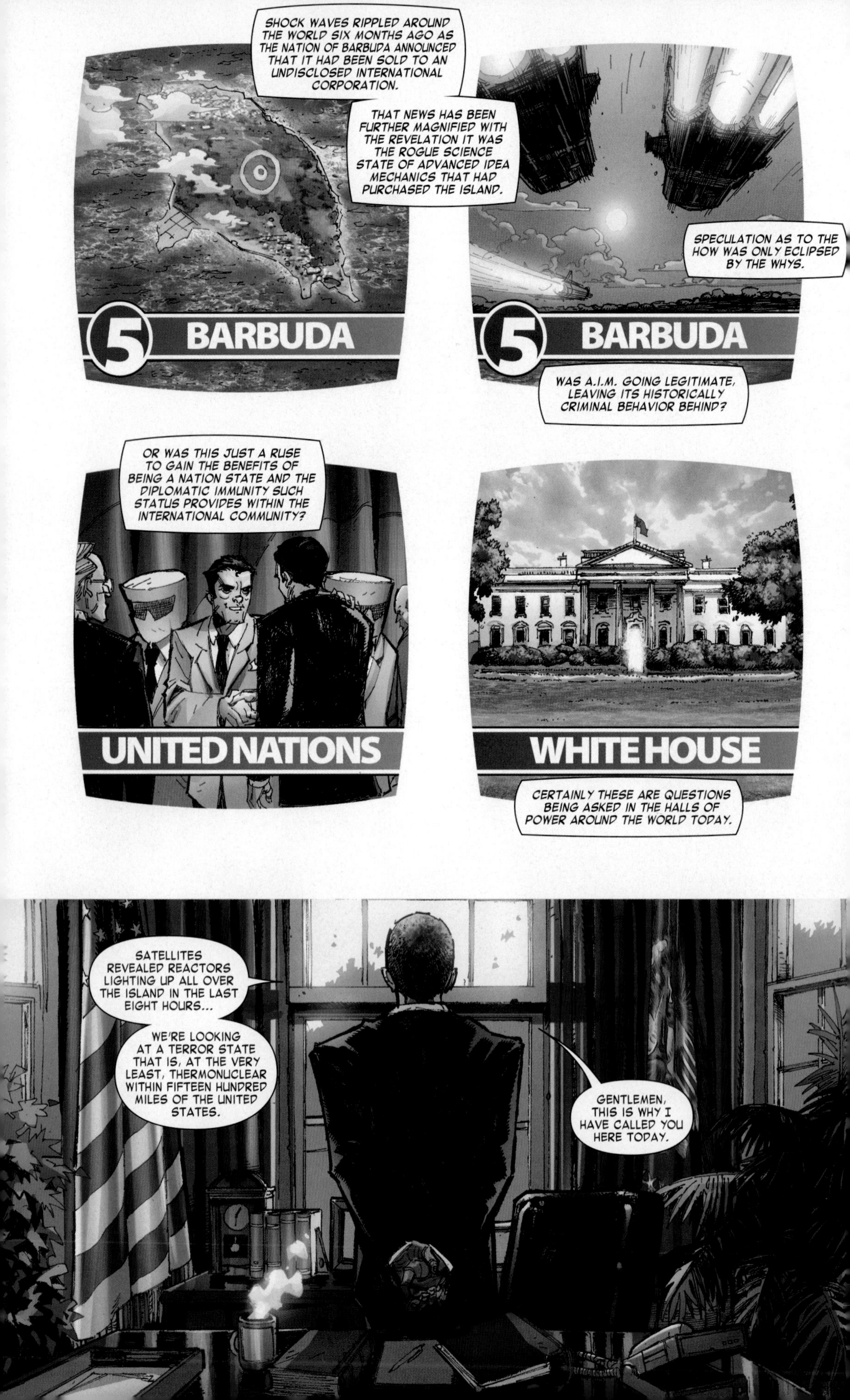
SHOCK WAVES RIPPLED AROUND THE WORLD SIX MONTHS AGO AS THE NATION OF BARBUDA ANNOUNCED THAT IT HAD BEEN SOLD TO AN UNDISCLOSED INTERNATIONAL CORPORATION.
THAT NEWS HAS BEEN FURTHER MAGNIFIED WITH THE REVELATION IT WAS THE ROGUE SCIENCE STATE OF ADVANCED IDEA MECHANICS THAT HAD PURCHASED THE ISLAND.
5 BARBUDA
SPECULATION AS TO THE HOW WAS ONLY ECLIPSED BY THE WHYS.
5 BARBUDA
WAS A.I.M. GOING LEGITIMATE, LEAVING ITS HISTORICALLY CRIMINAL BEHAVIOR BEHIND?
OR WAS THIS JUST A RUSE TO GAIN THE BENEFITS OF BEING A NATION STATE AND THE DIPLOMATIC IMMUNITY SUCH STATUS PROVIDES WITHIN THE INTERNATIONAL COMMUNITY?
UNITED NATIONS
WHITE HOUSE
CERTAINLY THESE ARE QUESTIONS BEING ASKED IN THE HALLS OF POWER AROUND THE WORLD TODAY.
SATELLITES REVEALED REACTORS LIGHTING UP ALL OVER THE ISLAND IN THE LAST EIGHT HOURS...
WE'RE LOOKING AT A TERROR STATE THAT IS, AT THE VERY LEAST, THERMONUCLEAR WITHIN FIFTEEN HUNDRED MILES OF THE UNITED STATES.
GENTLEMEN, THIS IS WHY I HAVE CALLED YOU HERE TODAY.

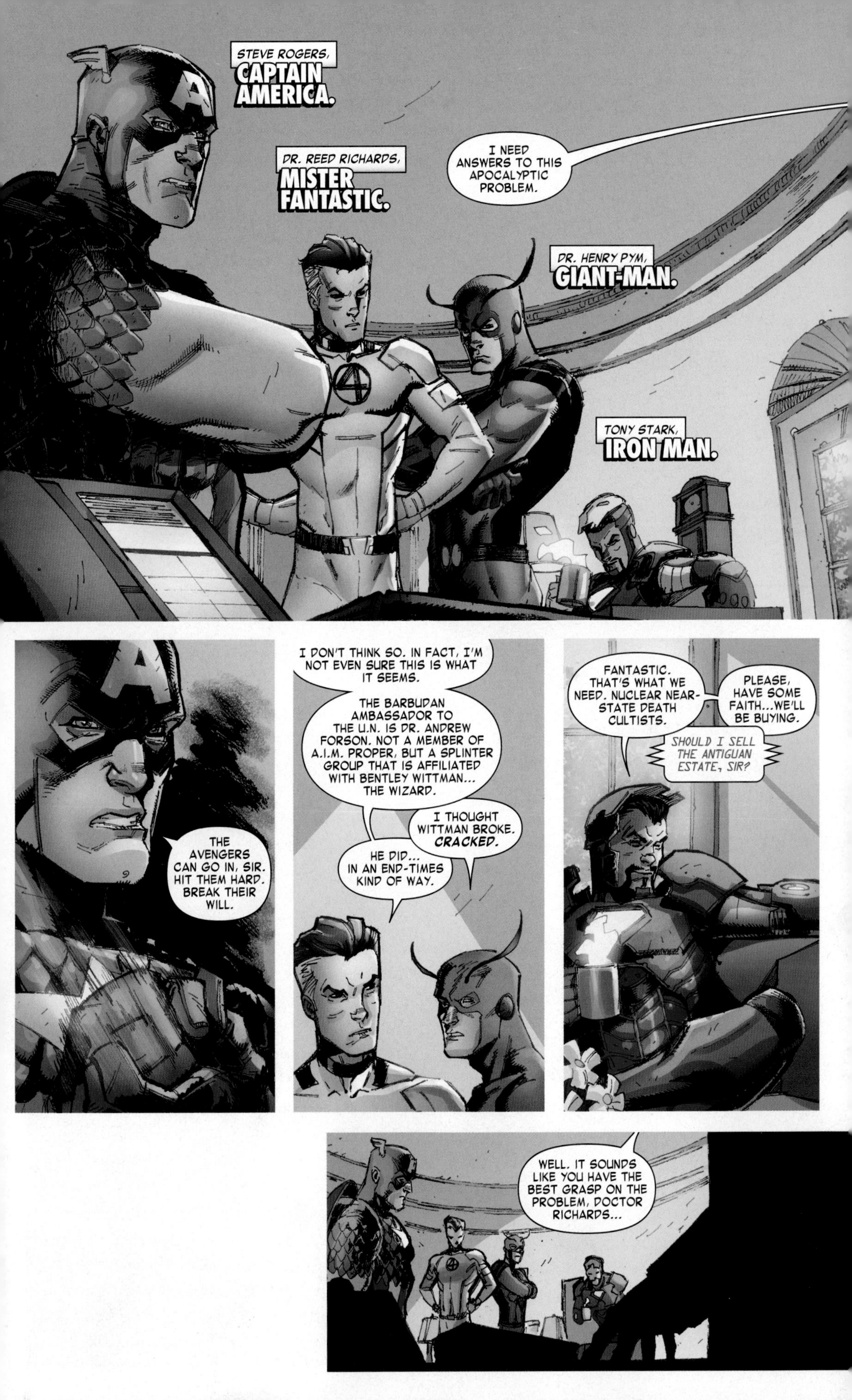
STEVE ROGERS,
CAPTAIN AMERICA.
DR. REED RICHARDS,
MISTER FANTASTIC.
I NEED ANSWERS TO THIS APOCALYPTIC PROBLEM.
DR. HENRY PYM,
GIANT-MAN.
TONY STARK,
IRON MAN.
THE AVENGERS CAN GO IN, SIR. HIT THEM HARD. BREAK THEIR WILL.
I DON'T THINK SO. IN FACT, I'M NOT EVEN SURE THIS IS WHAT IT SEEMS.
THE BARBUDAN AMBASSADOR TO THE U.N. IS DR. ANDREW FORSON. NOT A MEMBER OF A.I.M. PROPER, BUT A SPLINTER GROUP THAT IS AFFILIATED WITH BENTLEY WITTMAN... THE WIZARD.
I THOUGHT WITTMAN BROKE. CRACKED.
HE DID... IN AN END-TIMES KIND OF WAY.
FANTASTIC. THAT'S WHAT WE NEED. NUCLEAR NEAR-STATE DEATH CULTISTS.
PLEASE, HAVE SOME FAITH...WE'LL BE BUYING.
SHOULD I SELL THE ANTIGUAN ESTATE, SIR?
WELL. IT SOUNDS LIKE YOU HAVE THE BEST GRASP ON THE PROBLEM, DOCTOR RICHARDS...

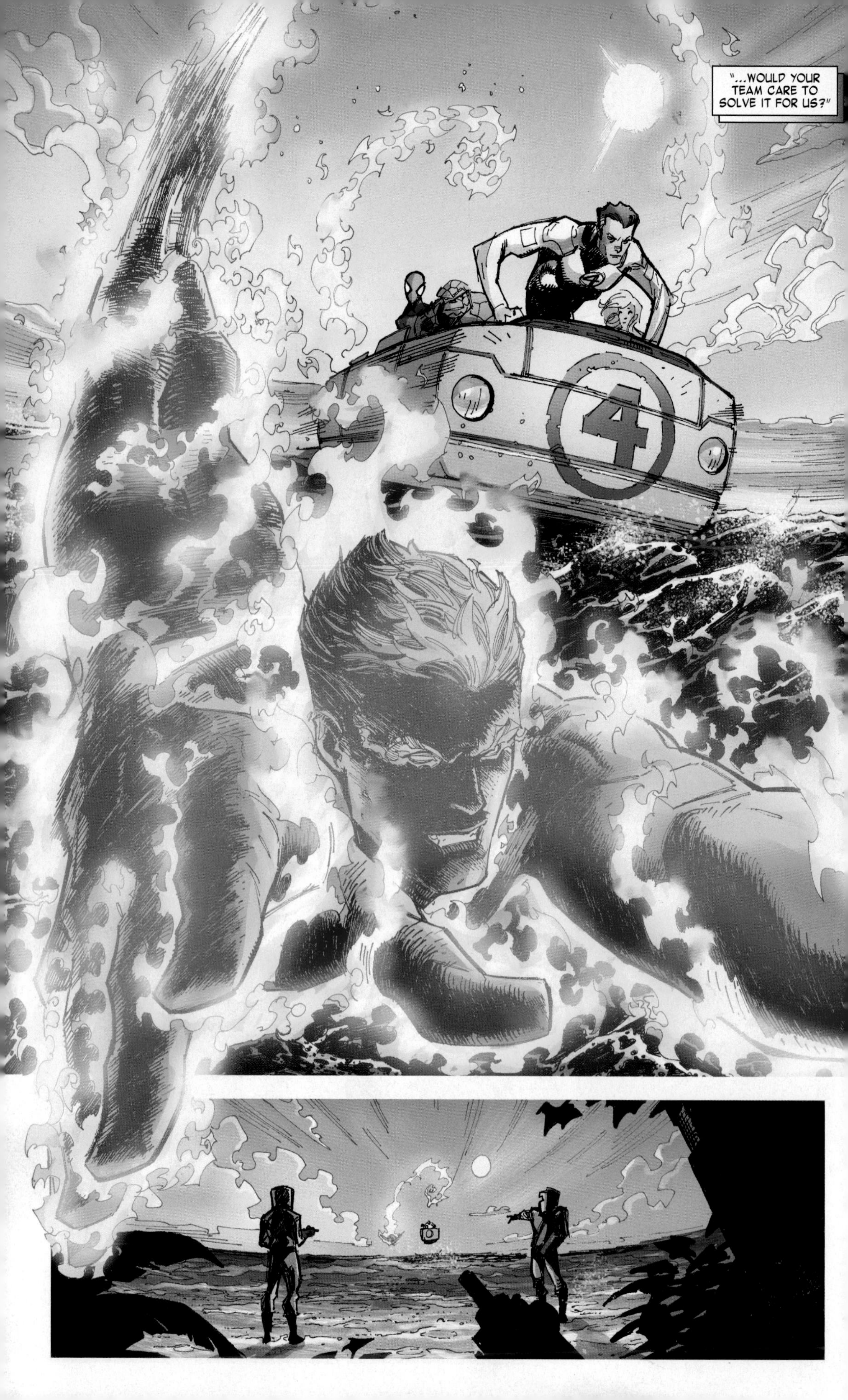
"...WOULD YOUR TEAM CARE TO SOLVE IT FOR US?"

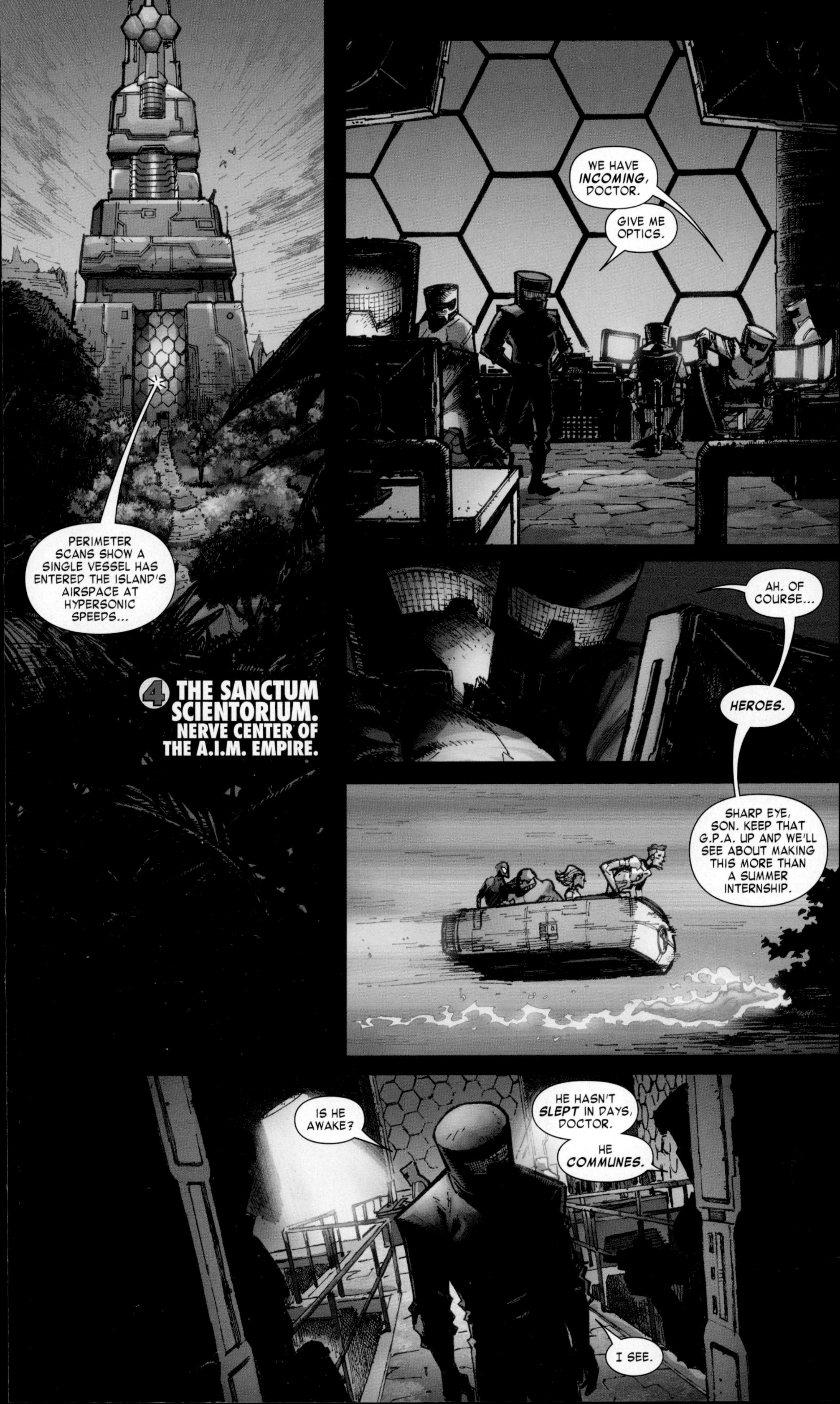
PERIMETER SCANS SHOW A SINGLE VESSEL HAS ENTERED THE ISLAND'S AIRSPACE AT HYPERSONIC SPEEDS...
THE SANCTUM SCIENTORIUM. NERVE CENTER OF THE A.I.M. EMPIRE.
WE HAVE INCOMING, DOCTOR.
GIVE ME OPTICS.
AH. OF COURSE...
HEROES.
SHARP EYE, SON. KEEP THAT G.P.A. UP AND WE'LL SEE ABOUT MAKING THIS MORE THAN A SUMMER INTERNSHIP.
IS HE AWAKE?
HE HASN'T SLEPT IN DAYS, DOCTOR.
HE COMMUNES.
I SEE.

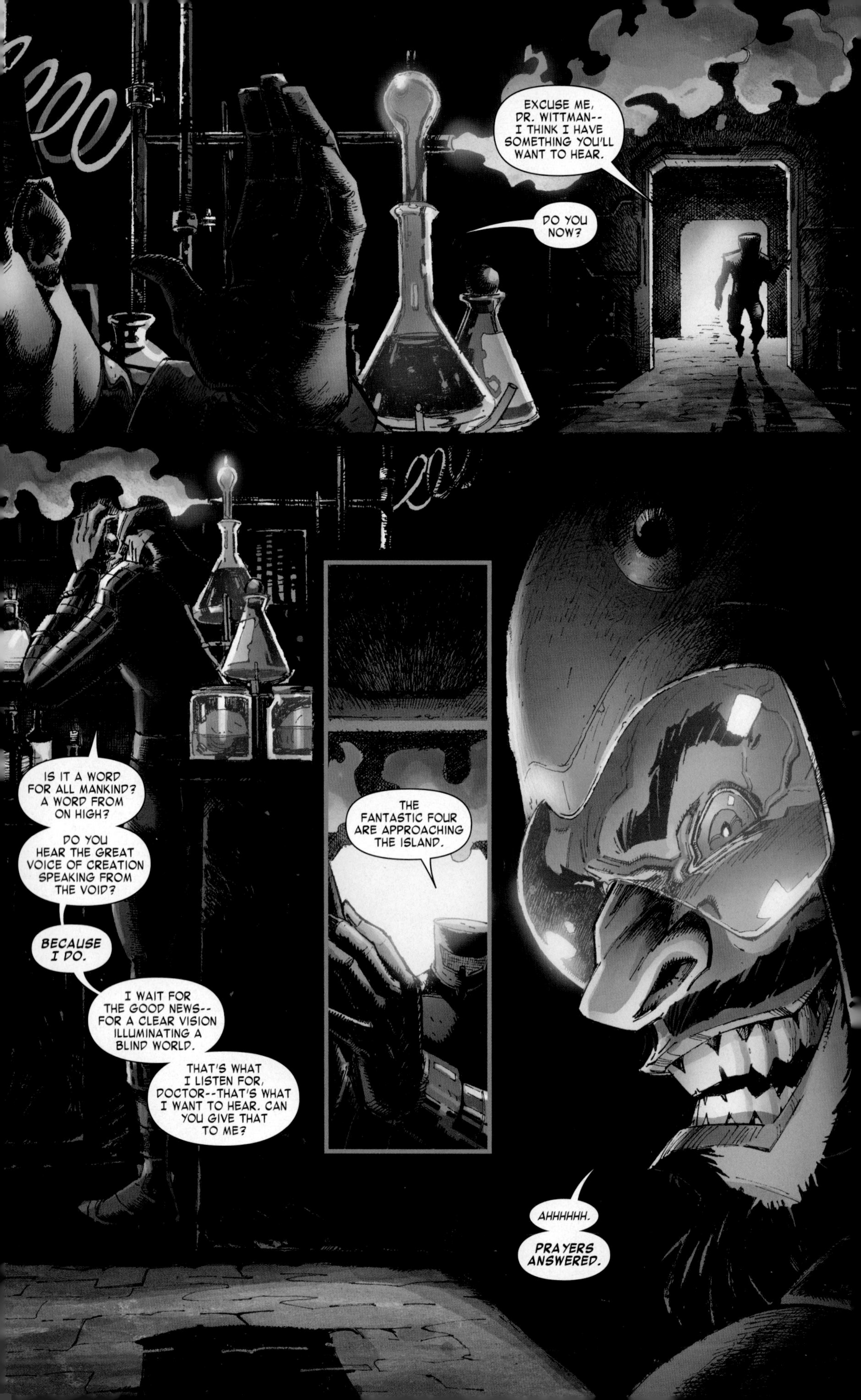
EXCUSE ME, DR. WITTMAN-- I THINK I HAVE SOMETHING YOU'LL WANT TO HEAR.
DO YOU NOW?
IS IT A WORD FOR ALL MANKIND? A WORD FROM ON HIGH?
DO YOU HEAR THE GREAT VOICE OF CREATION SPEAKING FROM THE VOID?
BECAUSE I DO.
I WAIT FOR THE GOOD NEWS-- FOR A CLEAR VISION ILLUMINATING A BLIND WORLD.
THAT'S WHAT I LISTEN FOR, DOCTOR--THAT'S WHAT I WANT TO HEAR. CAN YOU GIVE THAT TO ME?
THE FANTASTIC FOUR ARE APPROACHING THE ISLAND.
AHHHHHH.
PRAYERS ANSWERED.

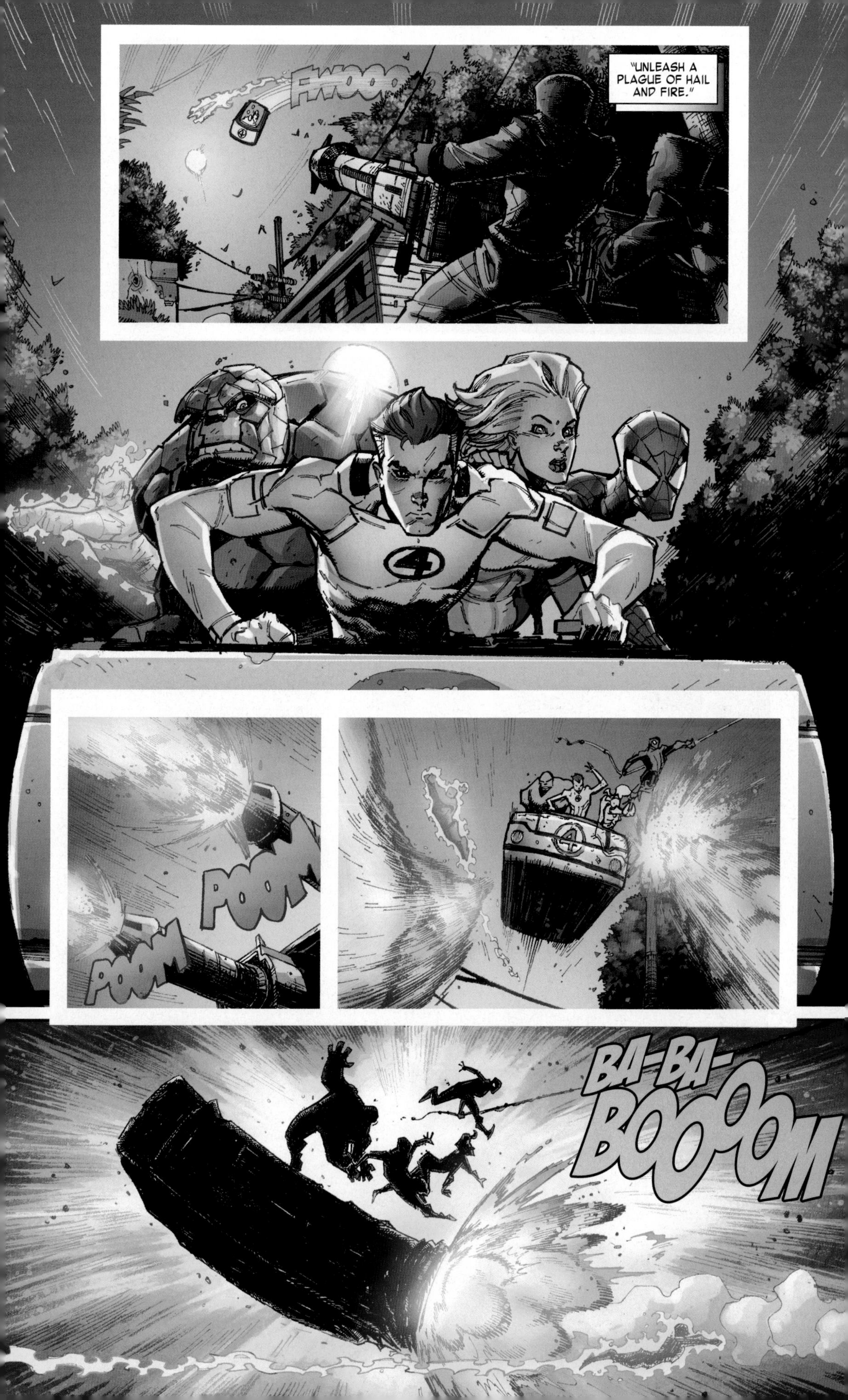
FWOOO
"UNLEASH A PLAGUE OF HAIL AND FIRE."
POOM
POOM
BA-BA-BOOOOM

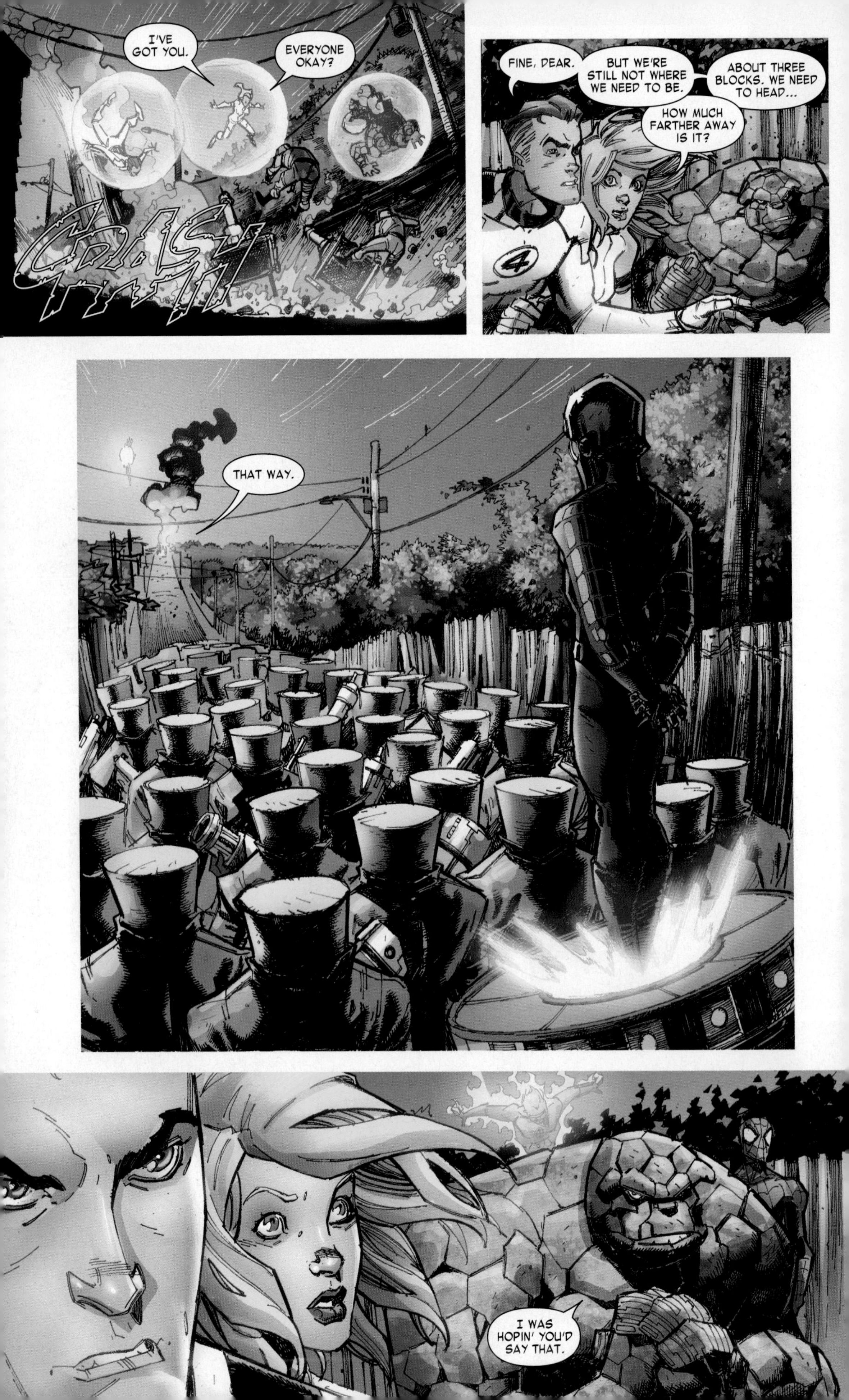
I'VE GOT YOU.
EVERYONE OKAY?
CRASH
FINE, DEAR.
BUT WE'RE STILL NOT WHERE WE NEED TO BE.
HOW MUCH FARTHER AWAY IS IT?
ABOUT THREE BLOCKS. WE NEED TO HEAD...
THAT WAY.
I WAS HOPIN' YOU'D SAY THAT.

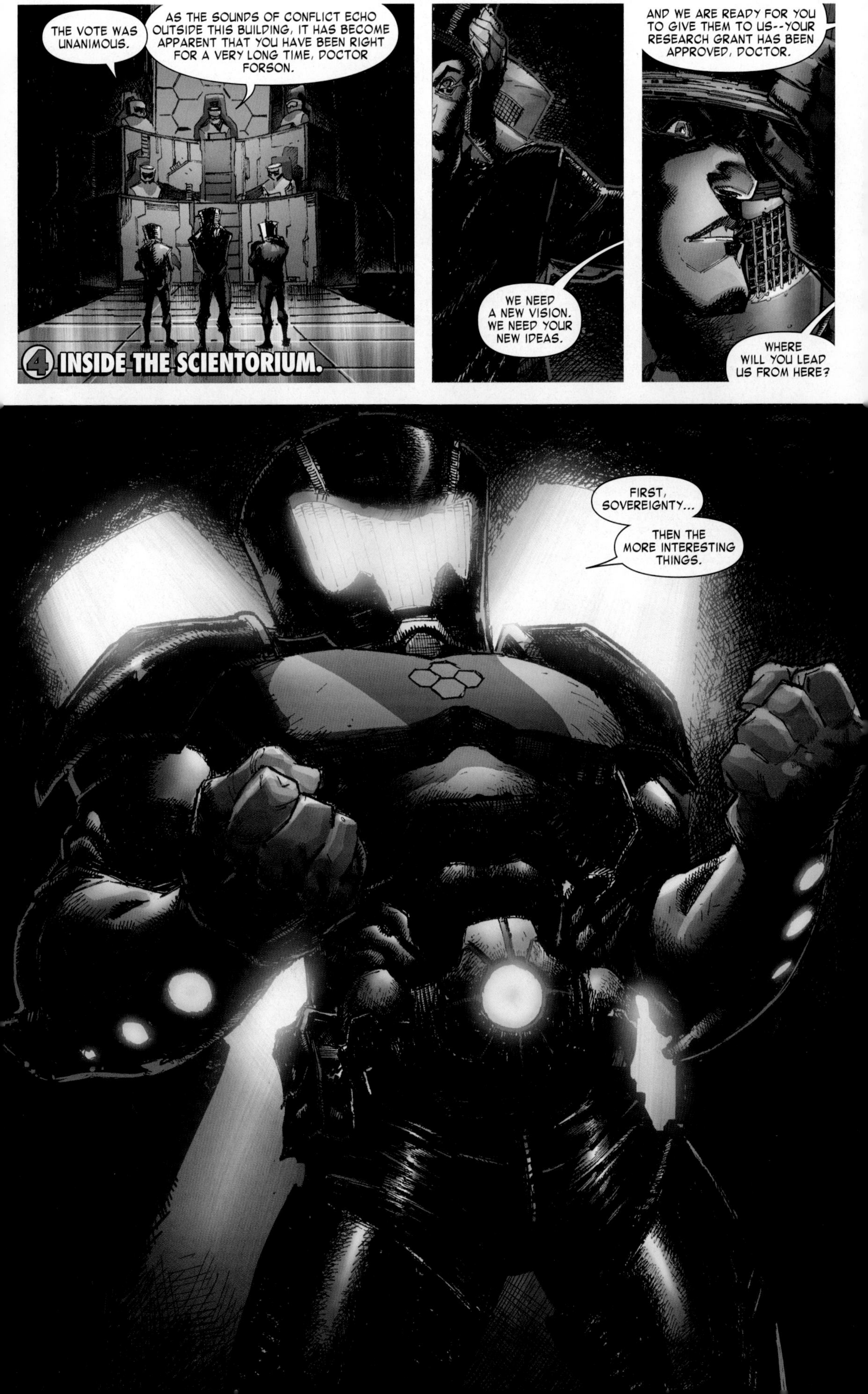

THE VOTE WAS UNANIMOUS.
AS THE SOUNDS OF CONFLICT ECHO OUTSIDE THIS BUILDING, IT HAS BECOME APPARENT THAT YOU HAVE BEEN RIGHT FOR A VERY LONG TIME, DOCTOR FORSON.
4 INSIDE THE SCIENTORIUM.
WE NEED A NEW VISION. WE NEED YOUR NEW IDEAS.
AND WE ARE READY FOR YOU TO GIVE THEM TO US--YOUR RESEARCH GRANT HAS BEEN APPROVED, DOCTOR.
WHERE WILL YOU LEAD US FROM HERE?
FIRST, SOVEREIGNTY...
THEN THE MORE INTERESTING THINGS.

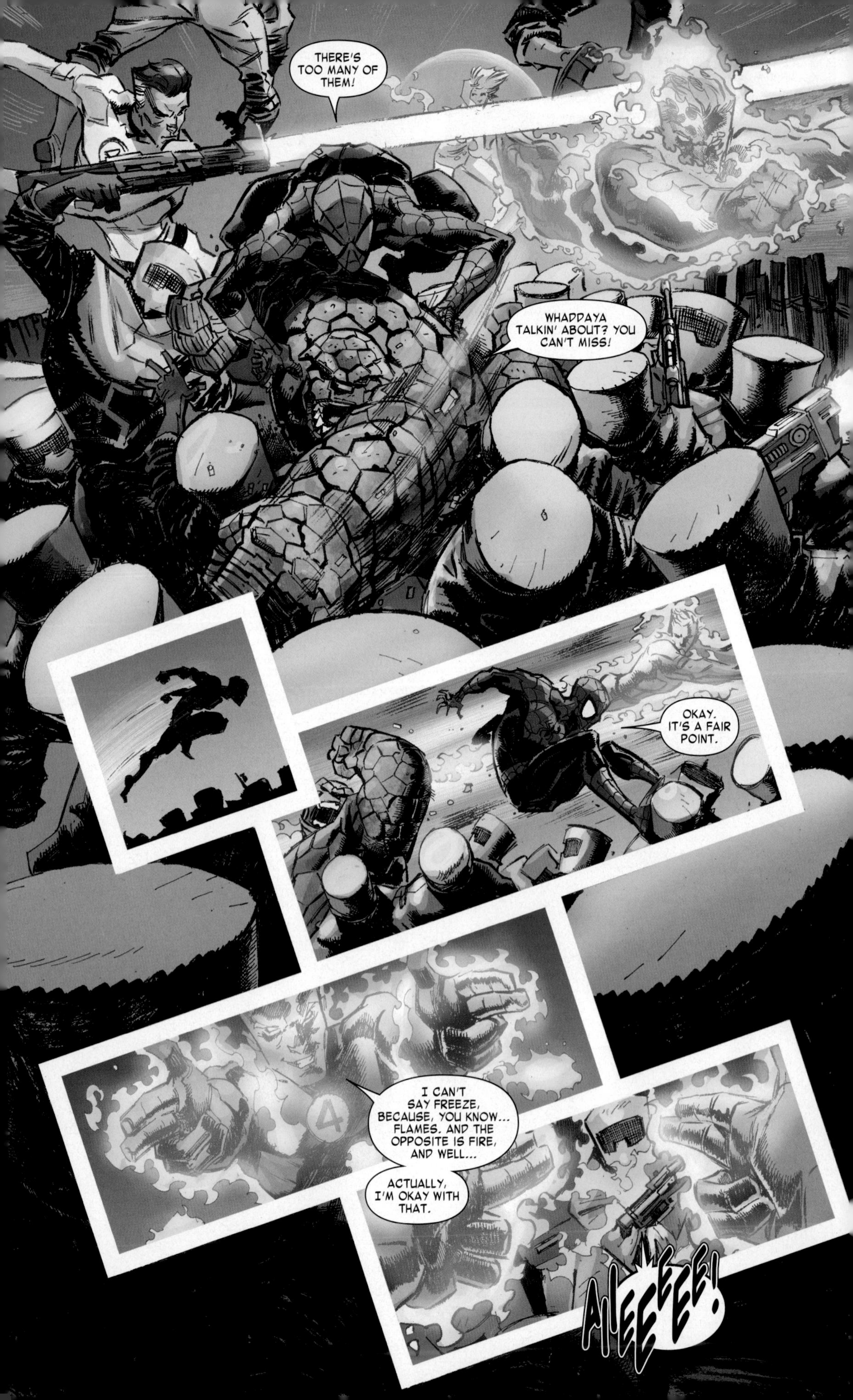
THERE'S TOO MANY OF THEM!
WHADDAYA TALKIN' ABOUT? YOU CAN'T MISS!
OKAY. IT'S A FAIR POINT.
I CAN'T SAY FREEZE, BECAUSE, YOU KNOW... FLAMES. AND THE OPPOSITE IS FIRE, AND WELL...
ACTUALLY, I'M OKAY WITH THAT.
AIEEEEE!

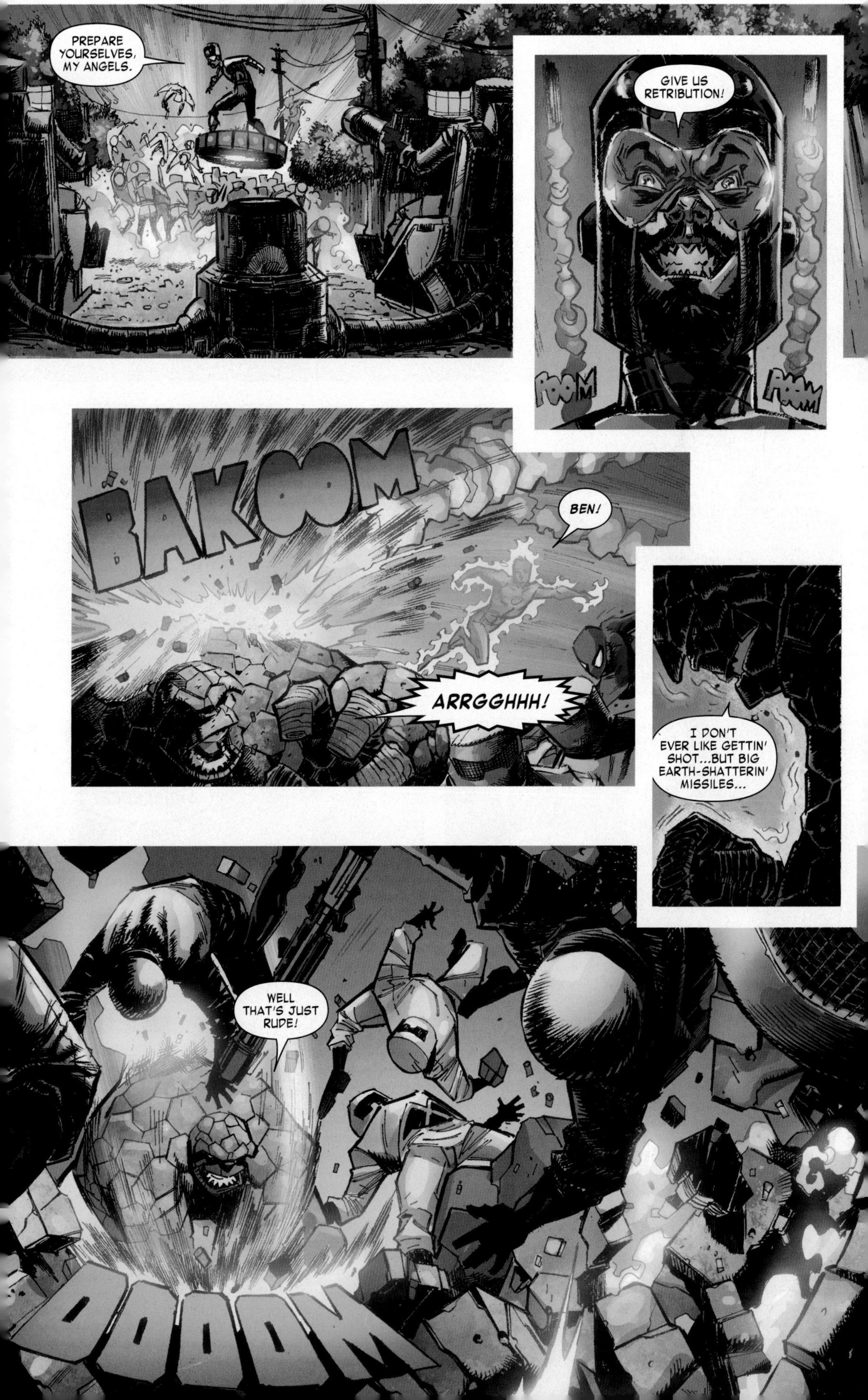
PREPARE YOURSELVES, MY ANGELS.
GIVE US RETRIBUTION!
POOM
POOM
BAKOOM
BEN!
ARRGGHHH!
I DON'T EVER LIKE GETTIN' SHOT...BUT BIG EARTH-SHATTERIN' MISSILES...
WELL THAT'S JUST RUDE!
DOOOM

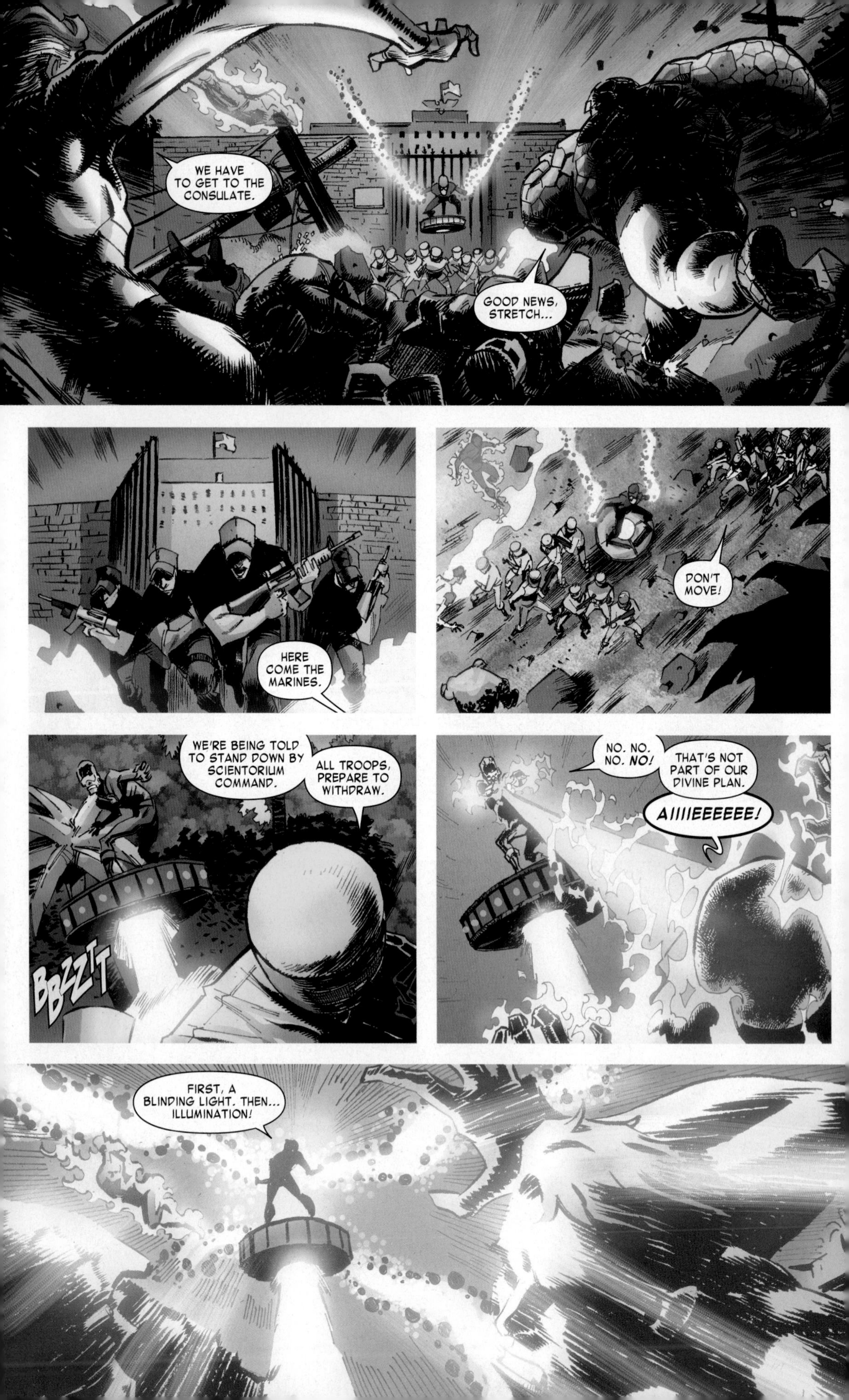
WE HAVE TO GET TO THE CONSULATE.
GOOD NEWS, STRETCH...
HERE COME THE MARINES.
DON'T MOVE!
WE'RE BEING TOLD TO STAND DOWN BY SCIENTORIUM COMMAND.
ALL TROOPS, PREPARE TO WITHDRAW.
BBZZTT
NO. NO. NO. NO!
THAT'S NOT PART OF OUR DIVINE PLAN.
AIIIIEEEEEE!
FIRST, A BLINDING LIGHT. THEN... ILLUMINATION!

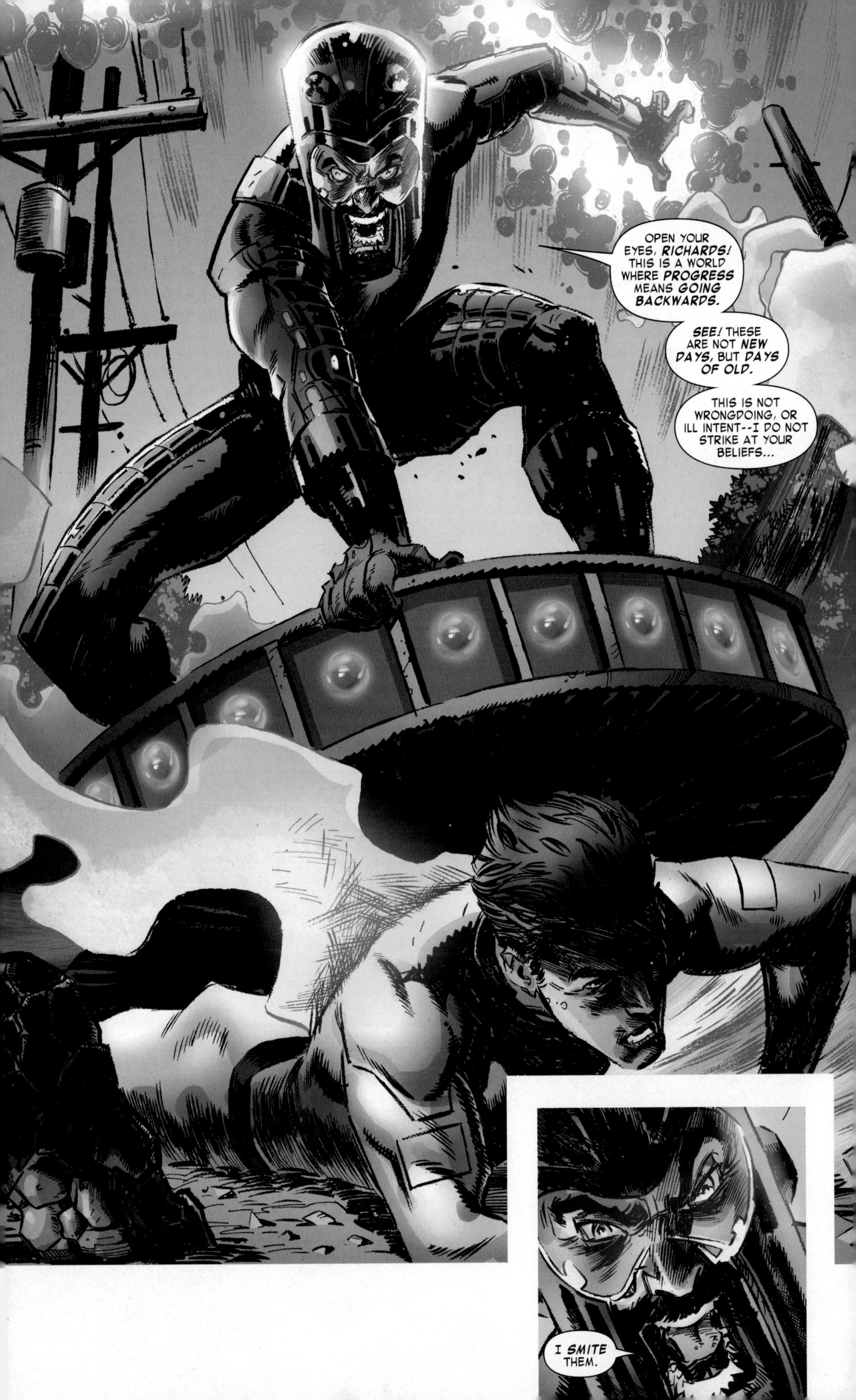
OPEN YOUR EYES, RICHARDS! THIS IS A WORLD WHERE PROGRESS MEANS GOING BACKWARDS.
SEE! THESE ARE NOT NEW DAYS, BUT DAYS OF OLD.
THIS IS NOT WRONGDOING, OR ILL INTENT--I DO NOT STRIKE AT YOUR BELIEFS...
I SMITE THEM.

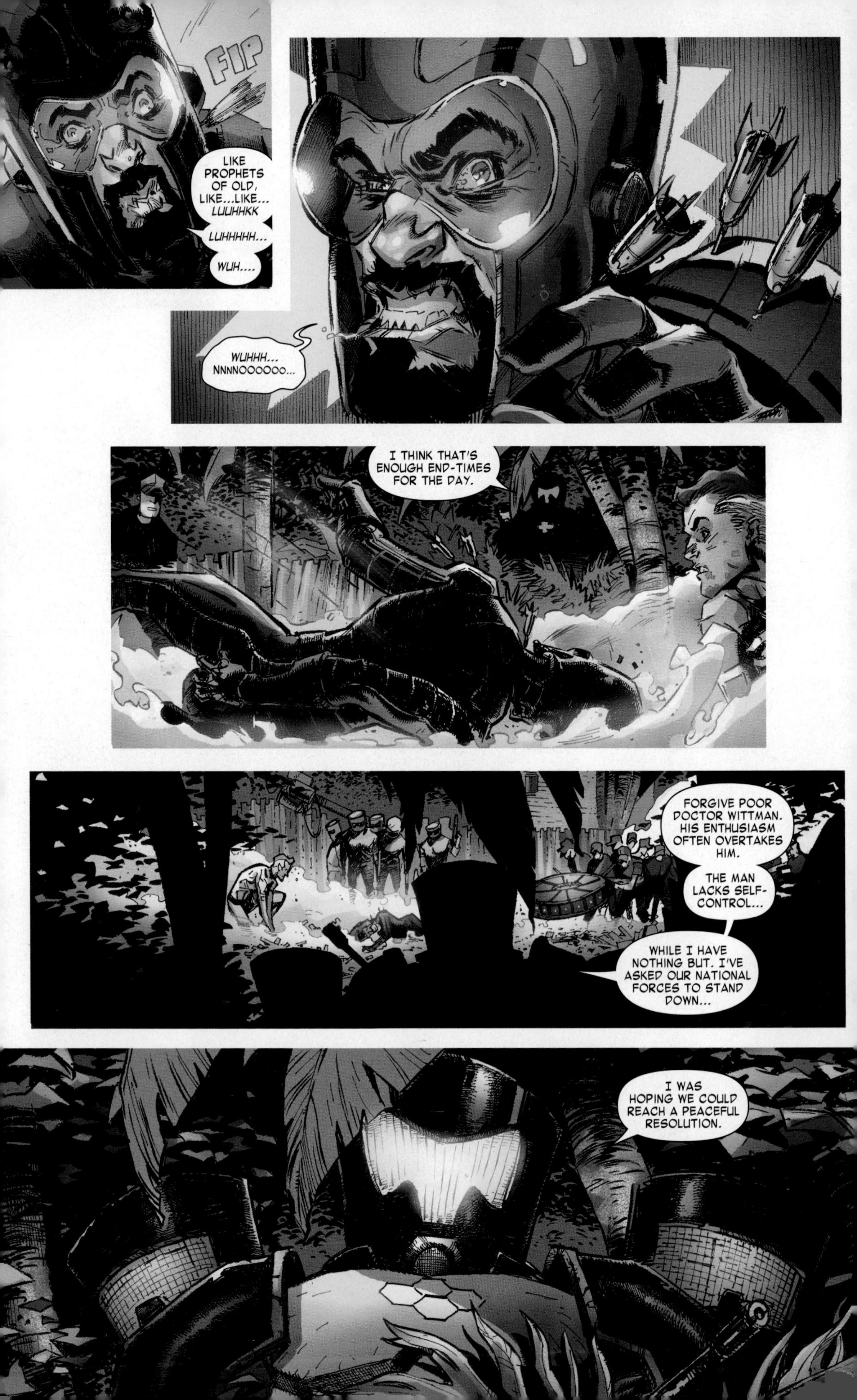
FIP
LIKE PROPHETS OF OLD, LIKE...LIKE... LUUHHKK
LUHHHHH...
WUH....
WUHHH... NNNNOOOOOO...
I THINK THAT'S ENOUGH END-TIMES FOR THE DAY.
FORGIVE POOR DOCTOR WITTMAN. HIS ENTHUSIASM OFTEN OVERTAKES HIM.
THE MAN LACKS SELF-CONTROL...
WHILE I HAVE NOTHING BUT. I'VE ASKED OUR NATIONAL FORCES TO STAND DOWN...
I WAS HOPING WE COULD REACH A PEACEFUL RESOLUTION.

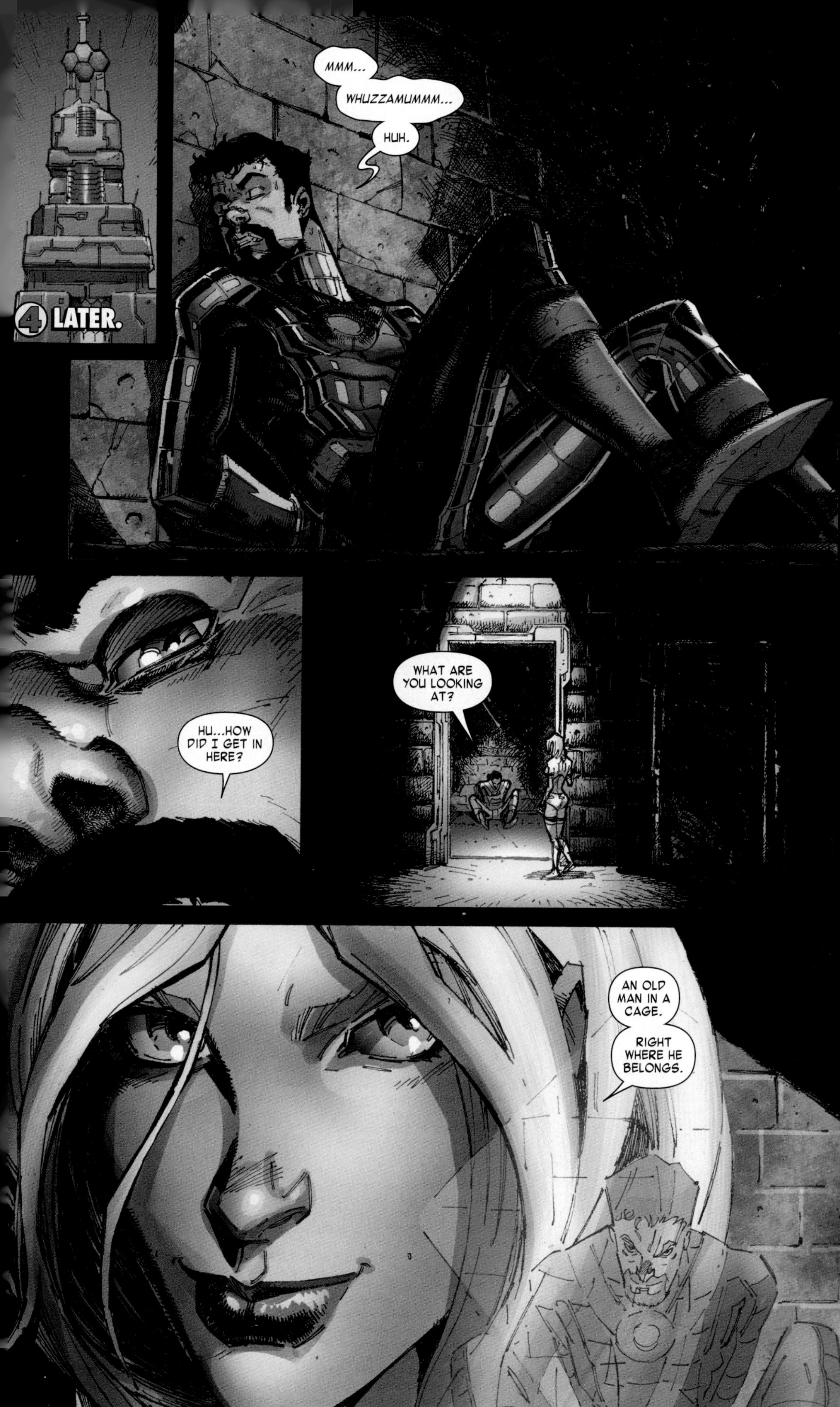
LATER.
MMM...
WHUZZAMUMMM...
HUH.
HU...HOW DID I GET IN HERE?
WHAT ARE YOU LOOKING AT?
AN OLD MAN IN A CAGE.
RIGHT WHERE HE BELONGS.

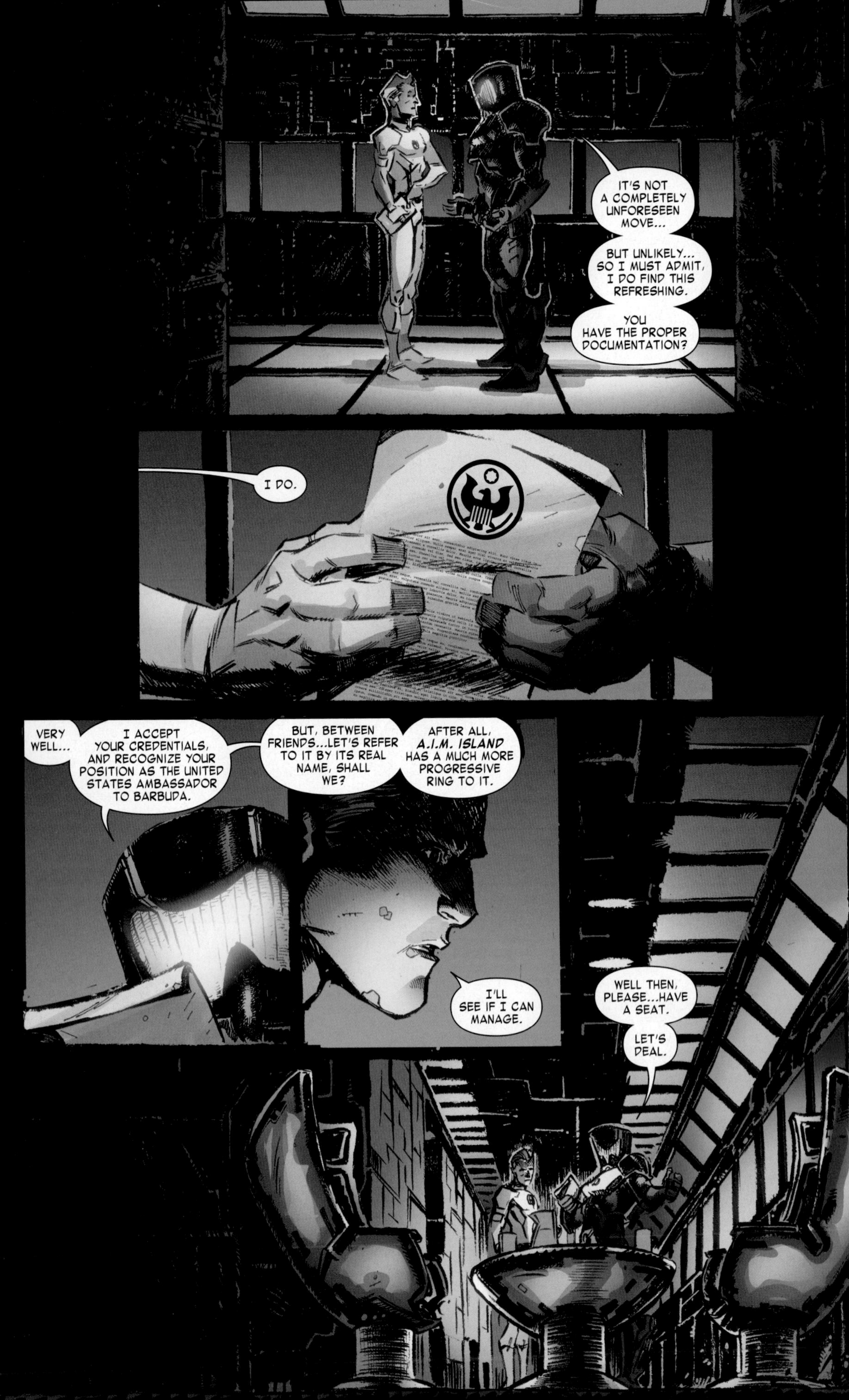
IT'S NOT A COMPLETELY UNFORESEEN MOVE...
BUT UNLIKELY... SO I MUST ADMIT, I DO FIND THIS REFRESHING.
YOU HAVE THE PROPER DOCUMENTATION?
I DO.
VERY WELL...
I ACCEPT YOUR CREDENTIALS, AND RECOGNIZE YOUR POSITION AS THE UNITED STATES AMBASSADOR TO BARBUDA.
BUT, BETWEEN FRIENDS...LET'S REFER TO IT BY ITS REAL NAME, SHALL WE?
AFTER ALL, *A.I.M. ISLAND* HAS A MUCH MORE PROGRESSIVE RING TO IT.
I'LL SEE IF I CAN MANAGE.
WELL THEN, PLEASE...HAVE A SEAT.
LET'S DEAL.

I'M JUST SAYING THAT THE SITUATION LEADS TO CERTAIN QUESTIONS BEING ASKED, AND THEN, ONCE ASKED, THE MIND BEGINS TO WANDER A BIT.

YOU KNOW, AT THE POSSIBILITIES.

FINE.

BUT I THINK THAT IT ONLY EXTENDS TO ACTUAL FAMILY MEMBERS.

SO IT WOULD ONLY AFFECT YOU, NOT BEN AND ME.

YEAH, AND I'M OKAY WITH THAT. SURE, YOU GUYS ARE SCREWED, BUT C'MON...

REALLY? YOU?

WE ALL KNOW THAT I'M THE ONE THAT'LL NEED IT THE MOST.

YOU'RE THE ONE WHO NEEDS IT MOST?

SERIOUSLY?

SPEEDING TICKETS, SPIDEY.

DIPLOMATIC IMMUNITY MEANS YOU DON'T HAVE TO PAY YOUR SPEEDING TICKETS.

HEY, CAN I ASK YOU GUYS SOMETHING?

UH-HUH.

SURE.

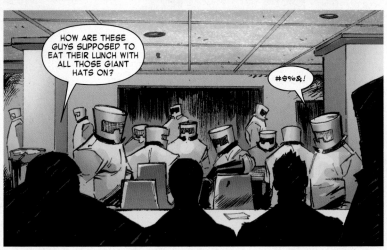

HOW ARE THESE GUYS SUPPOSED TO EAT THEIR LUNCH WITH ALL THOSE GIANT HATS ON?

#$%&!

UHHH, YEAH...

THIS IS BEEKEEPER 003. PLEASE TELL THE WATCH COMMANDER THAT, AH...

OUR COVER'S BEEN, UH, BLOWN.

BLOWN.

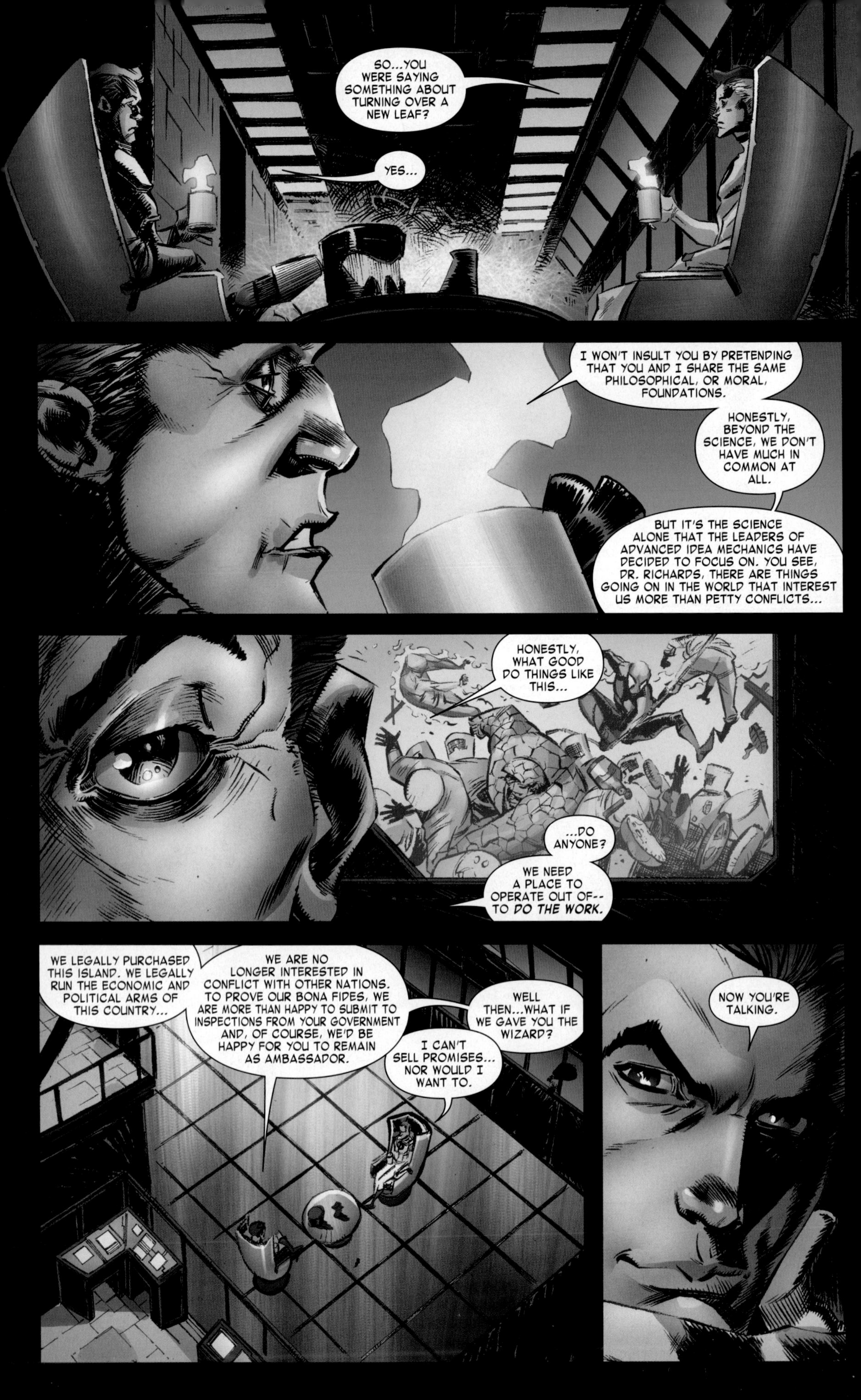
SO...YOU WERE SAYING SOMETHING ABOUT TURNING OVER A NEW LEAF?
YES...
I WON'T INSULT YOU BY PRETENDING THAT YOU AND I SHARE THE SAME PHILOSOPHICAL, OR MORAL, FOUNDATIONS.
HONESTLY, BEYOND THE SCIENCE, WE DON'T HAVE MUCH IN COMMON AT ALL.
BUT IT'S THE SCIENCE ALONE THAT THE LEADERS OF ADVANCED IDEA MECHANICS HAVE DECIDED TO FOCUS ON. YOU SEE, DR. RICHARDS, THERE ARE THINGS GOING ON IN THE WORLD THAT INTEREST US MORE THAN PETTY CONFLICTS...
HONESTLY, WHAT GOOD DO THINGS LIKE THIS...
...DO ANYONE?
WE NEED A PLACE TO OPERATE OUT OF--TO *DO THE WORK.*
WE LEGALLY PURCHASED THIS ISLAND. WE LEGALLY RUN THE ECONOMIC AND POLITICAL ARMS OF THIS COUNTRY...
WE ARE NO LONGER INTERESTED IN CONFLICT WITH OTHER NATIONS. TO PROVE OUR BONA FIDES, WE ARE MORE THAN HAPPY TO SUBMIT TO INSPECTIONS FROM YOUR GOVERNMENT AND, OF COURSE, WE'D BE HAPPY FOR YOU TO REMAIN AS AMBASSADOR.
WELL THEN...WHAT IF WE GAVE YOU THE WIZARD?
I CAN'T SELL PROMISES... NOR WOULD I WANT TO.
NOW YOU'RE TALKING.

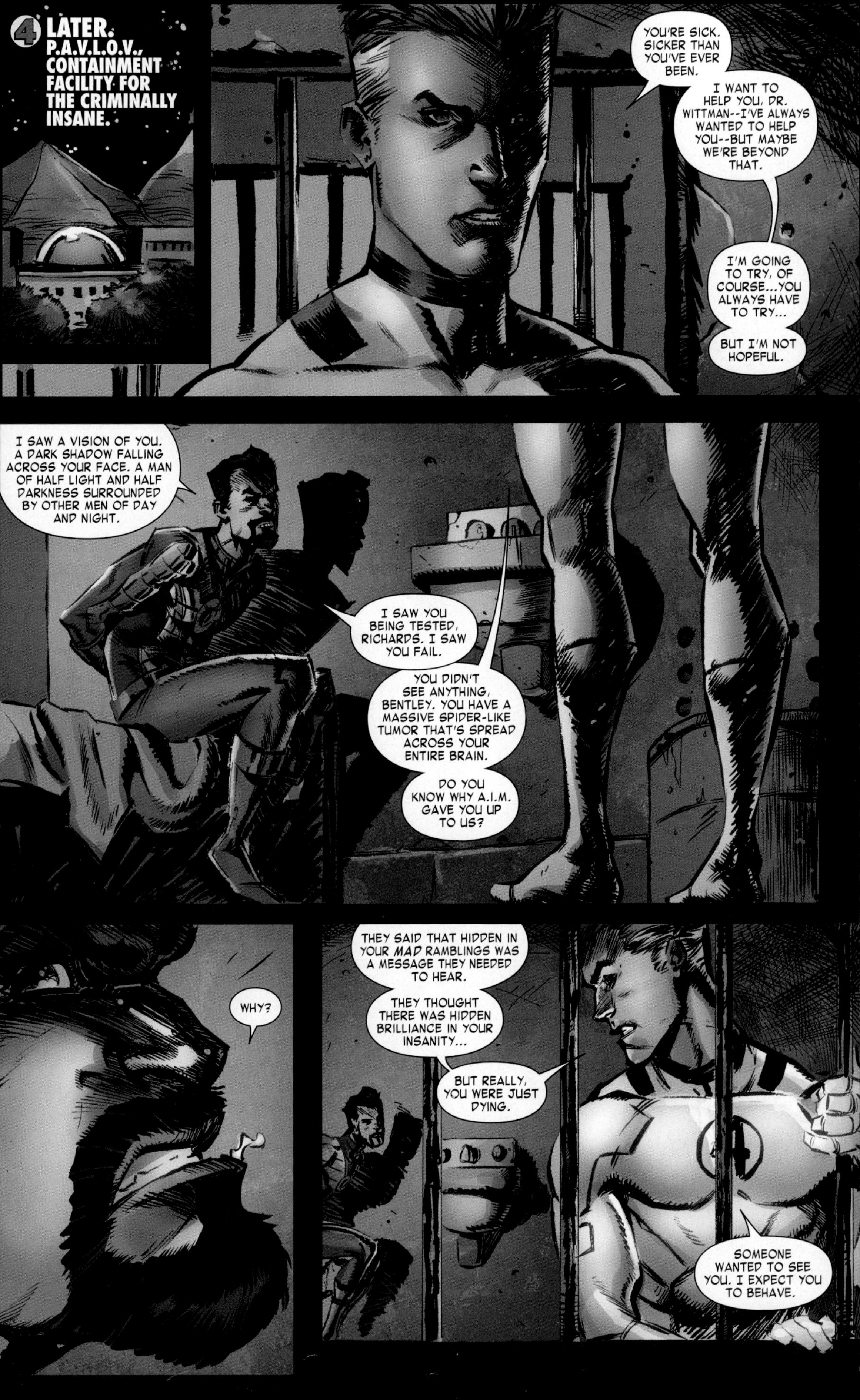

LATER. P.A.V.L.O.V., CONTAINMENT FACILITY FOR THE CRIMINALLY INSANE.
YOU'RE SICK. SICKER THAN YOU'VE EVER BEEN.
I WANT TO HELP YOU, DR. WITTMAN--I'VE ALWAYS WANTED TO HELP YOU--BUT MAYBE WE'RE BEYOND THAT.
I'M GOING TO TRY, OF COURSE...YOU ALWAYS HAVE TO TRY...
BUT I'M NOT HOPEFUL.
I SAW A VISION OF YOU. A DARK SHADOW FALLING ACROSS YOUR FACE. A MAN OF HALF LIGHT AND HALF DARKNESS SURROUNDED BY OTHER MEN OF DAY AND NIGHT.
I SAW YOU BEING TESTED, RICHARDS. I SAW YOU FAIL.
YOU DIDN'T SEE ANYTHING, BENTLEY. YOU HAVE A MASSIVE SPIDER-LIKE TUMOR THAT'S SPREAD ACROSS YOUR ENTIRE BRAIN.
DO YOU KNOW WHY A.I.M. GAVE YOU UP TO US?
WHY?
THEY SAID THAT HIDDEN IN YOUR *MAD* RAMBLINGS WAS A MESSAGE THEY NEEDED TO HEAR.
THEY THOUGHT THERE WAS HIDDEN BRILLIANCE IN YOUR INSANITY...
BUT REALLY, YOU WERE JUST DYING.
SOMEONE WANTED TO SEE YOU. I EXPECT YOU TO BEHAVE.

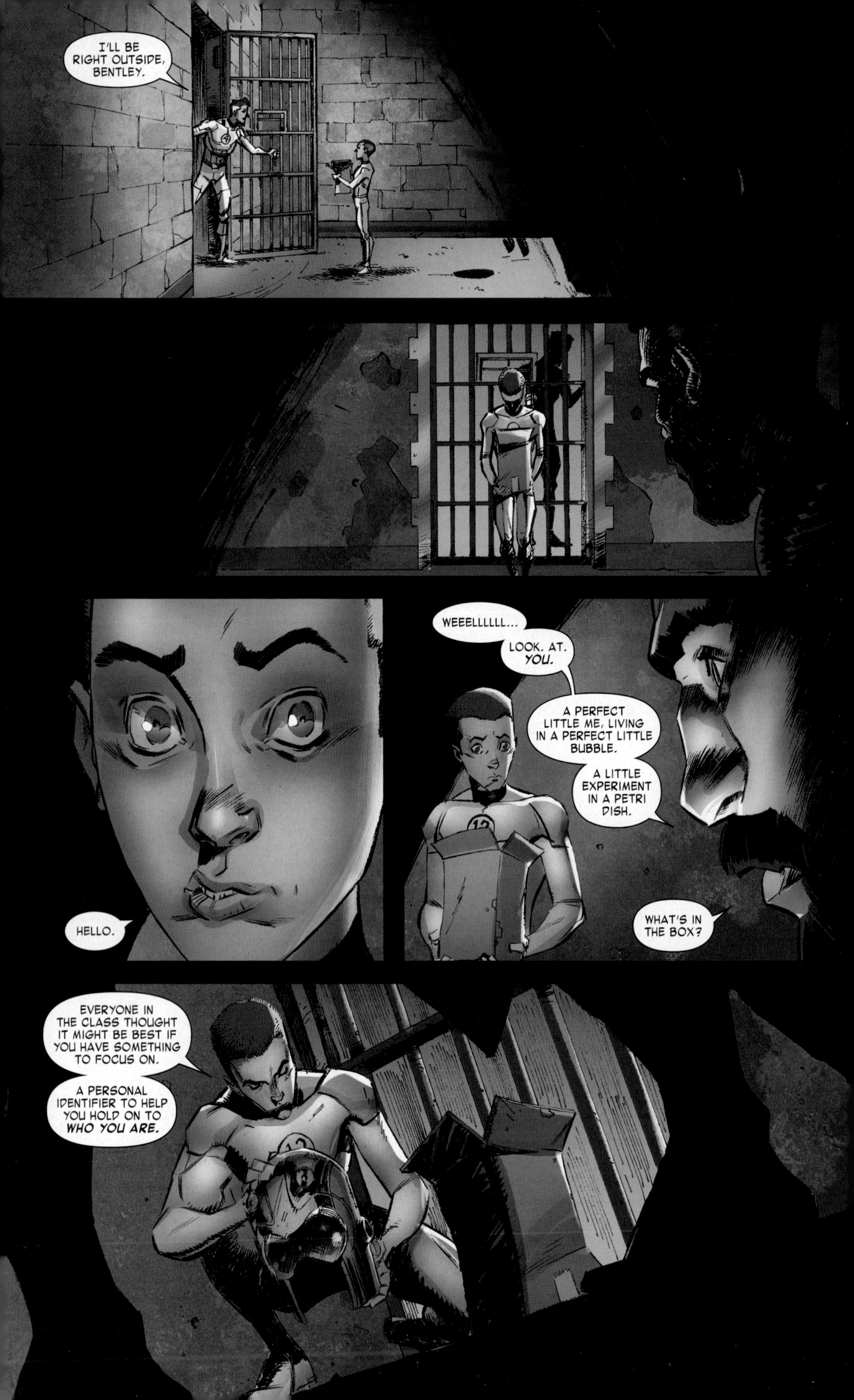
I'LL BE RIGHT OUTSIDE, BENTLEY.
HELLO.
WEEELLLLLL...
LOOK. AT. *YOU.*
A PERFECT LITTLE ME, LIVING IN A PERFECT LITTLE BUBBLE.
A LITTLE EXPERIMENT IN A PETRI DISH.
WHAT'S IN THE BOX?
EVERYONE IN THE CLASS THOUGHT IT MIGHT BE BEST IF YOU HAVE SOMETHING TO FOCUS ON.
A PERSONAL IDENTIFIER TO HELP YOU HOLD ON TO *WHO YOU ARE.*

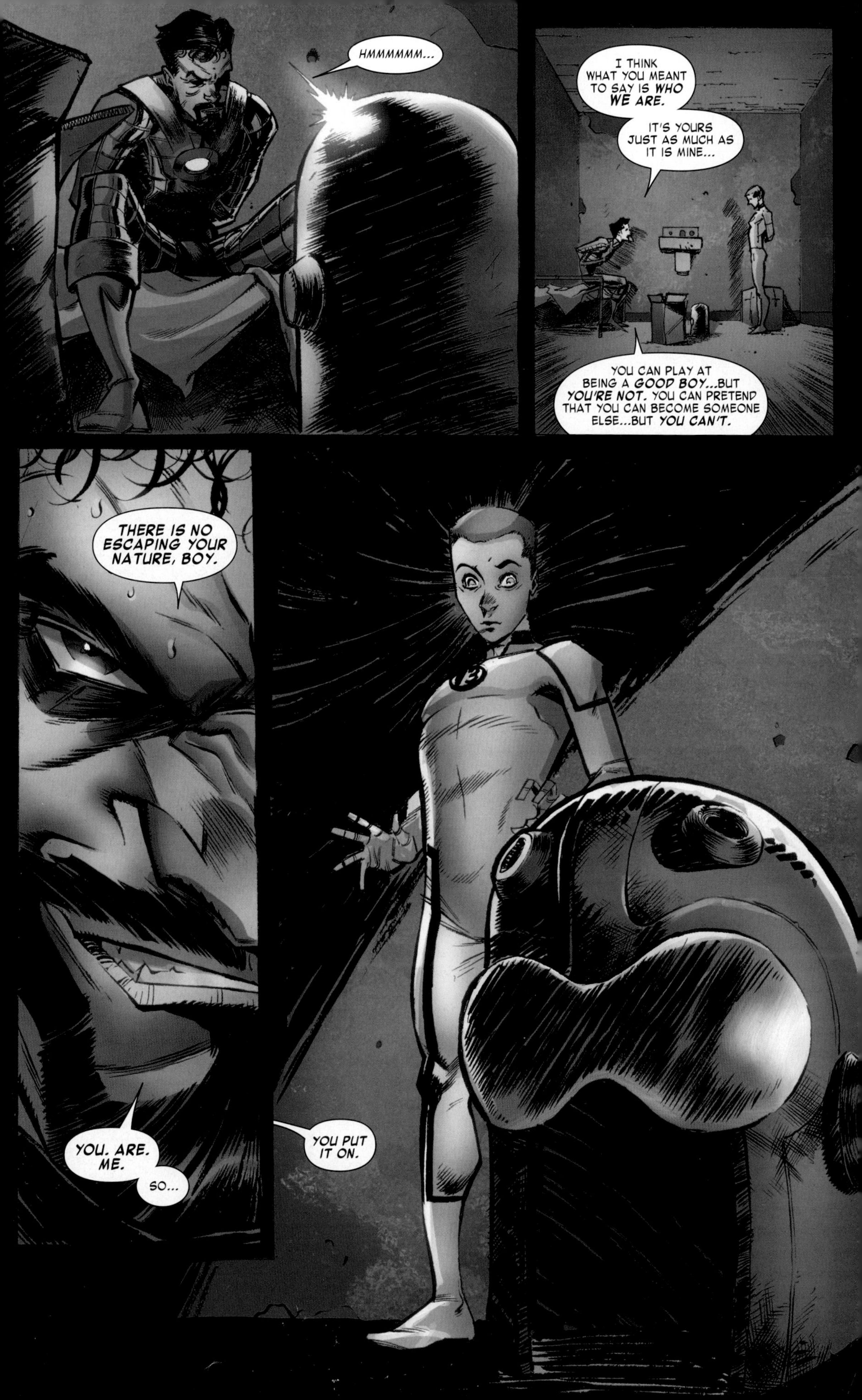
HMMMMMM...
I THINK WHAT YOU MEANT TO SAY IS WHO WE ARE.
IT'S YOURS JUST AS MUCH AS IT IS MINE...
YOU CAN PLAY AT BEING A GOOD BOY...BUT YOU'RE NOT. YOU CAN PRETEND THAT YOU CAN BECOME SOMEONE ELSE...BUT YOU CAN'T.
THERE IS NO ESCAPING YOUR NATURE, BOY.
YOU. ARE. ME.
SO...
YOU PUT IT ON.

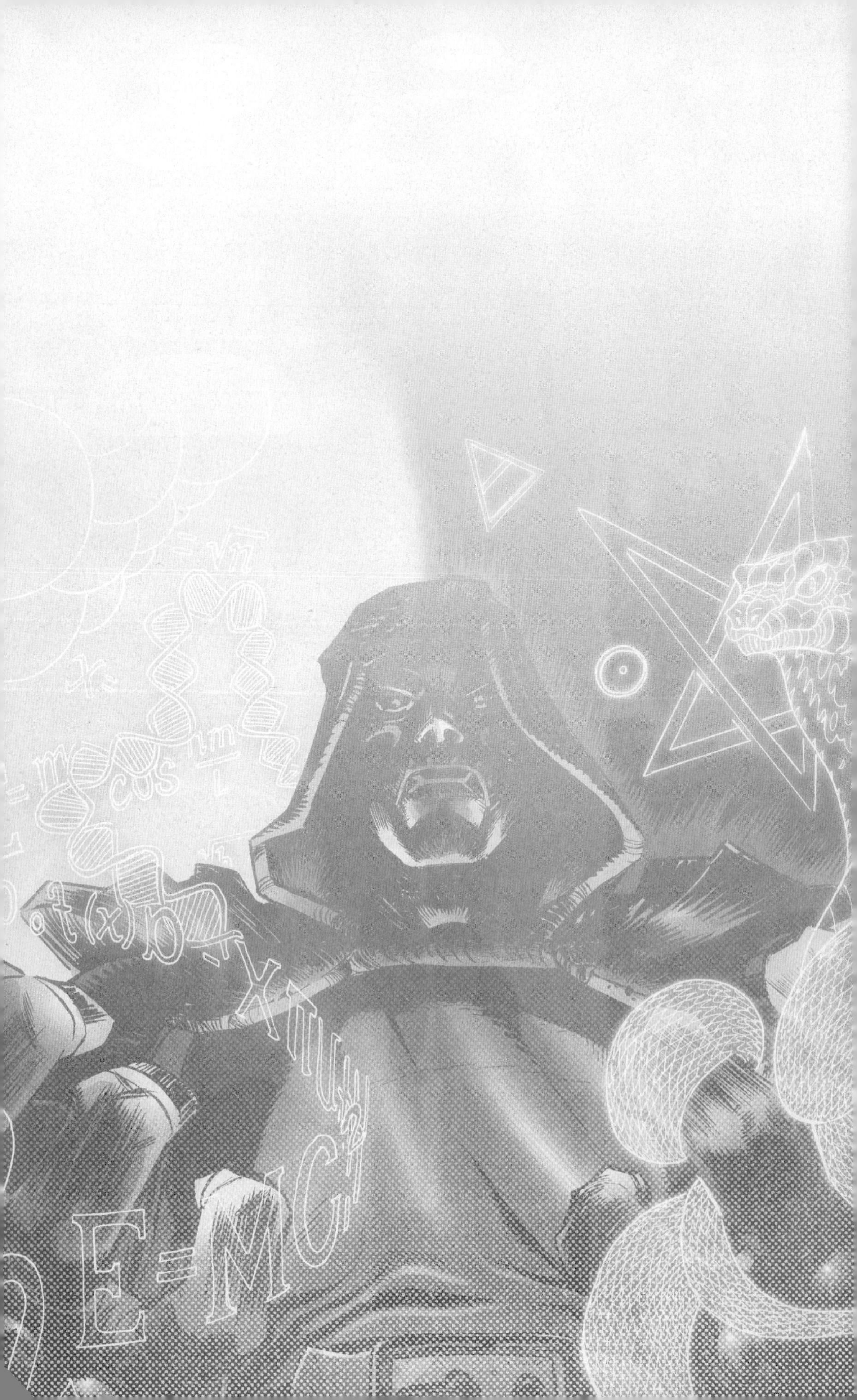

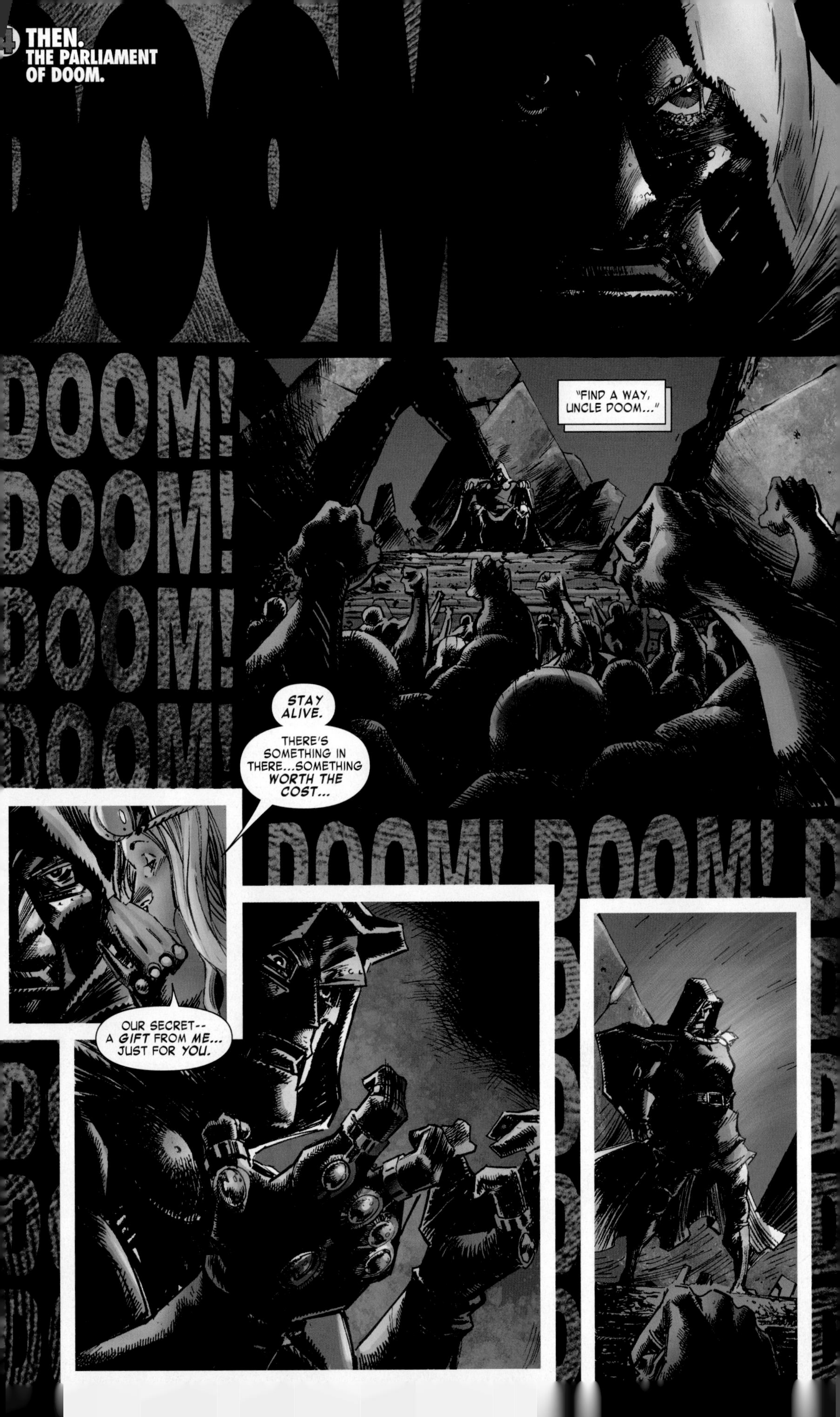
THEN. THE PARLIAMENT OF DOOM.
DOOM!
DOOM! DOOM! DOOM! DOOM!
"FIND A WAY, UNCLE DOOM..."
STAY ALIVE.
THERE'S SOMETHING IN THERE...SOMETHING WORTH THE COST...
DOOM! DOOM!
OUR SECRET-- A GIFT FROM ME... JUST FOR YOU.

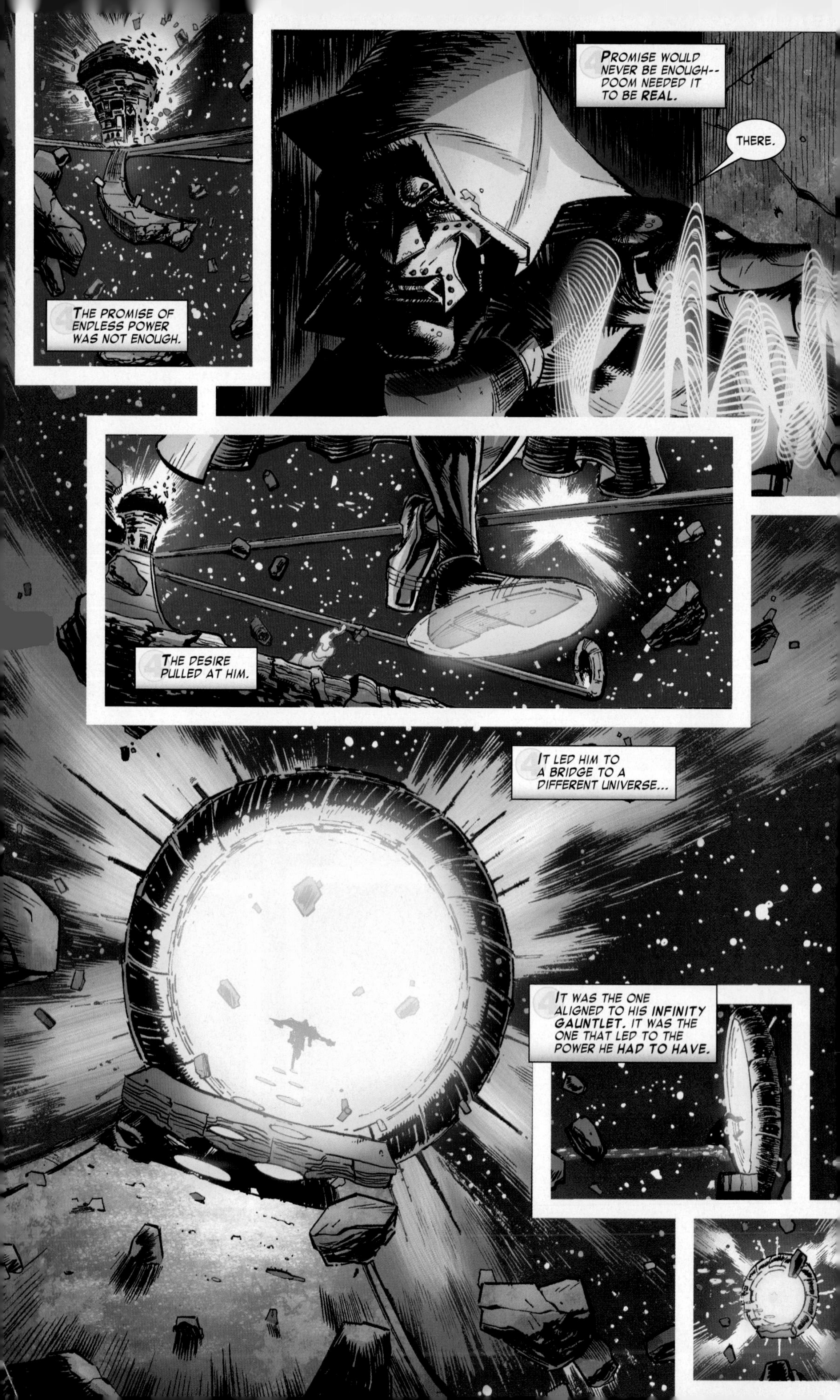
THE PROMISE OF ENDLESS POWER WAS NOT ENOUGH.
PROMISE WOULD NEVER BE ENOUGH-- DOOM NEEDED IT TO BE REAL.
THERE.
THE DESIRE PULLED AT HIM.
IT LED HIM TO A BRIDGE TO A DIFFERENT UNIVERSE...
IT WAS THE ONE ALIGNED TO HIS INFINITY GAUNTLET. IT WAS THE ONE THAT LED TO THE POWER HE HAD TO HAVE.

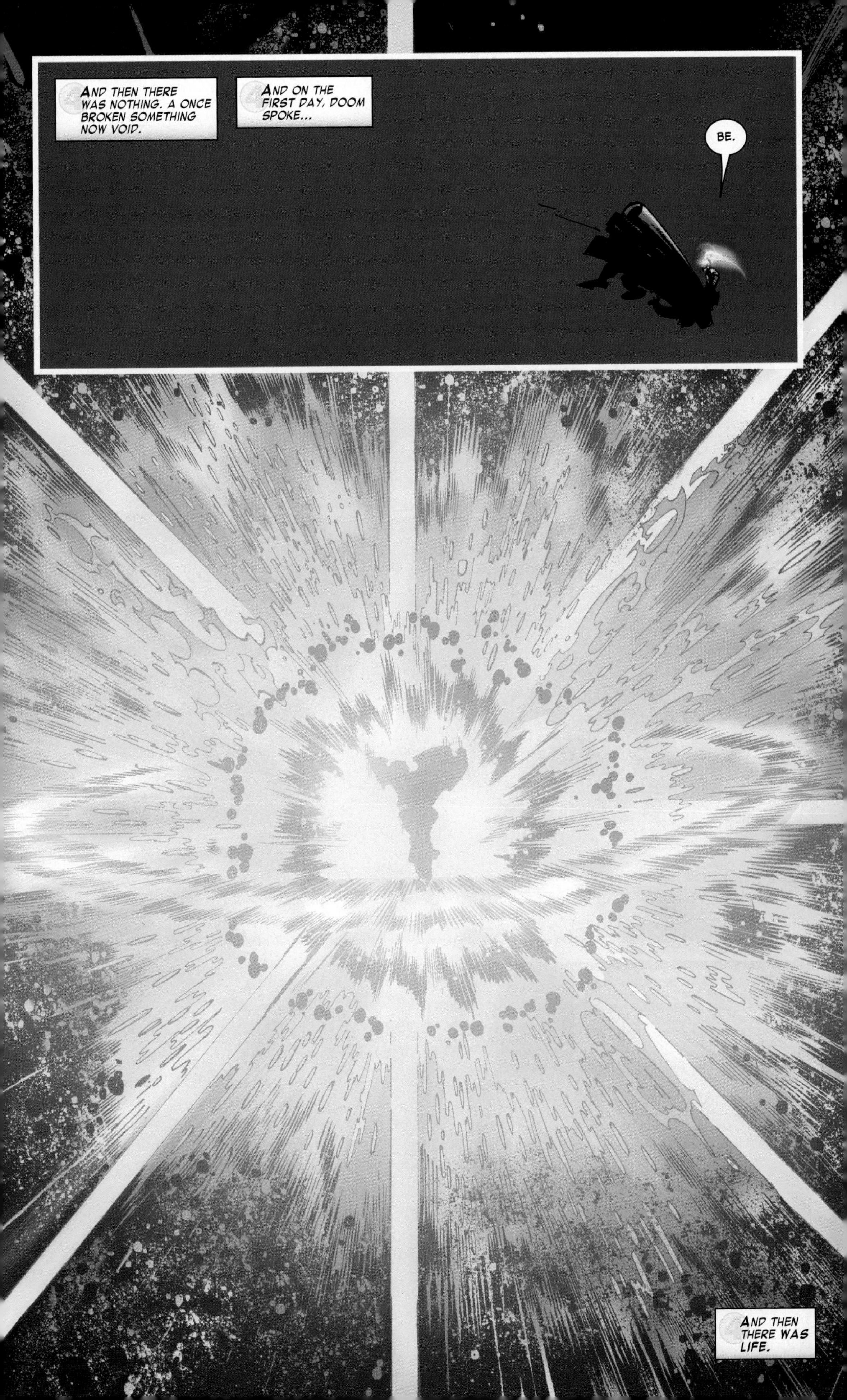

AND THEN THERE WAS NOTHING. A ONCE BROKEN SOMETHING NOW VOID.
AND ON THE FIRST DAY, DOOM SPOKE...
BE.
AND THEN THERE WAS LIFE.

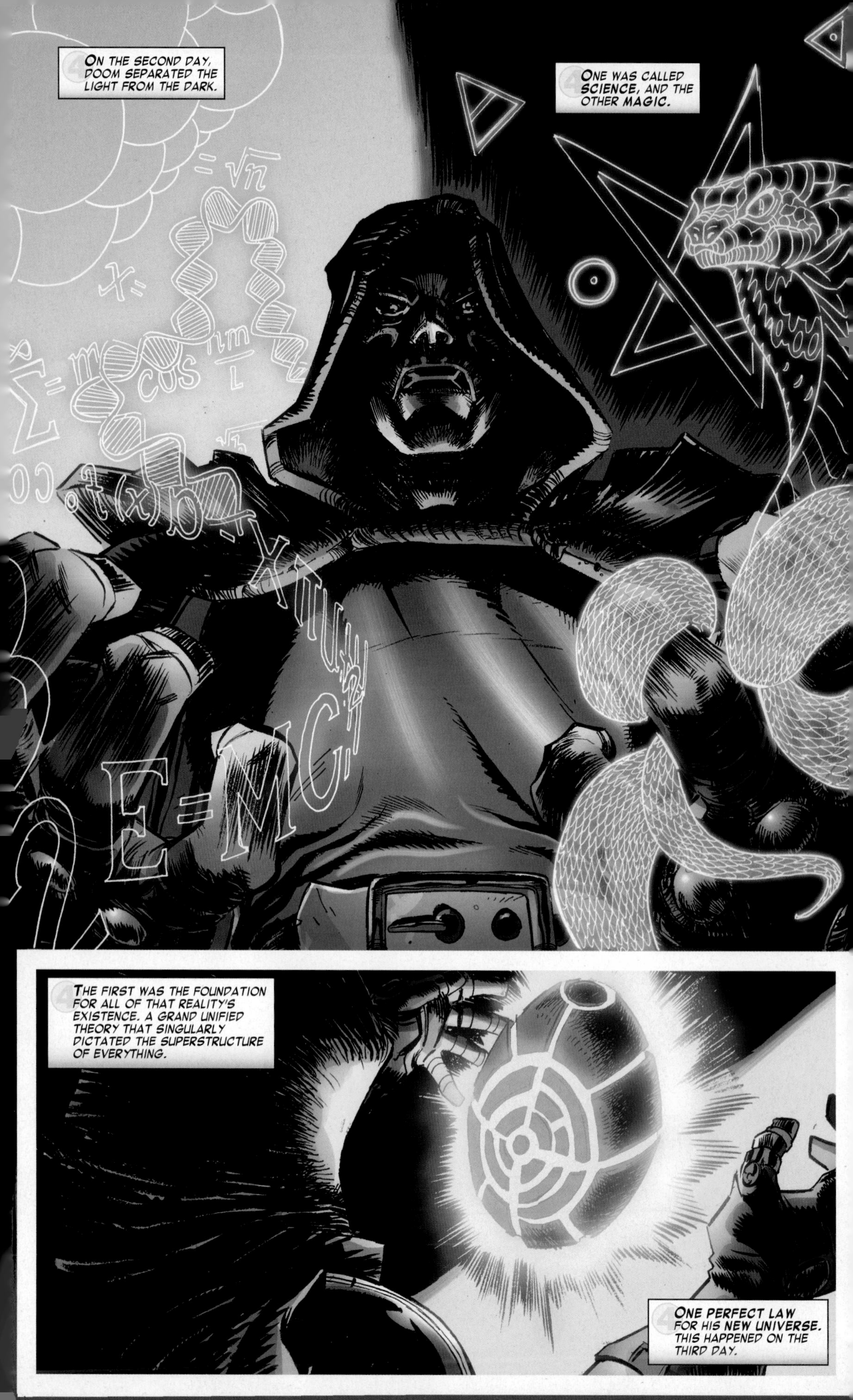
ON THE SECOND DAY, DOOM SEPARATED THE LIGHT FROM THE DARK.
ONE WAS CALLED SCIENCE, AND THE OTHER MAGIC.
THE FIRST WAS THE FOUNDATION FOR ALL OF THAT REALITY'S EXISTENCE. A GRAND UNIFIED THEORY THAT SINGULARLY DICTATED THE SUPERSTRUCTURE OF EVERYTHING.
ONE PERFECT LAW FOR HIS NEW UNIVERSE. THIS HAPPENED ON THE THIRD DAY.

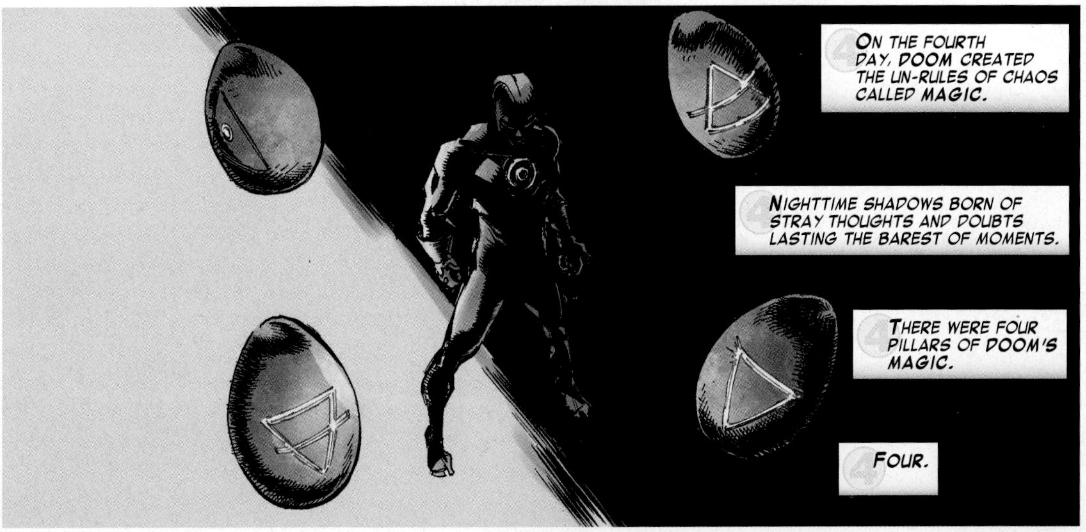
ON THE FOURTH DAY, DOOM CREATED THE UN-RULES OF CHAOS CALLED MAGIC.
NIGHTTIME SHADOWS BORN OF STRAY THOUGHTS AND DOUBTS LASTING THE BAREST OF MOMENTS.
THERE WERE FOUR PILLARS OF DOOM'S MAGIC.
FOUR.

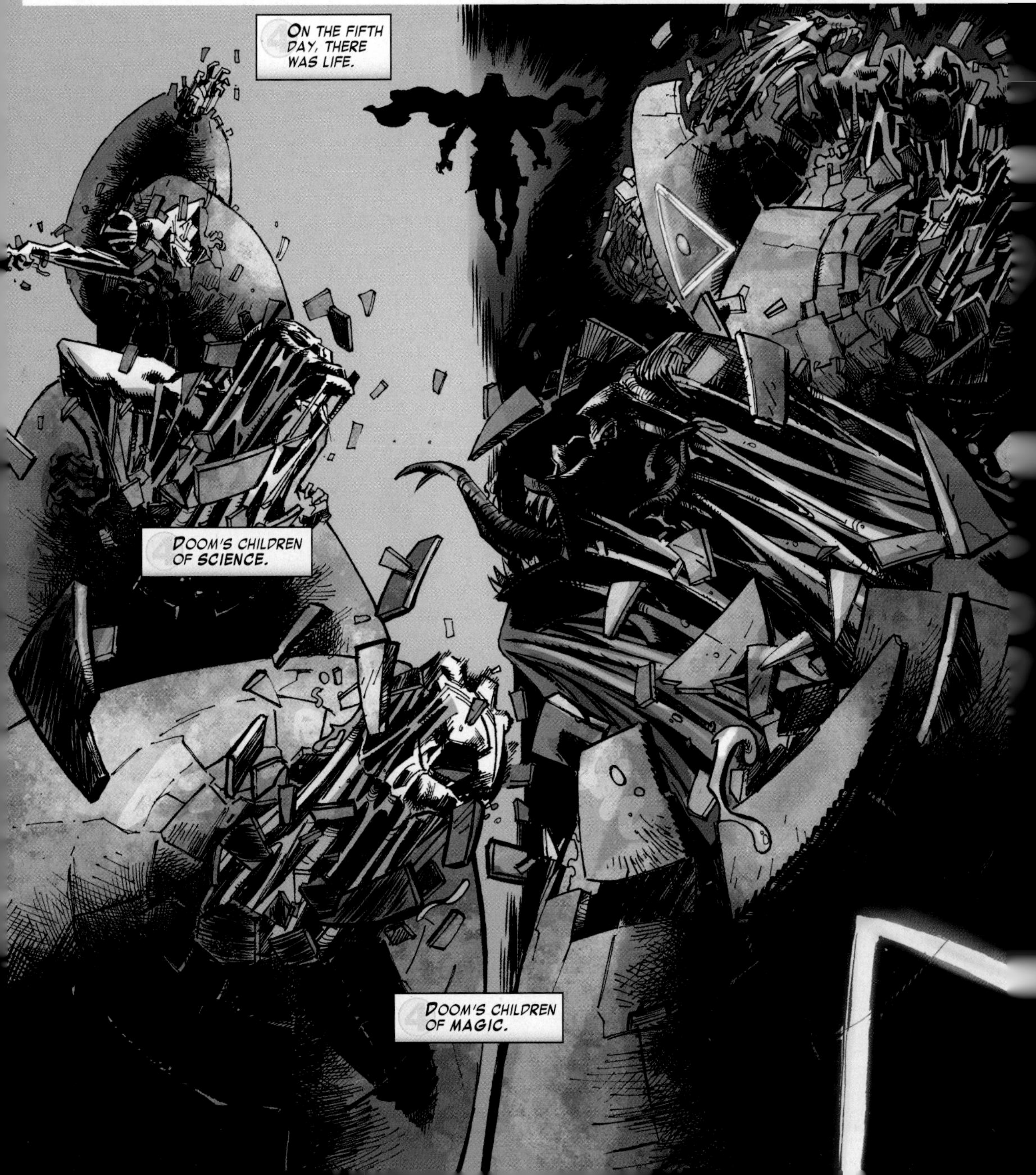
ON THE FIFTH DAY, THERE WAS LIFE.
DOOM'S CHILDREN OF SCIENCE.
DOOM'S CHILDREN OF MAGIC.

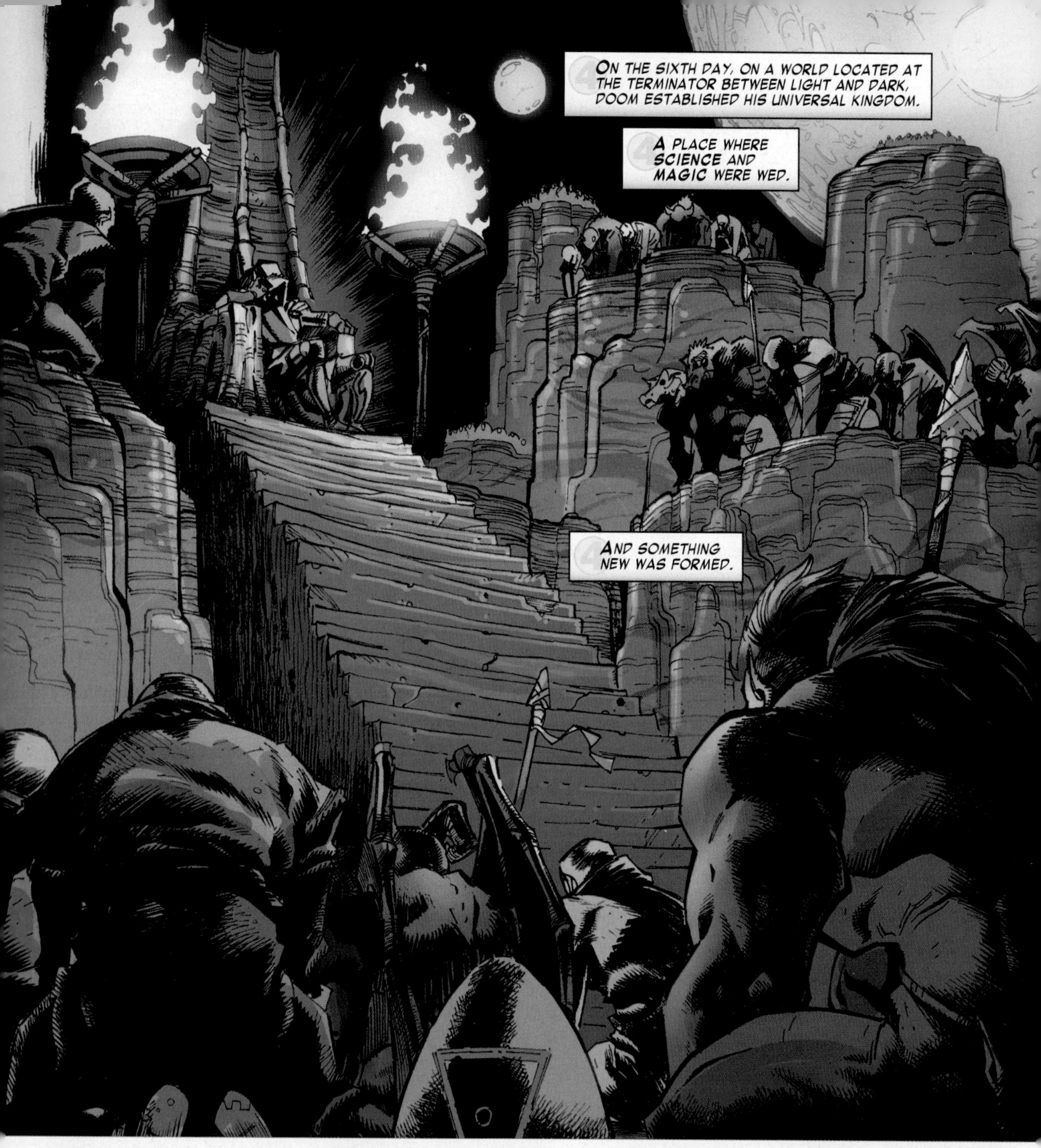
ON THE SIXTH DAY, ON A WORLD LOCATED AT THE TERMINATOR BETWEEN LIGHT AND DARK, DOOM ESTABLISHED HIS UNIVERSAL KINGDOM.
A PLACE WHERE SCIENCE AND MAGIC WERE WED.
AND SOMETHING NEW WAS FORMED.

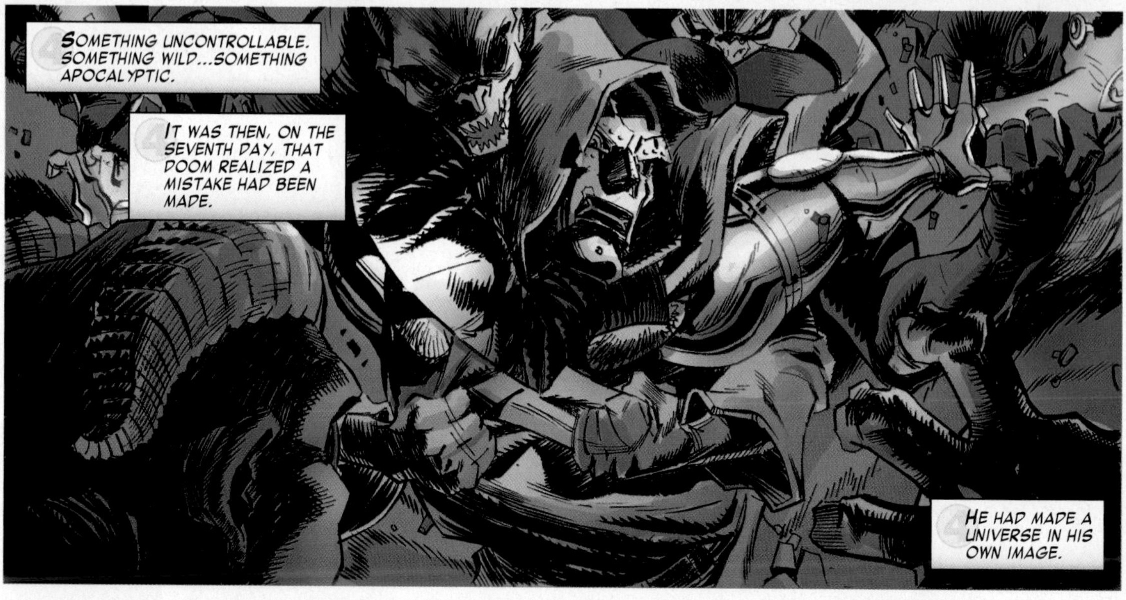
SOMETHING UNCONTROLLABLE. SOMETHING WILD...SOMETHING APOCALYPTIC.
IT WAS THEN, ON THE SEVENTH DAY, THAT DOOM REALIZED A MISTAKE HAD BEEN MADE.
HE HAD MADE A UNIVERSE IN HIS OWN IMAGE.

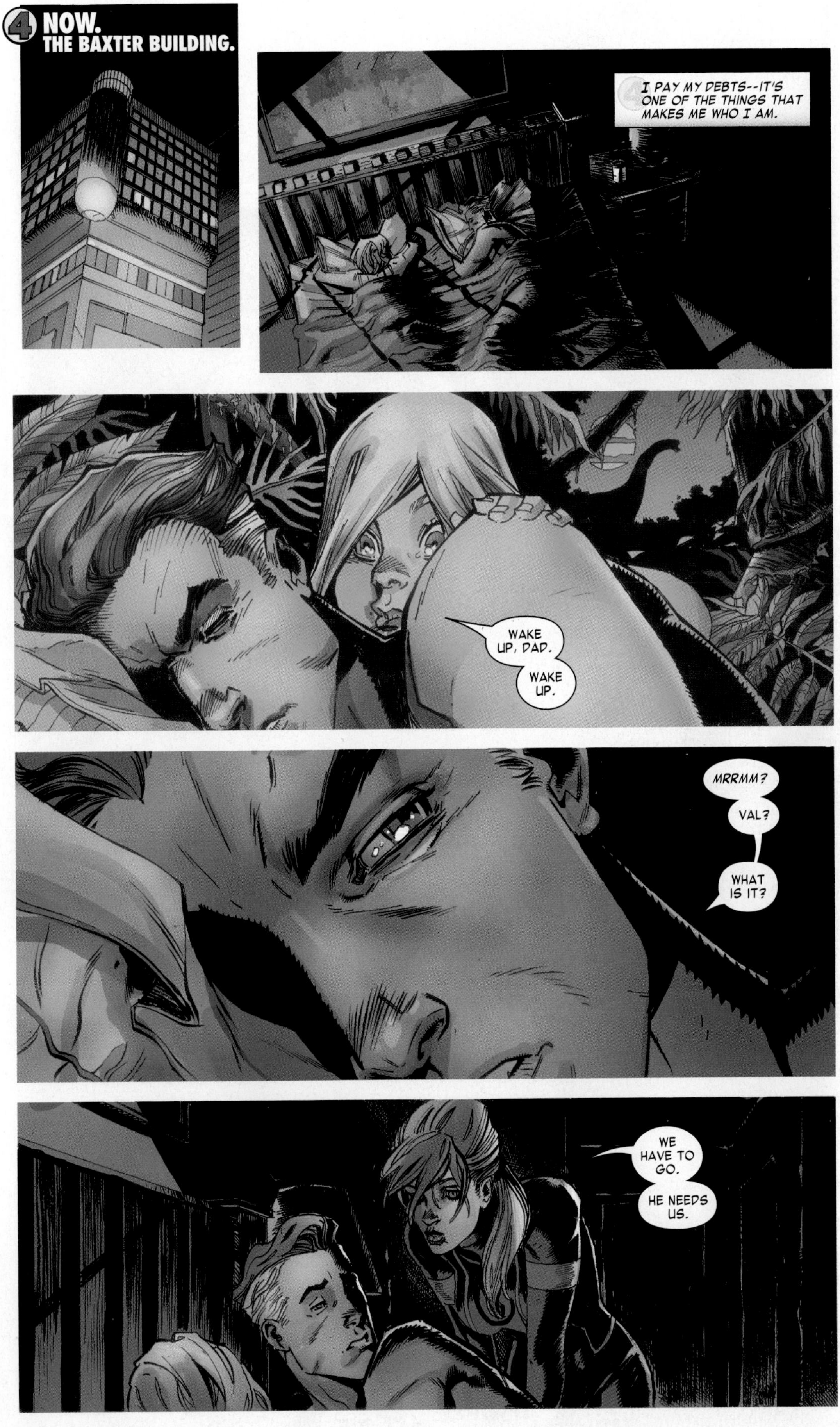
NOW.
THE BAXTER BUILDING.
I PAY MY DEBTS--IT'S ONE OF THE THINGS THAT MAKES ME WHO I AM.
WAKE UP, DAD.
WAKE UP.
MRRMM?
VAL?
WHAT IS IT?
WE HAVE TO GO.
HE NEEDS US.

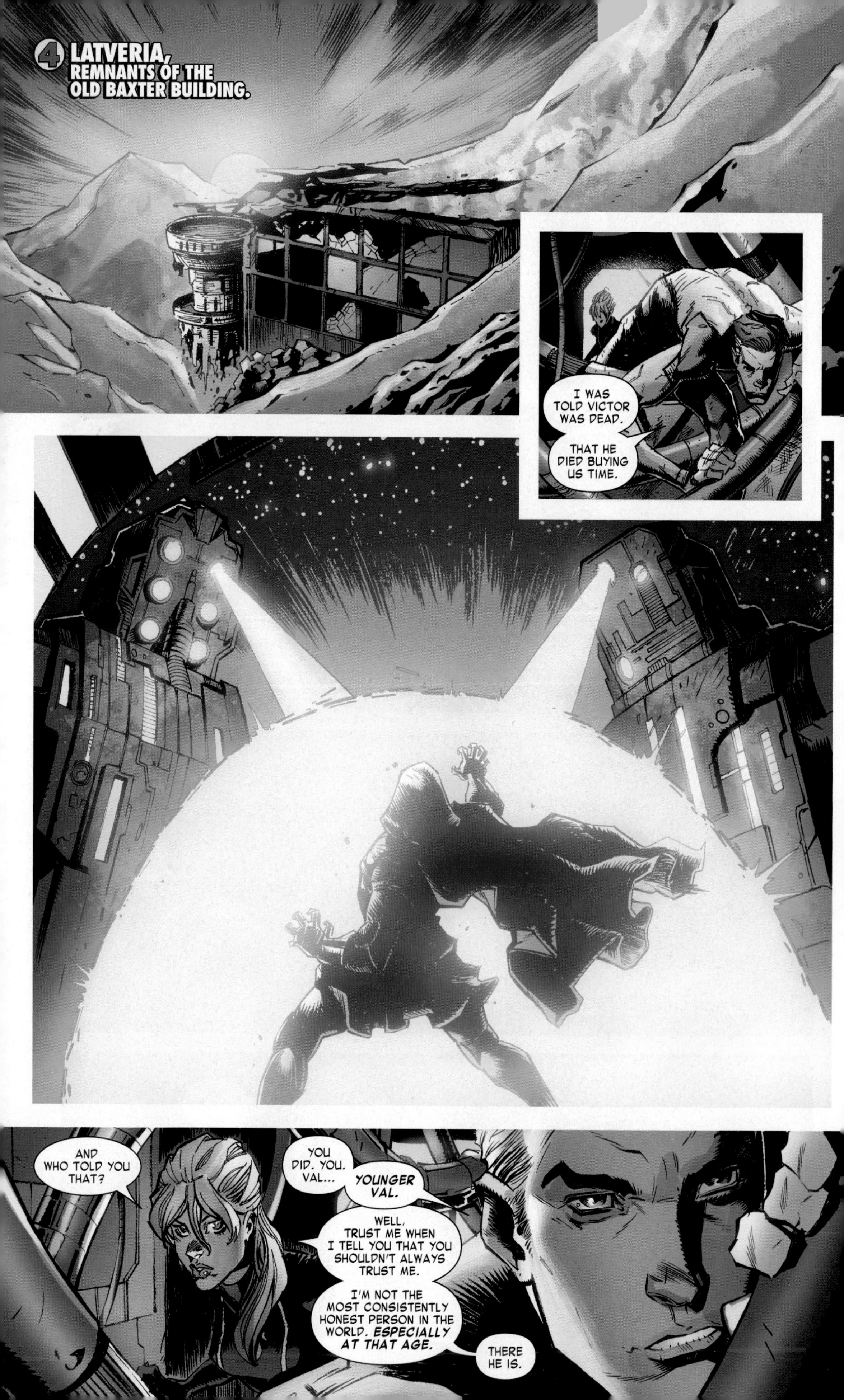
LATVERIA, REMNANTS OF THE OLD BAXTER BUILDING.
I WAS TOLD VICTOR WAS DEAD.
THAT HE DIED BUYING US TIME.
AND WHO TOLD YOU THAT?
YOU DID. YOU. VAL...
YOUNGER VAL.
WELL, TRUST ME WHEN I TELL YOU THAT YOU SHOULDN'T ALWAYS TRUST ME.
I'M NOT THE MOST CONSISTENTLY HONEST PERSON IN THE WORLD. ESPECIALLY AT THAT AGE.
THERE HE IS.

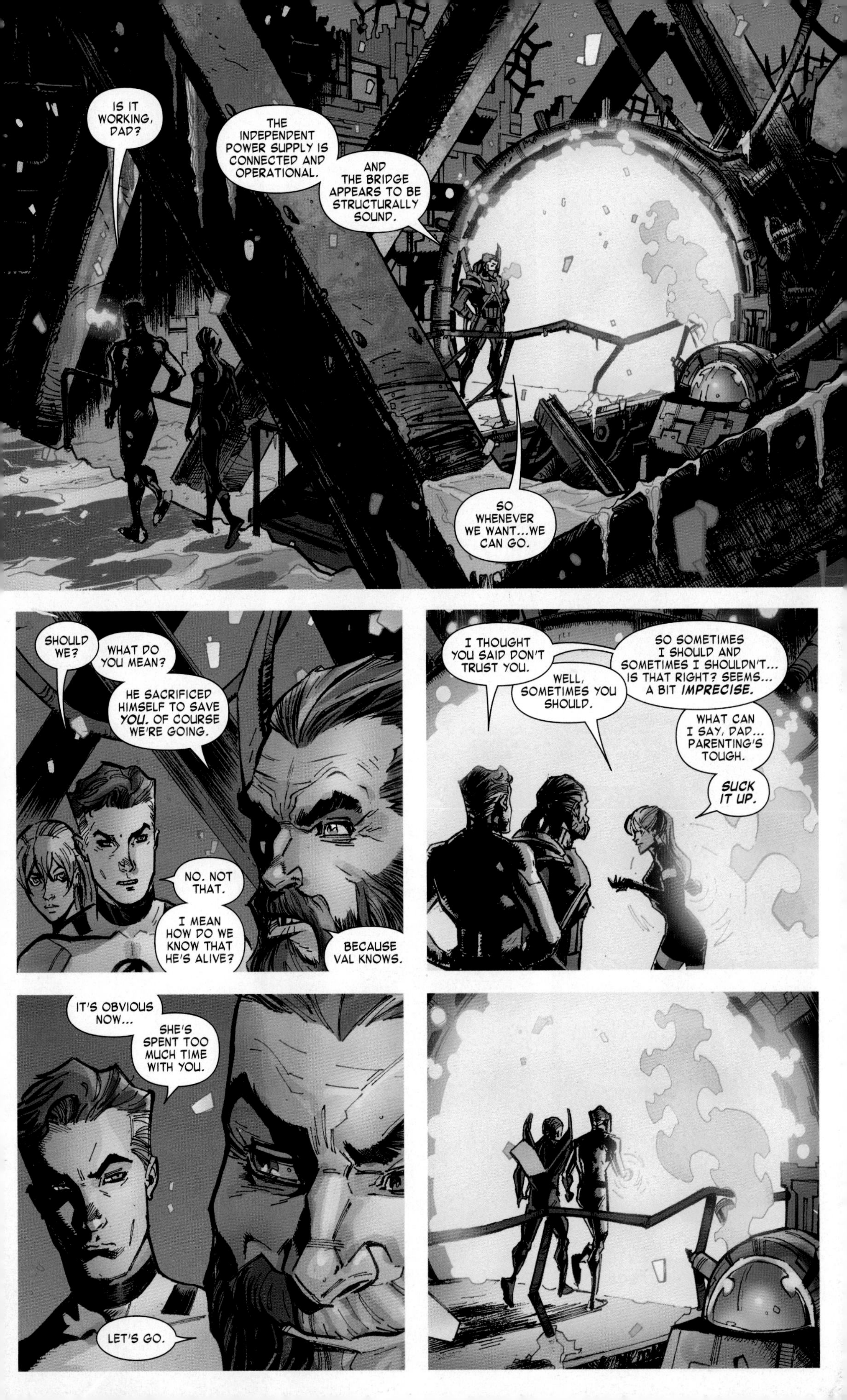
IS IT WORKING, DAD?
THE INDEPENDENT POWER SUPPLY IS CONNECTED AND OPERATIONAL.
AND THE BRIDGE APPEARS TO BE STRUCTURALLY SOUND.
SO WHENEVER WE WANT...WE CAN GO.
SHOULD WE?
WHAT DO YOU MEAN?
HE SACRIFICED HIMSELF TO SAVE *YOU.* OF COURSE WE'RE GOING.
NO. NOT THAT.
I MEAN HOW DO WE KNOW THAT HE'S ALIVE?
BECAUSE VAL KNOWS.
I THOUGHT YOU SAID DON'T TRUST YOU.
WELL, SOMETIMES YOU SHOULD.
SO SOMETIMES I SHOULD AND SOMETIMES I SHOULDN'T... IS THAT RIGHT? SEEMS... A BIT *IMPRECISE.*
WHAT CAN I SAY, DAD... PARENTING'S TOUGH.
SUCK IT UP.
IT'S OBVIOUS NOW...
SHE'S SPENT TOO MUCH TIME WITH YOU.
LET'S GO.

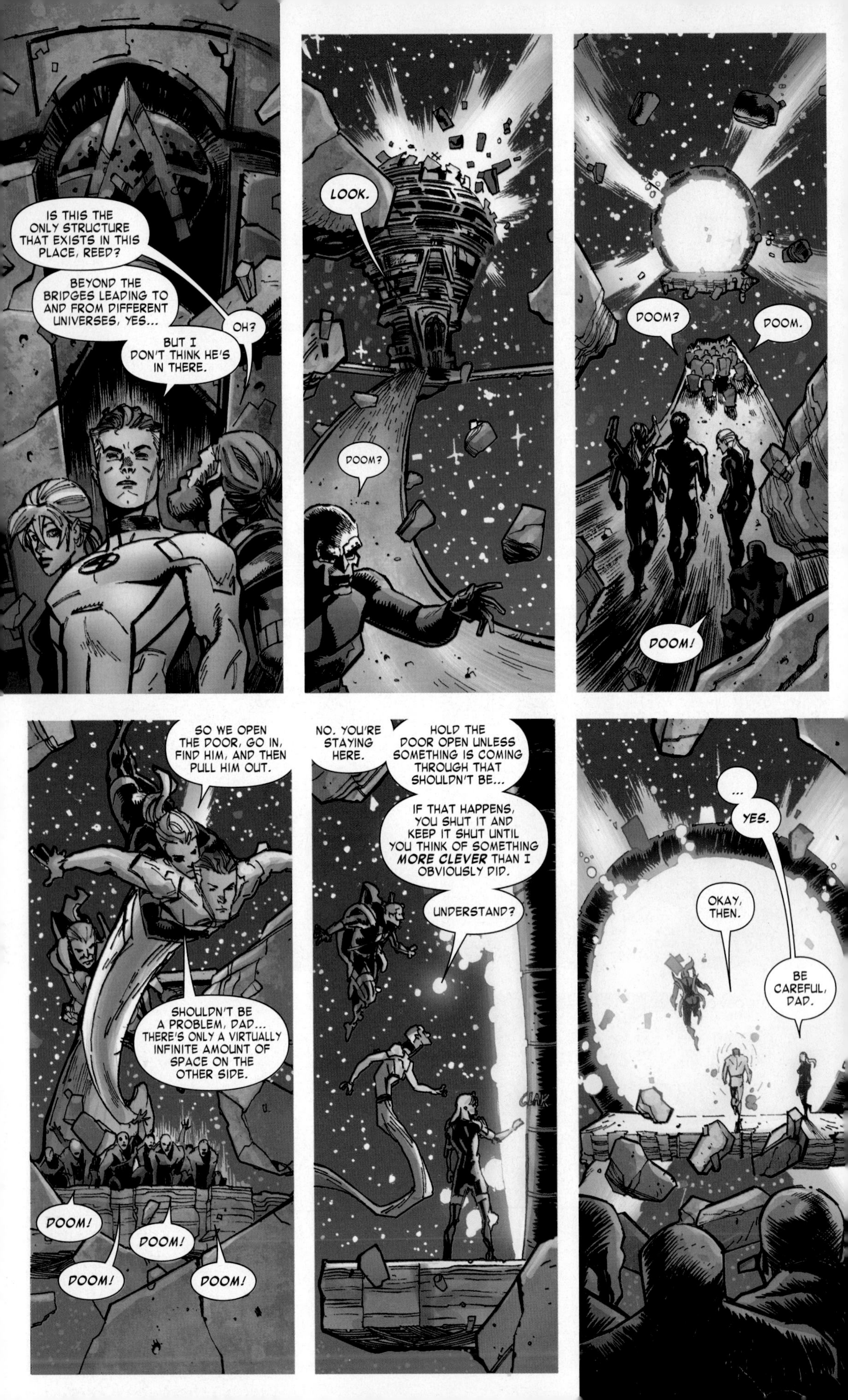
IS THIS THE ONLY STRUCTURE THAT EXISTS IN THIS PLACE, REED?
BEYOND THE BRIDGES LEADING TO AND FROM DIFFERENT UNIVERSES, YES...
OH?
BUT I DON'T THINK HE'S IN THERE.
LOOK.
DOOM?
DOOM?
DOOM.
DOOM!
SO WE OPEN THE DOOR, GO IN, FIND HIM, AND THEN PULL HIM OUT.
SHOULDN'T BE A PROBLEM, DAD... THERE'S ONLY A VIRTUALLY INFINITE AMOUNT OF SPACE ON THE OTHER SIDE.
DOOM!
DOOM!
DOOM!
DOOM!
NO. YOU'RE STAYING HERE.
HOLD THE DOOR OPEN UNLESS SOMETHING IS COMING THROUGH THAT SHOULDN'T BE...
IF THAT HAPPENS, YOU SHUT IT AND KEEP IT SHUT UNTIL YOU THINK OF SOMETHING MORE CLEVER THAN I OBVIOUSLY DID.
UNDERSTAND?
CLAK
...
YES.
OKAY, THEN.
BE CAREFUL, DAD.

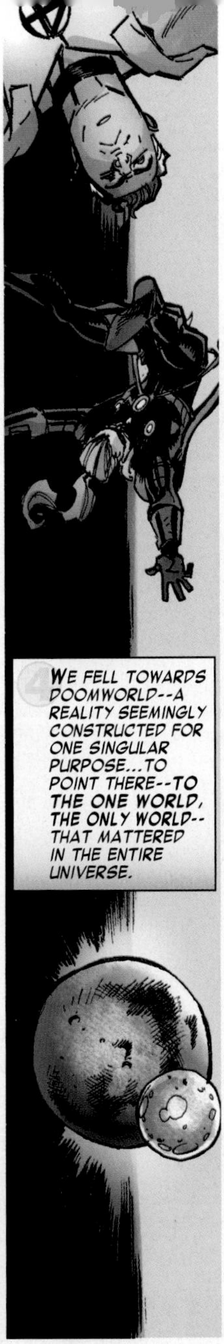
WE FELL TOWARDS DOOMWORLD--A REALITY SEEMINGLY CONSTRUCTED FOR ONE SINGULAR PURPOSE...TO POINT THERE--TO THE ONE WORLD, THE ONLY WORLD--THAT MATTERED IN THE ENTIRE UNIVERSE.

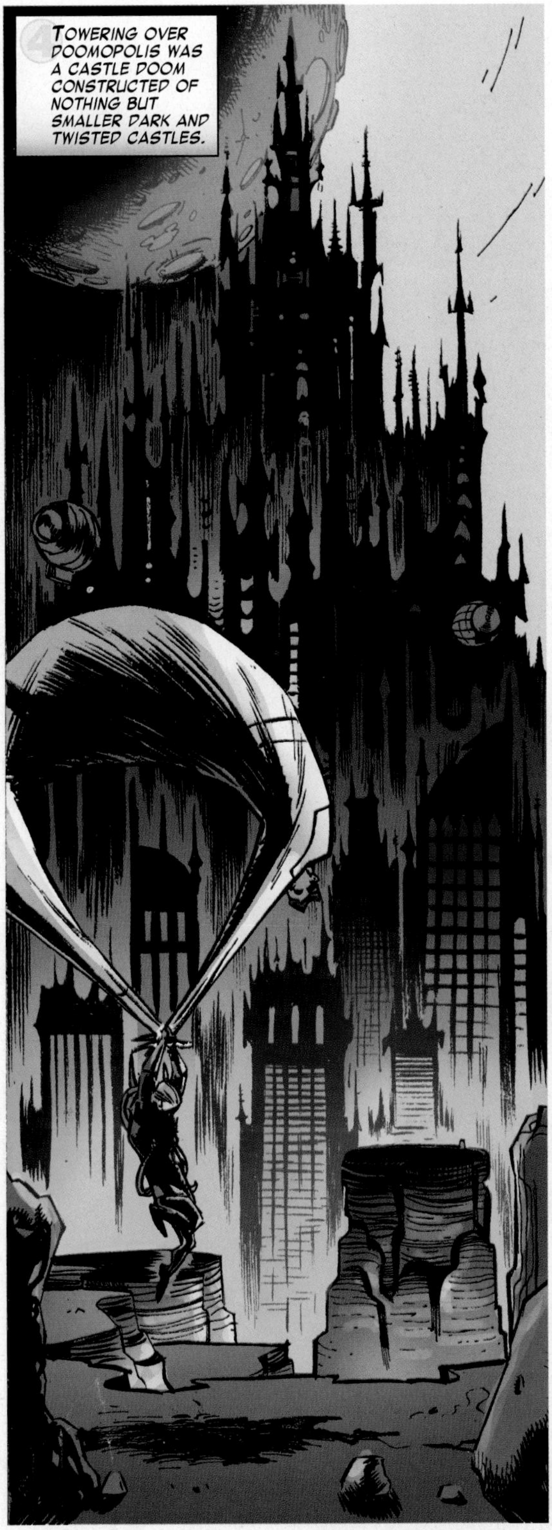
TOWERING OVER DOOMOPOLIS WAS A CASTLE DOOM CONSTRUCTED OF NOTHING BUT SMALLER DARK AND TWISTED CASTLES.

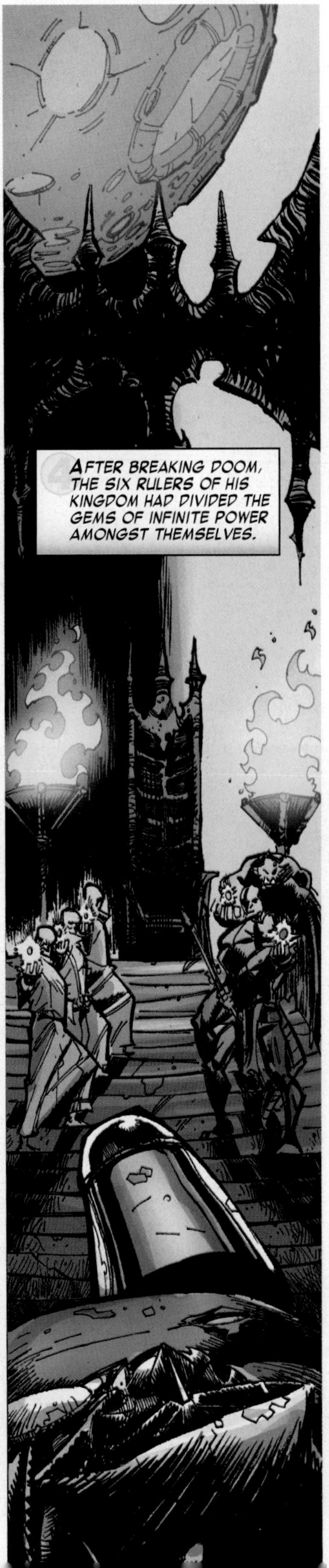
AFTER BREAKING DOOM, THE SIX RULERS OF HIS KINGDOM HAD DIVIDED THE GEMS OF INFINITE POWER AMONGST THEMSELVES.

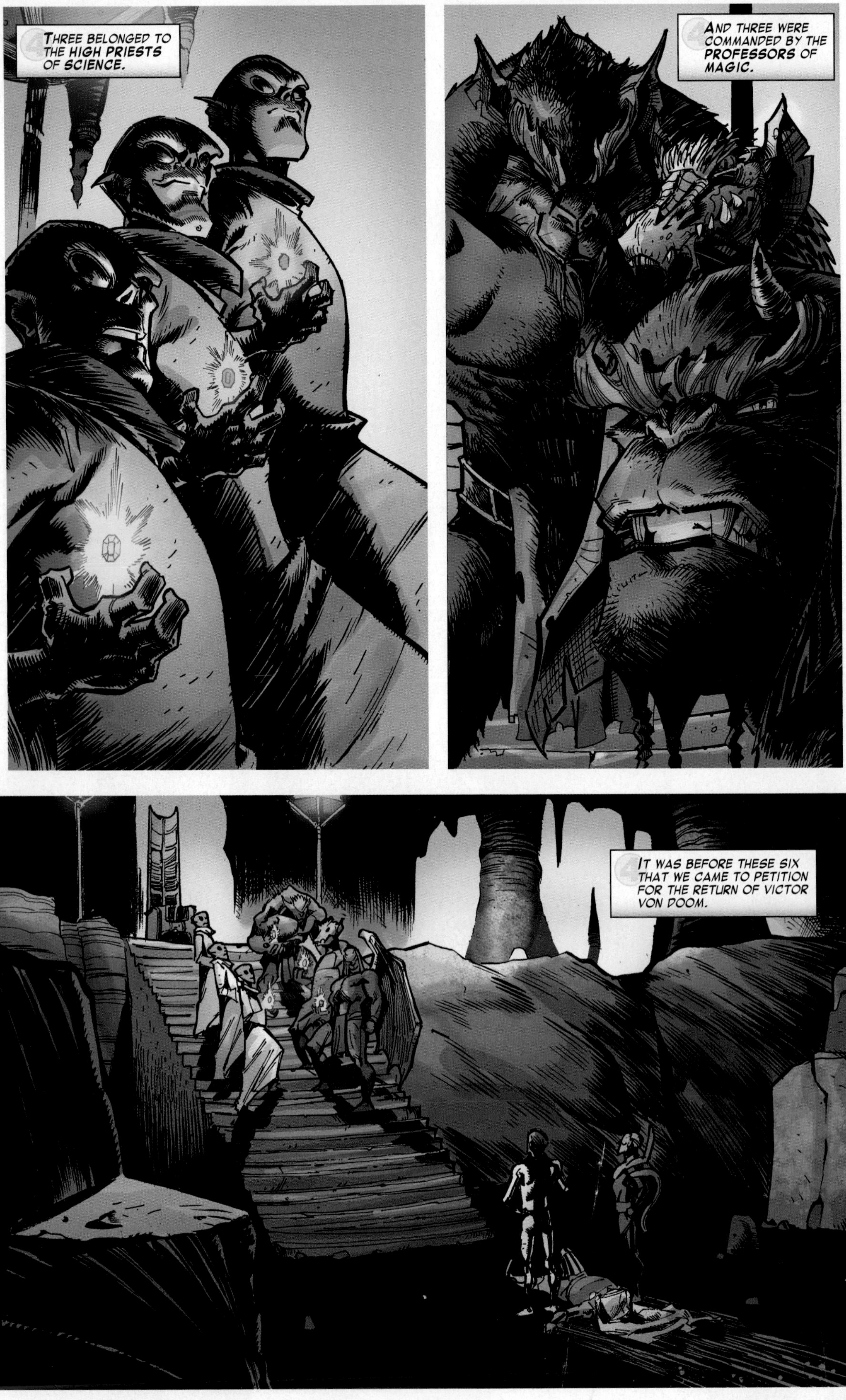
THREE BELONGED TO THE HIGH PRIESTS OF SCIENCE.
AND THREE WERE COMMANDED BY THE PROFESSORS OF MAGIC.
IT WAS BEFORE THESE SIX THAT WE CAME TO PETITION FOR THE RETURN OF VICTOR VON DOOM.

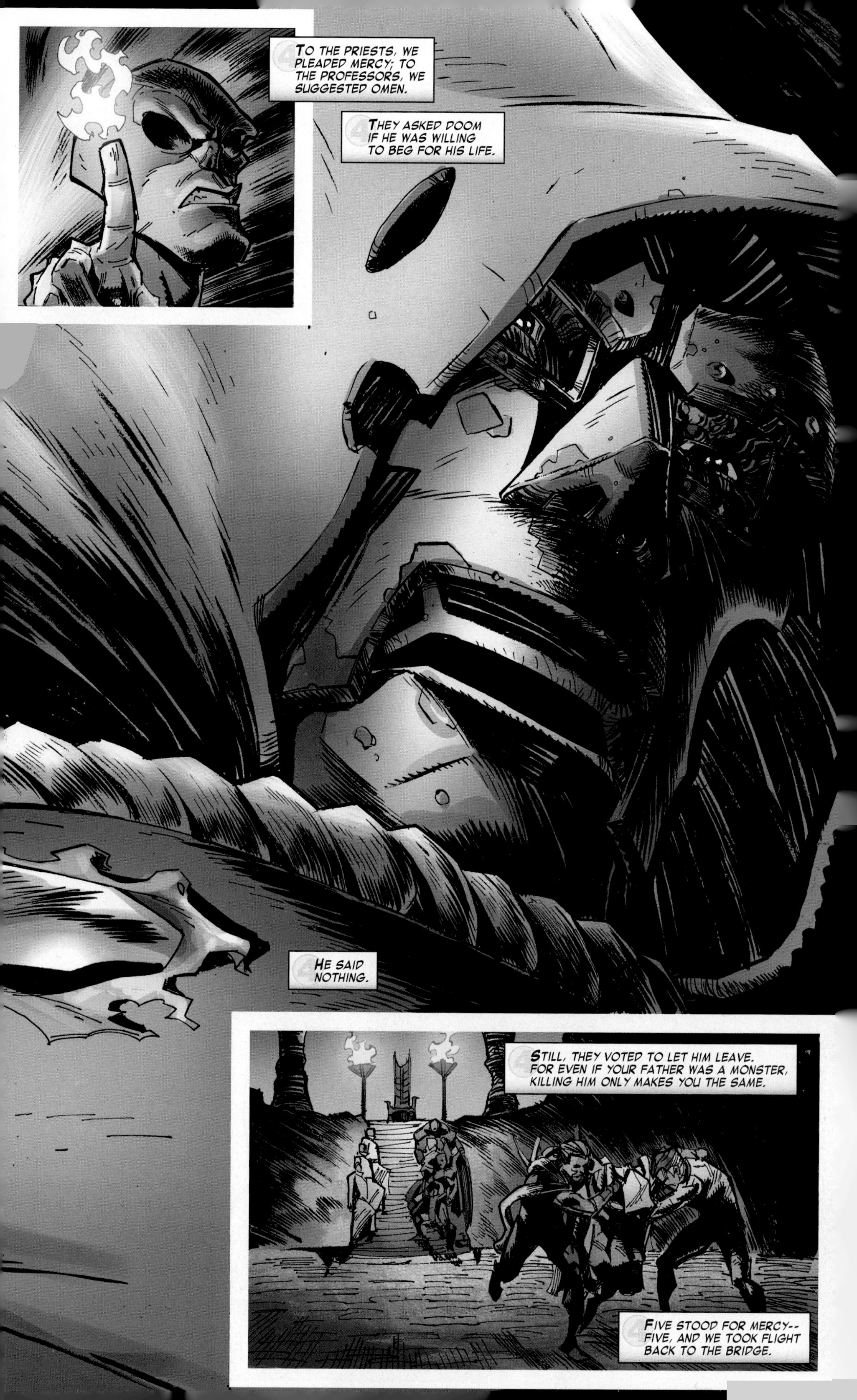
TO THE PRIESTS, WE PLEADED MERCY; TO THE PROFESSORS, WE SUGGESTED OMEN.
THEY ASKED DOOM IF HE WAS WILLING TO BEG FOR HIS LIFE.
HE SAID NOTHING.
STILL, THEY VOTED TO LET HIM LEAVE. FOR EVEN IF YOUR FATHER WAS A MONSTER, KILLING HIM ONLY MAKES YOU THE SAME.
FIVE STOOD FOR MERCY-- FIVE, AND WE TOOK FLIGHT BACK TO THE BRIDGE.

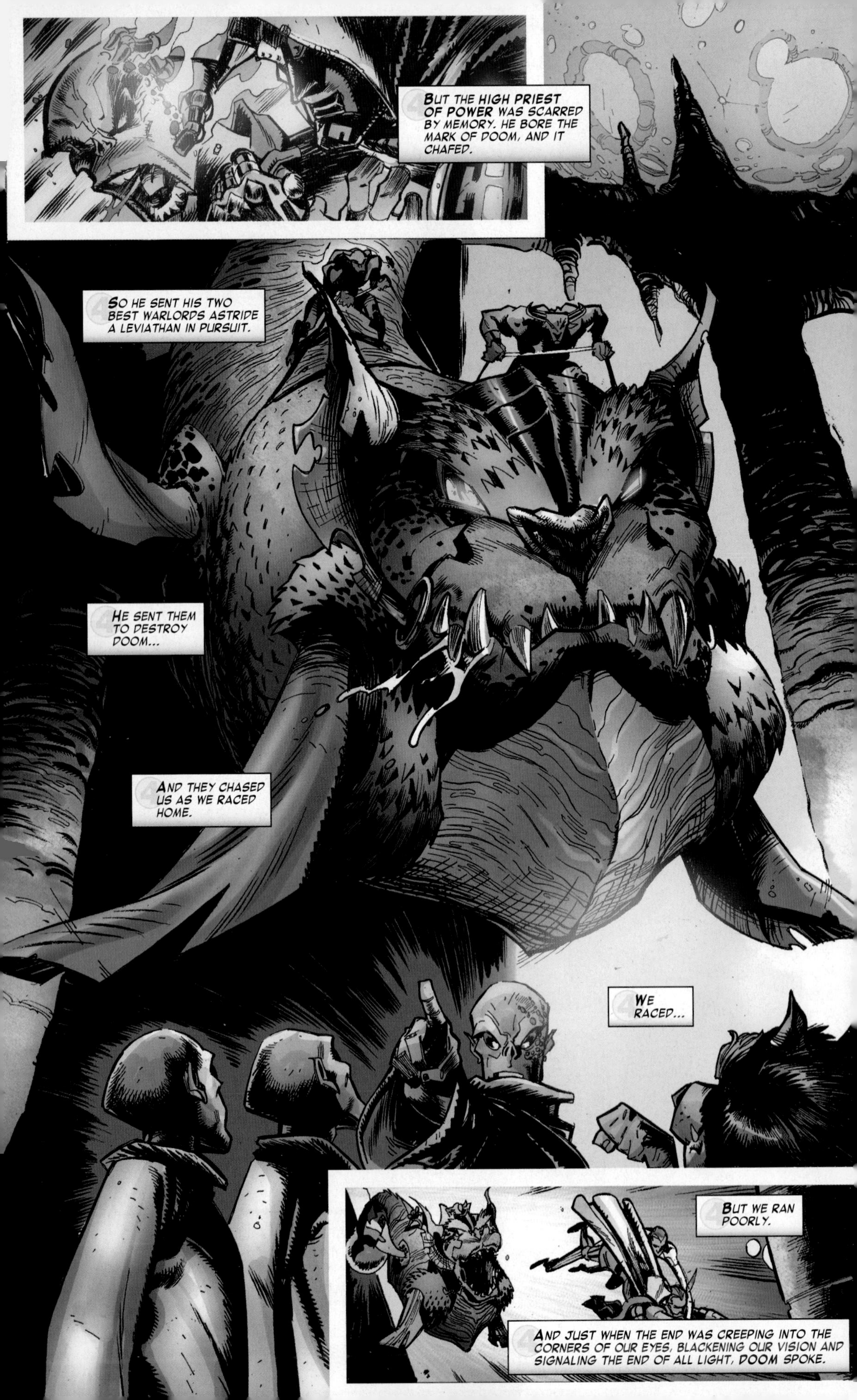
BUT THE HIGH PRIEST OF POWER WAS SCARRED BY MEMORY. HE BORE THE MARK OF DOOM, AND IT CHAFED.
SO HE SENT HIS TWO BEST WARLORDS ASTRIDE A LEVIATHAN IN PURSUIT.
HE SENT THEM TO DESTROY DOOM...
AND THEY CHASED US AS WE RACED HOME.
WE RACED...
BUT WE RAN POORLY.
AND JUST WHEN THE END WAS CREEPING INTO THE CORNERS OF OUR EYES, BLACKENING OUR VISION AND SIGNALING THE END OF ALL LIGHT, DOOM SPOKE.

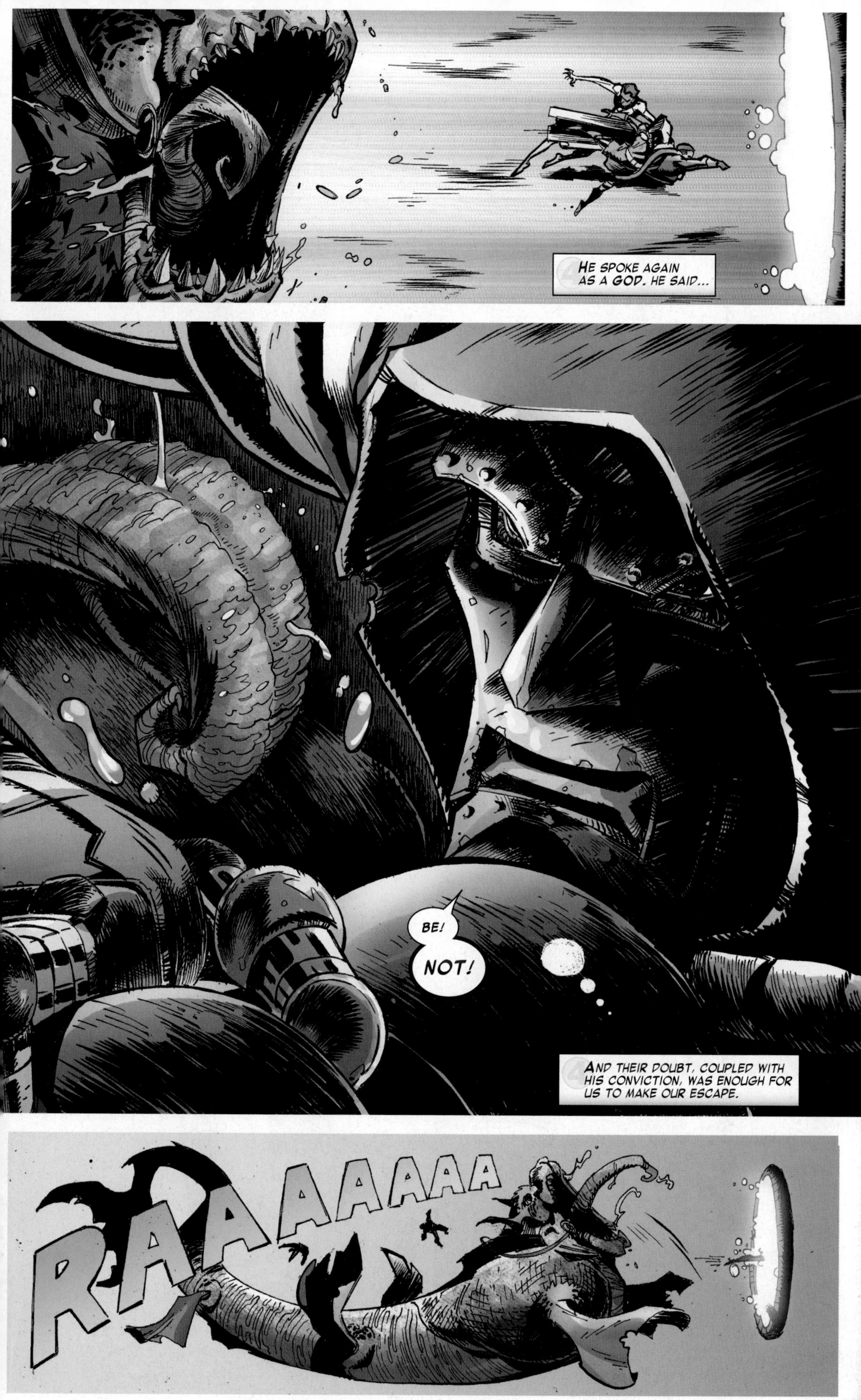
HE SPOKE AGAIN AS A GOD. HE SAID...
BE!
NOT!
AND THEIR DOUBT, COUPLED WITH HIS CONVICTION, WAS ENOUGH FOR US TO MAKE OUR ESCAPE.
RAAAAAAA

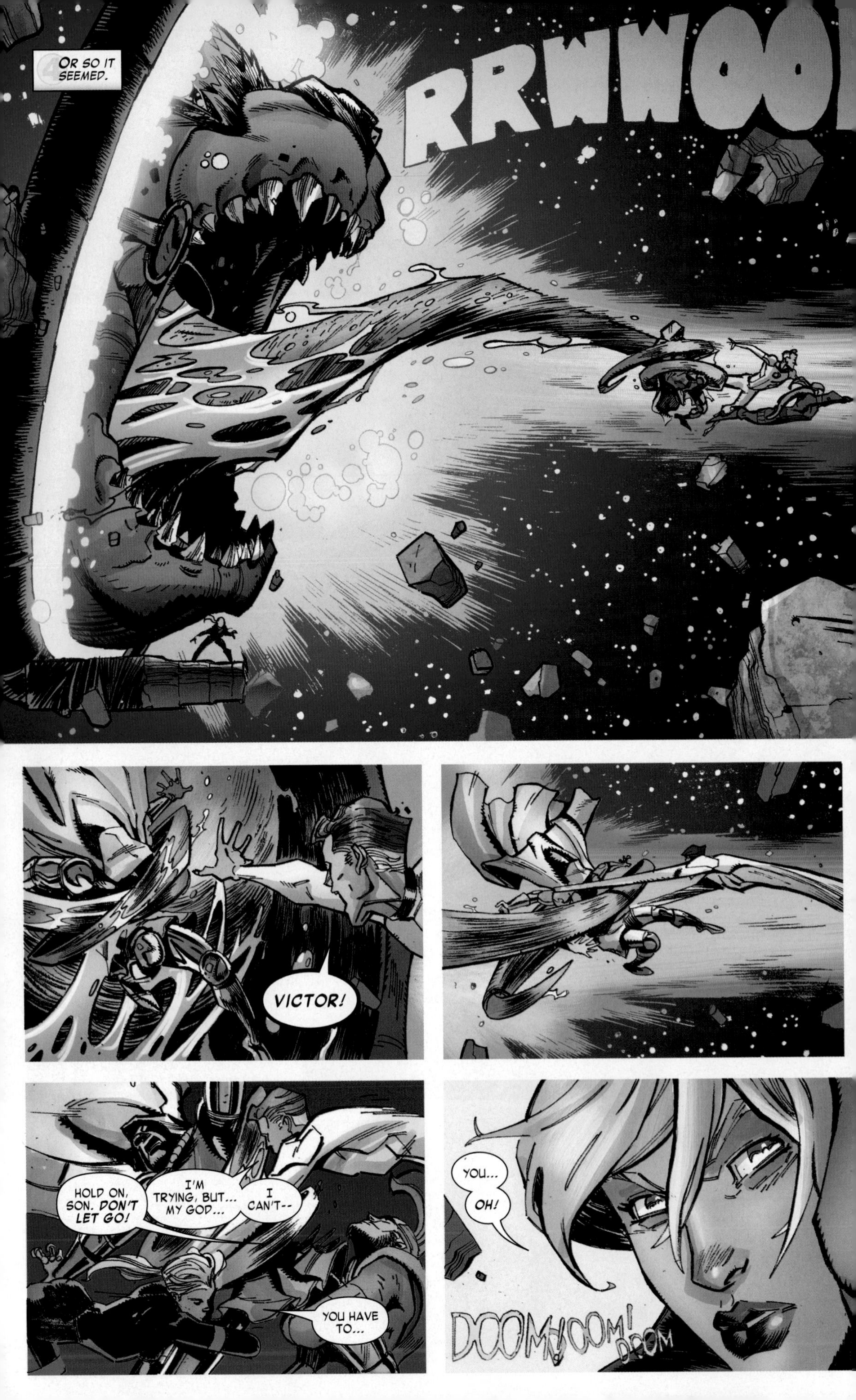
OR SO IT SEEMED.
RRWHOO
VICTOR!
HOLD ON, SON. DON'T LET GO!
I'M TRYING, BUT... MY GOD...
I CAN'T--
YOU HAVE TO...
YOU...
OH!
DOOM! DOOM! DOOM

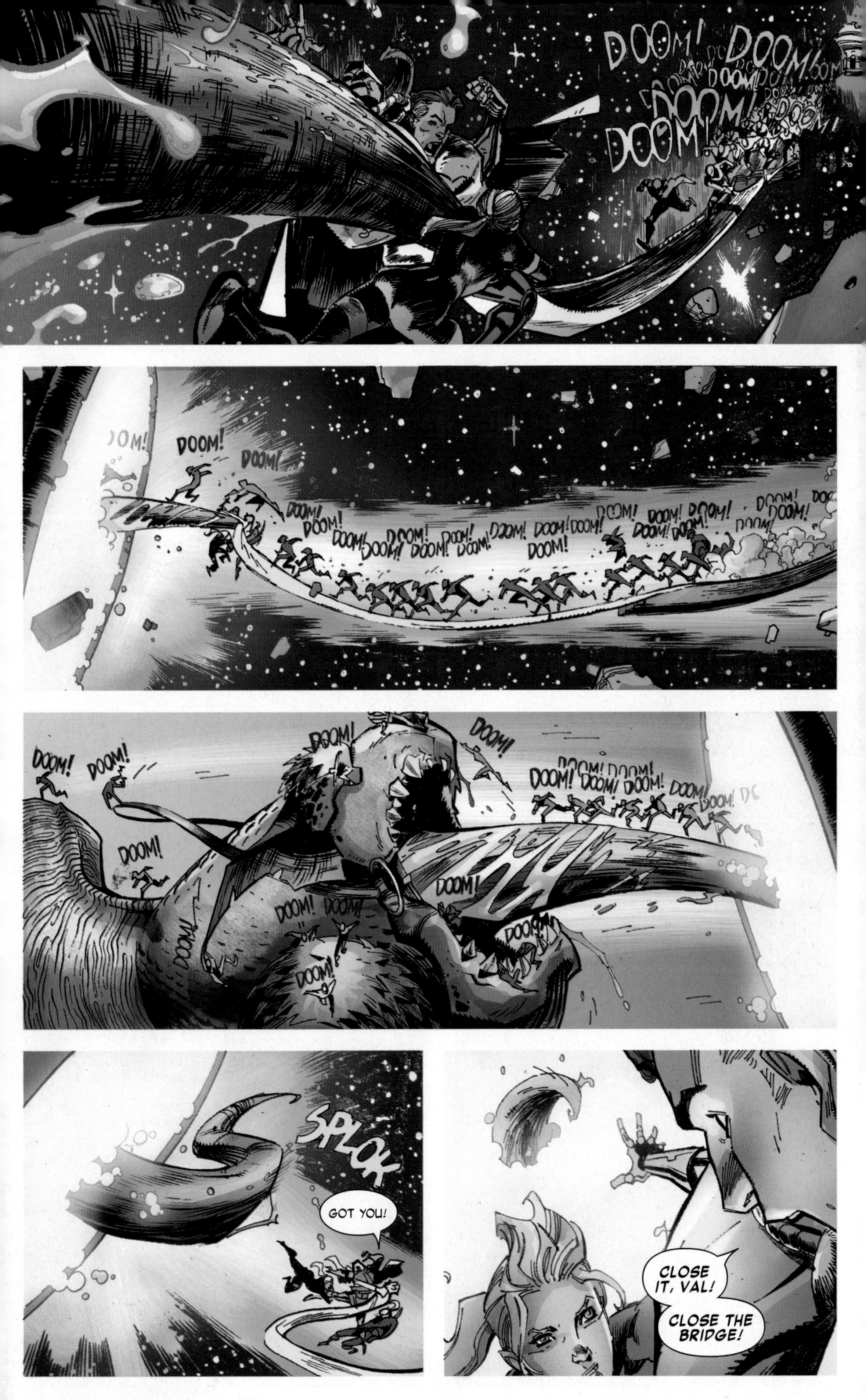
DOOM! DOOM! DOOM! DOOM! DOOM!
DOOM! DOOM! DOOM! DOOM! DOOM! DOOM! DOOM! DOOM! DOOM! DOOM! DOOM! DOOM! DOOM! DOOM! DOOM!
DOOM! DOOM! DOOM! DOOM! DOOM! DOOM! DOOM! DOOM! DOOM! DOOM! DOOM! DOOM! DOOM! DOOM! DOOM! DOOM!
SPLOK
GOT YOU!
CLOSE IT, VAL!
CLOSE THE BRIDGE!

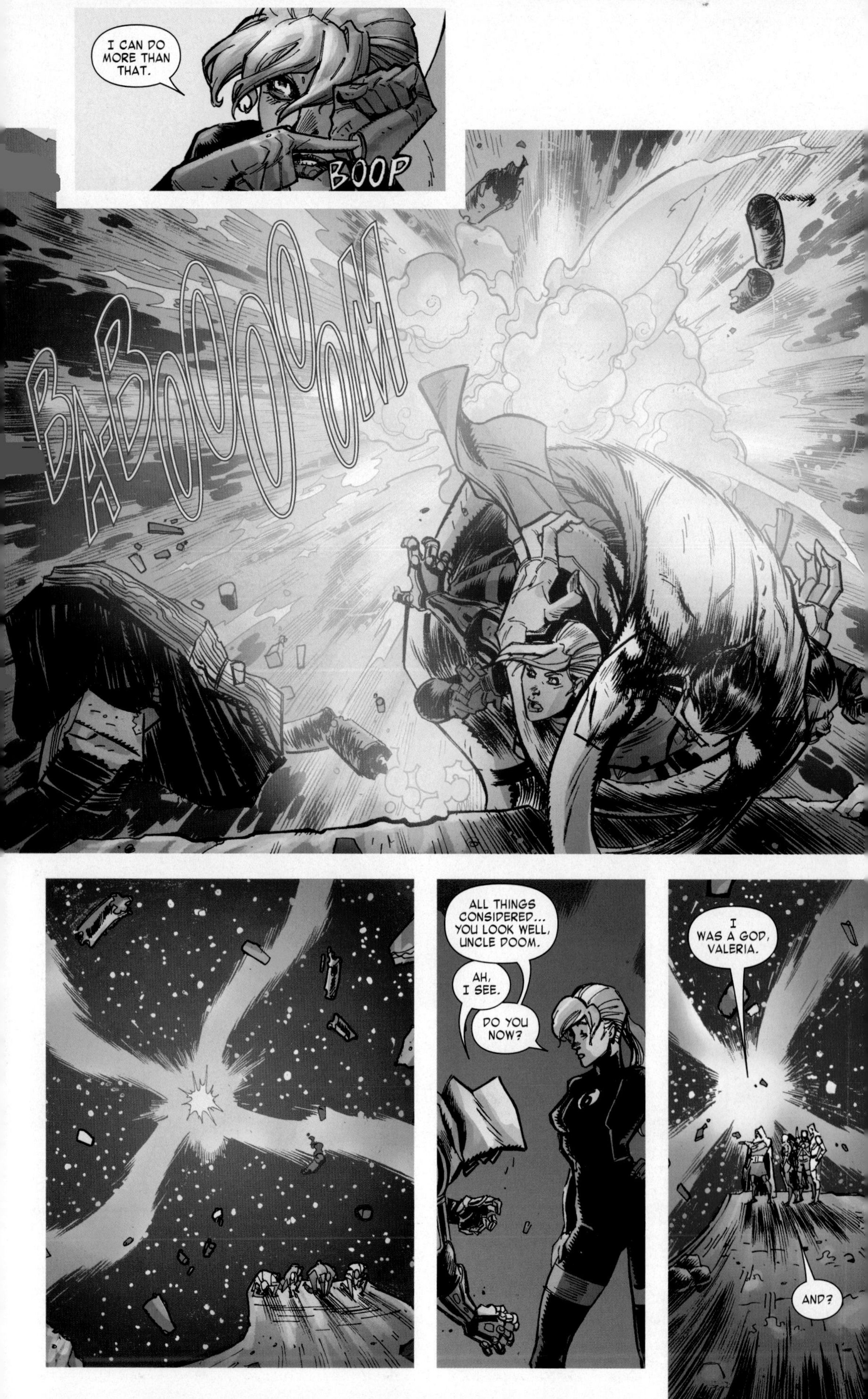
I CAN DO MORE THAN THAT.
BOOP
BABOOOOOM
ALL THINGS CONSIDERED... YOU LOOK WELL, UNCLE DOOM.
AH, I SEE.
DO YOU NOW?
I WAS A GOD, VALERIA.
AND?

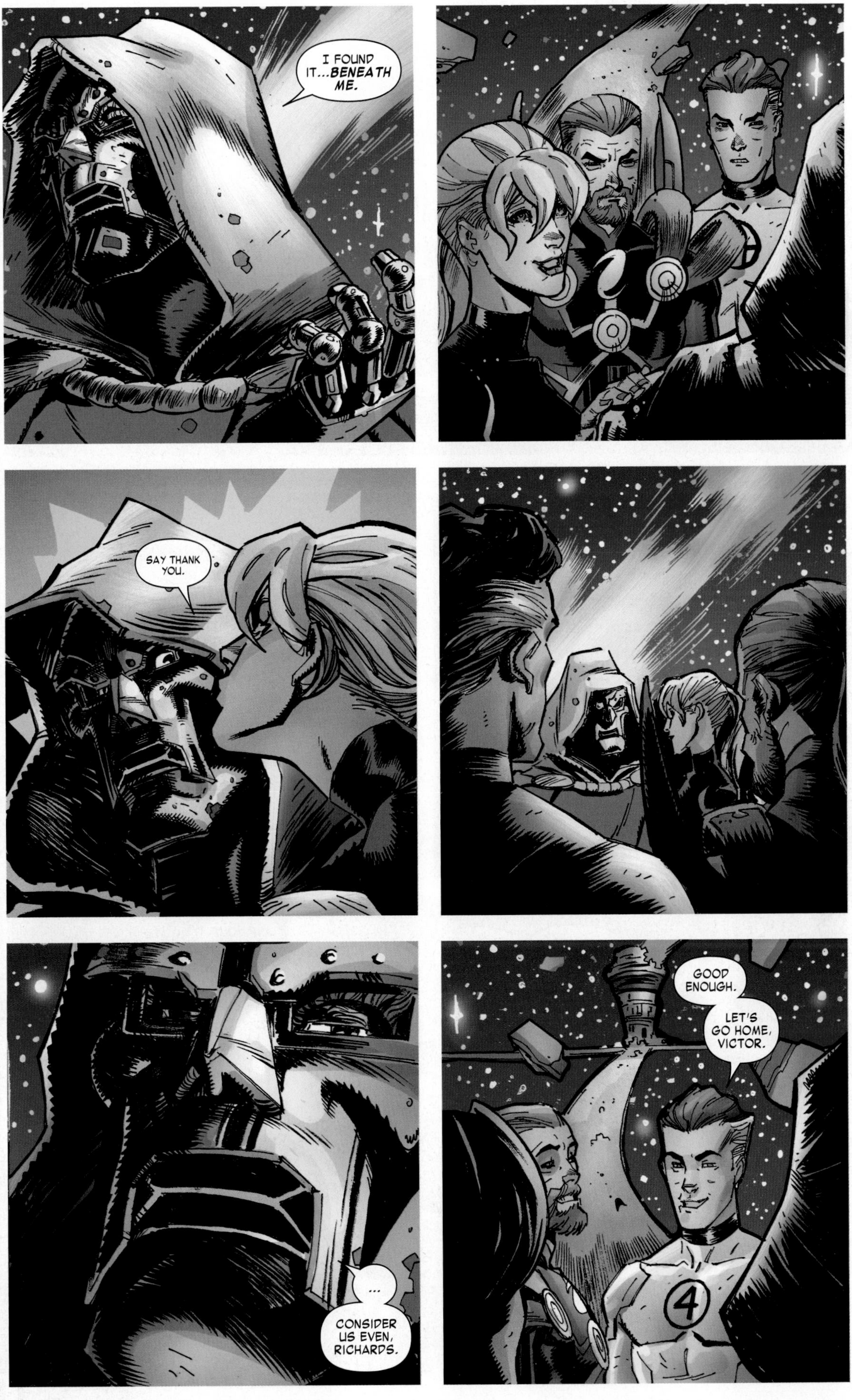
I FOUND IT...BENEATH ME.
SAY THANK YOU.
...
CONSIDER US EVEN, RICHARDS.
GOOD ENOUGH.
LET'S GO HOME, VICTOR.

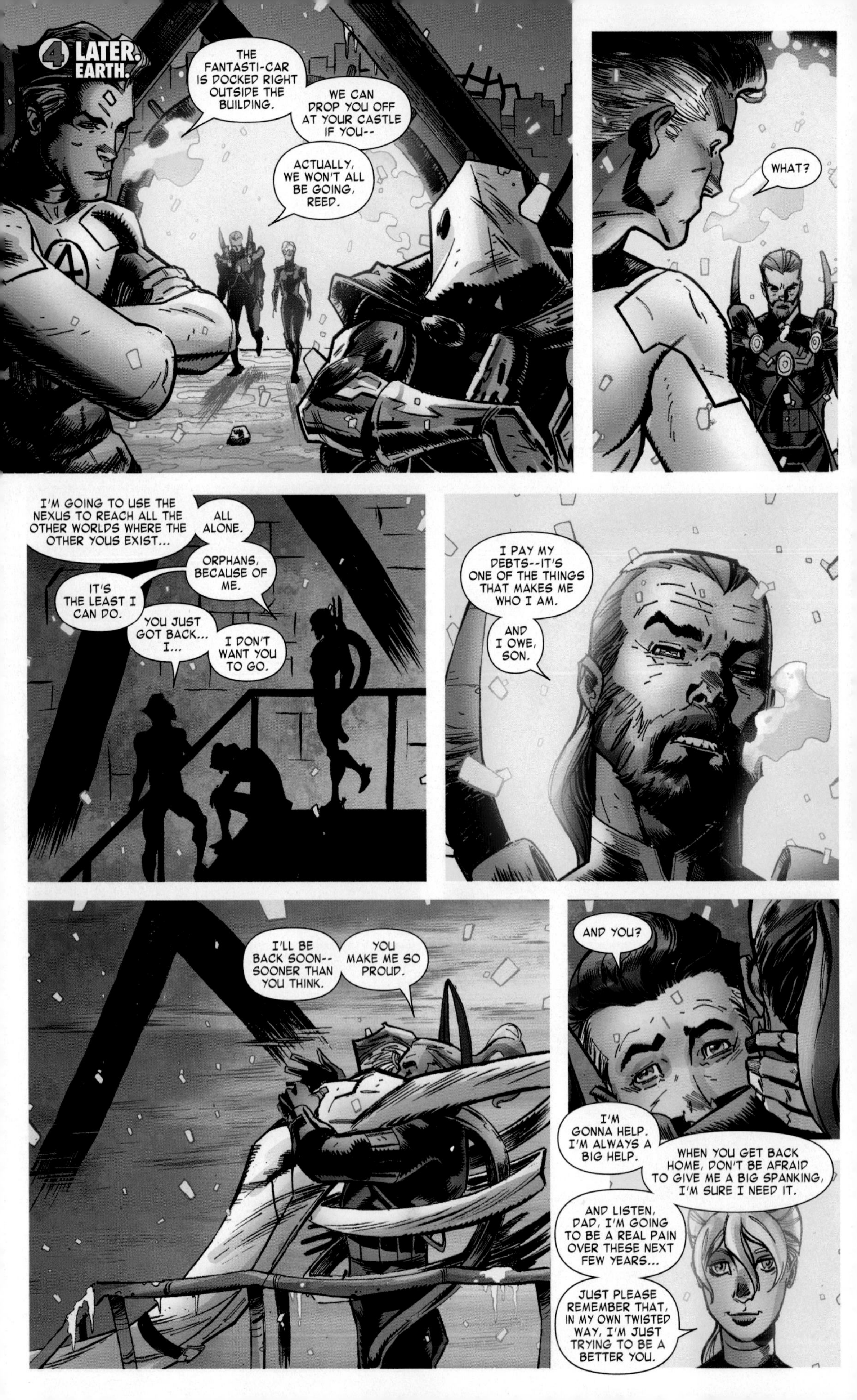
4 LATER. EARTH.
THE FANTASTI-CAR IS DOCKED RIGHT OUTSIDE THE BUILDING.
WE CAN DROP YOU OFF AT YOUR CASTLE IF YOU--
ACTUALLY, WE WON'T ALL BE GOING, REED.
WHAT?
I'M GOING TO USE THE NEXUS TO REACH ALL THE OTHER WORLDS WHERE THE OTHER YOUS EXIST...
ALL ALONE.
ORPHANS, BECAUSE OF ME.
IT'S THE LEAST I CAN DO.
YOU JUST GOT BACK... I...
I DON'T WANT YOU TO GO.
I PAY MY DEBTS--IT'S ONE OF THE THINGS THAT MAKES ME WHO I AM.
AND I OWE, SON.
I'LL BE BACK SOON-- SOONER THAN YOU THINK.
YOU MAKE ME SO PROUD.
AND YOU?
I'M GONNA HELP. I'M ALWAYS A BIG HELP.
WHEN YOU GET BACK HOME, DON'T BE AFRAID TO GIVE ME A BIG SPANKING, I'M SURE I NEED IT.
AND LISTEN, DAD, I'M GOING TO BE A REAL PAIN OVER THESE NEXT FEW YEARS...
JUST PLEASE REMEMBER THAT, IN MY OWN TWISTED WAY, I'M JUST TRYING TO BE A BETTER YOU.

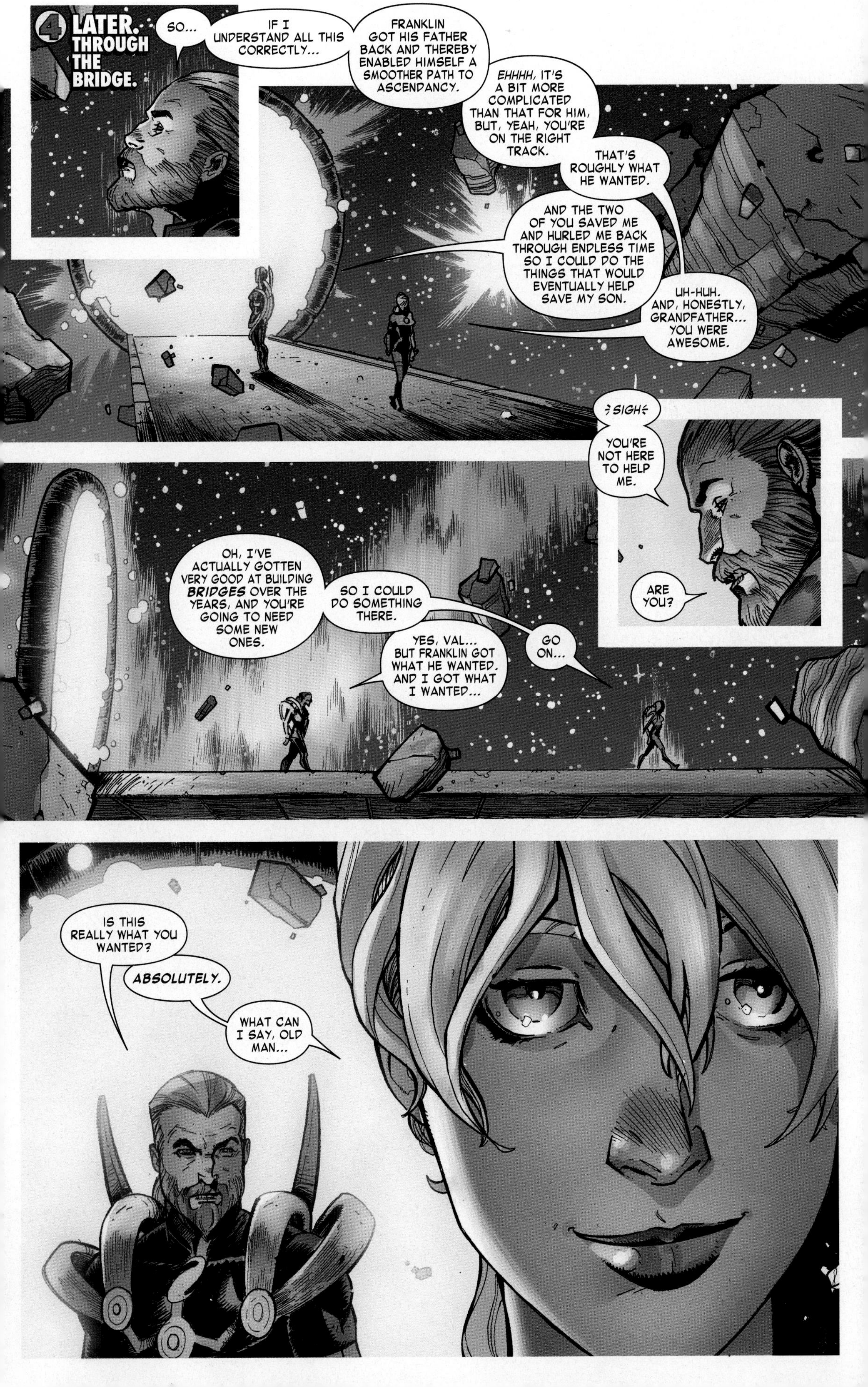
4
LATER. THROUGH THE BRIDGE.
SO...
IF I UNDERSTAND ALL THIS CORRECTLY...
FRANKLIN GOT HIS FATHER BACK AND THEREBY ENABLED HIMSELF A SMOOTHER PATH TO ASCENDANCY.
EHHHH, IT'S A BIT MORE COMPLICATED THAN THAT FOR HIM, BUT, YEAH, YOU'RE ON THE RIGHT TRACK.
THAT'S ROUGHLY WHAT HE WANTED.
AND THE TWO OF YOU SAVED ME AND HURLED ME BACK THROUGH ENDLESS TIME SO I COULD DO THE THINGS THAT WOULD EVENTUALLY HELP SAVE MY SON.
UH-HUH. AND, HONESTLY, GRANDFATHER... YOU WERE AWESOME.
SIGH
YOU'RE NOT HERE TO HELP ME.
ARE YOU?
OH, I'VE ACTUALLY GOTTEN VERY GOOD AT BUILDING BRIDGES OVER THE YEARS, AND YOU'RE GOING TO NEED SOME NEW ONES.
SO I COULD DO SOMETHING THERE.
GO ON...
YES, VAL... BUT FRANKLIN GOT WHAT HE WANTED. AND I GOT WHAT I WANTED...
IS THIS REALLY WHAT YOU WANTED?
ABSOLUTELY.
WHAT CAN I SAY, OLD MAN...

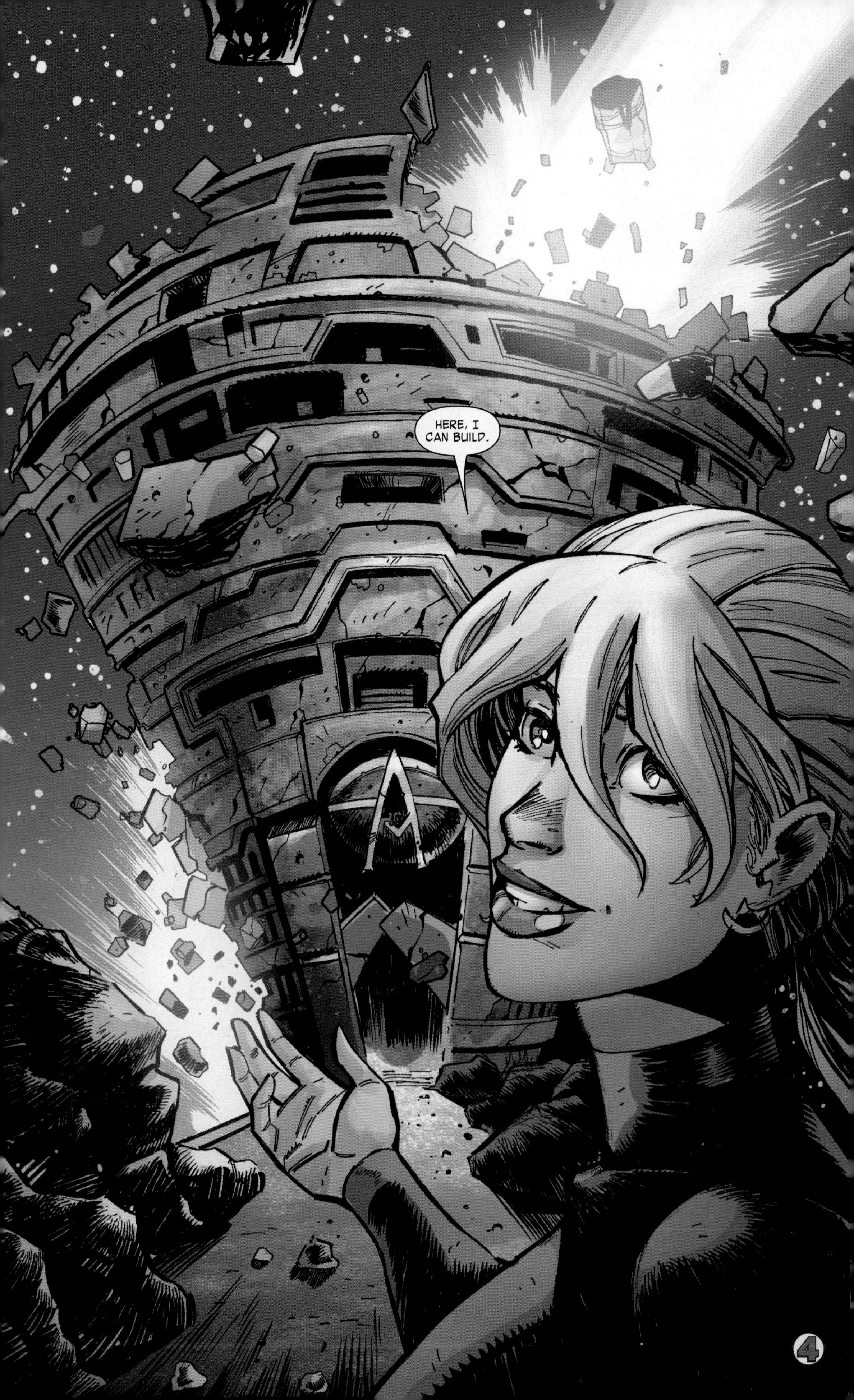
HERE, I CAN BUILD.
4

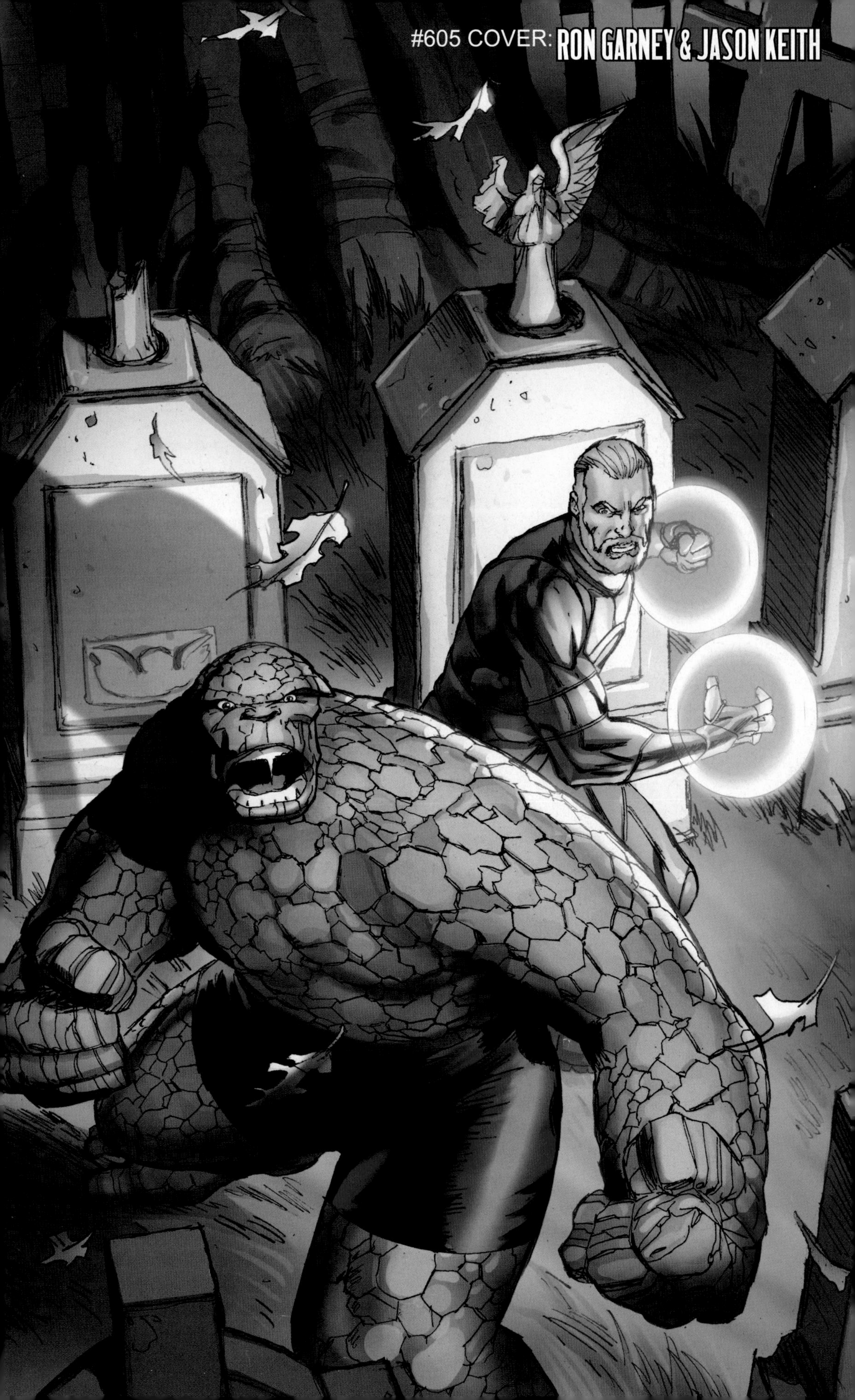

#605 COVER: **RON GARNEY & JASON KEITH**

#605.1 COVER: MIKE CHOI & GURU-eFX

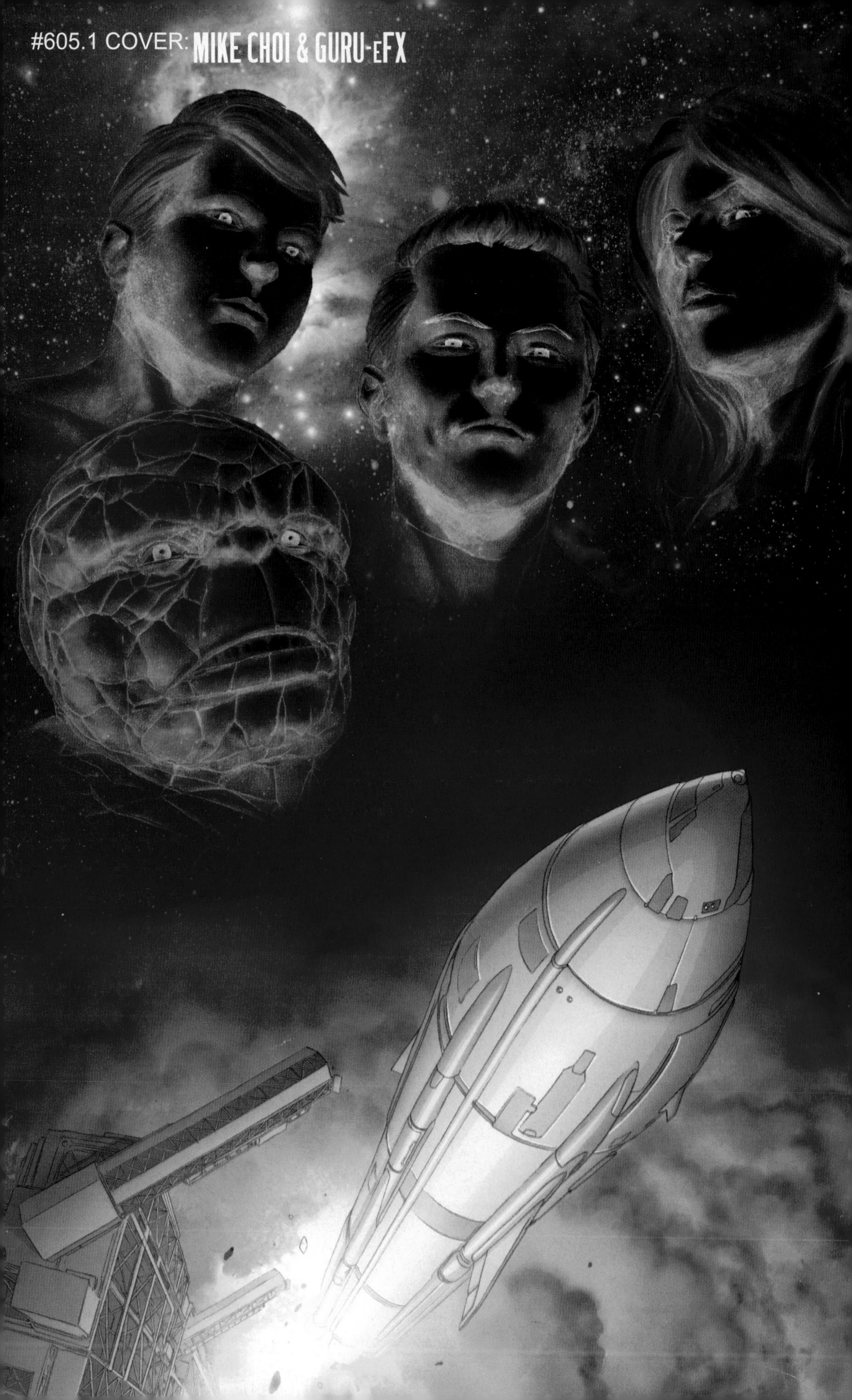

#606 COVER: MIKE CHOI & GURU-eFX

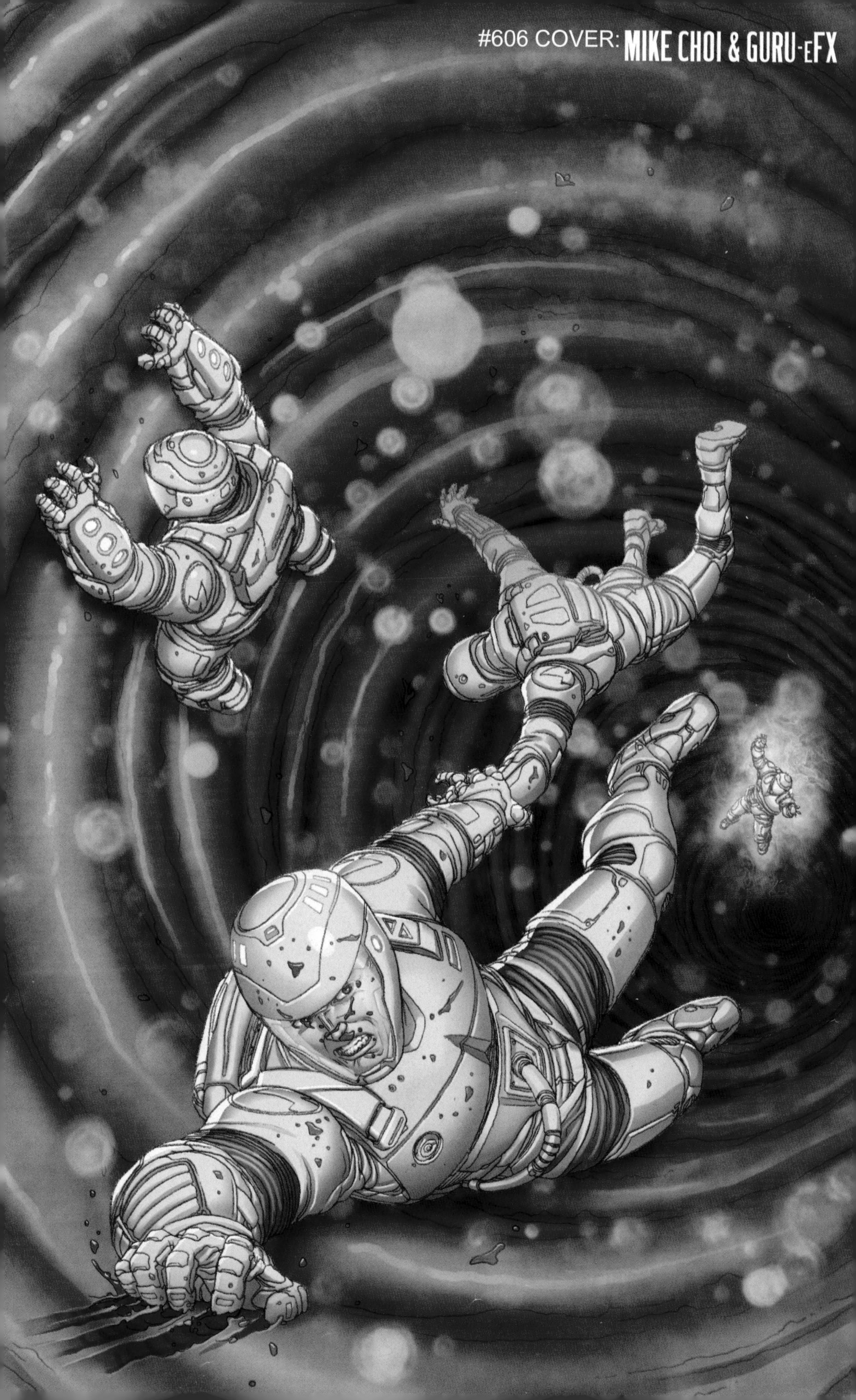

#607 COVER: MIKE CHOI & GURU-eFX

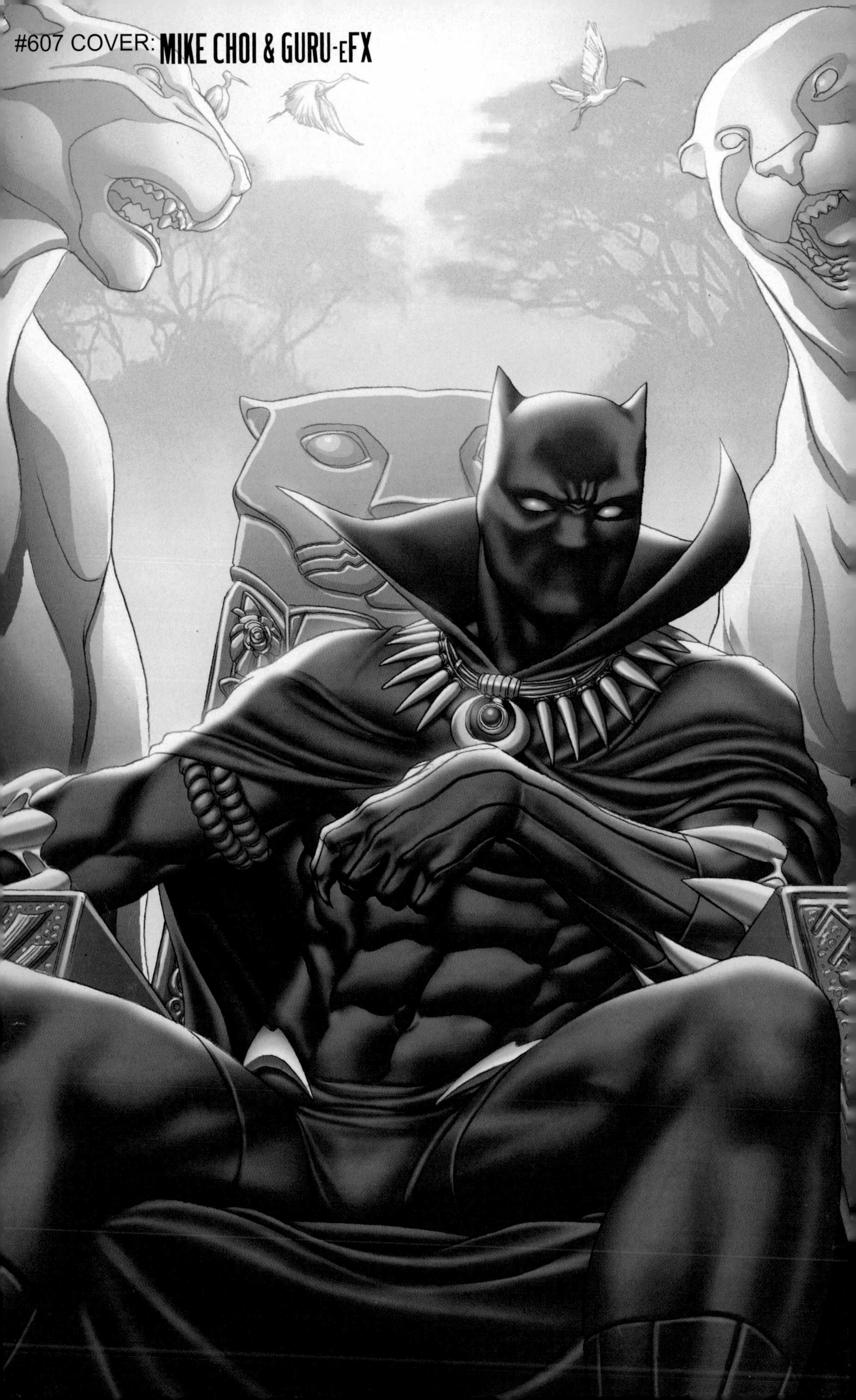

#608 COVER: FRANK CHO & JASON KEITH

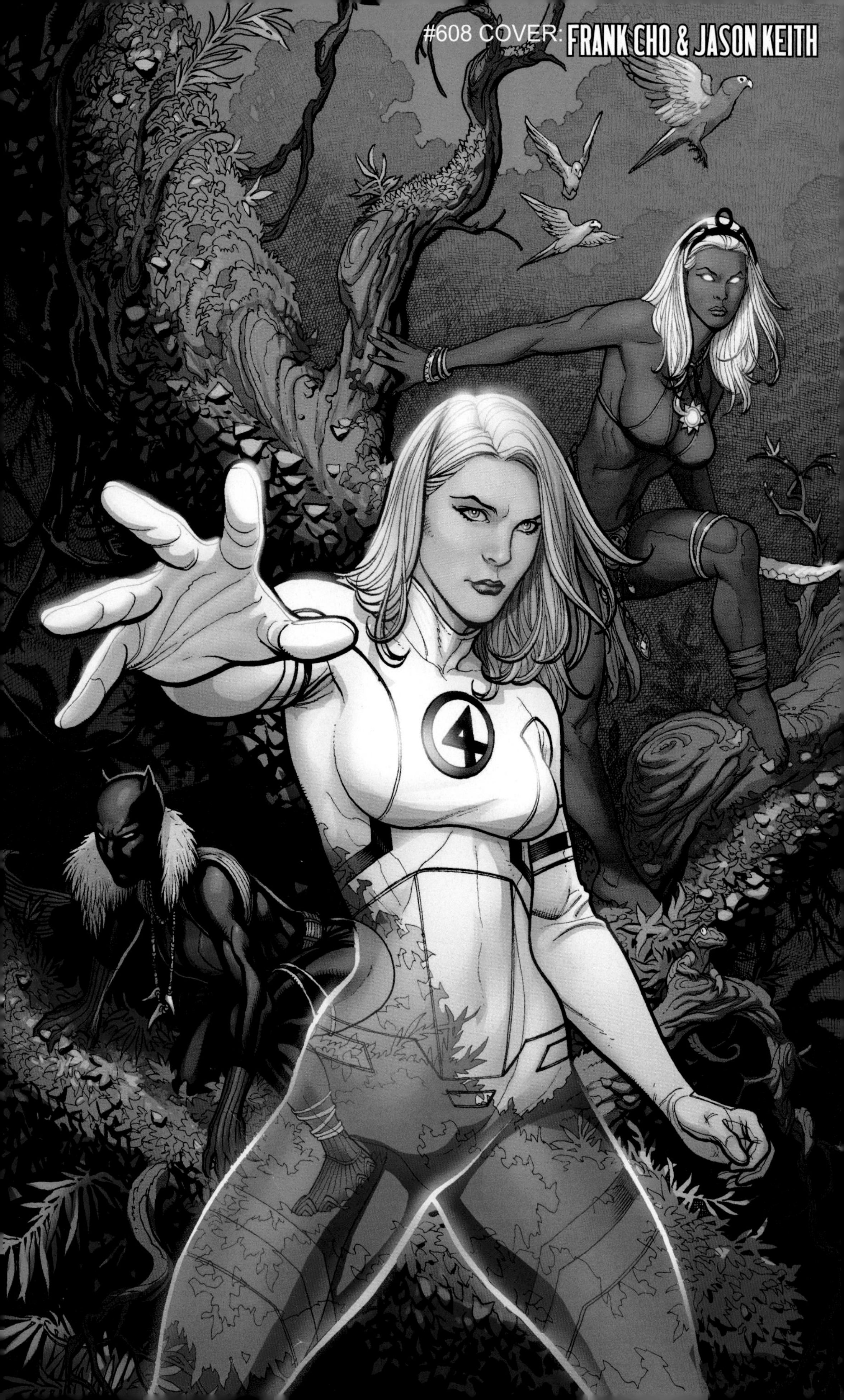

#609 COVER: RYAN STEGMAN & PAUL MOUNTS

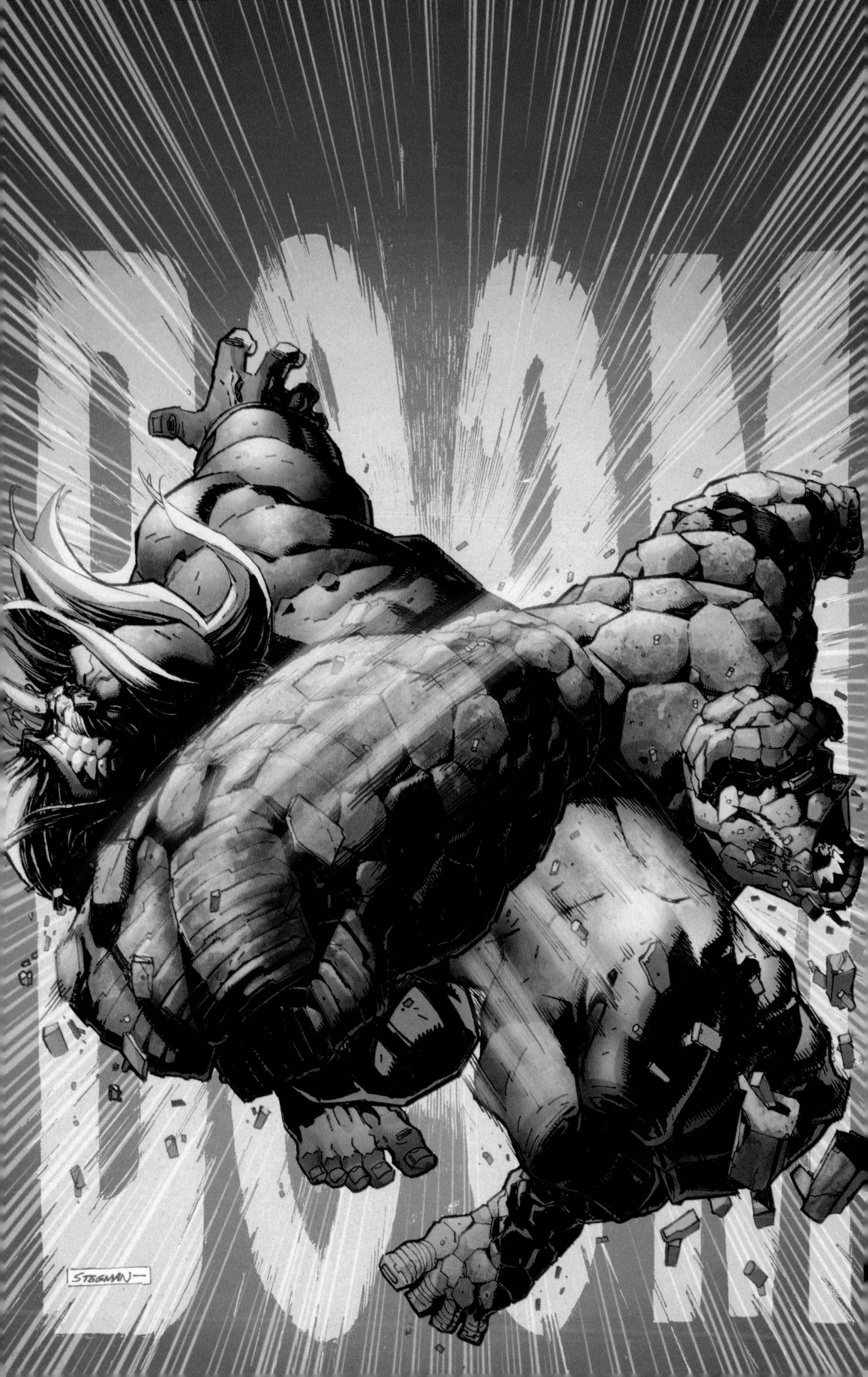
STEGMAN

#610 COVER: RYAN STEGMAN & PAUL MOUNTS

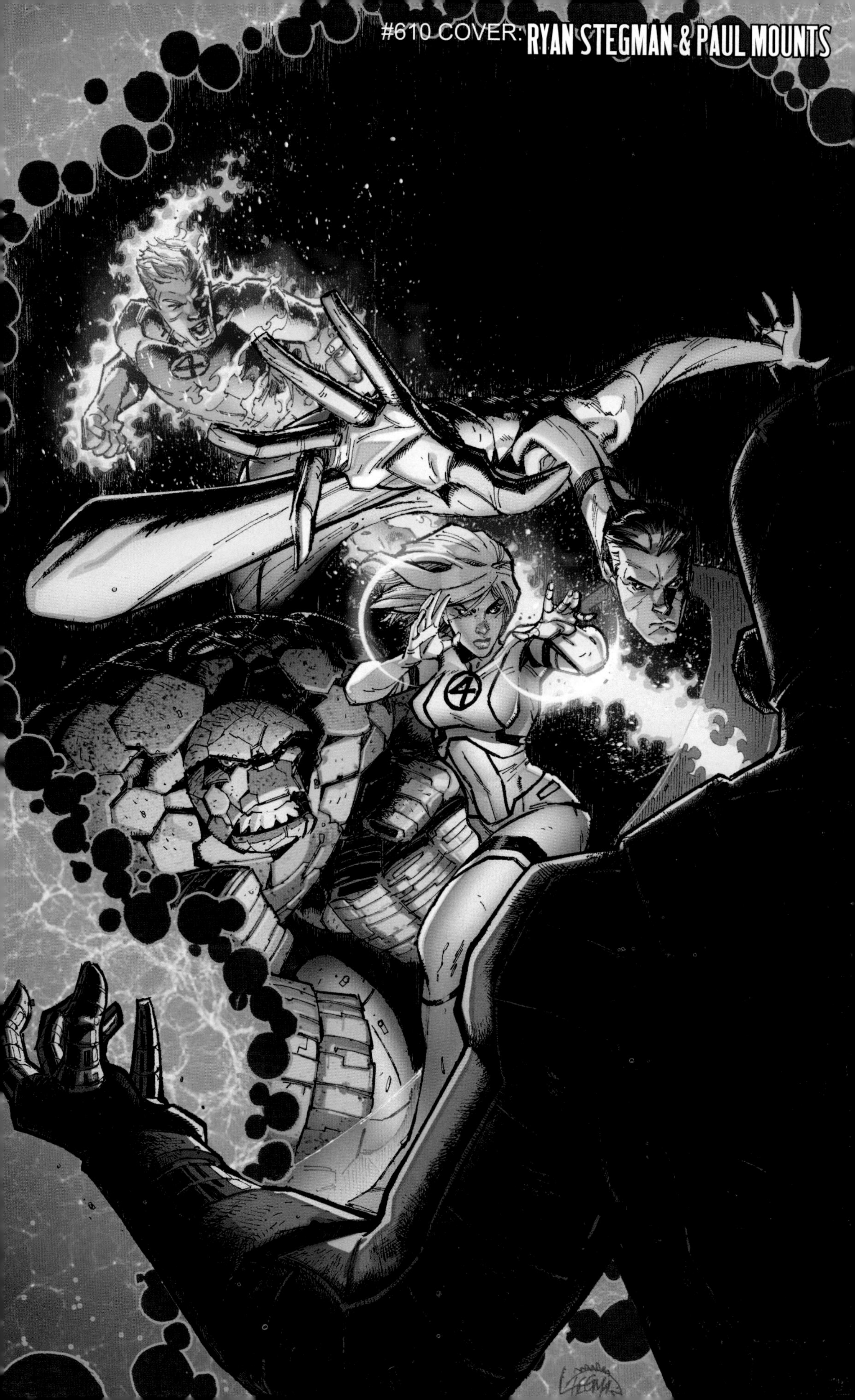

#611 COVER: RYAN STEGMAN & PAUL MOUNTS

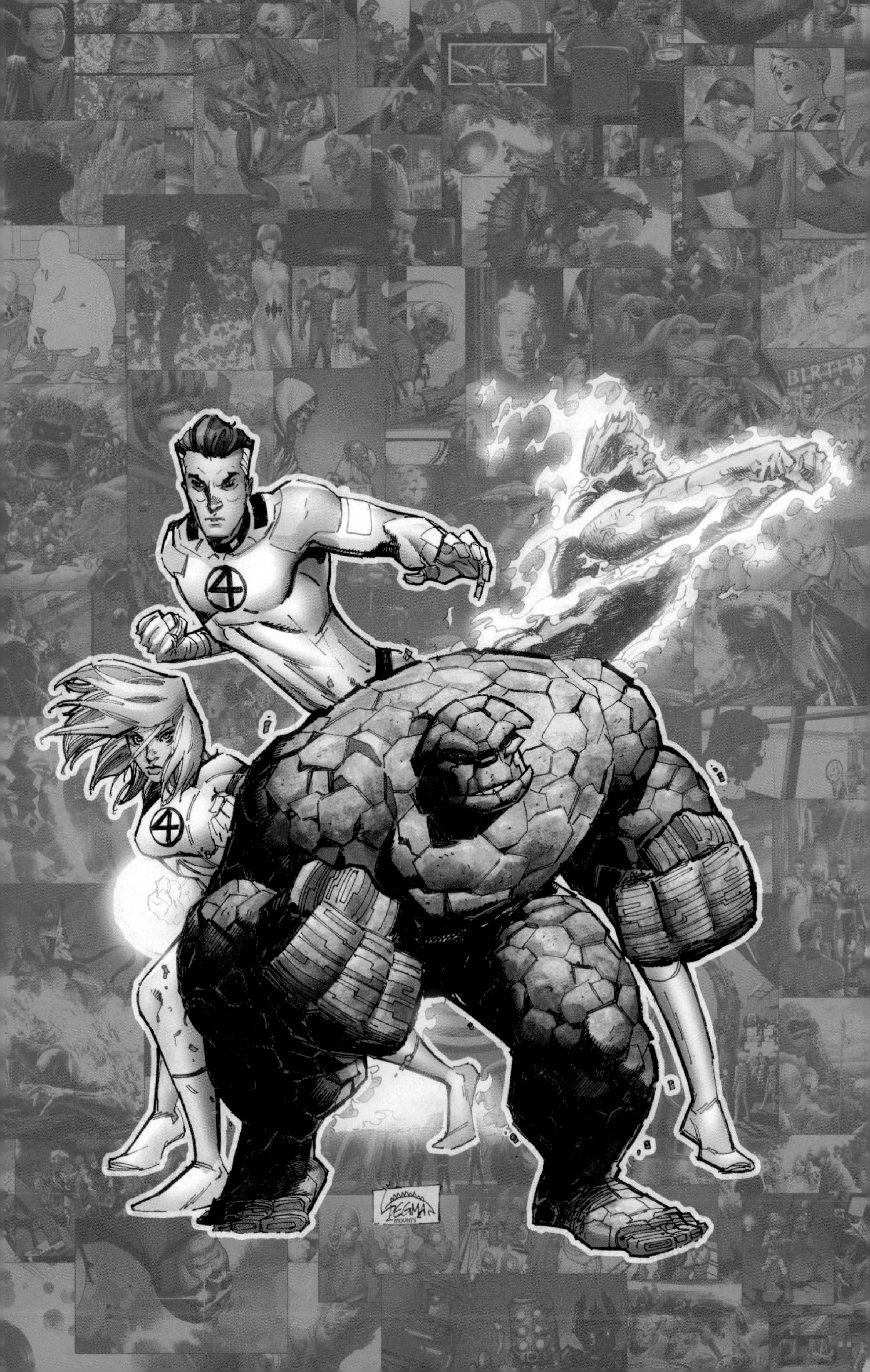